PERSPECTIVES

ON ISRAEL AND THE CHURCH

4 VIEWS

PERSPECTIVES
ON ISRAEL AND THE CHURCH
4 VIEWS

CHAD O. BRAND   TOM PRATT JR.

ROBERT L. REYMOND   ROBERT L. SAUCY

ROBERT L. THOMAS

EDITED BY CHAD O. BRAND

ACADEMIC

NASHVILLE, TENNESSEE

Perspectives on Israel and the Church: 4 Views
Copyright © 2015 Chad Brand

B&H Publishing Group
Nashville, Tennessee

All rights reserved

ISBN: 978-0-8054-4526-8

Dewey Decimal Classification: 296
Subject Heading: JUDAISM—RELATIONS—CHRISTIANITY \ ISRAEL \ CHURCH

Printed in the United States of America

1 2 3 4 5 6 7 8 9 10 • 20 19 18 17 16 15

VP

Contents

Contributors vii

Introduction 1
 By Chad O. Brand

Chapter 1: The Traditional Covenantal View 17
 By Robert L. Reymond
 Response by Robert L. Thomas 69
 Response by Robert L. Saucy 75
 Response by Chad O. Brand and Tom Pratt Jr. 82

Chapter 2: The Traditional Dispensational View 87
 By Robert L. Thomas
 Response by Robert L. Reymond 136
 Response by Robert L. Saucy 143
 Response by Chad O. Brand and Tom Pratt Jr. 149

Chapter 3: The Progressive Dispensational View 155
 By Robert L. Saucy
 Response by Robert L. Reymond 209
 Response by Robert L. Thomas 217
 Response by Chad O. Brand and Tom Pratt Jr. 224

Chapter 4: The Progressive Covenantal View 231
 By Chad O. Brand and Tom Pratt Jr.
 Response by Robert L. Reymond 281
 Response by Robert L. Thomas 286
 Response by Robert L. Saucy 292

Name Index 299

Subject Index 303

Scripture Index 305

Contributors

Chad O. **Brand** has served as a pastor and has taught theology and church history for more than twenty years at three Baptist colleges and seminaries.

Tom Pratt Jr. is president of Eagle Rock Ministries and is a Bible teacher, preacher, and freelance writer.

Robert L. Reymond (1932–2013) was professor of Theology emeritus at Knox Theological Seminary.

Robert L. Saucy is distinguished professor of Systematic Theology at Talbot School of Theology at Biola University.

Robert L. Thomas is professor of New Testament emeritus at The Masters Seminary.

Introduction

BY CHAD O. BRAND

Since very early in Christian history, the question of the relation of the church to Israel has been an important topic. It is a topic that graces the pages of the New Testament and is, arguably, an issue that is found in incipient form in the Old Testament as well. The early church fathers debated this relationship, as has the church throughout the ages. The debate continues today, having heated up in the late nineteenth century, especially between theologians in the covenantal (Reformed Calvinism, Zwinglianism, etc.) tradition and those from the newer dispensational tradition. In this introduction, I will provide a brief history of this conversation and then pose the key questions that the authors of these chapters were asked to address.

Historical Survey

The earliest Christians were Jews. That is abundantly clear from the book of Acts, but it is also clear that Gentile Christianity was not far behind (see Acts 8 for the first recorded Samaritan conversions and Acts 10 for the first recorded Gentile evangelism). Many key Jewish leaders, especially in the Herod-and-Pilate-dominated Judean region, attempted to repress this early

—1

Christian movement, at least in part because it constituted a threat to their own political and economic status. Even when the apostle to the Gentiles carried the gospel to Galatia, then to Asia, Macedonia, Achaia, and other "Gentile" places, Jewish opposition dogged his steps. Early on, this set Jews and Christians (both Jewish and Gentile) in opposition to one another.

That opposition continued in the postapostolic setting. One contributing factor was that a number of the early Christian thinkers were trained in the philosophical schools of the time, and their Greek orientation often conflicted with the Hebrew Scriptures.[1] An early example of this is the so-called *Epistle of Barnabas*. Likely written by Christians in Alexandria (a city heavily under the influence of Greek philosophical thought) around AD 130, the epistle interprets the Old Testament in an allegorical fashion, thus coping with the conflict between Hebrew and Greek thinking by converting Hebraic thought into Greek. In addition, the short work claims that Moses' throwing down of the tablets at the foot of Sinai was meant to show that the Jews would one day abandon the covenant, and that the covenant would then be transferred to the church.[2] The letter also states that Christ was manifested in order that the Israelites might be "perfected in their iniquities, and that we, being constituted heirs through Him, might receive the testament of the Lord Jesus."[3] The church, in effect, *replaces* Israel as the locus of the covenant, with no indication that Israel is still precious in God's sight.

Other second-century church fathers held similar views. Justin Martyr was one of those trained in Greek thought, specifically middle Platonism. In his *Dialogue with Trypho*, Justin claims that Jesus is the true heir of Israel and that the Jews have been rejected so that we who follow Jesus might be the "true Israelitic Race."[4] Exemplary Old Testament figures are treated as

---

[1] Our survey will be only representative, not exhaustive.

[2] *Epistle of Barnabas*, 4.7–9, Ante-Nicene Fathers, vol. 1, ed. Philip Schaff (New York: Christian Literature Co., 1885). Unless noted otherwise, our sources from the period before AD 325 are from *The Ante-Nicene Fathers* (10 vols., series ed. A. Cleveland Coxe, Alexander Roberts, James Donaldson, Philip Schaff, Henry Wace [New York: Christian Literature Co., 1885]). The set was first published by T&T Clark in Edinburgh, appearing in individual volumes from 1867–1873.

[3] *Epistle of Barnabas*, 14.5, Ante-Nicene Fathers, vol. 1.

[4] Justin Martyr, *Dialogue with Trypho, A Jew*, 135.

Christians, and circumcision is not the sign of the covenant so much as a harbinger of Israel's breaking the covenant.[5] Irenaeus was not as critical of Judaism as others in his day, his interpretation of the Old Testament in a more literal way being crucial to his criticism of Gnosticism, but he held out little hope for any future for the people of Israel. He preferred to see Old Testament expectations of a future time of glory as fulfilled only in the future glory of the church.[6]

In the third century Tertullian argued that Judaism is now made to serve the church, since the Jews are a "contumacious people," and since the covenant has been taken from them.[7] Origen followed the example of the *Epistle of Barnabas* (and the Jewish philosopher Philo) in employing an allegorical hermeneutic with reference to Old Testament interpretation, though not exclusively so. This was in part because Origen was deeply involved in constructing an *apologia* for the Christian faith over against its detractors in Alexandria, men such as Celsus. They regularly reminded him of "immoral" texts in the Old Testament, such as Lot's incest with his daughters and David's adultery. An allegorical hermeneutic allowed Origen to sanitize such texts and to show, to his satisfaction, that the "real meaning" was not to be found in the story as such, but beneath the story.[8] Because he was a foe of Gnosticism (and for other reasons), Origen did not denigrate the literal meaning of the Old Testament; he just did not find that meaning to be of the highest concern. In his most important work, Origen distinguished between "corporeal" Israel and "spiritual" Israel (the church), thus originating the tendency found in much later hermeneutics of "spiritualizing" the promises of God to Israel so that they apply to the church in a nonliteral way.[9] For Origen, Israel was no longer the people of God but rather was like a divorced wife in whom something unseemly has been found, while the church is the new bride.[10] This was a full-blown "replacement theology," and this spiritualizing

---

[5]   Ibid., 16.2.

[6]   Irenaeus, *Against Heresies*, 5.34.

[7]   Tertullian, *An Answer to the Jews*, 2–3.

[8]   Everett Ferguson, *Church History, Volume One: From Christ to Pre-Reformation* (Grand Rapids: Zondervan, 2005), 132–36.

[9]   Origen, *On First Principles*, 2.4.22.

[10] Origen, *Commentary on Matthew*, 14.22.

approach would be taken up by Augustine and especially by many later representatives of the amillennial school of interpretation.[11]

In his early writings, Augustine (fourth and early fifth centuries) followed the basic approach to eschatology hammered out by Justin Martyr and others, known as Chiliasm or premillennialism.[12] He conceived of history as consisting of six ages, followed by a "golden age" in which there would be peace and cosmic renewal.[13] The seventh age would be the millennium, interpreted in broadly literal fashion, though not lasting a thousand years since it would have no end. Here the church would be purged of all of its ills, and rest would finally be achieved. Somewhat oddly, Augustine did not believe that this was the eternal state, since it would happen in history and would be the prelude to an eternal time of bliss.[14] But, in his final years, writing his *magnum opus*, *The City of God*, Augustine adopted a different view. Here he argues that the millennium of Revelation 20 is symbolic of "all the years of the Christian era."[15] The "first resurrection" of Rev 20:4 is the conversion of the Christian that occurs at baptism, while the "second resurrection" (Rev 20:5) is the resurrection of the body at the Second Advent of Christ.[16] This book thus first set forth the schema that would later be known as amillennialism.

What of his attitude toward Israel? In the same work the African Father speaks of the Israelites as being faithful to the Lord in Egypt, in that they did not worship Neptune when delivered through the Red Sea, nor did they develop a shrine to the goddess "Mannia" when they received food by God's mercy in the wilderness. But eventually they were "seduced by impious gods" and "at last putting to death the Christ." If they had not done this, "they would have remained in the same kingdom which, even if it did not grow in extent, would have grown in happiness."[17] They

[11] One major exception to this kind of "spiritualizing" tendency among amillennialists is Anthony Hoekema, *The Bible and the Future* (Grand Rapids: Eerdmans, 1979).

[12] Brian E. Daley, *The Hope of the Early Church: A Handbook of Patristic Eschatology* (Cambridge: Cambridge University Press, 1991), 133.

[13] Augustine, *On Genesis: A Refutation of the Manichees, Unfinished Literal Commentary on Genesis* (New York: New City, 2004), 1.35–41.

[14] Daley, *Hope of the Early Church*, 133.

[15] Augustine, *The City of God against the Pagans*, trans. R. W. Dyson (Cambridge: Cambridge University Press, 1998), 20.7.

[16] Ibid., 20.5, 20.9.

[17] Ibid., 4.34.

did not, and so now are dispersed "by the providence of the true God."[18] That is not the end of it for Augustine, however. Though he is careful not to set dates or to be too specific about the actual way these things will happen, he did articulate a list of things that would happen at the end: the return of Elijah, the conversion of the Jewish people to faith in Christ, the persecution of the saints by Antichrist, the Second Advent of Jesus, the resurrection of the dead, the separation of the righteous from the impenitent, the renewal of this world, and the final judgment, not necessarily in that order.[19] With his hopefulness for the conversion of the Jews, Augustine softened the negativism toward these people that we have seen with some of his forefathers, which is all the more remarkable when you know that his "father in the faith," Ambrose, actually promoted the persecution of Jews in Milan. Still, Augustine further championed the view earlier advocated by the *Epistle of Barnabas* and Origen that the church has now replaced Israel as the people of God.

In the sixteenth and seventeenth centuries a fully developed covenantal (or, federal) theology grew out of the work of the Reformers who were most associated with the Calvin (as opposed to the Luther) wing of the Reformation. This covenant theology can trace some of its roots back to the *Epistle of Barnabas*, and the writings of Justin and Augustine, in the sense that the covenantal theologians agree that the new covenant spoken of in Scripture was not effected in national Israel, but in Christ, and then bequeathed to the church at Pentecost.[20] John Calvin often wrote about the covenants in the Bible, but his theology, following a trinitarian and biblical/exegetical contour, did not itself reflect the full-blown covenantalism of his followers in the next century. The Zurich Reformers, Zwingli and Bullinger, came closer to establishing this approach to systematic and biblical theology.[21] Johannes Cocceius, professor at the University

[18] Ibid.
[19] Ibid., 20.30.
[20] For a helpful discussion of some of the historical issues related to the new covenant, see Bruce A. Ware, "The New Covenant and the People(s) of God," in *Dispensationalism, Israel and the Church: The Search for Definition*, ed. Craig A. Blaising and Darrell L. Bock (Grand Rapids: Zondervan, 1992), 68–97.
[21] Robert Reymond, *A New Systematic Theology of the Christian Faith* (Nashville: Thomas Nelson, 1998), 503–4.

of Leyden from 1650 until his death in 1669, contended that the Bible presents a redemptive-historical understanding of salvation enshrined in three covenants: the covenant of works made with Adam, the covenant of grace made with Moses, and the new covenant effected through Christ.[22] But it was among English Calvinists, especially James Ussher and then the Westminster Assembly (1644–48), that covenant theology in its mature form came to be defined.[23]

In its developed form, covenant theology came to affirm that God's relation to humans could be understood in reference to three covenants: "the pre-temporal 'covenant of redemption' (*pactum salutis*) between the persons of the Godhead; the 'covenant of works' (*foederus naturae*) made with Adam before the Fall on behalf of the entire human race; and the 'covenant of grace' (*foederus gratiae*) made through Christ with all who believe, namely, the elect."[24] The Westminster Confession articulates the covenant of grace in this manner:

> Man, by his fall, having made himself incapable of life by [the covenant of works], the Lord was pleased to make a second, commonly called the covenant of grace, wherein He freely offereth unto sinners life and salvation by Jesus Christ; requiring of them faith in Him, that they may be saved, and promising to give unto all of those that are ordained unto eternal life His Holy Spirit to make them willing and able to believe.

This confession of faith proclaims "the unity of the covenant of grace and the oneness of the people of God in all ages."[25] The covenant of grace subsumes within itself all of the biblical covenants that are enjoined in the postfallen condition of humanity (Noahic, Abrahamic, Mosaic, Davidic, and the new covenant). At the heart of covenant theology is the conviction that the "genealogical principle" articulated in the Abrahamic covenant, codified

---

[22] Peter Golding, *Covenant Theology: The Key of Theology in the Reformed Thought and Tradition* (Ross-shire, UK: Christian Focus, 2004), 48.
[23] Reymond, *New Systematic Theology*, 504–5; Golding, *Covenant Theology*, 47–54.
[24] Peter J. Gentry and Stephen J. Wellum, *Kingdom through Covenant: A Biblical-Theological Understanding of the Covenants* (Wheaton: Crossway, 2012), 57.
[25] Reymond, *New Systematic Theology*, 506.

in the command to circumcise the male children (Gen 17:9–14), continues into the new covenant, though circumcision is now replaced by the baptism of all children.[26] Further, the church now has virtually replaced Israel in the economy of salvation, though some covenant theologians still hold out hope for a future ingathering of Jews into the church.[27] In effect, in covenant theology, the new covenant is a *renewal* of the Abrahamic covenant rather than being something inherently *new*.[28] Covenant theology has been very influential especially in Presbyterian and Reformed circles and somewhat influential among Calvinists in other traditions.[29]

Believers' church advocates (Baptists and others) contend that the genealogical principle is misguided. They argue that there are no clear NT texts that advocate infant baptism, and they further insist that the idea that baptism in the NT is a corollary to circumcision in the OT is an unfounded assumption. While some Baptists have adopted certain elements of covenant theology, especially its Calvinistic soteriology, most have not historically affirmed the basic hermeneutical emphasis that binds covenant theology together. So, while some of them have accepted the idea of the three-fold covenant (articulated above), they do not accept the genealogical principle.

In the early nineteenth century, a theological system gained popularity that grew out of insights from previous thinkers but was itself essentially new. Borrowing from the premillennialism of the early church and from some of Luther's ideas about the contrast between gospel and law, J. N. Darby and others first in England and then in America developed the system that came to be known as dispensational theology.[30] Dispensationalism has gone through

[26] Reymond, *New Systematic Theology*, 935–50; Gentry and Wellum, *Kingdom through Covenant*, 63.

[27] See, for example, John Murray, "The Last Things," in *Collected Writings of John Murray, Volume 2: Systematic Theology*, ed. Iain Murray (Carlisle, PA: Banner of Truth, 1977), 409–10.

[28] Gentry and Wellum, *Kingdom through Covenant*, 63, 223–300.

[29] In this volume, the chapter by Robert Reymond lays out the covenant theology position.

[30] On the history of dispensationalism, see especially Timothy P. Weber, *Living in the Shadow of the Second Coming: American Premillennialism 1875–1982*, enlarged ed. (Chicago: University of Chicago Press, 1987), 13–127; Richard R. Reiter, "A History of the Development of the Rapture Positions," in *Three Views on the Rapture: Pre-, Mid-,*

a series of developments since the time of Darby, so that Blaising and Bock can speak of "classical," "revised," and "progressive" dispensationalism.[31] In 1965 Charles Ryrie published what would turn out to be the standard treatment on dispensationalism from the "revised" school.[32] In that book he listed three basic themes that make dispensationalism distinctive: a consistently literal hermeneutic, a focus on the glory of God, and, most famously, his identification of the *sine qua non* of the system: "What then is the *sine qua non* of dispensationalism? . . . A dispensationalist keeps Israel and the Church distinct."[33] That conviction can be read back into "classical" dispensationalism and is found, to a lesser degree, in the "progressive" dispensationalist authors.[34] For dispensational theologians, then, promises made in the Old Testament to Israel, in some manner, must be fulfilled with reference to Israel and not the church. So, for traditional dispensationalist authors (and to some degree the "progressives") the promises of land as an "eternal promise" (e.g., Gen 15:17–21) must be literally fulfilled in the future by Israel once again inhabiting its ancient homeland, whether in this age, in the millennial kingdom, or in the new heavens and new earth.[35] Wellum and Gentry refer to this as the "land principle" and note that, whereas covenant interpreters see the genealogical principle as being continuous across the ages, dispensational interpreters see the land principle as the point of continuity between the Abrahamic and Mosaic covenants on the one hand and the new covenant on the other, at least in its future application.[36] This view is buttressed in more traditional dispensational circles (what Blaising and Bock call "classical" and "revised") by the belief that the church constitutes a "parenthesis" or,

---

or Post-Tribulational? (Grand Rapids: Zondervan, 1984), 9–44; Craig A. Blaising and Darrell L. Bock, *Progressive Dispensationalism* (Wheaton: Bridgepoint, 1993), 9–56.

[31] Blaising and Bock, *Progressive Dispensationalism*, 21–56.

[32] Note that Ryrie did not use that terminology, but he did offer some "correctives" to the older writers, represented by Darby, Scofield, and others.

[33] Charles Ryrie, *Dispensationalism Today* (Chicago: Moody, 1965), 44–45.

[34] In this volume, see the chapter by Robert Thomas as a statement by a "revised" dispensationalist (to use the term coined by Blaising and Bock though not necessarily endorsed by Thomas) and the chapter by Robert Saucy espousing "progressive" dispensationalism.

[35] Dispensationalists differ as to whether that promise will be fulfilled in the millennium or in the eternal state. Compare, for instance, the arguments of Thomas and Saucy in this volume.

[36] Gentry and Wellum, *Kingdom through Covenant*, 42–44.

better, an "intercalation" in the plan of God for Israel.[37] One difference between the "progressive" dispensationalists and the traditionalists in the movement is that the "progressives" see *some* application of the promises in the OT to Israel being applied to the church.[38] The rejection of Jesus/Messiah by Israel in the Gospels resulted in God offering the kingdom to whoever would receive it, whether Jews or Gentiles, but the future age of tribulation[39] and especially millennium will constitute a return to the covenant with Israel, in some manner.[40]

As to the other principles that Ryrie articulated as the distinctive features of dispensationalism, its "literal hermeneutic" and its goal as the glory of God, a couple of things need to be noted. First, the claim to a literal hermeneutic is not always followed by dispensational thinkers. John Walvoord, for instance, sees the seven churches in Revelation 2–3 as representative progressive ages in church history, an idea that has little or no foundation in the actual words of the text.[41] What dispensational thinkers generally insist on with the literal hermeneutic claim is that *Israel is Israel* and the church is the church; that is, the literal hermeneutic idea becomes a buttress for the land principle. As to the other principle, the glory of God, covenant theology is every bit as committed to that principle as dispensationalism is, as is readily obvious in any standard work of covenant theology.

[37] Lewis Sperry Chafer, *Systematic Theology*, 8 vols. (Dallas: Dallas Seminary Press, 1948), 4:40.

[38] Ware, "The New Covenant and the People(s) of God," in Blaising and Bock, *Dispensationalism, Israel and the Church*, 84–91.

[39] Not all "progressive" dispensationalists hold to a pretribulational rapture. See T. Van McLain, "The Pretribulation Rapture: A Doubtful Doctrine," in *Looking into the Future: Evangelical Studies in Eschatology*, ed. David W. Baker, ETS Studies (Grand Rapids: Baker, 2001), 233–45.

[40] Dispensationalists hold varying views on how this will work, with Ryrie seeing the millennium as constituted of mortal Jews living their lives out under the rule of King Jesus, while Blaising and Bock see the millennial "saints" as resurrected Jews (Israelites) in glorified bodies ruling with Christ over the Gentile nations made up of mortals who survive the great tribulation and their progeny. See Ryrie, *Dispensationalism Today*, 132–76; Blaising and Bock, *Progressive Dispensationalism*, 270–77. Some "progressive" dispensationalists see the millennium as glorified Israelites and Christians dwelling together under Christ's rule. See David L. Turner, "The New Jerusalem in Revelation 21:1–22:5: Consummation of a Biblical Continuum," in *Dispensationalism, Israel and the Church*, 264–92.

[41] John Walvoord, *The Revelation of Jesus Christ* (Chicago: Moody, 1966), 50–100. The idea serves a theological purpose for Walvoord, since the last church in the series is Laodicea, virtually an "apostate" church, and Walvoord's version of dispensationalism affirms the idea that the rapture happens in the context of a mostly apostate Christianity.

There is also the issue of "dispensations." Dispensationalists have disagreed over how many there are and over how hard the lines are between the dispensations. The *Scofield Reference Bible* famously argued for seven (see discussion of this in the various chapters of this book), but not all have agreed. There is further disagreement over the actual differences between the dispensations. Again Scofield *seemed* to argue for different means of salvation in the several dispensations, but "revised" and "progressive" dispensationalists have generally moved away from that idea.[42] In addition, even covenant theologians have argued for different eras in redemptive history—at least two: the covenant of works and the covenant of grace—though they tend to *flatten out* the biblical covenants, seeing the new covenant, as we pointed out above, as a virtual renewal of the Abrahamic covenant.[43]

In the past sixty or so years, a "mediating" position, or perhaps simply a *different* position, has come to the fore in several permutations.[44] Based on the work of several German scholars, especially Werner Kummel and Oscar Cullmann, but entering American scholarship early on through the writings of G. Eldon Ladd,[45] this view is distinct from both of the other positions in its ecclesiology and eschatology. Ladd agrees with dispensationalism's premillennialism, but not with its view of the pretribulational rapture of the church.[46] Also in contrast to dispensationalism, Ladd argues for the unity of Israel and the church: "The olive

---

[42] Scofield wrote that salvation under the old covenant came by keeping the law. See *Scofield Reference Bible*, note on Gen 12:1. Ryrie and others have contended that Scofield misspoke on this issue and would have written otherwise had he anticipated the fallout. See Ryrie, *Dispensationalism Today*, 110–31. Others have argued otherwise. See Daniel P. Fuller, "The Hermeneutics of Dispensationalism," PhD diss., Northern Baptist Theological Seminary, 1957, 164.

[43] Gentry and Wellum, *Kingdom through Covenant*, 63, and throughout their discussion.

[44] I would argue that this "mediating" position has been around for a long time, but it only became self-identified in its contrast to developed dispensationalism.

[45] Werner Kummel, *Promise and Fulfillment: The Eschatological Message of Jesus*, Studies in Biblical Theology (London: SCM, 1957); Oscar Cullmann, *Christ and Time: The Primitive Christian Conception of Time and History*, rev. ed., trans. F. Filson (Philadelphia: Westminster, 1964); G. Eldon Ladd, *The Presence of the Future: The Eschatology of Biblical Realism*, rev. ed. (Grand Rapids: Eerdmans, 1974); Ladd, *The Blessed Hope: A Biblical Study of the Second Advent and the Rapture* (Grand Rapids: Eerdmans, 1956); Ladd, *A Theology of the New Testament* (Grand Rapids: Eerdmans, 1974).

[46] Ladd, *Blessed Hope*, 61–136.

tree is one people of God."[47] One other issue related to dispensationalism that we have not covered, but that was of deep concern to Ladd, was dispensationalism's separatist ecclesiology. In part because of their polemic against liberalism, many (though certainly not all) dispensationalist leaders have separated out from denominational life and some, like Darby, have actually created new ecclesiological structures. Ladd rejected this separatism and the superficial ethical positions that he saw as entailed in this separatism.[48] Progressive dispensationalism has likewise not continued these ecclesiological or ethical practices.

Over against covenant theology, Ladd argues for a "believer's" relationship to both the sacraments of baptism and the Lord's Supper. Baptism is the "rite of admission" into the church, and "it symbolizes the believer's union with Christ in which he dies to his old life and is raised up to walk in newness of life."[49] He further states about baptism and circumcision, "It is not at all clear that Paul conceived of baptism as the Christian equivalent to circumcision."[50] What is clear in this is that Ladd is opposed to both the general ecclesiology of covenant theology, at least as to its genealogical principle, and to much of its eschatology, since he is premillennial, though not pretribulational. Ladd represents a position that is neither covenantal nor dispensational.

Over the past decades, others have joined the effort to carve out a position that is neither covenantal nor dispensational. Sometimes referred to as "new covenant theology" or "progressive covenantalism," this approach rejects both the land principle and the genealogical principle and asserts that Christ himself is the fulfillment of OT expectations.[51] Gentry and Wellum, as

[47] Ladd, *Theology of the New Testament*, 538.
[48] On this, see especially John A. D'Elia, *A Place at the Table: George Eldon Ladd and the Rehabilitation of Evangelical Scholarship in America* (Oxford: Oxford University Press, 2008), 175–78.
[49] Ladd, *Theology of the New Testament*, 547–48. Ladd prefers the term "rite" to the term "sacrament."
[50] Ibid., 548.
[51] Representative works include Tom Wells and Fred Zaspel, *New Covenant Theology* (Frederick, MD: New Covenant Media, 2002); Jason C. Meyer, *The End of the Law: Mosaic Covenant in Pauline Theology*, NAC Studies in Bible & Theology, ed. E. Ray Clendenen (Nashville: B&H Academic, 2009); John G. Reisinger, *Abraham's Four Seeds* (Frederick, MD: New Covenant Media, 1998); Gentry and Wellum, *Kingdom through Covenant*. These works follow similar hermeneutical approaches but differ from one another in theological and pastoral application.

representatives, forge a *via media* between covenantal and dispensational theology and stress the unity of the Bible by tracing the redemptive-historical thread through the progressive covenants of Scripture. They view each covenant (Adamic, Noahic, Abrahamic, Mosaic, Davidic, new covenant) as progressively building on previous covenants but also as refining (my term) them in certain ways to address what is now *new* in progressive revelation.[52] This approach is based on the idea that "Jesus and the new covenant must become the hermeneutical lens by which we interpret the fulfillment of the types of the Old Testament."[53] For dispensationalism the key terms seem to be Jesus and Israel, for covenantalism the key terms seem to be Jesus and the church, while for "progressive covenantalism" the key term seems to be just *Jesus.* "The hopes and fears of all the years" are met in him and him alone.[54]

Four Views on Israel and the Church

The authors in this volume were asked to address several issues in relation to Israel and the church. Each has addressed the exegetical issues related to Israel and its relationship to God. They have also looked at what is distinctively new in the coming of the church of the Lord Jesus Christ. They have analyzed these issues specifically in relationship to the doctrines of ecclesiology and eschatology, the two areas of systematic theology that impinge most on the topic of Israel and the church. They have also addressed the issue of the modern state of Israel, and whether or not it has some role to play in the carrying out of God's plan of salvation for the world.

The essays are presented in the historical order that the various positions arose, reflected in the earlier part of this introduction. One way to view the difference between the positions is in terms of Richard Lints's three "horizons" of context: textual,

---

[52] See especially Gentry and Wellum, *Kingdom through Covenant,* 591–716.
[53] Ibid., 608.
[54] Though we did not have access to the book by Gentry and Wellum while writing our essay for this volume, this is the basic position that Tom Pratt and I take in our chapter.

epochal, and canonical.[55] The *textual horizon* is the immediate context. One "cannot read all of the Bible at once,"[56] so the reader has to look at such things as grammar, genre, syntax, figures of speech, and other valid hermeneutical details. The second context is the *epochal horizon*, where texts are read in light of where they are in redemption history. As Lints has observed, "Redemption is an activity of God that unfolds over time. This unfolding movement in the biblical text is profoundly important to the accomplishment of its purposes."[57] Early revelation treats redemption somewhat differently than later Scripture. Circumcision, sacrifices, dietary laws, and other issues give way to fulfillment in Christ. There are also shifts that occur within the Old Testament and even within the short span of the New Testament. Third is what Lints terms the *canonical horizon*. Scripture must be read as a unified revelation, from first to last. The four approaches to the question of the church and Israel can each be seen to utilize these three horizons in different and distinct ways, but the key to understanding the differences lies mainly in Lints's second horizon, the *epochal*.

The first approach to Israel and the church in our volume is the traditional covenantal view. Robert Reymond argues for the covenantal view, contending for a greater degree of *continuity* between the old and new covenants than is characteristic of dispensationalism. In regard to the church/Israel debate, this continuity can be seen in the correlation between circumcision and baptism, with infant baptism being the analogue of circumcision—what I denominated as the "generational principle" earlier in this introduction. It can also be seen in the insistence that the church is the "new Israel," and, in Reymond's words, that the church now *replaces* Israel as the people of God (see p. 49). "There is no distinction between Jew and Gentile today, since God is calling out to himself a people from both groups," says O. Palmer Robertson, who then goes on to note that this "no distinction" will continue even in the age(s) to

[55] Richard Lints, *The Fabric of Theology: A Prolegomenon to Evangelical Theology* (Grand Rapids: Eerdmans, 1993), 259–311.
[56] Gentry and Wellum, *Kingdom through Covenant*, 93.
[57] Lints, *Fabric of Theology*, 262.

come.[58] The epochal horizon for Reymond hardly moves from Old Testament to New Testament, with the discontinuity being primarily the replacement of the church for Israel and the permanent gift of the Holy Spirit to all believers. There is no future for Israel as Israel, though Reymond and others in the covenantal tradition do believe there will be a future ingathering of Jewish persons into the church.

The second essay in this volume explicates the traditional dispensational position. Dispensationalists contend for a greater degree of *discontinuity* between Old and New Testaments, as well as a very different perspective on the relationship between the church and Israel. Robert Thomas sees the church as a parenthesis in God's overall strategy with reference to the covenant with Israel. After the rapture of the church, the covenant with Israel will be resumed with the 144,000 Jews in the tribulation period, and then continue on into the millennium with Israel ruling with Christ during the thousand years. He further notes, "Revelation 21:12,14 shows that Israel will have a role distinct from the church even in the new Jerusalem, the eternal state. As the special object of God's choice, she will ever be distinctive" (see p. 135). For Thomas, the epochal horizon from Old Testament to New Testament is a very large shift, as God's focus moves from Israel to another congregation, the church, but it is a move that will be somewhat, though not completely, reversed in the *eschaton* as the new congregation will also enjoy the blessings of eschatological bliss. Thomas also affirms the land principle, the continuity between the Testaments resides in the promise of land to Israel, and in fact affirms that as an eternal promise.[59]

The third view that has arisen chronologically, the progressive dispensational view, is articulated by Robert Saucy and maintains the land principle of traditional dispensationalism but modifies it by construing it as only lasting though the millennium, and not as an eternal distinction between Israel and the church. The epochal horizon is thus seen as moving from Israel

---

[58] O. Palmer Robertson, "Hermeneutics of Continuity," in *Continuity and Discontinuity: Perspectives on the Relationship between the Old and New Testaments*, ed. John S. Feinberg (Westchester, IL: Crossway, 1988), 102.

[59] Gentry and Wellum, *Kingdom through Covenant*, 86.

to the church in the new covenant, but then back to Israel for tribulation and millennium, and then back to a unified people in the eternal state. Promises to Israel in the Old Testament are in some sense fulfilled in Christ but also in another sense still fulfilled in a literal way in the millennium.[60] Finally, the fourth essay in this volume, by Tom Pratt and me, takes the progressive covenantal (inaugurated eschatology) or new covenant position, articulated by Ladd and now in a modified form by people like Zaspel and Wellum. We affirm with traditional covenantalism that there is a continuity between the Old and New Testaments in terms of a people of God and that the church is now the people of God, but we reject the notion of "replacement," since Israel is still the apple of God's eye and will be a subject of eschatological salvation. The new covenant position also rejects the genealogical principle of baptism being the analogue of circumcision since there is no description or prescription of infant baptism in the New Testament and since all texts relating to baptism presume that the persons being baptized are disciples of the Lord. This position also rejects the notion that there is a distinction between the two peoples of God in the millennium or the eternal state, as Paul argues in Ephesians 2 and other places, God has broken down the wall that divides the people of the Lord.[61] The epochal horizon is thus permanently shifted to the church with the coming of the Spirit at Pentecost, though God still has a concern for his old covenant people. This view also affirms that the "newness" of the new covenant includes the permanent indwelling of the Holy Spirit and the fact that Christ is the fulfillment of all Old Testament promises.

I commend these essays now to you, the reader. I believe you will learn much. But, even more, it is my prayer that this exercise will lead you to greater depth of worship and to a more impassioned commitment to proclaim the gospel of our Lord and Savior, Jesus Christ.

---

[60] It ought to be noted that there is a considerable range of opinions on controversial points among progressive dispensationalists, but Saucy is certainly one of the most respected voices in that circle.

[61] Ladd, *A Theology of the New Testament*, 480–87.

CHAPTER 1

The Traditional Covenantal View

BY ROBERT L. REYMOND

Historic Covenant Theology: What It Is

Historic covenant theology has three main characteristics. (1) It stresses the unity and continuity of redemptive history from Gen 3:15 to the farthest reaches of the future over against traditional and Dallas dispensationalism that stress the disunity and discontinuity of redemptive history. (2) It asserts the unity of the covenant of grace and the oneness of God's people in all ages over against traditional and Dallas dispensationalism, which maintain that there are two distinct peoples of God, namely, Israel and the Christian church, with two distinct destinies, namely, the glorified land of Israel for the former and a glorified heaven for the latter. (3) It insists that Old Testament saints were saved precisely the same way that New Testament saints are being saved, namely, through conscious faith in the (anticipated) sacrificial work of the promised Messiah on their behalf as that work was foresignified by Old Testament promises, prophecies, sacrifices, circumcision, the paschal lamb, and other types and ordinances delivered to the Jewish people, over against traditional and Dallas dispensationalism, which teach that saving faith in God has been manifested in "different ways" throughout the ages, depending on the dispensation.[1]

A Brief History of Historic Covenant Theology

"The doctrine of the covenants is a peculiarly Reformed doctrine,"[2] writes Geerhardus Vos, because with the Reformation in general came a serious return to the much neglected study of Scripture that prevailed throughout the Middle Ages. Using the grammatical/historical canons of hermeneutics, the Swiss Reformers, Ulrich Zwingli (1484–1531), Johann Heinrich Bullinger (1504–75), and John Calvin (1509–64), in particular returned to the Bible's root idea of God's glory both in creation and particularly in salvation. It was natural, then, that they would develop the biblical covenants as the successive historical instrumentalities whereby God determined to bring glory to himself by the salvation of the elect through the mediatorial work of his Son and the ministrations of his Spirit and his spoken and written Word. Covenant theology emerged, then, on Swiss soil,[3] particularly in German-speaking Zurich in the writings of

---

[1] See my book *Behold the Conquering Lamb* (Ross-shire, Scotland: Christian Focus, 2006).

[2] Geerhardus Vos, "The Doctrine of the Covenant in Reformed Theology," in *Redemptive History and Biblical Interpretation: The Shorter Writings of Geerhardus Vos*, ed. Richard B. Gaffin Jr. (Phillipsburg, NJ: P&R, 1980), 234.

[3] This should not be taken to mean that covenant theology is simply "manmade" and appeared on the scene for the first time in church history during the Reformation. The Swiss Reformers knew well the early patristic literature, citing the early church fathers extensively, particularly Augustine, and they found in them many nuances of covenant theology. But, it is a sad fact that after Augustine, biblical study languished, and as a result the church fathers more and more favored a sacerdotal theology and failed to develop a covenant theology. Geerhardus Vos has rightly noted in his "The Doctrine of the Covenant," that once the Reformers turned the church back to the study of Scripture and insisted that God should receive the preeminence in all things, particularly with respect to man and his relation to God,

> [this principle] immediately divided into three parts: 1. All of man's work has to rest on an antecedent work of God; 2. In all of his works man has to show forth God's image and be a means for the revelation of God's virtues; 3. The latter should not occur unconsciously or passively, but the revelation of God's virtues must proceed by way of understanding and will and by way of the conscious life, and actively come to external expression (242).

Vos then proceeds to show how this threefold demand was addressed in the doctrine of the covenant, with the eternal *covenant of redemption* becoming the resting place for all three requirements, and the *covenant of works* and the *covenant of grace* that flows

Zwingli—who, as a result of his debates with the Anabaptists, made the concept of covenant the main argument for the Reformed understanding of infant baptism—and in Bullinger's *Decades*, five books of ten sermons each that were structured by the covenant idea.

Also, in his *A Brief Exposition of the One and Eternal Testament or Covenant of God* (1534), the first treatise in church history on the covenant as such, Bullinger argued throughout that the entirety of Scripture must be viewed in light of the Abrahamic covenant, in which God graciously offers to give himself to men and in turn requires that men walk before him and be perfect (Gen 17:1).[4] In French-speaking Geneva, Calvin, in his *Institutes of the Christian Religion*, 2.10.1–5, 8, set forth the covenant idea, employing when need called for it both the unity of the covenant and the oneness of God's people in all ages, but because he developed his *Institutes* along Trinitarian lines the covenant concept, although there, is not the architectonic or governing principle of his *Institutes*.[5]

out of the covenant of redemption each in its own way fulfilling the demands of all three parts (242–67).

[4] For an English translation see Charles S. McCoy and J. Wayne Baker, eds., *Fountainhead of Federalism: Heinrich Bullinger and the Covenant Tradition* (Louisville: WJK, 1991), 101–38.

The common view that "all things Protestant" originated with Martin Luther is wrong. William Cunningham rightly observes in his article, "Zwingle, and the Doctrine of the Sacraments," in *The Reformers and the Theology of the Reformation* (1862; repr., London: Banner of Truth, 1967), 213–14:

The important movement of which Zwingle might be said to be the originator and the head, was wholly independent of Luther; that is to say, Luther was in no way whatever, directly or indirectly, the cause of the occasion of Zwingle being led to embrace the views which he promulgated, or to adopt the course which he pursued. Zwingle had been led to embrace the leading principles of Protestant truth, and to preach them in 1516, the year before the publication of Luther's Theses; and it is quite certain, that all along he continued to think and act for himself, on his own judgement and responsibility, deriving his views from his own personal and independent study of the word of God. This fact shows how inaccurate it is to identify the Reformation with Luther, as if all the Reformers derived their opinions from him [Of course, Calvin, being a second-generation Reformer, did drink at the wells of soteric Lutheranism in the beginning of his career.—RLR], and merely followed his example in abandoning the Church of Rome, and organizing churches apart from her communion. Many at this time, in different parts of Europe, were led to study the sacred Scriptures, and were led further to derive from this study views of divine truth substantially the same, and decidedly opposed to those generally inculcated in the Church of Rome.

[5] Paul Helm in his article, "Calvin and the Covenant: Unity and Continuity," in *Evangelical Quarterly* 55 (1981): 65–81, marshals evidence that shows that all the

The influence of the Zurich Reformers of German Switzerland and of the Geneva Reformer of French Switzerland was widespread and lasting. They influenced the Heidelberg theologians, Caspar Olevianus (1536–87) and Zacharias Ursinus (1534–83), both men having spent time in Zurich and both having studied with Calvin in Geneva. Olevianus wrote *The Substance of the Covenant of Grace Between God and the Elect* (1585) and Ursinus applied the covenant concept in his *Larger Catechism* (1612). Their ideas, respectively, of a precreation covenant between God the Father and God the Son for the salvation of men and of a prefall covenant of law between God and Adam that promised life for perfect obedience and threatened death for disobedience, resulted in the developed covenant theology of Dutch Reformed theologians Johannes Cocceius (1603–69), who wrote *Doctrine of the Covenant and Testaments of God* (1648), and Herman Witsius (1636–1708), who wrote *The Economy of the Covenants Between God and Man* (1685).

The Swiss Reformers also influenced the development of covenant theology in England. Many preachers and scholars had fled to Zurich and Geneva during the reign of Queen Mary, and Bullinger and Calvin maintained correspondence with them when they returned to England. Accordingly, Robert Rollock and Robert Howie in Scotland; Thomas Cartwright, John Preston, Thomas Blake, and John Ball in England; and James Ussher in Ireland all developed and wrote their theologies along covenantal lines. Bullinger's *Decades* were also translated into English in 1577 and became the official guide for clergy who had not obtained a master's degree. Influenced as they were by the labors of these men, the framers of the Westminster Confession of Faith in 1646 placed the concept of the covenants in the foreground of that confessional deliverance, giving creedal status to the covenant of works and the covenant of grace.

About the former, the Confession states: "The first covenant made with man was a covenant of works, wherein life was promised to Adam; and in him to his posterity, upon condition of

essential features of covenant theology—the eternal covenant of redemption between the Father and the Son, the covenant of works (in elementary form) between God and Adam, and the covenant of grace between God and the redeemed—have clear roots in Calvin's theological thought.

perfect and personal obedience" (VII.ii). About the latter—the tangible, concrete expression in creation history of the redemptive aspects of God's eternal plan of salvation—the Confession states: "Man, by his fall, having made himself incapable of life by [the first covenant], the Lord was pleased to make a second, commonly called the covenant of grace,[6] wherein He freely offereth unto sinners life and salvation by Jesus Christ; requiring of them faith in Him, that they may be saved, and promising to give unto all those that are ordained to eternal life His Holy Spirit, to make them willing, and able to believe" (VII.iii).

Without using the phrase in so many words, the Westminster Confession of Faith then clearly asserts the unity of the covenant and the oneness of God's people in all ages:

> VII.v: This [second] covenant was differently administered in the time of the law, and in the time of the gospel: under the law, it was administered by promises, prophecies, sacrifices, circumcision, the paschal lamb, and other types and ordinances delivered to the people of the Jews, all foresignifying Christ to come; which were, for the time, sufficient and efficacious, through the operation of the Spirit, to instruct and build up the elect in faith in the promised Messiah, by whom they had full remission of sins, and eternal salvation; and [it] is called the Old Testament.

> VII.vi: Under the gospel, when Christ, the substance was exhibited, the ordinances in which this covenant is dispensed are the preaching of the Word, and the administration of the sacraments of Baptism and the Lord's Supper: which, though few in number [compared to the Old Testament], and administered with more simplicity, and less outward glory, yet, in them, it is held forth in more fullness, evidence, and spiritual efficacy, to all

---

6   This second covenant, designated the "covenant of grace," while it is such for the elect sinner who becomes the pensioner of its benefits, was for Christ, the Mediator and Head of this covenant, the original "covenant of works," requiring of him the same perfect and personal obedience that it required of Adam. As the "last Adam" and "second Man from heaven" (1 Cor 15:45, 47), he perfectly met the obligations of the covenant of works that Adam failed to meet.

nations, both Jews and Gentiles, and [it] is called the New Testament. *There are not therefore two covenants of grace, differing in substance, but one and the same, under various dispensations.*

The Westminster Confession of Faith makes the same points later, albeit in a more directly salvific setting and in different words, when it declares:

VIII.vi: Although the work of redemption was not actually wrought by Christ till after His Incarnation, yet the virtue, efficacy and benefits thereof were communicated unto the elect, in all ages, successively from the beginning of the world, in and by those promises, types, and sacrifices, where [Christ] was revealed, and signified to be the seed of the woman which should bruise the serpent's head; and the Lamb slain from the beginning of the world, being yesterday and today the same, and forever.

. . .

XIX.iii: . . . God was pleased to give to the people of Israel . . . ceremonial laws containing several typical ordinances . . . prefiguring Christ, his graces, actions, sufferings, and benefits. . . .

While the influence of the work of the Westminster Assembly was short-lived in England itself—the Savoy Declaration of 1658, a modification of the Confession to suit English congregational polity, being the exception here—stifled as it was by the restoration of Charles II to the English throne in 1660, its Confession of Faith and its Larger and Shorter Catechisms were adopted by the Church of Scotland and in the New World by the Presbyterian churches in colonial America. Through these churches the covenant theology of the Reformers and the Westminster Assembly has had a growing influence over Protestant theology in general around the world, even in churches that have never formally adopted as their own the covenant theology of the Westminster Confession of Faith and Catechisms.

Historic Covenant Theology versus Traditional and Dallas Dispensationalism

Over against historic covenant theology's representation of the covenant of grace as being one in all ages, through the execution of which is created the one people of God, that is, the church, comprised of all the elect of all ages, stands the dispensational school's interpretation of redemptive history. While dispensational scholars differ over how many dispensations or consecutive "rules of life" one may find in Scripture, all of them would agree with the Dallas Theological Seminary (DTS) Doctrinal Statement, the largest dispensational seminary in the United States, if not in the world, that

> three of these dispensations or rules of life are the subject of extended revelation in the Scriptures, viz., the dispensation of the Mosaic law, the present dispensation of grace, and the future dispensation of the millennial kingdom.[7]

Of these three dispensations, the DTS Doctrinal Statement immediately affirms: "We believe that these are distinct and are not to be intermingled or confused, as they are chronologically successive." Moreover, while the DTS Doctrinal Statement affirms, "Salvation in the divine reckoning is always 'by grace through faith,' and rests upon the basis of the shed blood of Christ," it qualifies this affirmation by declaring

> that it was historically impossible that [Old Testament saints][8] should have had as the conscious object of their faith the incarnate, crucified Son, the Lamb of God (John 1:29), and that it is evident that they did not comprehend as we do that the sacrifices depicted the person and work of Christ [and] that they did not understand the redemptive significance of the prophecies and types concerning the sufferings of Christ (1 Pet 1:10–12); therefore, we believe that their faith toward God was manifested in other ways as is shown by the long record

---

[7] "DTS Doctrinal Statement," http://www.dts.edu/about/doctrinalstatement.
[8] This would include even such men as Moses, David, and Isaiah.

in Hebrews 11:1–40 [which manifested faith] counted unto them for righteousness.

The DTS Doctrinal Statement does not clearly explain why these things were historically impossible for Old Testament saints, but the *New Scofield Reference Bible* (1967) provides us with the traditional dispensational explanation in its note on Jesus' proclamation, "Repent, for the kingdom of heaven is at hand" (NKJV) in Matt 4:17:

> The Bible expression "at hand" is never a positive affirmation that the person or thing said to be at hand will immediately appear, but only *that no known or predicted event must intervene.* When Christ appeared to the Jewish people, the next thing, in the order of revelation as it then stood, should have been the setting up of the Davidic kingdom. In the knowledge of God, *not yet disclosed,* lay the rejection of the kingdom and the King, the long period of the mystery form of the kingdom, the world-wide preaching of the cross, and the out-calling of the Church. But this was as yet locked up in the secret counsels of God (Mt. 13:11, 17; Eph. 3:3–12). (Emphasis supplied)

The DTS Doctrinal Statement echoes essentially these points in somewhat different language when it states:

> . . . in fulfillment of prophecy[9] [the eternal Son of God] came first to Israel as her Messiah-King, and . . . being rejected of that nation, He, *according to the eternal counsels of God,*[10] gave his life as a ransom for all. (Emphasis supplied)

Of course, if no one before the time of Jesus' public ministry knew about the rejection of the Messiah, this present age, the world-wide proclamation of the cross, or the out-calling of the church, then the faith of the Old Testament saint could not have been directed toward the person and work of the *suffering* Christ as its

---

[9] See Scofield's phrase, "in the order of revelation as it then stood."
[10] See Scofield's phrase, "locked up in the secret counsels of God."

saving object. But, one should know that this has not been the historic confession of the church that has not hesitated to sing:

> In the cross of Christ I glory,
> Towering o'er the wrecks of time;
> All the light of sacred story,
> Gathers round its head sublime.[11]

It is difficult to conceive of two evangelical perspectives on Old Testament faith that differ more radically than do these two, being mutually exclusive in the following ways: (1) The covenantal perspective stressing the continuity, the dispensational perspective stressing the discontinuity of redemptive history; and (2) the covenantal perspective insisting that Old Testament saints were saved through conscious faith in the anticipated sacrificial work of the promised Messiah, the dispensational perspective insisting, since the Old Testament saints did not know about the Messiah's future sacrificial work because God had not revealed it to them, that they were saved through a general "faith toward God . . . expressed in other ways" that was *devoid* of any conscious awareness that "without the shedding of [Messiah's] blood there is no forgiveness" (Heb 9:22 HCSB), even a faith that expressly *excluded* faith in the Messiah's death as the object of saving faith. But, what this dispensational assertion means is that the content of the Old Testament saints' "ways [plural] of faith," depending on the dispensation in which they found themselves, was one thing, and the content of the New Testament saint's faith is something else entirely. But, this means, although traditional dispensationalists may wish to deny it, that Scripture endorses different "plans of salvation," depending on the dispensation in which the Old Testament saint found himself. Clearly, if the Westminster Confession of Faith is right, the dispensational vision is wrong; if the dispensational vision is right, the Westminster Confession of Faith is wrong. Both cannot be right. I would argue that the following five arguments place beyond all reasonable doubt the Westminster position:

---

[11] "In the Cross of Christ I Glory" by John Bowring (1792–1872).

1. Once the covenant of grace that had been inaugurated in Gen 3:15 had come to expression in the spiritual promises of the Abrahamic covenant, this covenant became salvifically definitive for all ages to come (more on this point later).

2. The exodus from Egypt—the Old Testament type *par excellence* of New Testament redemption—by divine arrangement preexhibited the same great salvific principles that governed Christ's work of atonement in the New Testament, in both its accomplished and applied aspects, thereby teaching the elect in Israel about salvation by grace through faith in the atoning work of the Messiah's paschal mediation (see 1 Cor 5:7). In both its purpose and execution the exodus redemption originated in the sovereign, loving, electing grace of God (Deut 7:6–8). It was accomplished by the power of God and not by the strength of man (Exod 3:19–20; 15:1–18). And, it delivered only those who availed themselves of the expiation of sin afforded by the covering of the blood of the paschal lamb (Exod 12:12–13, 21–27).

3. According to the New Testament writers, Moses and the prophets prophesied about the events of the New Testament age, including the death and resurrection of Jesus Christ (Luke 22:37; 24:25–27; John 1:29; 5:39, 46; 13:18; 19:24, 28, 36–37; 20:9; Acts 3:17–18; 10:43; 13:27–30; 17:2–3; 26:22–23; 28:22–23; 1 Cor 15:3–4). Even a quick perusal of these passages will place beyond all doubt that, according to the New Testament, the Old Testament prophets wrote about a suffering Messiah. And, I think we may presume that what they wrote about, they proclaimed in the marketplaces of Israel.

4. The church of Jesus Christ is the present-day expression of the one people of God whose roots go back to Abraham (Acts 15:16–17; Rom 11:16–24; Gal 6:16; Eph 2:11–13; Phil 3:3).

5. The requisite condition for salvation is identical in the Old and New Testaments: The elect of God were saved, are saved, and will be saved only by grace through faith in either the anticipated (OT) or accomplished (NT) work of the Messiah (see Gen 3:21; 4:3–5; 15:6; the elaborate protocols of the Levitical sacrificial system that schooled Israel in the great principle of forgiveness through the substitutionary death of an unblemished sacrifice; Pss 16:9–11; 22:16; 32:1–2; Isa 7:14; 9:6; 52:13–53:13; John 1:29; 8:56; 2 Tim 3:15; Heb 11:26–27).

I should note in passing that historic covenantal paedobaptists ground their practice of infant baptism in this unity of the covenant and the oneness of God's people in all ages. They believe, because throughout Old Testament history as well as the New Testament age children of parents within the covenant of grace are expressly represented as possessing covenant status in the community of the faithful, that the baptism of their infants and young children is a justifiable deduction from the following three *undeniable* biblical truths:

1. Infant males received the sign and seal of the covenant of grace under its Old Testament administration.

2. The covenant of grace, as we have just argued, has continuity and organic unity through Scripture; the people of God are essentially one in all ages.

3. One can find no repeal in the New Testament of the *almost two-thousand-year-long* Old Testament practice of placing the sign of the covenant of grace upon covenant children. G. C. Berkouwer comments: "Against those who asked for a direct scriptural proof in which infant baptism was divinely commanded, the Reformers . . . pointed at the injustice of this question. In response, they asked their critics precisely where the Bible says

that this fundamental Covenant relation is broken in the New Covenant."[12] John Murray likewise queries:

"Does the New Testament revoke or does it provide any intimation of revoking so expressly authorized a principle as that of the inclusion of infants in the covenant and their participation in the covenant sign and seal? . . . Has [this practice] been discontinued? Our answer to these questions must be, that we find no evidence of revocation. In view of the fact that the new covenant is based upon and is the unfolding of the Abrahamic covenant, in view of the basic identity of meaning attaching to circumcision and baptism, in view of the unity and continuity of the covenant of grace administered in both dispensations, we can affirm with confidence that evidence of revocation or repeal is mandatory if the practice or principle has been discontinued under the New Testament."[13]

And David C. Jones writes: "Since the new covenant is characterized by greater, not lesser, privilege and blessing, one would expect to find some definite word if the established practice (1900 years in place) was supposed to be discontinued. What one finds instead of repeal are definite indications that God continues to work within the solidarity of the family in covenant relationship" (see Luke 18:15–17; Acts 2:39; 16:15; 16:31–34; 1 Cor 1:16; 7:14).[14]

I do not intend to suggest by the five reasons given above for the unity of the covenant and the oneness of God's people in all ages that Old Testament saints possessed all the information about Christ that the New Testament contains about his person and work. Nor am I maintaining that all of the elect of the Old Testament understood as much as Christians today do about Christ, although it must be said, given the shockingly small amount of knowledge that many if not most Christians have about Christ and his salvation today, that many Old Testament saints

[12] G. C. Berkouwer, *The Sacraments*, trans. Hugo Bekker (Grand Rapids: Eerdmans, 1969), 175.

[13] John Murray, *Christian Baptism* (Philadelphia: P&R, 1962), 52–53.

[14] David C. Jones, unpublished classroom lecture on baptism given at Covenant Theological Seminary, St. Louis, Missouri.

doubtless had a *deeper* understanding of the things of Christ than these poorly taught Christians. David, for example, spoke explicitly of the death and resurrection of the Messiah in Psalms 2, 16, and 22, and Isaiah spoke explicitly of the Messiah's death in Isaiah 53. But, while Vos rightly observed that "it is unhistorical to carry back into the O.T. mind our developed doctrinal consciousness of these matters,"[15] it is possible to address the issue of the Old Testament saints' understanding of redemption so one-sidedly from the biblical-theological perspective that the hermeneutics of that discipline overpower the "analogy of faith" principle of systematic theology. As a result, neither the teaching of the Old Testament itself, nor what the New Testament writers expressly report or imply that the Old Testament saints knew about the suffering Messiah and his bodily resurrection from the dead, is given its just due. That is to say, when one takes into account all the data amassed in these five reasons, particularly Jesus' declaration that Abraham "rejoiced at the thought of seeing my day; he saw it and was glad" (John 8:56 NIV), and the New Testament reiterations that the Old Testament Scriptures testified that "the Messiah would suffer and rise from the dead" (Luke 24:25–27, 45–47 HCSB), one must conclude that the Old Testament saints knew much more about the Messiah's suffering than is generally credited to them, and infinitely more than the Dallas Statement would allow them, since it maintains that they knew nothing about his suffering.

Traditional dispensationalists have employed Jesus' "mystery of the kingdom of heaven" parables in Matthew 13 and Eph 3:3–12 as proof that the Old Testament saints could not have known about the "rejection of the kingdom and the King, the long period of the mystery-form of the kingdom, the world-wide preaching of the cross, and the out-calling of the church" (excerpted from Scofield's statement quoted above). Accordingly, something must be said about these passages.

First, while I admit that the Matthew 13 parables, in keeping with the biblical word "mystery" found therein (see 13:11, 17, 34–35), revealed some truths about the kingdom of God that had not been clearly revealed to mankind prior to

---

[15] Geerhardus Vos, *Biblical Theology* (Grand Rapids: Eerdmans, 1948), 64.

Jesus' instruction, I do not believe that the Messiah's rejection was among those truths first revealed in them. Rather, he informed them by these parables, in keeping with his total teaching about the kingdom of God, that while the kingdom of God would certainly appear someday in great power and glory as Daniel 2 had predicted, it had already first appeared in grace with his first coming, and that in its grace modality it would know gradual growth, largely in the internal, invisible sphere of the spiritual life, and would tolerate both imperfections in its subjects and resistance from the world system. In its "mystery" form, George E. Ladd explains,

> The kingdom has come among men but not with power that compels every knee to bow before its glory; it is rather like seed cast on the ground which may be fruitful or unfruitful depending on its reception (Matt 13:3–8). The kingdom has come, but the present order is not disrupted; the sons of the kingdom and the sons of the evil one grow together in the world until the harvest (Matt 13:24–30, 36–43). The kingdom of God has indeed come to men, not as a new glorious order, but like the proverbial mustard seed. However, its insignificance must not be despised. This same kingdom will one day be a great tree (Matt 13:31–32). Instead of a world-transforming power, the kingdom is present in an almost imperceptible form like a bit of leaven hidden in a bowl of dough. However, this same kingdom will yet fill the earth as the leavened dough fills the bowl (Matt 13:33). . . .
>
> The coming of the kingdom of God in humility instead of glory was an utterly new and amazing revelation. Yet, said Jesus, men should not be deceived. Although the present manifestation of the kingdom is in humility—indeed, its bearer was put to death as a condemned criminal—it is nevertheless the kingdom of God, and, like buried treasure or a priceless pearl, its acquisition merits any cost or sacrifice (Matt 13:44–46). The fact that the present activity of the kingdom will initiate a movement that will include evil men as well as good should not lead

to misunderstanding its true nature. It is the kingdom of God; it will one day divide the good from the evil in eschatological salvation and judgment (Matt 13:47–50).[16]

In sum, Jesus taught by his "mystery of the kingdom" parables that he was offering men not the kingdom of God in power, but that spiritual reign of God in their hearts that brings "righteousness, peace, and joy in the Holy Spirit" (Rom 14:17 HCSB)—a reign that men could resist and which the majority of Jews did in fact reject because of unbelief.

Second, regarding Eph 3:2–12 and Col 1:25–27, which say essentially the same thing, traditional dispensationalists cite them because both refer to the "mystery . . . that was not made known to men in other generations as it has now been revealed by the Spirit to God's holy apostles and prophets," and "that has been kept hidden for ages and generations, but is now disclosed to the saints" (NIV). But, neither teaches that the "mystery" that was kept secret from men (not in an absolute sense, of course; see Paul's "as it has now been revealed") was the rejection of the King and his suffering. Rather, according to Eph 3:2–12, what was not disclosed as clearly as it has now been disclosed is that *in the kingdom of grace, Gentiles were to be fellow-heirs, fellow-members of the body, and fellow-partakers with the Jews of the promise in Christ.* In sum, this passage teaches that Gentiles would be on a footing of perfect equality with Jews in Christ's body, the church. In the Colossians 1 passage, Paul speaks again of the corporate inclusion of Gentiles within the body of Christ, but he did not teach the radical conclusions that dispensationalists draw from it, namely, that Old Testament saints did not know that the Messiah would be rejected and suffer, or that a distinction should be drawn between Old Testament Israel under law and the New Testament church under grace.

I do not find the DTS Doctrinal Statement making these specific exegetical mistakes that the earlier traditional dispensationalists made in their interpretation of the passages cited above, but the statement is incorrect when it bases its assertion that the Old Testament saints "did not understand the redemptive

[16] George E. Ladd, "Kingdom of Christ, God, Heaven," in *Evangelical Dictionary of Theology*, ed. Walter A. Elwell (Grand Rapids: Baker, 1984), 609–10.

significance of the prophecies and types concerning the suffering of Christ" on 1 Pet 1:10–12. I state categorically that Peter does not teach this in these verses. Rather, he states that it was "the time and circumstances," *not* the "who"[17] (*tina ē poion kairon*— literally, "what sort of or what kind of time"), surrounding the Messiah's suffering, *not* his suffering per se, and the glories that would follow that they were investigating intently and with great care. Again, Peter does not say that the Old Testament prophets were ignorant of the Messiah's suffering as such. This fact is borne out by Peter's description of God's revelation that came in response to the prophets' intense searching into the revelation that they already possessed about him. God revealed to them, not *whose* sufferings they were speaking about—this they clearly knew already—but *when* the Messiah's sufferings were to occur. His sufferings, God informed them, were to occur not in their own time, that is, not in the age of the prophets, but in the age following the age of the prophets, namely, in the age of fulfillment, that is, in this present age, the age in which men would preach the gospel by the Holy Spirit sent from heaven.

Further, I do not think the DTS Doctrinal Statement handles the great faith chapter of Hebrews 11 accurately when it declares that the faith of the heroes treated there was a faith in God that manifested itself in ways other than trust in the suffering Messiah. The author of Hebrews informs us that theirs was a living faith in God that moved them to right actions. But, to conclude from the fact that the author of Hebrews does not mention in each instance faith in the suffering Messiah as an aspect of their faith that they did not have such a faith is a *non sequitur*. Further, it is exegetically erroneous, for the Scripture expressly tells us that by faith Abel offered a more excellent sacrifice than Cain, even the firstborn of his flock (Gen 4:4) that typified Christ, that by faith Abraham rejoiced to see Christ's day; indeed, he saw it and was glad (John 8:56), that by faith Moses

---

[17] The NASB and the ETV offer a terribly misleading translation here by their "what person or time." Peter's "or" is not disjunctive, as if two contrasting questions are referred to, but conjunctive; that is, only one question concerned them, the question of time that could be asked either way: "What sort of or what kind of time period do his sufferings occur in?" Either way the issue with which they were concerned was the issue of the *time* of the Messiah's sufferings, not *whether* he would suffer. That they already knew.

regarded *the reproach of the Messiah*[18] greater wealth than the treasures of Egypt (11:26) and that by faith he kept the Passover and sprinkled the blood so that the Destroyer might not touch them (11:28). These Old Testament saints understood the concept of substitutionary atonement, and it is hardly a giant step to conclude with the framers of the Westminster Confession that

> the promises, prophecies, sacrifices, circumcision, the paschal lamb, and other types and ordinances delivered to the people of the Jews, *all foresignifying Christ to come*; . . . were, for the time, sufficient and efficacious, *through the operation of the Spirit*, to instruct and build up the elect in faith in the promised Messiah, by whom they had full remission of sins, and eternal salvation. (VII.v, emphasis supplied)

Spatial limitations will not allow me to enter here into a discussion of dispensationalism's highly debatable teachings respecting its pretribulationism or its peculiar brand of premillennialism that entails the reestablishment of the Jewish theocracy and that future theocracy's requirements of circumcision (Ezek 44:9) and the Levitical ceremonialism of animal sacrifices (Ezek 43–44) in its alleged millennial temple of Ezekiel 40–48. But, one would think that the author of Hebrews' teaching, first, from the fact that the inadequate Aaronic priestly system (Heb 7:11; 8:6–7; 9:9, 13–14; 10:1–2, 12–14) was replaced by the priestly system after the order of Melchizedek, and second, that Christ as the priest forever after the order of Melchizedek offered himself up "once for all" to take away sin by the sacrifice of himself (Heb 7:27; 9:12, 25–26, 28; 10:10–14) would give sufficient reasons to the dispensationalist to question his literal interpretation of Ezekiel's temple vision.

The solution to all the difficulties that dispensationalism creates for itself is the glorious doctrine of the unity of the covenant of grace and the oneness of the people of God in all ages as the Westminster Confession of Faith so clearly affirms. In its representation of the one covenant of grace as salvifically normative for men throughout all time, the Westminster Confession of Faith avoids the salvific discontinuities of the dispensational

---

[18] The word "reproach" is an allusion to the tragic dimension in Messiah's ministry that Psalm 2 and Isaiah 53 envision.

system, takes seriously what the New Testament teaches concerning the faith of the Old Testament saints, and retains faith in the Messiah's atoning work—first in its *anticipated* Old Testament character and then in its *accomplished* New Testament character—as the necessary conscious ground of salvation in all ages.

Before I take up the issue of historic covenant theology's understanding of Israel's future, I should note that the movement designated by its advocates as "progressive dispensationalism" has appeared within dispensational circles in recent years.[19] This "progressive" vision of dispensationalism denies the "offer, rejection, postponement, and only *future*-fulfillment of the kingdom" motif of traditional dispensationalism and acknowledges that the church is fulfilling spiritual promises made to Old Testament Israel. In short, these dispensationalists place more emphasis on the continuities between the dispensations than did earlier traditional dispensationalists.[20] No one can say, of course, whether "progressive dispensationalism" with its implicit rejection of traditional dispensationalism's "keystone" doctrine, namely, its rigid separation of Israel and the church, will forever remain dispensationalism and not become a form of covenantal premillennialism. Indeed, Walter A. Elwell asserts: "The newer [progressive] dispensationalism looks so much like nondispensational premillennialism that one struggles to see any real difference."[21] But, at the present time "progressive dispensationalism" is still clearly in the dispensational fold with its commitment and declarations and is a long distance away from historic covenant theology. Al Mawhinney got it right when he remarked in a gathering of theologians at an annual meeting of the Evangelical Theological Society: "The authors [of *progressive dispensationalism*] are not covenant theologians in sheep's clothing. . . . They are pursuing significant changes within their own tradition." I will say more about this view in my response to Saucy's contribution to this volume, but now I must turn to a

---

[19] This position is urged and defended in this present volume by Robert L. Saucy.
[20] See Robert L. Saucy, *The Case for Progressive Dispensationalism* (Grand Rapids: Zondervan, 1993), and Craig A. Blaising and Darrell L. Bock, *Progressive Dispensationalism* (Wheaton: Victor, 1993).
[21] Walter A. Elwell, "Dispensationalists of the Third Kind," *Christianity Today* 38, no. 10 (September 12, 1994): 28.

discussion of historic covenant theology's understanding of Old Testament Israel and its future.

Israel's Future and the Current Challenge Facing Historic Covenant Theology

An effort is underway today to convince evangelicals in the US that the political state of Israel rightfully owns *in perpetuity* the so-called Holy Land[22] at the eastern end of the Mediterranean Sea by virtue of God's bequeathing it to Abraham and his descendants in the Old Testament. This effort today is being made not so much by the secular leadership of the state of Israel as by popular dispensational preachers and televangelists such as John Hagee,[23] founder and pastor of the Cornerstone Church in San Antonio, Texas.[24]

Apparently convinced by this huge propaganda effort, former President Clinton, after citing the words of his desperately ill Baptist pastor to him, "If you abandon Israel, God will never

---

[22] I say "so-called" because the phrase "holy land" occurs only twice in Scripture (Ps 78:54; Zech 2:12), and even here the word "land" needs to be supplied in both instances. The former verse speaks of "the boundary of his holiness," the Hebrew word for "boundary" being a metonymy for what is within the boundary, while the latter verse (Matt 2:16) reads "the ground of holiness," that is, "holy ground." Apart from holy God's manifested presence in it, there is nothing holy about the "Holy Land." But, wherever God manifests his presence, that place is holy, as God taught Moses at the burning bush in Sinai (Exod 3:1–6).

[23] According to Julia Duin, "San Antonio Fundamentalist Battles Anti-Semitism," in *The Houston Chronicle* (April 30, 1988): 1, Hagee does not believe that Jews must trust Christ in order to go to heaven: "The Jewish people have a relationship to God through the law as given through Moses. I believe that every Gentile person can only come to God through the cross of Christ. I believe that every Jewish person who lives in the light of the Torah . . . has a relationship with God and will come to redemption." This *radically* dispensational statement is heretical in its denial that faith in Christ is *universally* essential for salvation. Hagee does not seem to understand that salvation for everyone is a matter of grace, *not* race.

[24] Others include televangelist Kenneth Copeland; Paul and Matt Crouch of the Trinity Broadcasting Network (TBN); Jack Hayford, founder and pastor of the Church on the Way in Van Nuys, CA, and president of the Foursquare Gospel Church; Benny Hinn, pastor of the World Healing Center Church in Dallas, TX; Rod Parsley, pastor of the World Harvest Church in Columbus, OH; and Pat Robertson, founder and chief executive officer of Christian Broadcasting Network (CBN) and the Bible teacher on the 700 Club. Pat Robertson stated on public television on January 5, 2006, that Prime Minister Ariel Sharon of Israel suffered his massive stroke at the hand of God because he was in the process of giving a portion of Israel's land to the Palestinians in exchange for peace. He later apologized for his statement.

forgive you," declared before the Israeli Knesset in Jerusalem on October 27, 1994: "... it is God's will that Israel, the biblical home of the people of Israel, continue forever and ever,"[25] a statement that enters deeply into biblical hermeneutics concerning the nature of the church and the kingdom of God, not to mention biblical eschatology (note his "forever and ever"). President Clinton concluded his speech by saying, "Your journey is our journey [note: not "our journey is your journey"], and America will stand with you now and always," a statement that illustrates this nation's deep involvement in Middle East politics in general and its specific political commitment to Israel in the Israeli/ Palestinian conflict in particular in a way that cannot but affect the course of world politics.

President Clinton's statement is bad politics based on equally bad theology. I say this because, as I shall now argue, all of God's land promises to Israel in the Old Testament are to be viewed in terms of shadow, type, and prophecy in contrast to the reality, substance, and fulfillment of which the New Testament speaks. Consequently, contrary to Hagee, who insists, "Israel has a Bible mandate to the land, a divine covenant for the land of Israel, forever . . . [and] Christians have a Bible mandate to be supportive of Israel,"[26] I will argue that it is we Christians as members of Christ's messianic kingdom who are the real heirs to the land promises of Holy Scripture, but in their *fulfilled* paradisiacal character.[27] Hagee terms this view "replacement theology" because, he says, it "replaces" in the economy of God the Jewish people who are, he says, "God's centerpiece" and "the apple of his eye" (Zech 2:8 NIV) with the church of Jesus Christ. Of course, Hagee's perception of ethnic Israel is in error because *ethnic* Israel per se was *never* the centerpiece of God's covenant program since, according to the apostle Paul, God's promises *always* encompassed only the true spiritual Israel (that is, elect Israel)

---

[25] See *Vital Speeches* 61, no. 3 (November 15, 1994): 3, 70.

[26] David Horovitz, "Most evangelicals are seeing the error of 'replacement theology,'" http://davidhorovitz.com/articles/most-evangelicals-are-seeing-the-error-of-replacement-theology (March 21, 2006). Hagee urges pastors within the covenantal tradition to throw away their "replacement sermons."

[27] I happily acknowledge my great debt to O. Palmer Robertson, *The Israel of God: Yesterday, Today, and Tomorrow* (Phillipsburg, NJ: P&R, 2000), 3–31, for many of the thoughts in this section.

within ethnic Israel (Rom 9:6–13), and the land promises of the Old Testament, as we will show, were *always* to be viewed *typologically* of something more glorious to come. Nevertheless, Hagee has thrown down the dispensational gauntlet, and it is high time that covenant theologians picked it up and responded to him biblically. This is what I propose to do now. But, I offer a word of caution to Christians who will read this book and this chapter in it: reflect carefully on what you read before you accept or reject what I write. Do not reject what I write here merely because you may not have read any of this before. Think it through and, as the Bereans did, "examined the Scriptures daily to see if these things were so" (Acts 17:11 HCSB). And, I would urge any non-Christian Jews as well who may read this chapter not to be put off by it, but to read carefully what I now write. To them I would ask, in the words of the apostle Paul: "Have I now become your enemy by telling you the truth?" (Gal 4:16 HCSB). So, with these caveats I will begin with a discussion of the Abrahamic Covenant.

The Abrahamic Covenant as the Antidote to Hagee's Primary Error of Dispensationalism

With the call of Abraham in Genesis 12, the covenant of grace inaugurated in Gen 3:15 underwent a remarkable advance. The instrument of that advance is the covenant that God made with Abraham that guaranteed and secured soteric blessing for "all the families of the earth" (Gen 12:3 NASB). So significant are the promises of grace in the Abrahamic covenant, found in Gen 12:1–3; 13:14–16; 15:18–21; 17:1–16; and 22:16–18, that it is not an overstatement to declare these verses, from the covenantal perspective, the most important verses in the Bible. The fact that the Bible sweeps across the thousands of years between the creation of man and the call of Abraham in only eleven chapters, with the call of Abraham coming in Genesis 12, suggests that God intended the information given in Genesis 1–11 to be preparatory "background" to the revelation of the Abrahamic covenant. Revelation subsequent to it discloses that *all that God has done savingly in grace since the revelation of the Abrahamic covenant is the result and product of it*. In other words, once

the covenant of grace came to expression in the salvific promises of the Abrahamic covenant—that God would be the God of
Abraham and his spiritual descendants (Gen 17:7), and that in
Abraham all the families of the earth would be blessed—*everything that God has done since to this present moment he has
done in order to fulfill his covenant promises to Abraham* (and
thereby the eternal plan of redemption).

If this representation of the salvific significance of the
Abrahamic covenant seems an overstatement, the following declarations from later revelation should suffice to justify it:

1. It is the Abrahamic covenant and none other that God
   later confirmed with Isaac (Gen 17:19; 26:3–4) and with
   Jacob (Gen 28:13–15; 35:12).

2. The Scriptures state that God redeemed Jacob's descendants from Egypt in order to keep his covenant promise
   to the patriarchs: "God heard their groaning and he remembered his covenant with Abraham, with Isaac, and
   with Jacob" (Exod 2:24; see also 4:5).

3. Again and again throughout Israel's history the inspired
   authors of Scripture trace God's continuing extension of grace and mercy to Israel directly to his fidelity
   to his covenant promises to Abraham (Exod 32:12–14;
   33:1; Lev 26:42; Deut 1:8; 4:31; 7:8; 9:27; 29:12–13; Josh
   21:44; 24:3–4; 2 Kgs 13:23; 1 Chr 16:15–17; Ps 105:8–10,
   42–43; Mic 7:20; Neh 9:7–8).

4. When we come to the New Testament, it is no different.
   Both Mary and Zechariah declared the first coming of
   Jesus Christ, including the very act of incarnation, to be
   a vital constituent part of the fulfillment of God's gracious covenant promise to Abraham. Mary, in Luke 1:54–
   55, said: "He has helped his servant Israel, remembering
   to be merciful to Abraham and his descendants forever,
   even as he said to our fathers" (NIV). Zechariah in Luke
   1:68, 72–73 (NIV) said: "Praise be to the Lord, the God
   of Israel, because he has come . . . to remember his holy

covenant, the oath he swore to our father Abraham" (NIV).

I may note in passing that, whereas Christians today mainly celebrate only the incarnation of God's Son at Christmas time, Mary and Zechariah, placing this event within the covenantal metanarrative of Scripture, saw reason in Christ's coming to celebrate the larger truth of God's *covenant fidelity* to his people. In their awareness of the broader significance of the event and the words of praise that this awareness evoked from them we see biblical theology at its best being worked out and expressed.

5. Jesus, himself the Seed of Abraham (Matt 1:1; Gal 3:16), declared that Abraham "rejoiced at the thought of seeing my day; he saw it and was glad" (John 8:56 NIV).

6. Peter declared that God sent Jesus to bless the Jewish nation in keeping with the promise he gave to Abraham in Gen 12:3, in turning them away from their iniquities (Acts 3:25–26).

7. Paul declared that God, when he promised Abraham that "all peoples on earth will be blessed through you" (Gen 12:3 NIV), was declaring that he was going to justify the Gentiles by faith and was announcing the gospel in advance to Abraham (Gal 3:8). Accordingly, he stated that all believers in Christ "are blessed [with justification through faith] along with Abraham" (Gal 3:9 NIV).

8. Paul also declared: "Christ became a Servant of the circumcision . . . in order to confirm the promises made to the patriarchs so that the Gentiles might glorify God for his mercy" (Rom 15:8–9 author's translation).

9. Paul further declared that Christ died on the cross, bearing the law's curse, "in order that the blessing given to Abraham might come to the Gentiles in Christ Jesus, in order that we [both Jews and Gentiles] might receive the

promise of the Spirit through faith" (Gal 3:14 author's translation).

10. Paul expressly declared that the Mosaic law, introduced several centuries after God gave his covenant promises to Abraham and to his Seed (Christ), "does not set aside the covenant previously established by God [with Abraham] and thus do away with the promise" (Gal 3:17 NIV).

11. Paul also declared (1) that Abraham is the "father of all who believe" among both Jews and Gentiles (Rom 4:11–12), and (2) that all who belong to Christ "are Abraham's seed, and heirs according to the promise"(NIV) that God gave to Abraham (Gal 3:29).

12. Finally, Christ described the future state of glory in terms of the redeemed who "will take their place at the feast with Abraham, Isaac, and Jacob in the kingdom of heaven" (Matt 8:11 NIV).

What these facts mean is that the promise of God, covenantally given to Abraham, that he would be the God of Abraham and of his spiritual descendants after him forever (Gen 17:7–8), extends temporally to the farthest reaches of the future and encompasses the entire community of the redeemed and the renewed cosmos. This is just to say that the Abrahamic covenant, in the specific prospect it holds forth of the salvation of the entire church of God, is identical with the soteric program of the covenant of grace. It also means that the blessings of the covenant of grace that believers in Christ enjoy today under the sanctions of the New Testament economy are founded upon the covenant that God made with Abraham. Said another way, the "new covenant," whose Mediator is Jesus Christ, is simply the administrative "extension and unfolding of the Abrahamic covenant"[28] in redemptive history. The church of Jesus Christ, then, *not* ethnic Israel, is the present-day expression of the one people of God whose roots go back to Abraham.

---

[28] Murray, *Christian Baptism*, 46.

THE TRADITIONAL COVENANTAL VIEW — **41**

These facts also highlight the unity of the one covenant of grace and the oneness of God's people in all ages over against the discontinuities injected into redemptive history by the dispensational error that lies at the root of all the bad "land theology" being espoused today concerning Israel's "perpetual divine right" to the "holy land."[29] That is to say, God's redemptive purpose, first disclosed in Gen 3:15, once it had come to expression in the terms of the Abrahamic covenant, was *continuously* advanced thereafter by the successive covenants with Israel at Sinai and later on the plains of Moab, with David, and finally by the new covenant.

Accordingly, in his letter to the Gentile churches in Galatia, Paul described those who repudiate Judaistic legalism and who "never boast except in the cross of our Lord Jesus Christ," that is, Christ's church, as "the Israel of God" (Gal 6:12–16 NIV).[30] In his Ephesian letter, Paul told those Gentile believers that God had, in Christ, made them citizens of Israel and beneficiaries of the covenants of the promise (Eph 2:11–13). And in his letter to the Philippians, Paul declared that those "who worship by the Spirit of God, who glory in Christ Jesus, and who put no confidence in the flesh" are "the [true] circumcision" (Phil 3:3 NIV). So, clearly, the church of Jesus Christ is the present-day, true Israel of God.

I will now turn directly to the issue Hagee raises concerning the ownership of the land of Israel.

The Garden of Eden, the Prototypical Paradise of God

O. Palmer Robertson begins his treatise on the significance of the land as a theological idea by stating,

> The concept of a land that belongs to God's people originated in Paradise. This simple fact, so often overlooked, plays a critical role in evaluating the significance of the land throughout redemptive history and its consummate fulfillment. Land did not begin to be

---

[29] For the redemptive implications of this bad "land theology," see Knox Theological Seminary's "An Open Letter to Evangelicals and Other Interested Parties: The People of God, the Land of Israel, and the Impartiality of the Gospel," posted on the seminary's website, http://www.knoxseminary.edu, under "Wittenberg Door."

[30] See Robertson, *The Israel of God*, 40–41, for his exposition of the phrase "the Israel of God" in Gal 6:16.

theologically significant with the promise given to Abraham. Instead, the patriarch's hope of possessing a land arose out of the concept of restoration to the original state from which man had fallen. The original idea of land as paradise significantly shaped the expectations associated with redemption. As the place of blessedness arising from unbroken fellowship and communion with God, the land of paradise became the goal toward which redeemed humanity was returning.[31]

In the Edenic paradise of Genesis 2, we see God, whose garden it was (Ezek 28:13; 31:8)—the garden that became, in the history of redemption, the prototypical ideal (Gen 13:10) and microcosmic type of the macrocosmic antitypical paradise of God (Isa 51:3; Rev 2:7), thereby drawing the land promises of Scripture from Gen 3:15 onward within the sphere of redemption—we see God placing Adam and Eve within it to tend and to keep it and to enjoy communion with him (Gen 2:8). But, the paradisiacal nature of Eden was lost in and by Adam's fall, and our first parents were expelled from this land of blessing. But, the idea of paradise was renewed, first, by God's inaugurating with the guilty pair a second covenant—the covenant of grace of Gen 3:15—and, second, by his covenant with Abraham of Gen 12:1–3 to redeem a people from their fallen condition and to transform the cosmos. Just as Adam and Eve had known God's blessing in Eden, so also God would bless his redeemed people in another Eden, a land flowing with milk and honey, that lay somewhere ahead of them in the future.

The Typological Nature of the Land Promises

Undoubtedly, temporal, earthly promises of a land were given to Abraham and his descendants in the Abrahamic covenant (Gen 12:7; 13:15, 17; 15:18; 17:8). But, the land promises were never primary and central to the covenant's intention, and God never envisioned the literal fulfillment of these promises under Old Testament conditions as primary. Rather, the fulfillment of the land promises must be viewed, as we stated earlier, as arising

---

[31] Ibid., 4.

from the more basic and essential redemptive promises. For their fulfillment they await the final and complete salvation of God's elect and the recreation of the universe in the eschaton (Rom 8:19–23). I say this because the Bible declares that Abraham dwelt in the land as "in a foreign country" (Heb 11:9) and that he never inherited any land during his lifetime (Acts 7:5), which is just to say that Abraham believed that the fulfillment of God's land promises lay antitypically in the *eschatological* future.

Was this really Abraham's understanding of God's land promise? Or, did he think that God's promise entailed the small portion of land bounded on the west and the east by the Mediterranean Sea and the Jordan Valley and generally on the north and the south between the Sea of Galilee and the southern tip of the Dead Sea? Hardly. Was his faith even such that he would have been satisfied in knowing that someday his offspring would inherit the land "from the river of Egypt [not the Nile River but the *Wadi el Arish*] to the great river, the Euphrates" (Gen 15:18 NIV)?[32] Again we must respond: Hardly. His entire life experience of walking by faith and not by sight (see the recurring phrase "by faith Abraham" in Heb 11:8–9, 17) taught him to look beyond the temporal circumstances in which he lived. *To understand Abraham's concept of God's land promise to him, we must give special heed to the insights of the writers of the New Testament.* Just as Paul declared that the events of Israel's redemptive history were "types" for believers during this age (1 Cor 10:6), just as Paul said the religious festivals of the old covenant were "a shadow of things to come" (Col 2:17 NKJV), just as the author of Hebrews stated that the administration of redemption under the old covenant was "but a shadow of the good things to come" (Heb 10:1 NKJV), so also he taught that Abraham knew that God's land promises in their fulfillment entailed something far more glorious—namely, a better and heavenly homeland, whose designer and builder is God—than the land of Israel per se, which served only as the type of their fulfillment:

---

[32] These particular divine promises have already been fulfilled by the conquest of the land under Joshua and then by Solomon's reign (Josh 21:43–45; 23:14; 1 Kgs 4:24). They do not require fulfillment in and by a future Jewish millennium.

> By faith Abraham . . . went to live in the land of promise, *as in a foreign land,* living in tents with Isaac and Jacob, heirs with him of the same promise. For he was looking forward to the city that has foundations, whose designer and builder is God . . . These all died in faith, *not having received the things promised,*[33] but having seen them and greeted them from afar, and have acknowledged that they were *strangers and exiles on the earth.* For people who speak thus make it clear that they are seeking a homeland . . . a *better* country, that is, a *heavenly* one. Therefore, God is not ashamed to be called their God, for he has prepared for them a city. (Heb 11:8–16, emphasis supplied)[34]

Quite plainly, Abraham understood that the land promised to him actually had both its *origin* and its antitypical *fulfillment* in the heavenly, eternal reality that lay still in the future. Possession of a particular tract of land in ancient times might have significance from a number of perspectives with respect to God's redemptive working in the world, but clearly the land promise under the Abrahamic covenant served simply as a type anticipating the future reality of the coming of the messianic kingdom, with the Messiah himself assuming the throne of David in heaven,[35] ruling the universe after his resurrection/ascension, and reigning until all his enemies have been put under his feet.

How was it possible for Abraham to have the view of the land promise that the author of Hebrews ascribed to him? What led him to "spiritualize" the promise to make it entail future heavenly, kingdom realities? The answer lies in the fact that he took seriously God's promise to him that "in [him] *all the families*

---

[33] Abraham owned only the plot of ground, the field of Mach-pelah, that he purchased from the Hittites living in the land. It was for a burial ground for Sarah, his wife (Genesis 23)

[34] Unless noted otherwise, Scripture quotations are from the English Standard Version.

[35] Because any throne he, as the messianic Son of David (Matt 9:27; 20:30–31; 21:9; 22:41–46; Luke 1:31–33), would sit upon would be "the throne of David," Jesus Christ's present session at the right hand of God has invested the throne of God in heaven with a messianic character; that is to say, God's throne is "the throne of David." And, *this* Davidic throne is the throne of the only "Jerusalem" that matters today, namely, "the Jerusalem above," the glorified church of Jesus Christ (see Gal 4:26; Heb 12:22; Rev 21:9–26).

of the earth will be blessed" (Gen 12:3 NASB).³⁶ Therefore, he perceived that the promise to him and his offspring (who ultimately is Christ; see Gal 3:16) entailed that in Christ "he would be heir [not of a small parcel of land but] of the [glorified] world [*kosmou*]" (Rom 4:13 NASB). Plainly, Abraham understood that God's land promise meant God would someday restore the entire cosmos to its former paradisiacal glory, and in that he placed his hope and patiently waited for it. His faith and understanding would have been satisfied with nothing less.

In the middle of the second millennium BC, God separated Abraham's descendents and formed them into a nation at Sinai. But, although their founding document, the "book of the covenant," was glorious (2 Cor 3:7, 9, 11), God made it clear at the point of Israel's national establishment, by means of the fading radiance of Moses' face (Exod 34:29–35), that theirs was to be an age of only provisional and passing glory that would fade away when the greater glory of Christ came (2 Cor 3:7–16). So Moses, too, and his contemporaries wandered in the wilderness of Sinai for forty years, and died in faith, not having received the fulfillment of the promise (Heb 11:39).

Under Joshua's leadership, the Israelites conquered the land, receiving in a limited fashion the paradise God had promised. But, it quickly became obvious that this territory could not be the ultimate paradise. Undefeated Canaanites remained in the land. And because of Israel's sin throughout the united and divided kingdom periods, finally the land was devastated by the Assyrians and the Neo-Babylonians; the indwelling glory departed from Solomon's temple (Ezek 9:3; 10:1–22), which was then destroyed; and the people were banished and came to be known as *lo-ammi*, meaning "not-my-people" (Hos 1:9). The once fruitful land took on the appearance of a desert, a dwelling place of jackals, owls, and scorpions. Paradise, even in its old covenant shadow form, was taken from them.

Even the restoration after the Babylonian captivity under Ezra and Nehemiah, designated by biblical scholars today as the

---

³⁶ Paul tells us in Gal 3:8 that when God made this promise to Abraham, he was in effect "preaching the gospel beforehand to Abraham"—that is, he was declaring that he would justify the Gentiles by faith alone apart from law-keeping.

Second Temple period, could not be paradise. But, the return to the land and the rebuilding of the temple pointed the way to it. The glory of that tiny temple, Haggai prophesied, would someday be greater than the glory of the Solomonic temple. What did this seemingly hyperbolic language mean? It meant that God still had something better for them than a temporal land and a material temple. The promise of the land would be fulfilled by nothing less than *a restored paradise on a cosmic scale*. As Isaiah predicted, someday the wolf would lie down with the lamb, the leopard would lie down with the goat, the calf and the lion would live in peace, and a little child would lead them. The nursing child would play over the hole of the cobra, and the weaned child would place his hand on the adder's den, and the earth would be full of the knowledge of the Lord as the waters cover the places of the sea (Isa 11:6–9). No more would sin and sorrow reign nor thorns infest the ground. Then, writes Paul in Rom 9:25–26:

> Those who were not [God's] people [not only from the Jews but also from the Gentiles, Rom 9:24] [he] will call "my people," and her who was not beloved [he] will call "beloved." And in the very place where it was said to them, "You are not my people," there they will be called "sons of the living God."

Jesus' Teaching about the Land and about the Future of Ethnic Israel

Now, what about Jesus? Did he teach anything about the land and about the future of ethnic Israel? Indeed, he did! What he taught should dispel any lingering doubts that anyone may still have concerning what I advocate in this chapter.

First, what about the land in Jesus' teaching? When Christ came two thousand years ago, the biblical perspective of the land underwent a radical advance. By inaugurating his public ministry in Galilee of the Gentiles along the public trade route ("the way of the sea") in accordance with the prophecy in Isaiah 9:1 (see Matt 4:12–16), Jesus was making a statement. *That* land would serve as the springboard to all nations. It is interesting, too, that, after his bodily resurrection from the dead, Jesus instructed his disciples to leave Jerusalem and to meet him in Galilee, in which venue he issued his Great Commission (Matt 28:7, 10, 16). Clearly, the implication is that the kingdom of God—the central theme of Jesus' teaching—would encompass a realm that extended well beyond the borders of ancient Israel. As Paul so pointedly indicated, from the new covenant perspective, God's promise to Abraham meant that he would become heir of the whole world (Rom 4:13). Jesus' pointing his ministry toward the whole world rather than confining it to the land of Canaan cleared the way for the "old covenant type" to be replaced by the "new covenant antitype." Teaching that the kingdom of God had appeared in its grace modality with his first coming, and that it would appear in its power modality at his second coming, he focused the imagery of a return to a land flowing with milk and honey upon a rejuvenation that would embrace the *whole* of God's created order. It was not Canaan as such that would benefit in the establishment of Messiah's kingdom. The *whole* cosmos would rejoice in the renewal brought about by this newness of life resident in the messianic kingdom.[37]

Second, what about the future of ethnic Israel in Jesus' teaching? In his parable of the wicked farmers, found in Matt 21:33–45; Mark 12:1–12; and Luke 20:9–19, Jesus tells the story of a landowner who leased his vineyard to some farmers and then went into another country. When the time arrived for him to receive his rental fee in the form of the fruit of the vineyard, the landowner sent servant after servant to his tenants, only to have each one of them beaten, stoned, or killed. *Last of all* he sent his son—Luke says his "beloved son"; Mark says "*still one other*, a beloved son"—saying: "They will respect my son." But, when the tenants saw the landowner's son, they said, "This is the heir. Come, let's kill him, and inheritance will be ours." This they did, throwing his body out of the vineyard. When the landowner came, he destroyed the tenants and leased his vineyard to others. The interpretive intentions of the parable, as D. A. Carson notes,[38] are obvious on the face of it: the landowner is God the Father, the

---

[37] The thoughts expressed in the last four paragraphs I have adapted from O. Palmer Robertson, *Understanding the Land of the Bible* (Phillipsburg, NJ: P&R, 1966), 7–13.

[38] D. A. Carson, *Matthew* in *The Expositor's Bible Commentary* (Grand Rapids: Zondervan, 1984), 451.

vineyard the nation of Israel (Isa 5:7), the farmers Israel's leaders, the servants the prophets of the theocracy (Matt 23:37a), and the son Jesus himself.

The central teaching of the parable is obvious—as indeed it was to its original audience (Matt 21:45): after having sent his servants the prophets repeatedly in Old Testament times to the nation of Israel and its leaders to call the nation back to him from its sin and unbelief, only to have them rebuffed, persecuted, and often killed, God, the owner of Israel, had, in sending Jesus, the Second Person of the Godhead, moved beyond merely sending another servant. Listen once again to the pertinent verses in this connection: "Then *last of all* he sent his son" (Matt 21:37 NKJV) and ". . . having *one son*, his beloved, he also sent him to them *last*" (Mark 12:6 NKJV).

From Matthew's "last of all" and Mark's "last" it is clear that Jesus represented himself as God's *last*, his *final* ambassador, after whose sending none higher can come and nothing more can be done.[39] The Lord of the vineyard needs no further resources. As God's Son, the Son of God is the *highest* messenger of God conceivable. In sum, God had in Jesus *finally* (Matt 21:37: *hysteron*; Mark 12:6: *eschaton*) sent his own beloved Son, whom, Jesus taught in the parable, the nation would reject. But, the rejection of his Son, unlike the rejections of those servants before him, *was to entail neither God's continuance of dealing with the recalcitrant nation nor a mere change of politico-religious administration*. Rather, *his* rejection, Jesus taught, would eventuate in "the complete overthrow of the theocracy, and the rearing from the foundation up of a new structure [Christ's church] in which the Son would receive full vindication and supreme honor"[40] His words are as follows: "I tell you, the kingdom of God will be taken away from you and given to a people producing its fruits" (Matt 21:43) and "What will the owner of the vineyard do? He will

---

[39] This parable also carries implications concerning Muhammad's claim to be the last and greatest of God's prophets, even greater than Jesus. It shows him to be a false prophet. See my article, "What's Wrong with Islam," in *Contending for the Faith: Lines in the Sand that Strengthen the Church* (Ross-shire, Scotland: Mentor, 2005), 401–22.

[40] Geerhardus Vos, *The Self-Disclosure of Jesus* (repr. of 1926 ed.; Phillipsburg, NJ: P&R, 1978), 162.

come and destroy the tenants and give the vineyard to others" (Mark 12:9; see also Luke 20:16).

Here is a biblical "replacement theology," and it is Jesus himself who enunciated it: *National* Israel, except for its elect remnant, would be judged, and the special standing that it had enjoyed during the old dispensation would be transferred to the already existing and growing *international* church of Jesus Christ (whose roots go back to Abraham, indeed, to the divine promise of Gen 3:15) made up of both the elect Jewish remnant and elect Gentiles. So, as Jesus predicted, in time Israel's rulers rejected him and incited Rome to execute him as an insurrectionist and a false messiah. As he also predicted, the temple was again soon destroyed (see Matt 24:1–35), the people dispersed, and Israel ceased to exist as a political entity as Moses had predicted in Deut 28:15–68 (see also Deut 31:24–29).

Paul's Teaching about the Future of Ethnic Israel

In harmony with our Lord's "replacement theology" concerning ethnic Israel's future, Paul declared in 1 Thess 2:15–16 that the Jews who

> killed both the Lord Jesus and the prophets . . . displease God and oppose all mankind by hindering us from speaking to the Gentiles that they might be saved—so as always to fill up the measure of their sins. But God's wrath has come upon them *at last* [*eis telos*[41]]!

Since Paul wrote 1 Thessalonians in AD 50 or 51, it is unlikely that he intended by his phrase, "God's wrath has come upon them," the destruction of Jerusalem that occurred some twenty years later in AD 70. More likely, he was referring to the divine rejection of national Israel that Jesus referred to in his parable of the wicked farmers and elsewhere (Matt 23:38; 24:15–28), a rejection that Paul declared in Romans 11 had come to expression in God's hardening the *mass* of Israel, save for an elect Jewish

---

[41] BDAG, *"eis,"* 2.b (p. 998) properly views this prepositional phrase as an adverbial expression and suggests it should be translated, "forever, through all eternity." W. Bauer, F. W. Danker, W. F. Arndt, and F. W. Gingrich, *Greek-English Lexicon of the New Testament and Other Early Christian Literature*, 3rd ed. (Chicago: University of Chicago Press, 2000). Subsequent references will use BDAG.

remnant. If this is what Paul meant, it means that ethic Israel *en masse* today is in the same position in which the nations outside of Christ find themselves, namely, "separated from Christ, alienated from the [true] Israel [of God] and strangers to the covenants of promise, having no hope and without God in the world" (Eph 2:12). So, once again, Israel as a national entity is viewed as *lo-ammi*, "not my people," *only now with a finality about it*[42] save for the elect remnant (Rom 9:27–29).[43]

Someone might wonder here what has become of God's promises made to Israel as a nation; have they not proven to be ineffectual? This in turn raises the second question: If the promises of God to Israel proved ineffectual, what assurance does the Christian have that the divine promises made to him in Romans 3–8 will not also prove to be finally ineffectual as well? Accordingly, Paul addresses the issue of Israel's unbelief head-on. His explanation in one sentence is this: God's promises to Israel have not failed, simply because God never promised to save every Israelite; rather, he promised to save the elect (true) "Israel" within the nation of Israel (Rom 9:6). He proves this by underscoring the fact that from the beginning of God's dealings with Abraham and his seed, not all the natural seed of Abraham were accounted by God as "children of Abraham"—Ishmael, Abraham's firstborn, was excluded from

---

[42] When the Jewish crowd, having been persuaded by the chief priests and the elders to ask for Barabbas's release and for the crucifixion of Jesus, cried out in response to Pilate's declaration, "I am innocent of this man's blood," that "His blood be on us and on our children!" (Matt 27:20, 25 HCSB), they were affirming the Jews' collective guilt in the death of Jesus Christ and accepting full responsibility for his execution. William Hendriksen, in his *Exposition of the Gospel According to Matthew* (Grand Rapids: Baker, 1973), 957, writes:

> Though they do not realize it, [the Jewish people here] are in fact pronouncing a curse upon themselves, even involving in this curse their own posterity. By means of openly rejecting the Messiah, [they] cease to be in any special sense the people of God.

Thus, they were doing more than they realized: they were fulfilling Jesus' teaching in his parable of the wicked farmers in Matthew 21 and bringing to fulfillment his prophecy in Matthew 23–24 of the destruction of Jerusalem and the end of the Jewish nation as the people of God, save for the elect remnant.

[43] Robertson, *The Israel of God*, 174n3, rightly contends that the word "remnant" etymologically does not necessarily intend a small, insignificant number but simply that which is "left." But, when Isaiah declares: "Though the number of the sons of Israel be like the sand of the sea, it is the remnant that will be saved" (NASB), the implication still is that God has hardened the *mass* of ethnic Israel.

being a "child of promise" by sovereign reprobative divine arrangement (Rom 9:7–9).

Now, few Jews in Paul's day would have had any difficulty with the exclusion of Ishmael from God's gracious covenant. But, someone might have argued that Ishmael's rejection as a "child" of Abraham was due, first, to the fact that though he was Abraham's biological seed, he was also the son of Hagar the servant woman and not the son of Sarah, and second, to the fact that God foresaw that Ishmael would persecute "him that was born according to the Spirit" (Gal 4:29; see Gen 21:9; Ps 83:5–6). In other words, someone might argue that God drew the distinction he did between Isaac and Ishmael not because of a sovereign divine election of the former alone, but because they had two different earthly mothers and because of Ishmael's foreseen subsequent hostility to Isaac. The fact of the two mothers is true enough, and indeed this fact is not without *figurative* significance, as Paul himself argues in Gal 4:21–31. But, Paul clearly perceives that the principle operative in Isaac's selection over Ishmael is one of sovereign, unconditional discrimination and not one grounded in any way in human circumstances. Lest this elective principle that governed the choice of Isaac (and all the rest of the saved) be lost on his readers, Paul then moved beyond Isaac and Ishmael to a consideration of Jacob and Esau. Here there were not two mothers. In their case, there was one father (Isaac) and one mother (Rebekah). Moreover, in their case the two boys were twins, Esau—as Ishmael before him—even being the older and thus the person who normally would be shown the preferential treatment reserved for the firstborn son. The divine discrimination, Paul reminds his reader, was made *prior to their birth, before either had done anything good or bad.* Paul explicitly states in Rom 9:11–13,

> . . . before the twins were born or had done anything good or bad—in order that God's purpose in election might stand: not by works but by him who calls—she was told, "The older will serve the younger." Just as it is written:[44] "Jacob I loved, but Esau I hated." (NIV)

---

[44] Because Rom 9:13 is a quotation from Mal 1:2–3, which was written at the end of Old Testament canonical history, Arminian theologians contend that God's election

Clearly, for Paul both election ("Jacob I loved") and reprobation ("Esau I hated") are to be traced to God's sovereign discrimination between them.

We also learn from Rom 9:11–13 that the elective principle in God's eternal purpose serves and alone comports with the grace principle that governs all true salvation. Note Paul's statement again: ". . . in order that *God's purpose in election* might stand: *not by works but by him who calls*—she was told.*" Here we see the connection between God's grace and his elective purpose dramatically exhibited in his discrimination between Jacob and Esau, which, Paul points out, occurred *"before [mēpō]* the twins were born or had done anything good or bad" (Rom 9:11). Paul elucidates the *ratio* standing behind and governing the divine discrimination signalized in his phrase, "in order that God's 'according to [*kata*] election' purpose might stand [that is, might

---

of Jacob and his rejection of Esau are to be traced to God's prescience of Edom's sinful existence and despicable historical treatment of Israel (Ezek 35:5). But, for the following reasons, this interpretation intrudes the "works" element into Romans 9 that is foreign to Paul's entire argument and totally distorts his point:

(a) The Malachi context is against it. The very point the prophet is concerned to make is that, after his election of Jacob over Esau, God continued to love Jacob *in spite of* Jacob's (Israel's) similar history to that of Esau (Edom), as far as covenant faithfulness is concerned, and to reject Esau *because of* his wickedness.

(b) To inject into Paul's thought here to the slightest degree the notion of human merit or demerit as the ground for God's dealings with the twins is to ignore the plain statement of Paul: ". . . *before the twins were born or had done anything good or bad*—in order that God's purpose in election might stand, *not by works but by him who calls*—she was told . . . ."

(c) To inject into Paul's thought here the notion of human merit or demerit as the ground for God's dealings with the twins is also to make superfluous and irrelevant the following anticipated objection to Paul's position, captured in the question, "Is God unjust?" No one would even think of accusing God of injustice if he had related himself to Jacob and Esau on the basis of human merit or demerit. But, it is precisely because Paul had declared that God related himself to the twins not on the basis of human merit but solely in accordance with his own elective purpose that he anticipated the question: "Why does this not make God arbitrarily authoritarian and unjust?" It is doubtful whether any Arminian will ever be faced with the question that Paul anticipated here, simply because the Arminian doctrine of election is grounded in God's prescience of people's faith and good works. It is only the Calvinist, insisting as he does that God relates himself to the elect "out of his mere free grace and love, without any foresight of faith or good works, or perseverance in either of them, or any other thing in the creature, as conditions, or causes moving him thereunto; and all to the praise of his glorious grace" (Westminster Confession of Faith, III.v) who will face this specific charge that God is unjust.

remain immutable]," in terms of the following phrase, "not according to [ek] works but according to [ek] him who calls [unto salvation]."[45] This is equivalent to saying: "not according to works but according to grace." Paul is teaching here that God's elective purpose is not, as in paganism, "a blind unreadable fate" that "hangs, an impersonal mystery, even above the gods," but rather that his elective purpose serves the intelligible purpose of "bringing out the *gratuitous* character of grace."[46] In fact, Paul refers later to "the election of grace [*eklogēn charitos*]" (Rom 11:5 NKJV), that is, "the election *governed by* grace." The upshot of all this is just to say: "If unconditional election, then grace; if conditional election, then no grace!" To say "sovereign grace" is really to utter a redundancy, for to be gracious at all toward the creature undeserving of it *requires* God to be sovereign in his distributive exhibition of it.

So, Paul is quite clear that God broke no promise to the nation of Israel as a nation, clearly teaching in Rom 9:6–8,

> The word of God has [not] failed. For not all who are descended from Israel belong to Israel, and not all are children of Abraham because they are his offspring, but "Through Isaac shall your offspring be named." This means that *it is not the children of the flesh who are the children of God*, but the children of the promise are counted as offspring.

Accordingly, Paul writes in Rom 11:7–10:

> Israel failed to obtain what it was seeking [that is, a righteousness before God (Rom 9:31)]. The elect [remnant] obtained it, but the rest were hardened, as it is written, "God gave them a spirit of stupor, eyes that would not see and ears that would not hear, down to this very day." And David says, "Let their table become a snare and a trap, a stumbling block and a retribution for them; let

---

[45] See BDAG, "*ek*," 3.i (p. 297) for support for this rendering of the preposition.
[46] Geerhardus Vos, *Biblical Theology* (Grand Rapids: Eerdmans, 1954), 108, 110 (emphasis original).

their eyes be darkened so that they cannot see, and bend their backs *forever* [*dia pantos*[47]]."

But, because God, as I have already noted, has by no means rejected every Jew, choosing in grace a Jewish remnant (Rom 11:5), throughout this age elect Jews continue to be saved by being provoked "to jealousy" (Rom 11:11, 14 NKJV) by the multitudes of saved Gentiles, enjoying the spiritual blessings originally intended for their people and who, accordingly through faith in Jesus Christ, their Messiah, are being grafted back into their own "olive tree" (Rom 11:23–24 NKJV). The justification of Gentiles is then the primary avenue to the justification of the Jewish elect; indeed, *in this way (houtōs)*, Paul declares, "all Israel" will be saved (Rom 11:26 NKJV).[48]

Peter's Teaching about the Future of Ethnic Israel

Also in harmony with our Lord's "replacement theology" concerning ethnic Israel's future, Peter applied God's description of Israel in Exod 19:5–6: "you shall be my treasured possession; . . . and you shall be to me a kingdom of priests and a holy nation" to the church of Jesus Christ in 1 Pet 2:9: ". . . you are a chosen race, a royal priesthood, a holy nation, a people for his own possession, that you may proclaim the excellencies of him who called you out of darkness into his marvelous light," and he applied Hosea's description of Israel in Hos 1:6, 9–10, "I will no more have mercy on the house of Israel . . . you are not my people, and I am not your God. Yet . . . in the place where it was said to them, 'You are not my people,' it shall be said to them, 'Children of the living God,'" also to the church of Jesus Christ in 1 Pet 2:10: "Once you were not a people, but now you

---

[47] This phrase may also be translated "continually," but "continually" conveys the same sense as "forever" in this context.

[48] For my exposition of Romans 11 see my *A New Systematic Theology of the Christian Faith*, 2nd ed. (Nashville: Thomas Nelson, 2002), 1025–30. There I show exegetically that, just as God throughout this age is bringing the divinely determined full number (Rom 11:25) of elect Gentiles to faith in Christ, so throughout this age he is bringing the divinely determined full number (Rom 11:12) of elect Jews (the "remnant") also to faith in Christ, so that both "full numbers" are reached *in this age*. While Israel *as a nation* has no salvific covenant with God in this age, standing as it is under God's wrath, the remnant of elect Jews, as they are saved, are grafted by faith in Christ into the "cultivated olive tree" (Rom 11:17–24), that is, the true church; *there* they cease to be "Ishmael" but become the true "Israel of God."

are God's people; once you had not received mercy, but now you have received mercy."

Six Propositions

In light of this biblical data, we are now in a position to declare as biblical the following six propositions:[49]

1. The modern Jewish state is not a part of the messianic kingdom of Jesus Christ. Even though this particular political state, in God's general providence, came into being on May 14, 1948, the day when the "British Mandate over Palestine" expired, it would be a denial of Jesus' affirmation that his kingdom is "not of this world order" (John 18:36) to assert that modern Israel is a part of his messianic kingdom. To put it bluntly, the modern state of Israel is not true "Israel" at all (Rom 9:6–8) but is rather "the spiritual son of Hagar" (Gal 4:24–25) and thus is "Ishmaelitish" to the core, due to its lack of Abrahamic faith in Jesus Christ.[50] National Israel has accordingly forsaken any legitimate *biblical* claim to the land, any partitioning of which, along with reparations for property, should be negotiated today by the claimants to the land, not under *biblical* claims or threats of war but through the political peace process governed by international law.[51]

---

[49] I have adapted the first five propositions with some additions and alterations from Robertson, *The Israel of God*, 194. I am indebted to Ronald Kilpatrick, Knox Seminary librarian, for several of the thoughts of the sixth.

[50] Modern Israel must face the fact that to be the physical descendants of Abraham and to have Abrahamic blood flowing in their veins means nothing as far as acquiring God's approbation is concerned. John the Baptist warned: "Do not presume to say to yourselves, 'We have Abraham as our father,' for I tell you, God is able from these stones to raise up children to Abraham" (Matt 3:9). To the Jews who were seeking to kill him but who were saying at the same time, "Abraham is our father," Jesus said, "If you were Abraham's children, you would be doing what Abraham did [that is, you would rejoice to see my day]. . . . You are of your father the devil" (John 8:39–44, 56). The Jewish people must recall that Abraham had *two* sons—two, that is, of biblical importance, namely, Ishmael and Isaac, for in addition to these two he had six other sons by Keturah after Sarah's death (Gen 25:1–2)—which means that "not all are children of Abraham because they are his offspring"; that is to say, "it is not the children of the flesh who are the children of God, but the children of the promise are counted as offspring" (Rom 9:7–8).

[51] In such a partitioning process, the United States government should be even-handed in its policy decisions respecting the parties to the conflict, favoring neither the

2. The land promise of the Old Testament served in a *typological* role as a model of the consummate realization of the purposes of God for his redeemed people that encompasses "all the families of the earth" (Gen 12:3) and the entire cosmos (Rom 4:13), which means that Christians, as members of the messianic kingdom of God, are the real heirs, along with Abraham, of the land promise in its antitypical, consummated character.

3. Because of the inherently limited scope of the land promised in the Old Testament, it cannot be regarded as having continuing significance in the realm of redemption other than in its function as a model to teach that obedience and divine blessing go hand in hand, while disobedience and divine retribution also go hand in hand. Of course, many Christians, following the teachings of John Hagee and others, do not believe that the Old Testament land promises are "inherently limited" in scope; rather, they believe that God *unconditionally* promised Abraham's physical progeny that the so-called holy land would be theirs as a possession *forever*. But this is to overlook the following factors that qualify God's Old Testament land promises:

   a. First, Moses stated that the physical progeny's obedience to God's law was a basic requirement for inheriting and *continuing to possess* the land (Deut 4:25–31; 28:15–68). While the land promises may appear at times to be unconditional, they always contained the tacit requirement of obedience that had to be met for the promises to materialize and to come to lasting fruition (see the principle enunciated in Jer 18:7–10).

"spiritual Ishmaelites" nor the natural Ishmaelites. For instance, should a coalition of Muslim nations launch a nonprovoked attack on the nation of Israel in order to exterminate the Jewish population and to eliminate the Jewish state as a nation in the Middle East as some Muslim leaders have threatened to do, the United States government should condemn that coalition and side defensively with Israel. But should Israel launch a nonprovoked attack against her Palestinian enemies or the Muslim world, admittedly much less likely than the foregoing instance, the United States should be just as quick to condemn Israel and to do all that it can to protect the lives of Palestinians and Muslims.

b. Second, the Hebrew word for "everlasting," while admittedly it means "forever" in some contexts, may also denote in other contexts the limited duration of the age of promise, such as (1) God's declaration that circumcision was to be an "everlasting covenant" between him and his people in Gen 17:13 (but see Rom 2:25–29; Gal 2:3; 5:2–6; Col 2:11–12, where we are informed that "in Christ Jesus neither [outward] circumcision nor [outward] uncircumcision counts for anything," that "circumcision is a matter of the heart," and that circumcision, as a type, is fulfilled by Christian baptism, its new covenant antitype) and (2) God's declaration that the Passover Feast in Exod 12:17 was to be an "everlasting ordinance" (NKJV, but see 1 Cor 5:7, where we are informed that now "Christ is our Passover").[52]

c. Third, the New Testament, the documentary corpus in the progressiveness of revelation that describes prophetic fulfillment, nowhere refers to political Israel possessing the land forever; rather, it speaks of Abraham's believing covenant offspring as inheriting the world (Rom 4:13).

One passage requires comment here. After his resurrection, Jesus spent forty days with his disciples, speaking to them about the kingdom of God (Acts 1:3). Sometime during this period, the apostles asked him, "Lord, will you at this time restore the kingdom to Israel?" (Acts 1:6). Jesus responded, "It is not for you to know times or seasons that the Father has fixed by his own authority" (Acts 1:7). Because Christ did not deny in so many words that he would restore the kingdom to Israel, some scholars have argued

---

[52] Allan A Macrae, "('lm) III," in *Theological Wordbook of the Old Testament*, ed. R. Laird Harris, Gleason L. Archer, and Bruce K. Waltke (Chicago Moody, 1980), 2:673, declares: "That neither the Hebrew ['ōlām] nor the Greek word [aiōn] in itself contains the idea of endlessness is shown both by the fact that they sometimes refer to events or conditions that occurred at a definite point in the past, and also by the fact that sometimes it is thought desirable to repeat the word, not merely saying 'forever,' but 'forever and ever.'"

that this New Testament passage implies that ethnic Israel will in the future yet reign over the world from Jerusalem.[53] What shall we say about this contention? It is true that Jesus does not deny here that the kingdom would be restored to Israel, but then he does not affirm it either. This dispensational interpretation has all the weaknesses of any argument from silence. But, more must be said by way of response.

I admit that it is virtually certain that the apostles, speaking as they did of the kingdom being "restored to Israel," were probably thinking of the kingdom as a national entity with its government centered in Jerusalem and its domain encompassing the land of their fathers. But, theirs was both a misapprehension of the nature of the kingdom Jesus had in mind and a mixture of truth and error as the immediate context shows.

In the context immediately preceding their question, Jesus had been teaching them about the kingdom of God. And, as a major aspect of that teaching, "he ordered them not to depart from Jerusalem, but to wait for the promise of the Father," namely, the Spirit's baptismal outpouring that they would receive "not many days from now" (Acts 1:4). (It was doubtless Jesus' "not many days from now" reference that provoked their question: "Will you at this time restore the kingdom to Israel?") But, it is clear that they did not fully understand Jesus and were still thinking of the kingdom of God as a political "kingdom of Israel," for clearly Jesus' teaching about the coming of the kingdom "is synonymous with, or at least closely associated with, the coming of the Holy Spirit in power."[54] That is to say, Luke's close juxtaposition of these topics

---

[53] See Brent Kinman, "Debtor's Prison and the Future of Israel," *Journal of the Evangelical Theological Society* 42 (1999): 423. Kinman contends that Jesus' failure "to correct the disciples' misunderstanding" implies "confirmation of the premise of their question."

[54] Ben Witherington III, *The Acts of the Apostles: A Socio-Rhetorical Commentary* (Grand Rapids: Eerdmans, 1998), 109.

at the beginning of his Acts plainly suggests that what Jesus taught about the kingdom was that God's kingdom in this age was to be a *spiritual* kingdom as evidenced by "the promise of the Father," that is, the soon-to-be given baptism of the Spirit in fulfillment of Joel 2. Consequently, Jesus, the Lord of all humanity (Acts 10:36), by his statement in Acts 1:8, "turns their thoughts from curiosity as to times and seasons to a sober submission to the sovereign will of the Father, from the idea of reign to the duty of ministry, from the narrow horizon of Israel to the wide world,"[55] by instructing them that they would receive power when the Holy Spirit had come upon them and they would become his witnesses, not only in Jerusalem and all Judea, but also to the multi-ethnic Samaritans and to the ends of the earth, that is, to the wide world of the Gentiles, both of whom Jews hated.

But, by beginning their witness as preachers of the gospel, as they would in Jerusalem and Judea, the apostles would come to understand as the gospel went forth to distant lands that God had in a spiritual sense "restored" spiritual Israel to kingdom authority. As Robertson states,

[Jesus' statement in Acts 1:8] should not be regarded as peripheral to the question asked by the disciples. Instead, it is germane to the whole issue of restoration of the kingdom to Israel. The domain of this kingdom, the realm of the Messiah's rule, would indeed begin at Jerusalem, the focal point of Israel's life for centuries. So, unquestionably, Israel would be a primary participant in the coming [and expansion— RLR] of the messianic kingdom. . . .

At the same time, the domain of this kingdom cannot be contained within the Israel of the old covenant. Going even beyond Judea and Samaria, this kingdom would break through the bounds of Jewish

---

[55] Martin H. Franzmann, *The Word of the Lord Grows* (St. Louis, MO: Concordia, 1961), 8.

political concern and extend to the farthest corners of the earth. According to one insightful analysis of Jesus' statement to his disciples [Jesus in Acts 1:8 was] . . . indicating that their forthcoming mission to the "ends of the earth" would itself be an indication of Israel's restoration and the means whereby the truth of that restoration would be implemented upon the world stage. Israel was being restored through the resurrection of its Messiah and the forthcoming gift of the Spirit. The way in which Israel would then exert its hegemony over the world would not be through its own political independence, but rather through the rule and authority of Israel's Messiah. . . . Jesus' concern . . . was not for a political "kingdom of Israel" but rather for the "kingdom of God."[56]

Such, I submit, is a more sensitive way to read the disciples' question and Jesus' response to it than that of the dispensationalist.

4. The Old Testament predictions about the return of Israel to the land in terms of a geopolitical reestablishment of the state of Israel are more properly interpreted as types having consummating fulfillment at the antitypical "restoration of all things" that will accompany the resurrection of believers at the return of Christ (Acts 3:21; Rom 8:22–23). *To interpret these Old Testament predictions literally would be a retrogressive elevation of shadow over substance, of type over antitype.* Robertson concurs: "In this age of fulfillment, a retrogression to the limited forms of the old covenant must be neither expected nor promoted. Reality must not give way to shadow."[57]

5. The future messianic kingdom will embrace the whole of the newly recreated cosmos and will not experience a special manifestation that could be regarded *in any sense* as "Jewish" in the region of the so-called Holy Land or anywhere else.

---

[56] See P. W. L. Walker, *Jesus and the Holy City: New Testament Perspectives on Jerusalem* (Grand Rapids: Eerdmans, 1996), 292.
[57] Robertson, *The Israel of God*, 31.

Peter, the apostle to the circumcision (who surely would have had his ear tuned to any and every future privilege Jews might enjoy), when he wrote of future things in 2 Peter 3, said nothing about a *Jewish* millennium or about a restoration of a *Jewish* kingdom in the land of Israel; rather, he divided the whole of earth history into three periods: the *first* period—"the world of that time"—extending from the beginning of creation to the Genesis flood (2 Pet 3:5–6), that was destroyed by the flood; the *second* period—"the heavens and earth that now exist" (2 Pet 3:7)—extending from the flood to the final Day of the Lord, at which time the earth will be destroyed by fire (2 Pet 3:7) and the present heavens "will pass away with a roar, and the heavenly bodies will be burned up and dissolved" (2 Pet 3:10); and the *third* period—"new heavens and a new earth in which righteousness dwells" (2 Pet 3:13)—extending throughout eternity future. If he had believed in a Jewish millennium following this present age, it is legitimate to assert that 2 Peter 3 would have been the appropriate place to mention it, but he makes no mention of a millennium, much less a *Jewish* millennium; rather, he places the entirety of earth history within the three time frames I mentioned.

6. Biblical prophecy says nothing about the modern state of Israel. In fact, far from the formation of modern Israel being a fulfillment of biblical prophecy, it is, if anything, a major, if not *the* major, contemporary means today in the hand of God to sustain ethnic Israel in its divinely imposed hardening.

   Christian Zionists, to the contrary, claim that the establishment of Israel as a nation on May 14, 1948, fulfilled biblical prophecies. The following Old Testament prophecies are samples from a larger group of passages that these biblical interpreters say were fulfilled by the establishment of modern Israel in 1948:

- Jeremiah 29:14, it is said, predicted the founding of the modern state of Israel. But, the context of Jeremiah 29 makes it clear that the predicted "restoration" after the completion of the seventy years of Babylonian exile (29:10) refers to the return from exile under Zerubbabel in 536 BC.

- Isaiah 11:11, it is said, speaks of a "second time" that God would restore the remnant to the land, the first being the return from Babylon in 536 BC, and the second being the establishment of modern Israel in 1948. But the context of Isaiah 11 makes it clear that Israel's first deliverance was from Egypt under Moses (11:16), with its second restoration being from the nations into which Jews of the Assyrian/Babylonian captivities had spread over time during the Second Temple period that typically pointed forward to the antitypical rejuvenation of the entire cosmos in the eschaton.

- Zechariah 8:7, it is said, predicted that God "will save [his] people from the east country and from the west country, and . . . bring them to dwell in the midst of Jerusalem." It is, however, a reach to see this prediction as referring to the modern state of Israel. In fact, the passage speaks of the faithfulness and righteousness of the inhabitants of Jerusalem in that day (8:8), something that is definitely not true of present Jerusalem. Zechariah was predicting the return of exiles during the days of Ezra, Nehemiah, and after (see Ezra 7:1–10; Neh 11:1–2) that, again, pointed typically forward to the antitypical new paradise of God.

- Ezekiel 36:24–26, it is said, predicted that Israel would be restored to the land "in unbelief," which agrees with the situation in modern Israel today. But, the passage does not speak of a restoration "in unbelief." God does not bless disobedience. Verse 33 states: "On the day that I cleanse you from all your iniquities, I will cause the cities to be inhabited," clearly implying that those who are "restored" have first been spiritually cleansed, thereby meeting the requirement of Lev 26:40–42: "If they confess their iniquity . . . if then their uncircumcised heart is humbled, . . . *then* I will remember my covenant . . . and I will remember the land."

- Amos 9:14–15, it is said, declares that a condition of permanent national establishment would someday prevail that simply was not true of any Old Testament restoration. However, the restoration of Amos 9:14–15 envisions the return from exile during the Second Temple period and, given the fact that Amos 9:11–12 according to James (Acts 15:15–17) describes this church age, also depicts in pastoral terms—the only terms that could or would communicate to Amos's contemporaries—the eschatological rejuvenation of the cosmos and the "restoration of all things."[58]

Conclusion

What should we conclude from all this? The twin facts of ethnic Israel's unbelief and God's wrath exhibited toward ethnic Israel (1 Thess 2:15–16) pose a problem for Christians today. On the one hand, should not our attitude toward these people, through whom came not only our Old Testament Scriptures but also our Messiah and Savior according to the flesh (Rom 9:5), indeed, our very salvation (John 4:22), be one of gratitude? Should Christians not do everything in their power to make the lot of the Jewish people more acceptable to the world? On the other hand, was not the Jewish religious leadership "the hand holding the knife" in the crucifixion of their Messiah (with Rome's complicity in Jesus' crucifixion providing the "knife"), notwithstanding Roman Catholicism's absolution of Jews in that event? And have not Jews for the most part rejected their Messiah, the Savior of the world, declaring him to be only one in a long line of false messiahs, and do not these same Jews, when pressed, acknowledge that they regard Christians as idolaters, worshiping as they do him whom they regard as a "mere man"?

---

[58] I would urge anyone interested in reading further on this subject to consult O. Palmer Robertson's *The Israel of God: Yesterday, Today, and Tomorrow* (Phillipsburg, NJ: P&R, 2000) and his *The Christ of the Prophets* (Phillipsburg, NJ: P&R, 2004), chaps. 10–12.

In response to this problem, I would first say that no true Christian should or ever will advocate or support anything evenly remotely resembling ethnic discrimination against Jews. When he recalls the suffering that Jews experienced at the hands of Gentiles (but *not* at the hands of true Christians) in, for instance, the Jewish Holocaust, he can only weep until he has no tears left at the unspeakable horror of Adolf Hitler's "Final Solution" during World War II that attempted to solve for Europe its so-called "Jewish problem." The "solution" resulted in the mass destruction of 6 million Jews in the death camps, gas chambers, and mobile gas vans of the infamous cities of Auschwitz, Belzec, Bergen-Belsen, Birkenau, Buchenwald, Chelmno, Dachau, Majdanek, Sobibor, and Treblinka, which "solution" was accompanied by the wholesale plundering of Jewish real estate, art, gold, and other possessions. The "solution" was followed by the Nazi program codenamed *Aktion 1005* that attempted to conceal the evidence of the Jewish Holocaust from the world by destroying the remains of millions of Jewish dead. This program was so successful in its "cleanup" measures that the lack of full physical evidence of the number of Jewish dead has given inspiration to the lunatic fringe who claim the Holocaust never happened.[59] At the same time, in light of the fact that the only hope of salvation for the Jewish people resides in the provisions of the Christian gospel, it would be wrong, unloving, and un-Christian, for a true Christian to encourage or to support Israel in the establishment and maintenance of its *religious* "Jewishness" as the ground of its hope of approbation before God. This is simply to take seriously the uniqueness and finality of Jesus Christ as the only Savior and the only hope, not only of ethnic Israel, but also of *every* people group and *every* nation! The Bible denounces every hope for approbation before God that is not grounded in the person and work of Christ. Such approbation pursued through ethnicity or good works is futile

---

[59] Modern Israel, since May 14, 1948, does not have pure hands either in its treatment of the Palestinian people. Under the direction of David Ben-Gurion, the new state's first prime minister, Israel ruthlessly slaughtered many Palestinians living within its borders, destroyed their villages, and drove those remaining into refuge camps beyond its borders in a "purification" of the land that Palestinians today refer to as *al-Nakba*, The Catastrophe. For this inhumanity toward the Palestinians on Israel's part one must weep as well.

(Gal 2:16) and fatal. Therefore, the Jew, if he is ever to know genuine forgiveness by God, must be persuaded through our Christian witness to forsake the notion that his ethnic connection to the patriarchs and/or his allegiance to Torah make him acceptable to God (Rom 2:17–29; Gal 5:3–4).

It is a strange twist of thinking, if not downright disloyalty to the gospel, for Christians to aid and to abet the Jewish people in their retention of their *religious* distinctives that provide the ground of their hope for divine approbation, the holding on to which only solidifies them in their unbelief. And yet, in order that the blessing of Gen 12:3 might be theirs, and in order to escape the threatened curse enunciated in the same verse, many Christians fervently believe that they must support Zionist causes, whatever the cost, and must rejoice with every "Israeli advance" in the world, failing to realize as they do, that as long as they encourage the Jew to continue to hold his unbiblical perception of what constitutes "Jewishness,"[60] and that as long as the Jew continues to hold to Judaism as his religion (*contra* John Hagee), just so long will he continue to reject Jesus Christ, who is Israel's only hope of salvation. Should he miss Jesus, he will be eternally condemned.

The Roman Catholic Church, in spite of its efforts at *aggiornamento*—that is, its efforts to "modernize" itself[61]—has not

---

[60] In no uncertain terms Paul declared that "no one is a Jew who is merely one outwardly, nor is circumcision outward and physical. But a Jew is one inwardly, and circumcision is a matter of the heart, by the Spirit, and not by the letter" (Rom 2:28–29). Moreover, he taught that "the present Jerusalem," the enslaved city doomed for destruction in AD 70, is the "son of Hagar" bearing children for slavery whereas Christians both are and have "the Jerusalem above," where Jesus the Son of David sits and reigns, as their mother (Gal 4:25; see also Heb 12:22; Rev 21:9–26). And John says of the Jews of Smyrna who were slandering Christians before the Roman authorities that "Jews they are not" but rather are a "synagogue of Satan" (Rev 2:10).

[61] In spite of its efforts to modernize, the Vatican, after sixty plus years, still refuses to explain the public silence of Pope Pius XII (whose papal reign extended from 1939 until his death in 1958) in the face of the annihilation of Europe's Jews, despite repeated Allied requests that he speak out, as well as the sanctuary and aid given by high Roman church officials to Adolf Eichmann and other prominent Nazi murderers after the defeat of the Third Reich.

Vatican defenders of Pope Pius XII insist that he was a friend of the Jew, whose tireless work through quiet diplomacy saved the lives of hundreds of thousands of Jews. His critics, however, have portrayed him as a calculating politician who, at best, displayed a callous and near-criminal indifference to the plight of Europe's Jews and, at worst, was actually complicit in the Holocaust. The world will never know the full truth regarding this matter until the Vatican opens its Secret Archives to historians in search of the truth.

helped here either, declaring as recently as its 1994 *Catechism of the Catholic Church* that (1) because the faith of the Jewish people—catechetically described as "the first to hear the Word of God"—"unlike other non-Christian religions, is already a response to God's revelation in the Old Covenant" (paragraph 839),[62] (2) because to the Jews belong all the privileges outlined in Rom 9:4–5 (paragraph 839), and (3) because, with Christians, they "await the coming of the Messiah" (paragraph 840), the people of God include the Jewish people. It does not seem to bother Rome that the Jewish people, for the most part, deny the deity of Jesus Christ and thus the doctrine of the Trinity, or that they, save for the elect remnant, rejected their Messiah as a misguided prophet and a false messiah at best and a blasphemer at worst the first time he came, and had him crucified, and accordingly believe today that Christians are idolaters because we worship him whom they contend was simply a man, and that the Jewish people see no need for Christ's substitutionary atonement. According to Rome's teaching, they are still related salvifically to the people of God and may go to heaven!

Again, Christians are often told today that in their witness to their Jewish friends, they may assume that the Jews to whom they speak already believe the Old Testament and that it only remains to show them that Jesus Christ is the one about whom

---

In order to quell the controversy surrounding its beleaguered Pope, in October 1999 the Vatican created a commission of six independent historians (three Catholics, three Jews) to assess the conduct of Pope Pius XII and the Roman See during the war. Employing the only documents available to it, documents that were already in the public domain and that are mainly wartime diplomatic traffic, the commission concluded: "No serious historian could accept that the published, edited volumes [*Actes et Documents du Saint Seìge relatifs à la Seconde Guerre Mondiale*] could put us at the end of the story." It submitted to the Vatican a list of forty-seven questions, along with a request for supporting documentary evidence from the Vatican's Secret Archives such as "diaries, memoranda, appointment books, minutes of meetings, draft documents" and personal papers of senior wartime Vatican officials. After ten months, when it became clear that the Vatican had no intention of releasing the documents requested, the commission disbanded with its work unfinished. The Vatican's silence continues about this matter, as well as about its relationship to the murderous military regimes of Latin America. This suggests no "modernization" here; so much for the Roman church-state's *aggiornamento*!

[62] Theirs was indeed a response, a *negative* one, to God's revelation in the old covenant. To suggest that the faith of Christ-rejecting Jews is in any sense a proper response to the Old Testament revelation is surely an inaccurate appraisal of the situation. In light of the fact that the only hope of salvation for Jews resides in the provisions of the Christian gospel, it is simply gross wrong-headedness to encourage or to support them in their "Jewishness" or in their Zionist causes.

the Old Testament prophets spoke. This is surely an inaccurate appraisal of the actual situation. Most Jews today neither believe the Old Testament is the inspired Word of the living God nor know what the Old Testament teaches. We must think more carefully here, for no Jew can truly believe the Old Testament and not acknowledge Jesus Christ to be the Messiah, Savior, and Lord revealed therein. Jesus expressly declared to the Jewish religious leadership of his day, "If you believed Moses, you would believe me; for he wrote of me. But if you do not believe his writings, how will you believe my words?" (John 5:46–47). Luke reports that on the night of his bodily resurrection from the dead, Jesus "beginning with Moses and all the Prophets, . . . explained to them what was said in all the [Old Testament] Scriptures concerning himself" (Luke 24:27 NIV; see also John 13:18; 19:24, 28, 36–37; 20:9).[63] Later that same evening, to the disciples who had gathered together, with others with them, Jesus declared, "This is what I told you while I was still with you: Everything must be fulfilled that is written about me in the Law of Moses, the Prophets and the Psalms" (Luke 24:44). Jesus clearly taught that the Old Testament spoke about him.

Then Paul declares in 2 Cor 3:7–16 that an unlifted "veil" (*kalumma*) covers the hearts of unbelieving Jews when they read Moses, that is, the old covenant, a veil that can only be removed by Christ. The blindness that Israel experienced when beholding the radiant face of Moses, Paul writes, continues "to this day" as a veil over their hearts when they read the old covenant. That is to say, the Jewish people do not and never will read aright the Old Testament as long as they read it apart from its fulfillment in Christ and his saving work. They do not understand that the glory of God they seek in Torah has been surpassed by the greater glory to be found in Christ, and that the Old Testament must be read christologically, that is, from the present perspective of its fulfillment in Christ. The real truth of the matter is that no one—neither Jew, nor Gentile—who has heard of the

---

[63] Christians have often expressed the wish that they could have heard Jesus' interpretation of the Old Testament on that occasion. They can be assured, however, that both the apostles' sermons recorded in Acts and their apostolic letters reflect the major features of Christ's Emmaus road exposition by the way in which they interpret the Old Testament christologically.

Messiah and his atoning work and then rejects him, believes the Old Testament. When the modern Jew claims that he believes and follows Torah, even though he may even say that he sees grace taught therein, but at the same time also believes that he must live a certain way if he is to merit and remain a "son" of Torah, he does not believe the Old Testament and is denying the saving provision of which Torah actually speaks through the elaborate protocols of its Levitical sacrificial system, sacrifices which pointed typically to Jesus Christ, the Lamb of God, who takes away the sin of the world.

The sooner Christians realize that to bring the Jewish people to the Christian faith, they must convince them of the futility of any and every hope for God's approbation that is related to the fact that they have Abrahamic blood flowing in their veins (Matt 3:9; John 1:13), or that they are physically circumcised (Rom 2:25–29; Gal 5:2–4; 6:15), or that they are practicing "sons and daughters of Torah" (Rom 2:17–24; 3:9; Gal 3:10; 4:21–5:1), the sooner their witness to the Jewish people will become effective.

Thus, we must conclude that just as, for God, "as far as the gospel is concerned, [the Jewish people, with the exception of the remnant] are [regarded as his] enemies [for the salvific sake of non-Jews] . . . ; but as far as election is concerned, they are loved on account of the patriarchs" (Rom 11:28 NIV), so also, for Christians, they should love the Jews, by whose elect remnant, along with Gentile Christians, God will fulfill his elective promises to the patriarchs. But, Christians must also do everything they can, without being arrogant toward them (Rom 11:28), to bring the Jewish people to the place where they will forsake any and every religious distinctive in which they may be resting their hope for salvation. Christians must do this for the sake of the Jewish people and out of loyalty to the cause of the gospel. "How sad it would be," writes Robertson, "if evangelical Christians who profess to love the Jewish people should become a primary tool in misdirecting their faith and expectation"[64] toward a false hope and away from this world's only true Savior, who is Jesus Christ, the Jewish Messiah and only Savior of the world.

---

[64] Robertson, *The Israel of God*, 31.

Response by Robert L. Thomas

The Dependability of God's Promises

In my description of the dispensationalist perspective, I sought to emphasize the continuity of God's unconditional covenants with Israel. From Genesis to Revelation, Israel is always the center of attention now and will be in the future of God's dealings with his creation.

I find it interesting that Reymond equates Gen 3:15 with the covenant of grace in covenant theology. That was a direct promise to the serpent and Satan, not to humans, but it illustrates how God's unconditional promises will always be implemented: "And I will put enmity between you and the woman, and between your seed and her seed; he shall bruise you on the head, and you shall bruise him on the heel" (NASB). To illustrate the principle of God's inevitable fulfillment of his promises, one must only consult Rev 20:1–3, 10, which describes the final blow on the serpent's head:

> Then I saw an angel coming down from heaven, holding the key of the abyss and a great chain in his hand. And he laid hold of the dragon, the serpent of old, who is the devil and Satan, and bound him for a thousand years; and he threw him into the abyss, and shut *it* and sealed *it* over him, so that he would not deceive the nations any longer, until the thousand years were completed; after these things he must be released for a short time. . . . And the devil who deceived them was thrown into the lake of fire and brimstone, where the beast and the false prophet are also; and they will be tormented day and night forever and ever. (NASB)

Just as God's promise to the serpent was bound to be fulfilled, so are his unconditional promises to Abraham and his descendants, beginning in Genesis 12. Surely his promise to the serpent in the *Protevangelium* (i.e., "the first gospel") has significant implications for Adam and Eve and their descendants, but in the text of Genesis it was a promise made to the serpent.

The Durability of God's Abrahamic Covenant

The promises will be for Abraham and his physical descendants, not just his spiritual descendants, as Reymond at times has called them. In his approach he uses only NT Scripture as justification for a distinction between physical and spiritual. That step violates grammatical-historical principles in at least two ways. (1) When he writes about the "spiritual promises of the Abrahamic covenant," he derives his support from NT passages rather than the historical context of the Genesis statements about the covenant. For example, one cannot learn Abraham's understanding of the covenant and God's intention in Genesis by resorting to Paul's words in Eph 2:11–13. Paul's historical and theological circumstances were entirely different. The words of Genesis 12 must be understood as dictated by the historical context in the OT. Paul's historical and theological circumstances came much later and were different.

Terry cautions against the danger of trying to make passages parallel that are not parallel and the pitfall of mistaking likeness of sentiment for real parallelism.[65] Ramm joins him in emphasizing the need for objectivity:

> The true philological spirit, or critical spirit, or scholarly spirit, in Biblical interpretation has as its goal to discover the original meaning and intention of the text. Its goal is *exegesis*—to lead the meaning out of the text and shuns *exogesis*—bringing a meaning to the text. . . . It is very difficult for any person to approach the Holy Scriptures free from prejudices and assumptions which distort the text. The danger of having a set theological system is that in the interpretation of Scripture the system tends to govern the interpretation rather than the interpretation correcting the system. . . . Calvin said that the Holy Scripture is not a tennis ball that we may bounce around at will. Rather it is the Word of God

---

[65] Milton S. Terry, *Biblical Hermeneutics*, 2nd ed. (repr., Grand Rapids: Zondervan, n.d.), 222–23.

whose teachings must be learned by the most impartial and objective study of the text.[66]

Terry also warns that general analogy of faith cannot govern in places that have no real parallel and that stand unopposed by other parts.[67] Single revelations of divine truth without elaborations must be allowed. General analogy is of little help in such cases. One's goal in biblical interpretation is to let each passage speak for itself.

(2) At one point in his discussion, Reymond does acknowledge that Abraham understood the covenant in Genesis 12 to be a reference to his physical descendants. He notes that temporal earthly promises of a land to Abraham and his *physical* seed were among the provisions of the Abrahamic covenant (Gen 12:7; 13:15, 17; 15:18; 17:8). In assigning two meanings (physical and spiritual) in the same OT passage, he violates the traditional principle of single meaning. Terry affirms, "A fundamental principle in grammatico-historical exposition is that the words and sentences can have but one significance in one and the same connection. The moment we neglect this principle we drift out upon a sea of uncertainty and conjecture."[68] Not quite so long ago, Ramm advocated the same principle in different words: "But here we must remember the old adage: 'Interpretation is one, application is many.' This means that there is only one meaning to a passage of Scripture which is determined by careful study."[69] Summit II of the International Council on Biblical Inerrancy agreed with this principle: "We affirm that the meaning expressed in each biblical text is single, definite and fixed. We deny that the recognition of this single meaning eliminates the variety of its application."[70]

So it will be for Abraham and his descendants, not just his "spiritual descendants" as Reymond calls them. In his approach

---

[66] Bernard Ramm, *Protestant Biblical Interpretation: A Textbook of Hermeneutics*, 3rd rev. ed. (Grand Rapids: Baker, 1970), 115–16.

[67] Terry, *Biblical Hermeneutics*, 581.

[68] Ibid., 205.

[69] Ramm, *Protestant Biblical Interpretation*, 113.

[70] Article VII, "Articles of Affirmation and Denial," adopted by the International Council on Biblical Inerrancy, November 10–13, 1982. They can be read here: Accessed 9/30/13 http://www.modernreformation.org/default.php?page=articledisplay&var1=ArtRead&var2=1127&var3=main.

he uses only NT Scripture as justification for a distinction between physical and spiritual. That step violates grammatical-historical principles. When he writes about the "spiritual promises of the Abrahamic covenant," he derives his support from NT passages rather than the context of the Genesis statements, and he assigns the same passage two different meanings. He allows his analogy of faith to overpower principles of grammatical-historical hermeneutics by assigning two different meanings to the same statement of the Abrahamic covenant.

The same sovereign, elective, loving grace of God that he displayed in delivering Israel from Egyptian bondage was at work in his choosing Abram and his physical descendants as a special people to represent him to the human race. In the working out of the divine plan for the world, God made the choice on his own. Abraham did not merit being chosen.

The Church, a People of God Distinct from Israel

Reymond elaborates on the parable in Matt 21:33–45 and its parallels as a major support for the church's replacement of Israel as the one people of God. What he does not mention, however, are the words of Jesus near the end of the parable: "Therefore I say to you, the kingdom of God will be taken away from you and given to a people [*ethnos*, lit. "a nation"], producing the fruit of it" (Matt 21:43 NASB). Qualified lexicographers have identified *ethnos* in this verse as referring to Israel. What Reymond fails to consider is that in the NT the singular noun *ethnos*, when unqualified by other words such as "nation against nation" (Matt 24:7; Mark 13:8; Luke 21:10) and "every nation of humankind" (Acts 17:26), usually refers to Israel.[71] The singular noun frequently refers to Israel (cf. Luke 7:5; 23:2; John 11:48, 50–52; Acts 24:2, 10). The plural usually includes those outside Israel. This follows a similar pattern found in the OT. BDAG observes, "in Mt 21:43 ἔ. (not gentiles) in contrast to the leaders described vv. 23, 45,"[72] a BDAG comment coming under the category of "a body of persons united by kinship, culture, and common traditions." Quite obviously, Israel is the nation in view in Matt 21:43.

---

[71] See BDAG, 276–77.
[72] Ibid., 276.

What Jesus predicted to his adversaries in the parable of Matt 21:33–45 is the future generation of Israel who will gladly trust Jesus as their Messiah and Savior. This ingathering of Israelites will be an event that will transpire after the rapture of the church (Rev 3:10) and the beginning of the Day of the Lord (1 Thess 5:2). In other words, it will come after the period of Israel's rejection, which has characterized the nation for centuries.

Shortly after a series of parables in Matthew 21, but apparently on the same occasion in Jerusalem, Jesus proceeded to pronounce a series of woes on the scribes and Pharisees in Matthew 23. He closes the series with words directly to those Jewish leaders by addressing them with the second person plural pronoun "you." As he moves to a conclusion of the last "woe," he substitutes "this generation" (*tēn genean tautēn*) for the pronoun (Matt 23:36). BDAG correctly classifies use of the word "generation" (*genea*) under the heading "the sum total of those born at the same time, expanded to include all those living at a given time and freq. defined in terms of specific characteristics."[73] It also suggests, as an alternate rendering, "those exhibiting common characteristics of interests, 'race, kind.'"[74] It characterizes them as "an evil and adulterous generation (or race; cf. Matt 12:39)."[75]

That lexicon has captured a truth that commentators have sometimes missed. Jesus used *genea* as a qualitative term without chronological meaning. It does not refer to a span of time. Rather, it refers to a kind of Jewish people who could exist at any time since the call of Abraham. As Gundry writes, "generation" or "kind" (*genea*) refers to "the 'unbelieving and perverted' in the whole of human history,"[76] as BDAG indicates. In other words, *genea* refers to Jesus' listeners and any Jewish unbelieving people since the beginning of the Jewish race. His contemporary listeners, the scribes and Pharisees, were of the same ilk as unbelieving Israelites who murdered the prophets of old (Matt 23:31–36).

At the end of Matthew 23, Jesus spoke of Israel's future repentance, addressing Jerusalem to represent Israel's future change

---

[73] Ibid., 191.
[74] Ibid.
[75] Ibid., 191–92.
[76] Robert H. Gundry, *Matthew: A Commentary on His Literary and Theological Art* (Grand Rapids: Eerdmans, 1982), 472.

of heart at the time of his return: "For I say to you, from now on you will not see Me until you say, 'BLESSED IS HE WHO COMES IN THE NAME OF THE LORD!'" (Matt 23:39 NASB).

Later the same day, Jesus again used "this generation." BDAG correctly places this use of *genea* in the same category of meaning as in Matt 23:36.[77] When he said, "'Truly I say to you, this generation [i.e., kind] will not pass away until all these things take place'" (Matt 24:34), he spoke indirectly and prophetically of the future repentance of Israel in conjunction with his second coming. The context of Matthew 24–25 speaks of events of the seventieth week of Daniel (Dan 9:24–27). As that context notes, it will be a period of great suffering on earth, especially for Israel. The suffering will come through God's pouring out his wrath on unbelievers and those who persecute Israel. Yet somehow, through all of this, Israel will turn to faith in Christ as her Messiah and Savior. Until this future repentance, Israel as a whole will continue in unbelief.

Events connected with Christ's second advent will begin with the rapture of the church (Rev 3:10) and the beginning of the Day of the Lord (1 Thess 5:2). During this period of Israel's rejection, the Lord has chosen to raise up another people of God, whom he has called the church (Matt 16:18). As I have described in the dispensational perspective, both of these future happenings are imminent and will mark the beginning of the future seventieth week.

The Church and Israel in Contemporary Setting

Reymond frequently refers to John Hagee and other dispensationalists who support dispensationalism by citing the twentieth-century establishment of the nation of Israel in 1948 as fulfillment of biblical prophecy. Dispensationalists differ with one another about prophetic details. Some disagree in some respects with Hagee's position.

This response, for example, does not view the establishment of the modern state of Israel as a direct fulfillment of OT or NT prophecy. I do not think any biblical prediction will find fulfillment before the two happenings at the beginning of the future

---

[77] BDAG, 191.

seventieth week spoken of in Daniel 9.[78] That week was alluded to by Jesus at least twice in his Olivet Discourse (Matt 24:15; Mark 13:14), and likened by him to the beginning of birth pains (Matt 24:8; Mark 13:8) spoken about in the OT prophets. The two fulfillments to occur at the beginning of the week are, as mentioned above, the rapture of the church and the commencement of events of the Day of the Lord. A number of dispensationalists agree that these coincide with each other.[79]

Though not all dispensationalists see the twenty-first-century nation of Israel as fulfilling biblical prophecy, they do see it as perhaps a foreshadowing of how God will raise Israel to prominence among world powers during or at the end of the seventy weeks. The assurance that some day Israel will have that role raises the question of how God will, in his sovereign purpose, accomplish it. The fact that he has elevated the nation to such prominence even before the arrival of the seventy weeks is a reminder of his promise that Abraham's physical descendants will occupy the land promised to the patriarchs. Contemporary Israel occupies only a portion of the land now, but someday they will have it all.

A dispensationalist can rejoice for Israel and for the church. For the former group because "all Israel will be saved" (Rom 1:26 NASB) since "they are beloved for the sake of the fathers; for the gifts and the calling of God are irrevocable" (Rom 11:28–29 NASB). "The fathers" include Abraham, Isaac, and Jacob. For the church, rejoicing will come because some of the benefits from God's covenants with Israel have been extended to Gentile believers.

Response by Robert L. Saucy

As a progressive dispensationalist, I find Reymond's essay contains a great deal with which I can concur, some things I believe

---

[78] See John F. Walvoord, *The Thessalonian Epistles* (Findlay, OH: Dunham, 1955), 89; John F. Walvoord and Mark Hitchcock, *1 & 2 Thessalonians* (Chicago: Moody, 2011), 89, 91.

[79] See Jeffrey L. Townsend, "The Rapture in Revelation 3:10," in *When the Trumpet Sounds*, ed. Thomas Ice and Timothy Demy (Eugene, OR: Harvest House, 1995), 377.

are a misunderstanding of dispensationalism, and a number of things related to the topic of this book that I find problematic.

Before looking at specific issues more related to Israel and the church, a few comments on Reymond's concept of dispensationalism might be helpful. (I should note that my comments stem from my own understanding of dispensationalism and are not intended to speak for all dispensationalists.) Several times the essay accuses dispensationalists of teaching multiple ways of salvation. While the interpretations of certain texts thought to express distinctions between the dispensations of law and grace by earlier dispensationalists could possibly be understood that way, I do not believe this was ever a part of classic dispensationalism. Nor do I know of any expression of this teaching in any written work by dispensationalists today, traditional or progressive.[80] Dispensationalists, with all orthodox evangelicals, believe that salvation is by grace through faith alone on the basis of Christ's perfect life and sacrifice for us.

Different dispensations (or economies) are not different ways or means of salvation but differences in human expressions of saving faith. All evangelicals believe that the person who has genuine saving faith in God will seek to obey him. But, Scripture also teaches—and I would suggest that this is also common to evangelicals—that the righteousness set forth by God for his people is not always stipulated in the same commands. No Christian today follows the sacrifices commanded of Israel living under the old Mosaic covenant. It is also doubtful that many follow the dietary laws and other regulations, such as not reaping "to the very corners of your field" (Lev 19:9 NASB) or not wearing anything made of "two kinds of material mixed together" (Lev 19:19 NASB), and numerous others. While the righteous principles expressed in all of these commands are the eternal righteousness of God, this righteousness is expressed in different ways even as a child is no longer under the specific regulations of his parents once he becomes an adult. Nevertheless, as an adult he remains

---

[80] It is difficult to tell whether the statement attributed to pastor Hagee as an example of multiple ways of salvation is truly that (n. 20). Even if the statement is Hagee's words, and not those of the reporter, it does not clearly stipulate that Jewish people who "live in the light of the Torah" are redeemed (saved?), but rather that they "will come to redemption." The means of their redemption is thus not clearly stated.

under the same principles of good that his parents sought to inculcate in him through their rules when he was child (see Gal 3:23–25; 4:1–6).

For the covenant theology of Reymond, the crucial evidence of dispensationalism's multiple ways of salvation is its denial that Old Testament saints had "conscious faith in the (anticipated) sacrificial work of the promised Messiah on their behalf" (p. 17). Reymond asserts this "conscious faith" of Old Testament saints primarily on the basis that the sacrifice of the Messiah is predicted in the Old Testament through typology, sacrifices, and prophecy (see Isaiah 53).

There is no question about the prediction of the sacrificial death of Christ in the Old Testament. But demonstrating that Scripture teaches that all Old Testament saints understood this prophecy so that it was the "conscious" content of their faith is quite another matter, and, I believe, impossible to demonstrate.[81] God's people have always been saved through belief in the revelation of God to them, and that revelation has been progressive in its illumination of the specifics of his saving work through the Messiah. Is not something of this involved in the "revelation of the mystery which has been kept secret for long ages past, but now is manifested"—that is, the mystery of the gospel and Christ (Rom 16:25–26 NASB)?

This issue is one evidence of the inadequacy of traditional covenant theology to sufficiently recognize the historical developments in God's historical outworking of his plan of salvation. As a dispensationalist I have no problem with the theological covenants of covenant theology (redemption, works, grace) as

---

[81] No doubt the belief in a messianic figure that would bring final salvation for mankind based on Gen 3:15 was a common belief of Old Testament saints, although it is difficult to know the belief of some apparent believers such as the widow of Zarephath and Naaman the Syrian (Luke 4:26–27), and even Jethro, the father-in-law of Moses. But even with those more closely related to the covenant line it is difficult to see any mention of a crucified Messiah as the conscious object of their faith.

There is no explicit reference to a crucified Messiah in God's covenant promise to Abraham, which covenant theology rightly recognizes as the primary expression of salvation grace. And, four times the Scripture mentions the justifying faith of Abraham as belief in God's promises of vast descendants (Gen 15:5–6; Rom 4:3, 18–22; Gal 3:6), not belief in a crucified Messiah. Surely the disciples of Jesus were saved (except for Judas), but who of them had saving faith in the substitutionary death of the Messiah? Whenever Jesus tried to teach them that truth, they failed to understand and even rejected the thought (Matt 16:21–22; Mark 8:31–32; Luke 9:44–45; 18:31–34; see also Luke 23:19–21).

fundamental truth related to the central issue of salvation—that is, fundamental principles on how humans can be rightly related to God. The problem comes up when these theological covenants, which are essentially timeless—they apply to all human history—are made to level out all of the history of salvation and consequently fail to give adequate attention to the developments within that history signified by the successive historical covenants in the biblical story of salvation, namely, the Abrahamic, Mosaic, Davidic, and new covenants. I have no problem with saying that the covenant of grace runs throughout history since the fall of mankind in Adam, and that this makes all believers one in Christ. But I do not believe that the scriptural evidence indicates that this unity demands that all believers in all epochs must have the same conscious content of their saving faith in God's redemptive grace or that there is no real distinction between Israel and the church.

Now, in relation to the traditional covenant understanding of Israel and the church, because of space limitations, I will attempt to respond to the many texts and thoughts presented by focusing on two fundamental topics that underscore our disagreement—the meaning and purpose of Israel, and the correlative necessity of a millennial reign of Christ.

Reymond presents Israel as a national expression of the recipients of the blessing that ultimately is destined for all people (Gen 12:3). This appears to mean that national Israel was created and set apart from other nations as the special recipients of salvation through the covenant of grace.[82] While this element of a saving relationship in God's covenant with Israel is true, covenant theology fails to note another aspect of God's rationale for creating and relating to Israel in this special sense. God's call of Israel, as I have sought to demonstrate in my essay, was not only to salvation but also to mission—to be the nation through which God would bring the light of his saving revelation to all nations.

Reymond does little, if anything, with this important concept, which is found already in the covenant with Abraham, where the creation of "a great nation" inherently involved the ultimate goal

---

[82] This is not to suggest that all Israelites enjoyed salvation. The actual experience of a saving relationship with God entailed a response of faith, which not all Israelites had.

of the blessings for all of the families of the earth (Gen 12:2–3),[83] and made explicit in the Sinai covenant (Exod 19:6) and throughout the prophecies of the messianic days (see "And in Israel He shows forth His glory," Isa 44:23 [NASB]; see also 43:7; 60:7, 13, 21; Ezek 39:13; Zech 2:5).

It is absolutely vital to understand that dispensationalists see God's call of Israel related to a particular function and not a different saving relationship to God. Even as church elders have a particular function in the church and yet are no different than any believer in their saving relationship to God, so Israel has a different function in salvation history. Both Jewish believers and Gentile believers are equally the people of God and therefore one, no matter what nation they come.

While the church has a similar commission to witness, its witness cannot be that of a nation with which God openly displays his glory in historical acts before the eyes of the world, as at the exodus, and has promised to do so again at the return of Christ in defeating the nations arrayed against Israel and renewing that nation spiritually and nationally to be a showcase of his glory. Nor, according to the New Testament teaching of the course of this present age, will the church succeed in fulfilling the prophesied pilgrimage of nations to Zion (see Isa 2:1–4).

I do not understand the points cited from Jesus, Paul, and Peter as teaching a final rejection of Israel as that nation of the Old Testament history and prophecy and its replacement by the church. As I sought to show in my essay, Jesus' strong condemnation was aimed not at the nation as a whole but at its spiritual and political leaders. Moreover, he gave hints of a reversal of Israel's fortunes (see Matt 23:39).

Paul's teaching in Romans 9–11 likewise recognizes a present judgment of hardening over the bulk of Israel but also the presence of a faithful remnant that signifies that "God has not rejected his people whom he foreknew" (had a covenant relationship with) (Rom 11:2 NASB; see vv. 1–6). In this reference, Paul, with most modern commentators, refers to the ethnic

---

[83] For the grammatical evidence that the Hebrew syntax of Gen 12:1–3 indicates that all of what is said prior to the final statement, "all the families of the earth will be blessed" (v. 3 NASB), aims at this final goal, see William J. Dumbrell, *Covenant and Creation* (Nashville: Thomas Nelson, 1984), 65.

Israel of the Old Testament, which is also its meaning in all of its eleven uses in Romans 9–11.[84] Moreover, Paul clearly sees the same Israel that was judged in partial hardening later restored (not, of course, the same individuals but the entity of Israel— see Rom 11:11–12, 15, 24–31). In addition, as explained in my essay in this work, I do not think that Eph 2:11–13 teaches that the incorporation of Gentiles into the people of God "made them citizens of Israel," as Reymond states, nor that Gal 6:16, or any other Pauline text, is best understood as teaching the church as a new Israel. Similarly, Peter's use of similar language for believers in the church as that used in relation to Israel only points to the fact that the church and Israel have these similar characteristics (1 Pet 2:9). But, it does not necessitate the conclusion that the church has replaced Israel. If replacement theology were truly the apostolic teaching, one would expect it to be more plainly stated.

Importantly, and what is not really considered in covenant theology, is the fact that this history of Israel is all foretold in the prophecies of the Old Testament. The crucifixion of the Messiah was clearly predicted in the Old Testament, but so was the complicity of the unbelief of Israel in this crucifixion. However, rather than predicting that Israel's unbelief would lead to God's termination of his relationship with that nation, the Old Testament goes on to speak of a new covenant that would bring spiritual restoration and physical restoration of that nation, including possession of a national land. And, God would utilize that nation to reveal his glory to the nations with unprecedented salvation.[85] Thus, this future restoration of Israel is not "retrogressive elevation of shadow over substance" or a return to "the limited forms of the old covenant" (p. 60). It is all promised for the days of the Messiah under the *new covenant*.

It should be noted also that these prophecies of a literal restoration of Israel in a literal land indicate that they are more than a type of the paradisiacal reality of eternal things that Reymond

---

[84] See Rom 9:6 (2x), 27 (2x), 31; 10:19, 21; 11:2, 7, 25–26. See also Douglas Moo, *The Epistle to the Romans*, The New International Commentary on the New Testament (Grand Rapids: Eerdmans, 1996), 720–21.

[85] For the biblical evidence of these prophecies, see my *The Case for Progressive Dispensationalism* (Grand Rapids: Zondervan, 1993), chaps. 9 and 12.

sees. They are a historical reality yet to come in the history of salvation before the eternal state which I agree with Reymond will be "something more glorious." But I would suggest that the promised land for a restored Israel is no more a type than our present bodies or the present creation are types of our new bodies or the new creation. To be sure, all believers, including Abraham and all of the Old Testament saints of Israel, looked beyond the reality of this history in which all things deteriorate to the eternality of heavenly things in a totally new creation. And scriptural prophecy often focuses on that goal without giving a clear chronology of events leading to it. And well it should, for only that ultimate perfect goal can be the standard for those who will inhabit it (see 2 Pet 3:13–14).

This last point leads to the second major issue that underlies my disagreement with the traditional covenant theology perspective on Israel and the church, which I can only touch briefly—namely, the vast question of a temporary millennial kingdom of Christ reigning in glory on this earth as part of salvation history prior to the eternal state. Obviously, my dispensational perspective of Israel and the church entails a future period of salvation history, in which the Old Testament prophecies of a reign of Christ on earth while sin is still present take place (see Isa 2:2–4; Zech 14:9–19), and God's glory is manifest to the nations through Israel in a last wonderful age of salvation.

Nothing in the New Testament denies this future kingdom reign, and in truth, the New Testament not only affirms the fulfillment of the Old Testament covenant promises (Rom 9:3–5; 11:28–29) but expressly teaches a millennial reign following the return of Christ prior to the eternal state (see Rev 20:4–21:1). Such a reign of Christ in glory on earth prior to his handing over the messianic kingdom to the Father (1 Cor 15:24) completes the suffering-to-glory picture in Scripture of the Messiah's work. Moreover, it completes the fullness of messianic salvation (which must be accomplished prior to handing over the kingdom)—that is, the salvation of all of the structures of human life, socio-economic-political-cultural—as well as the present salvation. It is difficult for me to see how the present age of the church as the new Israel is the fulfillment of this picture.

In sum, my disagreement over the relation of Israel and the church in covenant theology is not with the theological covenants for which it is named but rather with applying those salvation principles to salvation history and thus minimizing the historical developments set forth in the historical biblical covenants.

Response by Chad O. Brand and Tom Pratt Jr.

Dr. Reymond has written an essay in his usual vigorous and bold style. He sets out the contrast between his covenantal approach to theology and that of dispensationalism in both its traditional form and in what Reymond calls "Dallas" dispensationalism. Covenant theology began with Zwingli, then was codified by his successor, Bullinger, and matured in the writings of Cocceius and the Westminster Divines. Reymond articulates the key elements of covenant theology (hereafter CT) as it is defined in the Westminster Confession before proceeding to articulate the implications for the topic of the relationship between Israel and the church.

He observes the differences between CT and dispensational theology (hereafter DT) when he states, "Over against historic covenant theology's representation of the covenant of grace as being one in all ages, through the execution of which is created the one people of God, that is, the church, comprised of all the elect of all ages, stands the dispensational school's interpretation of redemptive history" (p. 23). For Reymond, there is a substantial continuity between the testaments of Scripture, a continuity requiring the maintenance of the "genealogical principle"[86] in transferring infant circumcision from the old covenant to infant baptism in the new. We feel that there is a lack of justification for that position. The NT never describes children as being baptized, and the early church did not practice infant baptism. Kurt Aland, himself a paedobaptist, made the historical case that there is no evidence for infant baptism in the early church until after AD 200.[87]

---

[86] Peter J. Gentry and Stephen J. Wellum, *Kingdom through Covenant: A Biblical-Theological Understanding of the Covenants* (Wheaton: Crossway, 2012), 56–80.

[87] Kurt Aland, *Did the Early Church Baptize Infants?*, trans. G. R. Beasley-Murray (London: SCM, 1963), 102.

THE TRADITIONAL COVENANTAL VIEW — **83**

James Leo Garrett Jr. presents six reasons to affirm believer's baptism over against infant baptism. First, the NT is *silent* on the matter of infant baptism.[88] Even the so-called household baptisms in Acts never mention small children. Even Schleiermacher admitted that.[89] Garrett also notes that the prevailing NT sequence for evangelism is "preaching the gospel, hearing, confessing one's faith, and water baptism," thus abjuring infant baptism in the first place.[90] Then, he notes, some texts advanced by paedobaptist authors (such as 1 Cor 7:14) contain "no reference to infant baptism."[91] Fourthly, "infant baptism has been unnecessarily tied to a doctrine of *original guilt*."[92] Then, he notes that many have alleged that infant baptism has been tied to the European notion "of the *Volkskirche* or *Staatskirche* (state church) with its great masses of nonworshiping, nonpracticing church members who in effect have repudiated their baptism."[93] Finally, the case for believer's baptism rests on "New Testament Theology," that is, a comprehensive view of NT theology, emphasizing the "person and work of Christ, the nature and function of the church, and the last things ought to be employed for the comprehensive rationale for the baptism of believers."[94] With all of this we certainly concur.

This means that we cannot agree with Reymond when he writes:

1. Infant males received the sign and seal of the covenant of grace under its Old Testament administration.

2. The covenant of grace, as we have just argued, has continuity and organic unity through Scripture; the people of God are essentially one in all ages.

---

[88] James Leo Garrett Jr., *Systematic Theology: Biblical, Historical, and Evangelical*, vol. 2 (Grand Rapids: Eerdmans, 1995), 526.

[89] Friedrich Schleiermacher, *The Christian Faith*, English trans. of 2nd German ed., ed. H. R. Mackintosh and J. S. Stewart (Philadelphia: Fortress, 1976), 634–38.

[90] Garrett, *Systematic Theology*, 2:526.

[91] Ibid., 2:527.

[92] Ibid., emphasis in original.

[93] Ibid.

[94] Ibid., 2:528.

3. One can find no repeal in the New Testament of the *al-most two-thousand-year-long* Old Testament practice of placing the sign of the covenant of grace upon covenant children (see p. 27).

(see p. 27)

We are convinced that believer's (or *disciple's*) baptism is the correct understanding of the NT; and this is one of the disconti-nuities that stand between the old covenant and the new. To put it another way, the notion of inaugurating infants (or at least a subset of them, baby boys) into the covenant community is not one of the continuities between the OT and NT but one of the discontinuities. As Gentry and Wellum state, "No doubt there is a significant amount of continuity in the one people of God, but there is a significant amount of discontinuity as well by virtue of our Redeemer's work which has inaugurated the entire new cov-enant age, and who has brought to fulfillment all the promises, types, and covenants of the Old Testament."[95] We believe that there is a problem in DT in making the discontinuities too great, but in CT the other problem prevails of making the continuities too rigid.

It is important to recognize that the covenants of Scripture do not simply flatten out and remain intact across time. As one moves through the various biblical covenants diachronically, it becomes clear that successive covenants incorporate some of the material from previous covenants, but they generally dis-card material as well. So, the new covenant discards the com-mand to Abraham to circumcise male children (Rom 2:25–29; Gal 5:6). The new covenant also removes us from the yoke of the law (Rom 3:21–26). Both of those things were good in and of themselves, but a newer covenant supersedes them and changes the nature of how one relates to God. That is discontinuity over time and is an important aspect of how one interprets Scripture.

Another issue that Reymond raises is important for our con-sideration. He takes up the issue of "replacement theology" and makes it clear that he believes that the church replaces Israel as the people of God. Replacement theology has been a matter of concern for many who have addressed these issues over time.

---

[95] Gentry and Wellum, *Kingdom through Covenant*, 73.

Justin Martyr, as one example, wrote, "Christ is the Israel and the Jacob, even so we, who have been quarried out from the bowels of Christ, are the true Israelitic race."[96] While we are sympathetic to Justin's main point, we do not affirm replacement theology in its entirety, nor are we sympathetic with the term in the way that Reymond uses it. As we note in our response to Professor Saucy, the church does not replace Israel but rather extends Israel's scope to include all of those grafted into the original olive tree. To put it another way, "the church must be viewed neither as the replacement nor as the continuation of Israel but as something unique, which requires that we think of ethnic Israel as distinct from the church. . . ."[97] It is Christ who is the fulfillment of OT expectations. "This is why the entire New Testament is Christological in focus, since Jesus is the one that the covenants and prophets anticipate (e.g., Matt 5:17–18; 11:11–15; Rom 3:21, 31)."[98]

Traditional CT errs, in our view, in that it construes the genealogical principle as applicable to the church, in spite of the fact that there is no description or prescription for the baptism of infants in the NT, and in its notion that the church has now replaced Israel as the covenant people of God. Rather, it is Christ, "the hopes and fears of all the years," who has fulfilled all of the expectations of previous revelation.

---

[96] Justin Martyr, *Dialogue with Trypho*, Ante-Nicene Fathers, ed. A. Cleveland Coxe, Alexander Roberts, James Donaldson, and Philip Schaaf (Grand Rapids: Eerdmans, n.d.), 1:204.

[97] Gentry and Wellum, *Kingdom through Covenant*, 119.

[98] Ibid., 108.

CHAPTER 2

The Traditional
Dispensational View

BY ROBERT L. THOMAS

The following perspective on Israel and the church is exegetical rather than theological in nature. The goal is to implement hermeneutical principles of the traditional grammatical-historical interpretation in investigating the subject under discussion. Since those principles have come under a cloud of change and uncertainty in recent years,[1] the discussion will attempt at points to refresh the reader's memory regarding the principles as understood by orthodox Christianity through most of the time since the Reformation.

Because of limitations in a multiauthored volume, the treatment will select certain relevant areas for comment. Space will not permit a detailed discourse of all theological issues that may arise, but a theological explanation is feasible if the exegetical approach is sound.

---

[1] See Robert Thomas, *Evangelical Hermeneutics: The New Versus the Old* (Grand Rapids: Kregel, 2002), 13–62.

Israel in the OT

In dealing with matters pertaining to Israel and the church, one must start with the covenant that God made with Abraham. God promised that Abraham would become a great nation (Gen 12:2; see 13:16; 15:5; 17:1–2, 7; 22:17), that Abraham's descendants would possess a specific geographical territory (Gen 12:1, 7; see 13:14–15, 17; 15:17–21; 17:8), and that Abraham's descendants would become a source of worldwide blessing (Gen 12:3; see Gen 22:18).[2] God repeated these promises to Isaac (Gen 26:3–5, 24) and Jacob (Gen 28:3–4, 13–15; 36:10–12; 48:3–4), Abraham's son and grandson. The sole reason for the covenant was God's sovereign choice of Abraham and his descendants to fill such a role. The general nature of the covenant became more specific as time passed, when God added the Land (or Palestinian) covenant (Deut 29:1–30:20),[3] the Davidic covenant (2 Sam 7:12–16; see 2 Sam 23:5; Ps 89:3–4, 28, 34, 39),[4] and the new covenant (Jer 31:31–34; see Ezek 11:17–21; 16:60–63; 36:26–38).[5] These were all covenants God made with Abraham's physical descendants, who later became known as a nation bearing Jacob's new name "Israel" (Gen 32:28; 35:10). Each covenant made more specific certain aspects of the original covenant with Abraham. In following the biblical account, one marvels at God's unwavering faithfulness in his program for Israel, beginning with the call of Abraham and continuing to the very end.

The Land Promise in the Pentateuch

Of the promises made to Abraham, the land promise is the most specific, not lending itself to possible variations of interpretation. It fixed specific geographical boundaries and did not lend itself to generalizations, as did the promise of becoming a great nation and the promise of being a worldwide blessing. In light of

---

[2] Ron J. Bigalke Jr., "The Abrahamic Covenant," in *Progressive Dispensationalism: An Analysis of the Movement and Defense of Traditional Dispensationalism*, ed. Ron Bigalke (Lanham, MD: University Press of America, 2005), 43.

[3] Arnold G. Fruchtenbaum, "The Land Covenant," in Bigalke, *Progressive Dispensationalism*, 89.

[4] Thomas H. Cragoe, "The Davidic Covenant," in Bigalke, *Progressive Dispensationalism*, 99.

[5] Stephen R. Lewis, "The New Covenant: Enacted or Ratified?" in Bigalke, *Progressive Dispensationalism*, 136, 142n7.

the land promise's specificity, it will be given close attention. The land promise to Abraham has been summed up as follows:

> The Abrahamic Covenant, and the sub-covenants of land, seed and blessing, is fulfilled in the thousand-year kingdom period. The Jews will be in the land as fulfillment of the promise. The clear biblical teaching is that the Son of David will be reigning and ruling as promised on the literal throne of David in Jerusalem.[6]

When God promised Abraham that his seed would inherit this land, Abraham understood God's words the same way that Adam understood God's words in Gen 2:16–17: "From any tree of the garden you may eat freely; but from the tree of the knowledge of good and evil you shall not eat, for in the day that you eat from it you will surely die."[7] In a sinless environment, Adam accurately transmitted what God had told him to Eve because Eve's response to the serpent reflected an accurate knowledge: "From the fruit of the trees of the garden we may eat; but from the fruit of the tree which is in the middle of the garden, God has said, 'You shall not eat from it or touch it, or you will die'" (Gen 3:3). In a sinless environment, Eve's repetition of God's instructions to the serpent could not have been a deliberate distortion or an exaggeration. She did not report verbatim in what Moses recorded in Gen 2:16–17 but probably chose words from a more extended discussion between God and Adam that the Bible does not record. She committed no sin of misrepresentation at this point; her sin came a little later when she acted on the serpent's suggestion in eating the forbidden fruit. Before that suggestion, no distorted interpretation occurred. The first hermeneutical error in understanding what God had said came in the serpent's suggestion: "You surely will not die! For God knows that in the day you eat from it your eyes will be opened, and you will be like God, knowing good and evil" (Gen 3:4–5). The serpent imposed a certain preunderstanding of God's words on Eve, perhaps something like, "God just gave you life by creating you; surely He will

---

[6] Ron J. Bigalke Jr. and Mal Couch, "The Relationship Between Covenants and Dispensations," in Bigalke, *Progressive Dispensationalism*, 36.

[7] Unless noted otherwise, Scripture quotations are from the New American Standard Bible.

not take it away." Unfortunately, Eve and Adam took his bait, and the sad result is history.

At that point in history, national Israel had no existence. National Israel came into existence the moment that God said to Abram, "Go forth from your country, and from your relatives and from your father's house, to the land which I will show you; and I will make you a great nation, and I will bless you, and make your name great; and so you shall be a blessing; and I will bless those who bless you, and the one who curses you I will curse. And in you all the families of the earth will be blessed" (Gen 12:1–3). After Abram obeyed, God became more specific regarding the land: "To your descendants [seed] I will give this land" (Gen 12:7a).

How was Abram to understand God's words? They were plain enough. Historically, the geographical location was quite specific in this and later wordings of the land promise.[8] A literal approach interprets the words as God intended them and as Abram understood them. No typology. No spiritualizing. No symbolism. No preunderstanding of how the words must fit into a system of theology. No reading back into the words a later special revelation. To take the words in any other sense than what God intended and Abraham understood is a distortion. Though Abram's environment was not sinless as originally in the garden of Eden, God had not changed and was still perfectly capable of communicating clearly. He cannot lie and must be taken at his word. Abram understood God correctly, so Israel became a nation chosen by God and destined to possess a particular plot of land on the present earth's surface.

Vern Poythress, who argues for a heavy use of typology in the OT, would say a conclusion as to how God intended his promise to Abraham must be suspended because Scripture is not that precise and often includes ambiguities that are only clarified later when Scripture is fulfilled. He explains,

> God knows the end from the beginning. Therefore, as the divine author of the Bible he can establish a

---

[8] Genesis 15:18b–21 is quite specific: "To your descendants I have given this land, from the river of Egypt as far as the great river, the river Euphrates: the Kenite and the Kenizzite and the Kadmonite and the Hittite and the Perizzite and the Rephaim and the Amorite and the Canaanite and the Girgashite and the Jebusite."

relation between the type and its antitypical fulfillment. Since the fulfillment comes only later, the type becomes richer than what is available by ordinary means in Old Testament times. In other words the divine intention for a type may, in certain cases, be richer than what one can obtain by grammatical-historical interpretation. Such richness, properly conceived, will not *violate* grammatical-historical meaning, or go contrary to it.[9]

Poythress is mistaken in saying that if "the type becomes richer than what is available by ordinary means in Old Testament times," it does not violate grammatical-historical meaning. The single grammatical-historical meaning is set by the historical context in which words are spoken, never to be changed or added to. Adding meaning to the promises God made to Abraham or changing that meaning *does* violate the grammatical-historical meaning just as the serpent added to and/or changed the meaning of the words God spoke to Adam. Poythress's explanation assumes that the promises to Abraham were ambiguous and needed clarification, which they were not and did not.

God's land covenant with Israel in Deut 29:1–30:20 reaffirmed the land promise that God made to Abraham.[10] The land promise continues to receive reaffirmation throughout the OT, a point with which progressive dispensationalism advocate Robert Saucy agrees. Saucy even concurs that the NT continues to imply the validity of the land promise, though it does not do so as explicitly as the OT.[11] New covenant theologian John Reisinger also agrees regarding the OT focus on the land promise but disagrees regarding the NT.[12] By reading the NT—specifically Heb 4:11—back into the OT, Reisinger takes the land promise of the OT

---

[9] Vern S. Poythress, *Understanding Dispensationalists*, 2nd ed. (Phillipsburg, NJ: P&R, 1994), 90–91, emphasis in original.

[10] Fruchtenbaum, "The Land Covenant," in Bigalke, *Progressive Dispensationalism*, 88.

[11] Robert L. Saucy, *The Case for Progressive Dispensationalism: The Interface between Dispensation and Non-Dispensational Theology* (Grand Rapids: Zondervan, 1993), 50–57.

[12] John G. Reisinger, *Abraham's Four Seeds* (Frederick, MD: New Covenant Media, 1998), 39–40; 89–91.

to be a pledge of the spiritual rest promised to the believer.[13] He and Michael W. Adams—another new covenant theologian— agree that one cannot say that the land promise had already been fulfilled in Joshua's day (Josh 21:43–45)[14] because in David's day, a long time later, fulfillment of the land promise was still future (1 Chron 16:13–18).[15]

The Land Promise in the Psalms

The Psalms have plenty to say about the land promise to Abraham as the following will illustrate (emphasis added in each Scripture):

> For evildoers will be cut off, but *those who wait for the LORD, they will inherit the land.* Yet a little while and the wicked man will be no more; and you will look carefully for his place and he will not be there. But *the humble will inherit the land* and will delight themselves in abundant prosperity. . . . For *those blessed by Him will inherit the land,* but those cursed by Him will be cut off. . . . *The righteous will inherit the land* and dwell in it forever. (Ps 37:9–11, 22, 29)

> Surely *His salvation is near to those who fear Him, that glory may dwell in our land.* . . . Indeed, the LORD *will give what is good, and our laud will yield its produce.* (Ps 85:9, 12)

> *My eyes shall be upon the faithful of the land, that they may dwell with me;* he who walks in a blameless way is the one who will minister to me. He who practices deceit shall not dwell within my house; he who speaks falsehood shall not maintain his position before Me. *Every morning I will destroy all the wicked of the land, so as to cut off from the city of the LORD all those who do iniquity.* (Ps 101:6–8)

---

[13] Ibid., 87, 91–92; see also Michael W. Adams, "In Defense of the New Covenant: A Theological Response to Richard Barcellos's Book, *In Defense of the Decalogue: A Critique of New Covenant Theology,*" accessed 7/12/06, http://www.ncbf.net/PDF/Defense.pdf 9.

[14] Adams, "In Defense of the New Covenant," 8–9.

[15] Reisinger, *Abraham's Four Seeds*, 90–91.

He has remembered His covenant forever, the word which He commanded to a thousand generations, the covenant which He made with Abraham, and His oath to Isaac. Then He confirmed it to Jacob for a statute, to Israel as an everlasting covenant, saying, *"To you I will give the land of Canaan as the portion of your inheritance,"* when they were only a few men in number, very few, and strangers in it. (Ps 105:8–11)

The Land Promise in the Prophets

Eight illustrations provide examples of how plentiful the promises in the Prophets are. They continue an emphasis on the faithfulness of God in fulfilling his promises to Abraham, particularly his land promise (emphasis added in each Scripture):

In that day the LORD will start His threshing from the flowing stream of the Euphrates to the brook of Egypt, and you will be gathered up one by one, O sons of Israel. ... [T]hose who were perishing in the land of Assyria and who were scattered in the land of Egypt will come and worship the LORD *in the holy mountain at* Jerusalem. (Isa 27:12–13)

Again you will plant vineyards *on the hills of Samaria;* the planters will plant and will enjoy them. ... They will come and shout for joy *on the height of Zion.* (Jer 31:5, 12)

And you will know that I am the LORD, *when I bring you into the land of Israel, into the land which I swore to give to your forefathers.* (Ezek 20:42)

Thus says the Lord GOD, "When I gather the house of Israel from the peoples among whom they are scattered, and will manifest My holiness in them in the sight of the nations, then *they will live in their land which I gave to My servant Jacob.*" (Ezek 28:25)

I will make them and the places around My hill a blessing. And I will cause showers to come down in their season; they will be showers of blessing. Also the tree of the field will yield its fruit and the earth will

yield its increase, and *they will be secure on their land.*
(Jer 34:26–27)

You will live in the land that I gave to your forefathers; so you will be My people, and I will be your God.
(Ezek 36:28)

And in that day the mountains will drip with sweet wine, and the hills will flow with milk, and *all the brooks of Judah will flow with water; and a spring will go out from the house of the LORD to water the valley of Shittim.*
(Joel 3:18)

Also I will restore the captivity of My people Israel, and *they will rebuild the ruined cities and live in them;* they will also plant vineyards and drink their wine, and make gardens and eat their fruit. *I will also plant them on their land, and they will not again be rooted out from their land which I have given them,' says the LORD your God.* (Amos 9:14–15)

For God to say of himself, "I, the LORD, do not change; therefore you, O sons of Jacob, are not consumed" (Mal 3:6), after his many promises to Israel, is additional confirmation of the permanence and unchanging nature of his plan for this ethnic group.

Israel in the NT

Promises to Israel

The fact that Jesus' earthly ministry took place within the boundaries stipulated to Abraham and others in the OT implies that the land promise continued in its validity at the beginning of NT times. The question then turns on whether the NT ever reversed that promise or spiritualized it into something else. Covenant theology, new covenant theology, kingdom theology, and progressive dispensationalism for the most part[16] say that it

---

[16] Apparently, Craig Blaising and Darrell Bock merge Gentiles with Israel in Israel's future inheritance:

"We can illustrate this progressive dispensational view of the church in the case of Jewish Christians. A Jew who becomes a Christian today does not lose his or her relationship to Israel's future promises. Jewish Christians will join the Old Testament remnant of faith in the inheritance of Israel. Gentile Christians will be

did. Dispensationalism holds that nothing of that sort occurred. From Matthew through Revelation God's promises to Israel hold true. The only question is, which group of living Israelites will receive those promises? Certainly not those who were alive when Christ became a man and came to his own creation, and those who were his own people did not receive him (John 1:11). Christ himself told that group, "The kingdom of God shall be taken from you, and given to a nation bringing forth the fruits thereof" (Matt 21:43 KJV).[17] He identified the recipients of the kingdom of God as a future group of Israelites who will repent and embrace him fully as the Messiah.

Occasions When Jesus Might Have Canceled God's Promises to Abraham but Did Not

Occasion 1: Negative Response to John the Baptist's Call for Repentance. The NT continued promoting the promises to Abraham and David, as the angel's citing of the Davidic covenant

---

joined by saved Gentiles of earlier dispensations. All together, Jews and Gentiles will share the same blessings of the Spirit, as testified to by the relationship of Jew and Gentile in the church of this dispensation. The result will be that all peoples will be reconciled in peace, their ethnic and national differences being no cause for hostility. Earlier forms of dispensationalism, for all their emphasis on the future for Israel, excluded Jewish Christians from that future, postulating the church as a different people-group from Israel and Gentiles." *Progressive Dispensationalism: An Up-to-Date Handbook of Contemporary Dispensational Thought* (Wheaton: Victor, 1993), 50.

In its emphasis on only one people of God, progressive dispensationalism must make everyone, including Gentiles in the church and saved Gentiles from other dispensations, inheritors of Israel's promises. That does not make for a very "Israelitish" millennium, nor does it retain Israel's distinctiveness as recipients of the land promised to Abraham. It rather includes every believer in the inheritance promised to Israel, including the specific land promised, or else it denies Israel the specific land God promised her.

[17] This passage and its parallels (cf. Matt 21:33–45=Mark 12:1–12=Luke 20:9–19) are among the Scriptures mistakenly used by Robert L. Reymond to demonstrate that ethnic Israel has no claim on the land promises made to Abraham ("Who Really Owns the 'Holy Land'? Part 2," *The Trinity Review* 257 [July 2006]: 1–2). What Reymond fails to consider is that in the NT the singular noun *ethnos* when unqualified by other words such as "nation against nation" (Matt 24:7=Mark 13:8=Luke 21:10) and "every nation of humankind" (Acts 17:26) usually refers to Israel (BDAG, 276–77). The singular noun frequently refers to Israel (e.g., Luke 7:5; 23:2; John 11:48, 50–52; Acts 24:2, 10). The plural usually includes those outside Israel. This follows a similar pattern found in the OT. BDAG observes, "In Mt 21:43 [*ethnei*] (not gentiles) in contrast to the leaders described vv. 23, 45" (ibid., 276), a comment coming under the category of "a body of persons united by kinship, culture, and common traditions." Quite obviously, Israel is the nation in view in Matt 21:43.

to Mary (Luke 1:32–33)[18] and Zechariah's citing of the Abrahamic, Davidic, and new covenants of Israel verify (Luke 1:69, 73, 77).[19] OT covenants and prophecies brought a two-pronged expectation into the NT regarding the Jewish Messiah, that he would bring worldwide blessing by some day sitting on David's throne, ruling from Jerusalem over a worldwide kingdom (see 2 Sam 7:8–16; Ps 89:3–4), and that he would be rejected by his people and eventually suffer death for their sins (see Isa 52:13–53:12). John the Baptist preached two messages that featured the twofold expectation: "Repent, for the kingdom of heaven is at hand" (Matt 3:2 ESV), confirming the Davidic covenant, and "Behold, the Lamb of God, who takes away the sin of the world" (John 1:29 ESV),[20] confirming Israel's rejection of her Messiah. Israelites on earth at the time of the Messiah's first coming did not understand how those seemingly contradictory lines of prophecy would be fulfilled. The Baptist himself illustrated their confusion when he asked Jesus, "Are You the Expected One, or shall we look for someone else?" (Matt 11:3). John was expecting a conquering Messiah but at that particular moment was languishing in prison because of his proclamation and his relationship to Jesus (Matt 11:2).

In preparing the way for the King, John encountered resistance to his cry for repentance, a resistance mounted in particular by the leaders of the Jewish nation at that time. He refused to baptize them because they lacked evidence of the repentance needed in preparation for the King:

> But when he [i.e., John] saw many of the Pharisees and Sadducees coming for baptism, he said to them, "You brood of vipers, who warned you to flee from the wrath to come? Therefore bear fruit in keeping with

---

[18] Darrell Bock agrees with this understanding of Mary's words: "The Davidic throne is clearly a regal image drawn from the Davidic covenant's promise of a son, a house, and an everlasting rule (2 Sam. 7:8–16, esp. vv. 13, 16. . . .)" (Darrell L. Bock, *Luke 1:1–9:50*, Baker Exegetical Commentary on the New Testament [Grand Rapids: Baker, 1994], 114).

[19] John Nolland, *Luke 1–9:20*, Word Biblical Commentary 35A (Dallas: Word, 1989), 86–87, 89.

[20] Brown finds in the "lamb of God" designation of Jesus references to both the Suffering Servant of Isaiah 53 and the paschal lamb used in the Jewish Passover (Raymond E. Brown, *The Gospel According to John (i–xii)*, Anchor Bible [Garden City, NY: Doubleday, 1966], 60–63). From usage elsewhere in John's Gospel, his conclusion is correct.

repentance; and do not suppose that you can say to yourselves, 'We have Abraham for our father'; for I say to you that from these stones God is able to raise up children to Abraham. The axe is already laid at the root of the trees; therefore every tree that does not bear fruit is cut down and thrown into the fire." (Matt 3:7–10)

Here was an early hint that fulfillment of prophecies about a suffering Messiah might precede those about a reigning Messiah. How could the King come to a people whose leaders stood in rebellion against him?

Nevertheless, Jesus picked up and continued John's message, "Repent, for the kingdom of heaven is at hand" (Matt 4:17). The Davidic kingdom prophecies had not been cancelled but were still valid.

Occasion 2: Sabbath Controversies with Judaism's Leaders. Jesus encountered the same problems with Jewish leadership of his day as John the Baptist did. He discovered corruption in temple worship early in his ministry and had to use force to cleanse the temple from such practices (John 2:14–16). He had to engage Jewish leaders in three Sabbath controversies because of their superficial observances of the Sabbath (John 5:1–18; Matt 12:1–8=Mark 2:23–28=Luke 6:1–5; Matt 12:9–14=Mark 3:1–6=Luke 6:6–11). His Sermon on the Mount (Matthew 5–7) announced the failure of scribal and Pharisaic righteousness: "For I say to you that unless your righteousness surpasses that of the scribes and Pharisees, you will not enter the kingdom of heaven" (Matt 5:20). That sermon gave prerequisites for entering the future kingdom: the leaders did not meet those prerequisites. Even at that point, it must have been evident to the more discerning students of OT prophecy that the Davidic kingdom could not come until Israel's leaders were ready. Since they refused to repent, the Messiah would probably have to suffer before he could reign.

Yet, in that sermon Jesus told the listeners to pray, "Your kingdom come" (Matt 6:10a), and instructed them, "But seek first His kingdom and His righteousness, and all these things will be added to you" (Matt 6:33). The corruption in Judaism's leadership did not terminate promises God had made to Abraham and

David. In Jesus' program, Israel's promised kingdom was still a confirmed prospect.

Occasion 3: Absence of Centurion-like Faith in Israel. Shortly after he delivered the Sermon on the Mount, Jesus used a Gentile centurion to illustrate the type of response he wanted from Israel. The centurion was convinced of Jesus' authority and told Jesus so. Commenting on the centurion's conviction, Jesus said,

> Truly I say to you, I have not found such great faith with anyone in Israel. I say to you that many will come from east and west, and recline at the table with Abraham, Isaac and Jacob in the kingdom of heaven; but the sons of the kingdom will be cast out into the outer darkness; in that place there will be weeping and gnashing of teeth. (Matt 8:10–12)

As promised to Abraham, Jesus reiterated that Gentiles would have a role in the future kingdom with Abraham's descendants. But, unbelieving Israelites of his day would not be participants. His naming of Abraham, Isaac, and Jacob shows that promises to Abraham will play a leading role in that future period. Believing national Israel has a place reserved for her in the coming kingdom but not unbelieving Israelites of Jesus' day or of any day. Jesus' contemporary Israelites had failed the test and would be excluded but not so with national Israel. A future people of that lineage will respond positively to Jesus' messiahship and inherit the promises made to Abraham.

Occasion 4: The Unpardonable Sin. Following those harsh words regarding the exclusion of Jesus' contemporary Jews from the kingdom came another of Jesus' confrontations with scribes and Pharisees, a confrontation occasioned by his healing of a demon-possessed man who was blind and unable to speak. This time, the encounter reached a new level of intensity as the crowds were considering the possibility that Jesus might be the promised Son of David (Matt 12:23). The occasion was more significant because scribes had come all the way from Jerusalem to Galilee to entrap Jesus (Mark 3:22) and were suggesting that Jesus was possessed by Beelzebul and that the ruler of the demons gave him power to cast out demons.

In responding to the outlandish claims of the scribes, Jesus said, "If I cast out demons by the Spirit of God, then the kingdom of God has come upon you" (Matt 12:28). He used a verb ("has come upon you") that regarded the kingdom as already present in a potential sense because the King was already present. In some sense the kingdom in a "secret" sense was already present as Jesus' parables were about to attest.

At least two factors on this occasion marked the encounter as a turning point in Jesus' ministry to Israel. One factor was the way he labeled their blasphemy as an unforgivable and eternal sin (Matt 12:32; Mark 3:29). His contemporary Israelites had failed the test of repentance necessary for those who desired to enter the promised kingdom of David, necessitating an interim period of Israel's rejection until Israel on earth would repent of the nation's rejection. The other factor came later in the same day when Jesus initiated a ministry of teaching the crowds through parables (Matt 13:1–3a; Mark 4:1–2; Luke 8:4).[21] His parabolic ministry followed and was triggered by the Jewish leaders' rejection earlier in the same day as the parables began. That parabolic teaching allowed him to impart new truth to his disciples without casting his pearl before swine, and to hide the new truth from his adversaries and even to take away whatever understanding they already possessed (Matt 13:11–12).

Jesus called the new truths taught through parables "mysteries" ("secrets" in NIV; Matt 13:11; Mark 4:11; Luke 8:10). In what way were the truths kept secret previously? His listeners expected a kingdom with ideal conditions, including a reign of the promised Messiah, but the parables for the first time presented a new concept of the kingdom, according to which only one of four seeds fell on good soil and bore fruit, and in which tares grew alongside the wheat that was sown. The concept of evil alongside the good in the kingdom was hard for Jesus' disciples to grasp (see Matt 13:36) because the OT had not provided that kind of

---

[21] Gibbs concurs that the two episodes occurred on the same day: "The phrase 'on that day' [in Matt 13:1] connects Matthew's parables discourse closely to the preceding context, in which the crowds have been distinguished from Jesus' disciples, who are doing the will of Jesus' heavenly Father (12:50)" (Jeffrey A. Gibbs, *Matthew 11:2–20:34*, Concordia Commentary [Saint Louis: Concordia, 2010], 675). The unity of the parabolic chapter in Matthew with the continuity of events dealing with opposition to Christ in earlier portions of Matthew 12 is clear.

information about the kingdom. Jesus acknowledged to them that the prophesied OT kingdom would eventually come but only after this unexpected phase of the kingdom caused by Israel's rejection had run its course (Matt 13:43). Only then will the kind of kingdom the OT had led them to expect become a reality, with Daniel's prophecy of the righteous kingdom being fulfilled ("And those who have insight will shine brightly like the brightness of the expanse of heaven, and those who lead the many to righteousness, like the stars forever and ever," Dan 12:3).

Occasion 5: Prediction of the Messiah's Coming Crucifixion. Shortly after Christ divulged the secrets about the kingdom, and after another blasphemous accusation by his enemies (Matt 9:34), he, with his disciples, left Galilee to launch a ministry of about six months in regions around Galilee. He devoted this period especially to training the Twelve. Toward the end of the period, a series of revelatory events near Caesarea-Philippi amplified Jesus' response to Israel's unresponsiveness.

By this time, as seen in Peter's confession, the disciples had seen and heard enough to be fully assured of Jesus' Messiahship (Matt 16:16=Mark 8:29=Luke 9:20). Only the disciples had reached this conclusion; the rest of the Israelites identified him in other ways (Matt 16:13–14=Mark 8:27–28=Luke 9:18–19). Based on Peter's pronouncement, Jesus for the first time announced his future goal of building the church (Matt 16:18). He followed this with the first direct announcement of his coming suffering at the hands of the Jerusalem elders, chief priests, and scribes, his execution by them, and his resurrection on the third day (Matt 16:21=Mark 8:31=Luke 9:22). The church and his coming passion and resurrection were news to his disciples, who expected him to set up his kingdom immediately (see Luke 19:11). The OT had spoken specifically about his suffering but said nothing about a church that Jesus would build. By this series of revelations, he clarified that his fulfillment of suffering Messiah prophesies must come before the fulfillment of the kingdom-reign prophecies, but his disciples were slow to grasp that sequence. They still expected the Davidic kingdom to be next on the agenda. In fact, Peter reprimanded the Lord for his announcement of coming suffering (Matt 16:22=Mark 8:32).

Jesus could have used this occasion to tell the disciples that the church would replace Israel in God's program for the future, but he did not. Easily he could have said that Israel's role in his crucifixion was the end of the line for that nation and that the disciples and a new group of people taken from all nations would replace Israel and fulfill her promises. Such an announcement as that is conspicuously absent from Jesus' teaching at Caesarea-Philippi and everywhere else.

In case the announcement about his coming death discouraged them regarding God's promises to Israel, he went on to assure them that the OT kingdom promises would eventually be fulfilled. He did this by taking Peter, James, and John up to a high mountain and allowing them to witness his transfiguration and his session with Moses and Elijah (Matt 16:27–17:3=Mark 8:38–9:4=Luke 8:26–9:31). Here was a preview of the coming kingdom, which, as Peter later attested, came as a reassurance to the disciples:

> For we did not follow cleverly devised tales when we made known to you the power and coming of our Lord Jesus Christ, but we were eyewitnesses of His majesty. For when He received honor and glory from God the Father, such an utterance as this was made to Him by the Majestic Glory, "This is My beloved Son with whom I am well-pleased"—and we ourselves heard this utterance made from heaven when we were with Him on the holy mountain. So we have the prophetic word made more sure, to which you do well to pay attention as to a lamp shining in a dark place, until the day dawns and the morning star arises in your hearts. (2 Pet 1:16–19)

The prophecy of his occupying the future Davidic throne received dramatic confirmation through this experience of the three, even though his immediate future entailed rejection by the Jewish leadership. Israel's leadership role was still in God's program for the world in the future.

Occasion 6: Pronouncement of Pharisaic Blindness. After the six months with his disciples in regions around Galilee, Jesus went to Jerusalem for the Feast of Tabernacles. There he experienced a series of clashes that led Jewish leaders to try to stone him, but Jesus escaped (John 8:59). While Jesus was still in Judea, he healed a demon-possessed man, giving onlookers another opportunity to make a third blasphemous accusation (Luke 11:14–15).

About three months later, Jesus was still in Jerusalem for the Feast of Dedication. His healing of a blind man on the Sabbath once again provoked the anger of the Pharisees and was an occasion for another confrontation. The climax came when Jesus said, "For judgment I came into this world, so that those who do not see may see, and that those who see may become blind" (John 9:39). His Pharisaic listeners correctly interpreted his words as implying they were spiritually blind (John 9:40–41).

As a sequel to his accusation of blindness, Jesus proceeded to tell the allegory of the Good Shepherd and the thief (John 10:1–18). In the allegory, the man healed of blindness was one of the sheep, who were the godly remnant of Israel (10:4); the Pharisees were identified as thieves (10:1, 8), the stranger (10:5), and the hireling (10:12–13). The "fold" of which Jesus spoke (10:1, 16) represented the corrupt Judaism of Christ's day, from which he had led a believing remnant (10:3). The "other sheep" (10:16) were those of the Gentile world who were to believe in Christ. "One flock" (10:16) anticipated the formation of the body of Christ—the church which he purposed to build (Matt 16:18), composed of the godly remnant of Israel and Gentile believers. Jesus is both the door of access into the flock (10:7, 9) and the Good Shepherd who cares for the flock (10:11, 14). His claim of unity with the Father triggered another attempt by his opponents to stone him (John 10:30–31). This might have been another opportune time for Jesus to turn his back permanently on national Israel, but he did not.

Occasion 7: Jerusalem's Role in the Messiah's Coming Death. Jesus left Jerusalem and Judea after this encounter and spent about three months in and around Perea. Back in a territory controlled by Herod Antipas, some Pharisees warned Jesus about Herod's desire to kill him (Luke 13:31). He responded with a lament over Jerusalem and its desolate condition but acknowledged that some day the city would welcome the one who comes in the name of the Lord (Luke 13:34–35). His words about being welcomed by Israel in the future anticipated his second coming and a reception that will be in sharp contrast to the way Israel's leadership and people treated Jesus at his first coming. Still in the regions in and around Perea and on his way to Jerusalem, sensing that the time was near for a showdown with Israelite leadership, Jesus predicted for the third time his coming arrest, trial, crucifixion, and resurrection (Matt 20:17–19=Mark 10:32–34=Luke 18:31–33). Old Testament prophecies about the Messiah's suffering had to be fulfilled, but beyond that, he would be raised from the dead, ascend to heaven, and return to establish his earthly reign with ethnic Israel playing a prominent role.

At one point during the period, a rich young ruler came to Jesus to ask about obtaining eternal life (Matt 19:16=Mark 10:17=Luke 18:18), a request that Jesus equated to asking how to enter the kingdom of God (Matt 19:23=Mark 10:23=Luke 18:24). Jesus spoke of the difficulty for rich people to enter the kingdom (Matt 19:23=Mark 10:23=Luke 18:24) and repeated his warning about difficulty, this time for *anyone* to enter the kingdom (Mark 10:24). His disciples were puzzled at these words and asked, "Who can be saved?" (Matt 19:25=Mark 10:27=Luke 18:26). After assuring them that all things are possible for God, he went on to make a striking statement: "Truly I say to you, that you who have followed Me, in the regeneration when the Son of Man will sit on His glorious throne, you also shall sit upon twelve thrones, judging the twelve tribes of Israel" (Matt 19:28). In the continuing context of Christ's teaching, "the regeneration" spoke of the world's restored condition, when the Messiah will return to fulfill the long-anticipated OT promises of the Davidic kingdom. From the statement it is clear that the people of Israel will once again be central objects in God's dealings with the world, and these twelve disciples (excluding Judas Iscariot, of course) will occupy places of authority over Israel. Following Jesus' shocking statement about how difficult it is to enter the kingdom of God, this teaching must have been not only a relief to them but also a reassurance of Israel's future role in that kingdom. Jesus did not discontinue the hope of national Israel; he reinforced it.

Occasion 8: Further Corruption in Israel Noted. Then came the climax in the life of Jesus, often called Passion Week. The week began with Jesus' triumphal entry into Jerusalem (Matt 21:1–11=Mark 11:1–11=Luke 19:29–44=John 12:12–19). In unmistakable terms, Jesus on this occasion presented himself to Israel in the role of Davidic King, not as a Suffering Servant.[22] He took great pains to demonstrate his office as King of Israel in fulfillment of Zech 9:9, a point not missed by the crowds who called him the Son of David and the King (Matt 21:9=Mark 11:9–10=Luke 19:38=John 12:13, 15). The people as a whole were correct on this point—some day the Messiah will deliver Israel from foreign oppressors—but they failed by not complying with the spiritual requirement of repentance. The national aspirations of that group of Israelites were not mistaken about Israel's future but for spiritual reasons were doomed to disappointment, a failure that brought grief to Jesus even in his hour of great public acclamation (Luke 19:41).

John's Gospel locates another significant happening just before the triumphal entry, the anointing of Jesus with expensive perfume in preparation for his burial (John 12:2–8=Matt 26:6–13=Mark 14:3–9). Some of Jesus' disciples, including Judas Iscariot, were upset over the waste of the money that sale of the perfume would have brought, but Jesus commended the woman who anointed his head and feet. Jesus informed the men that "she did it to prepare Me for burial" (Matt 26:12), which must have surprised them greatly on the eve of his triumphal entry. Along

---

[22] In defense of his position that Jesus did offer the kingdom to Israel at his first coming, Robert L. Saucy writes,

> We suggest that the solution lies in the same realm as other problems related to the sovereign decree of God for history and the responsible actions of mankind. The idea that God could offer humankind a real choice and opportunity, knowing all the while that humankind would fail (and, in fact, having decreed a plan on the basis of that failure), is expressed in other passages of Scripture. In Eden, humankind was given a genuine opportunity to choose holiness, yet Scripture indicates that God's plan already included the sacrifice of Christ "from the creation of the world" (Rev 13:8; cf. Ac 2:23; 4:28). Thus in this instance, a similar unanswerable question as that related to the offer of the kingdom might be posed: What would have happened to the death of Christ if Adam and Eve had not sinned? (*The Case for Progressive Dispensationalism*, 92)

Just as the opportunity for Adam and Eve to remain innocent was valid, the offer to Israel of repentance and receiving the kingdom was valid even though the cross was inevitable because of OT prophecy that predicted it.

with the crowds, they were expecting the Davidic King, but Jesus was speaking about the Messiah whose suffering was necessitated—humanly speaking—by his unrepentant contemporaries.

The day after the triumphal entry, Jesus illustrated the absence of genuine piety in Israel of his day by the cursing of the fig tree (Matt 21:18–19a=Mark 11:12–14). Then, he showed Israel's corruption more vividly through his second cleansing of the temple (Matt 21:12–13=Mark 11:15–18=Luke 19:45–48). But, anticipation of his rule on the Davidic throne remained intact.

Occasion 9: Jesus' Woes Pronounced against the Scribes and Pharisees. On Tuesday of Passion Week, in responding to the chief priests', scribes', and elders' challenge of his authority, Jesus responded with several parables (Matt 21:28–22:14=Mark 12:1–12=Luke 20:9–19). Among the parables was included his statement, "Therefore I say to you, the kingdom of God will be taken away from you and given to a people [literally, 'a nation'], producing the fruit of it" (Matt 21:43). That is the same fruit, the fruit of repentance, that John's baptism had required earlier (Matt 3:8=Luke 3:8). When Jesus spoke of taking away the kingdom from "you" (i.e., Israel and her leadership) and giving it to another nation, he meant that the leadership, through its failure to repent, had forfeited that group of Israelites' chance of becoming a part of the promised Davidic kingdom.[23] Jesus' reference to another "nation" implied the prospect of a future time when Israel would repent and receive the kingdom.

Another action of Jesus, also on Tuesday, showed his wrath toward the scribes and Pharisees. That was his utterance of seven woes, apparently with them present to hear his negative pronouncements against them (Matt 23:1–36=Mark 12:38–40=Luke 20:45–47). The final woe condemns them for their false claim of opposing their ancestors who killed the prophets (Matt 23:29–30). Jesus labels that claim as untrue, saying that they bear witness against themselves because they are of the same ilk as their fathers and will not escape the sentence of Gehenna (Matt 23:31–33). He continues, "Therefore, behold, I am sending you prophets and wise men and scribes; some of them you will kill and crucify, and some of them you will scourge in your synagogues, and

---

[23] See note 16 above.

persecute from city to city, so that upon you may fall the guilt of all the righteous blood shed on earth, from the blood of righteous Abel to the blood of Zechariah, the son of Berechiah, whom you murdered between the temple and the altar" (Matt 23:34–35). In other words, Jesus predicts that they will continue the line of action of their unrepentant fathers and thereby become guilty of deeds committed throughout the history of rebellious Israel. He addresses his listeners with the plural personal pronoun "you," which views them as part of a larger group who murdered the righteous throughout the OT period. When he closes his remarks with "all these things will come upon this generation," he uses "this generation" as interchangeable with the plural "you." "This generation," therefore, is not a chronological term covering forty or so years; it is a qualitative term for unrepentant Israelites on the earth at any given time.

Jesus might have terminated God's promised program for Abraham's descendants at that point in Passion Week, but he did not. Instead, using the same collective second person pronoun, Jesus closed his seven woe-pronouncements with a lament over Jerusalem's spiritual desolation and anticipated the day when Israel will repent and say, "Blessed is He who comes in the name of the Lord!" (Matt 23:39). At his second advent, Israelites on earth, in the promised land, of which Jerusalem is the capital, will repent and welcome the Messiah. He implied that same anticipation later in the day, when he said, "Truly I say to you, this generation [i.e., unrepentant Israel] will not pass away until all these things take place" (Matt 24:34). By this he meant that Israel's rebellion against God would continue until the events of his second coming. At that time, Israel will repent.

As Jesus was leaving the temple after pronouncing the seven woes, his disciples' question about the temple buildings gave him occasion to prophesy about the coming destruction of the temple and other matters related to his return to earth (Matt 24:1–3=Mark 13:1–4=Luke 21:5–7). Jesus turned the disciples' attention to Israel's future, both their immediate future (Luke 21:12) and their distant future, particularly events in fulfillment of Daniel's seventieth week. In the latter case, he spoke of "the beginning of birth pangs" (Matt 24:8=Mark 13:8) and "the abomination of desolation" (Matt 24:15=Mark 13:14; cf. see Dan 9:27; 11:31; 12:11), which will immediately precede his return to earth (Matt 24:29–31=Mark 13:24–27=Luke 21:25–27). That will be a time of purging for Israel, a time of "Jacob's trouble [or distress]" (Jer 30:7). After the tribulation of those days, the Messiah will return, and a repentant Israel will enjoy her promised supremacy among the nations. From David's earthly throne, he will judge the survivors of the "great tribulation" (Matt 25:31).

Occasion 10: Some New Covenant Benefits Extended to Outsiders. On Thursday of Passion Week, Jesus participated with his disciples in the Passover meal. At this time, he identified Judas as the betrayer and predicted Peter's denials. The third of four cups at the Passover meal—taken after the supper—recalled God's promise of Israel's redemption: "I will also redeem you with an outstretched arm and with great judgments" (Exod 6:6). That cup became Jesus' symbol for the shedding of his blood for redemption (Matt 26:28; Mark 14:24; Luke 22:20; 1 Cor 11:25). His use of "many" in speaking of the "blood of the covenant, which is poured out for many for forgiveness of sins" (Matt 26:28; see Mark 14:24) in effect extended redemptive benefits of the new covenant beyond the boundaries of Israel to include Gentiles, a fact that 1 Cor 11:25 confirms, as Paul uses the statement in writing about the Lord's Supper to the predominantly Gentile church at Corinth.[24] The fourth and last cup to God's promise of

---

[24] When Jesus instituted the Lord's Supper, he worded his explanation of the cup to include not just Israel but all people: "for this is My blood of the covenant, which is poured out for many for forgiveness of sins" (Matt 26:28); "This cup which is poured out for you is the new covenant in My blood" (Luke 22:20); "This cup is the new covenant in My blood" (1 Cor 11:25).

That Jesus, by this statement, expanded the group to be benefited by the redemptive aspects of his sacrifice is evident from two features. (1) Jesus said his blood of the covenant—the new covenant, of course—was shed for *many*, not just for Israel. The adjective *pollōn* has a "comprehensive sense" in Matt 26:28 just as it does in Matt 20:28. W. D. Davies and Dale C. Allison Jr., *A Critical and Exegetical Commentary on the Gospel according to Saint Matthew* (Edinburgh: T&T Clark, 199), 3:95, 474; Donald A. Hagner, *Matthew 14–28*, Word Biblical Commentary, vol. 33B (Dallas: Word, 1995), 583, 773. It carries the force of "all," *pantōn*, the same as it does in 1 Tim 2:6 (see Rom 5:15, 19). In wording his statement this way, Jesus thereby extended certain benefits of the new covenant beyond the boundaries of Israel. (2) Paul quoted Jesus' words instituting the Lord's Supper in writing to a predominantly Gentile church (1 Cor 11:25). Here again is another indication of the extension of certain benefits beyond the scope of national Israel. The applicability of that to Gentiles in the church indicated that Jesus was extending those benefits to others who are not Israelites. The extended benefits of the new covenant were

Israel's restoration was omitted, as Jesus explained that he would not drink it until he does so in the coming kingdom of God (Matt 26:29=Mark 14:25=Luke 22:18). Clearly, Jesus was looking forward to Israel's promised kingdom when he spoke of the future. That kingdom will come when he comes to fulfill God's promise to Israel.

When he offered his contemporary fellow Jews the fulfillment of Abraham's promises, they resisted him, causing him to broaden his offer of spiritual blessings to the rest of humanity. Paul notes this transition in beneficiaries: "I say then, they [i.e., Israel] did not stumble so as to fall, did they? May it never be! But by their transgression salvation has come to the Gentiles, to make them jealous. Now if their transgression is riches for the world and their failure is riches for the Gentiles, how much more will their fulfillment be!" (Rom 11:11–12). Note how Jesus extended redemptive benefits of his death beyond the pale of Israel, but in doing so, he never revoked the OT promises made to the nation.

As Jesus continued his comments at the Last Supper, he delivered to his disciples what has been called "The Upper Room Discourse." The recipients of this discourse were the same as those who received the discourse on Tuesday evening, but the two discourses differed radically. On Tuesday, the disciples were told about the future of the national Israel of which they were a part. On Thursday, however, they were addressed as representatives of those who will become believers (i.e., the church) during the period of Jesus' absence (John 13:33, 36; 16:5–7; 17:20). Anticipations of the church, many of whose members are not Israelites, differ markedly from the national aspirations of Israel. That accounts for the differences between the two major discourses delivered during Passion Week. Prominent in Jesus' words to the apostles, who were to become the nucleus of the church on the day of Pentecost, were Jesus' promises of the coming of the Spirit (John 14:17, 26; 15:26; 16:13), to whom he also referred as the Helper (Greek, *parakletos*; John 14:16, 26; 15:26; 16:7). This was in fulfillment of "the promise of My Father"

---

not all-encompassing but rather pertained only to the forgiveness of sins. Jesus never extended the land benefits of the Abrahamic covenant to anyone but national Israel. Those belong exclusively to the generation of national Israel who, at his second coming, will embrace Jesus as Israel's promised Messiah.

(Luke 24:49) given through Jesus later during his postresurrection ministry. In speaking of the Spirit's ministry to the church, beginning on the day of Pentecost, Jesus was, in effect, extending to those outside Israel and to the believing remnant of Israel another benefit of God's new covenant with Israel (see Joel 2:28). Once again, however, the church does not represent the fulfillment of national Israel's new covenant.

Members of the body of Christ receive certain special benefits as a result of Israel's rejection of the Messiah at his first advent, but only believing Israelites at some time in the future can enjoy the full benefits of that covenant of which the church has only a taste.

Occasions When the Apostles Might Have Canceled God's Promises to Abraham But Did Not

In Acts and the Pauline Epistles, occasions arose when the apostles might have canceled God's promises to Israel but did not.

Occasion 1: Peter's Strong Words in Acts 3. Stephen Sizer has staunchly rejected the idea that Jews continue to enjoy a favored status with God, citing several passages in Acts. One passage is Acts 3:23, "Anyone who does not listen to him [Christ] will be completely cut off from among his people" (NIV). He concludes that if Peter's Jewish listeners "persisted in refusing to recognize Jesus as their Messiah, they would cease to be the people of God."[25] Sizer's explanation of these verses lacks persuasiveness, however. Acts 3:23 speaks of the cutting off of an individual from the nation, not the cutting off of the whole nation. Acts 3:19–21 shows quite clearly that promises to national Israel are still intact.

A statement of Peter in his Acts 3 sermon to a Jewish audience is specific: "Therefore repent and return, so that your sins may be wiped away, in order that times of refreshing may come from the presence of the Lord; and that He may send Jesus, the Christ appointed for you, whom heaven must receive until the period of restoration of all things about which God spoke by the mouth of His holy prophets from ancient

---

[25] Stephen Sizer, *Christian Zionism: Road Map to Armageddon* (Leicester: InterVarsity, 2004), 149.

time" (Acts 3:19–21). Like John the Baptist and Jesus, Peter called Israel to repent, promising that when they would, their sins would be forgiven, Jesus would return from heaven, bring times of refreshing, and restore all things that God had promised through the OT prophets. As Peter asserted to his Jewish listeners, those promises include those made to Abraham: "It is you who are the sons of the prophets and of the covenant which God made with your fathers, saying to Abraham, 'And in your seed all the families of the earth shall be blessed'" (Acts 3:25). In addressing the words to physical descendants of Abraham, Peter gave assurance that a future repentant group of Israelites would become a source of worldwide blessing. They would do so in fulfillment of the Land covenant, the Davidic covenant, and the new covenant.

Occasion 2: Peter's Encounter in a Gentile Household. Sizer also cites Peter's experience in the house of Cornelius and Peter's words, "I now realize how true it is that God does not show favoritism but accepts men from every nation who fear him and do what is right" (Acts 10:34–35 NIV). Sizer uses those words to prove that "it cannot logically be presumed that Jews continue to enjoy a favoured or exclusive status."[26] His conclusion at this point ignores Jesus' temporary turning from a ministry to unbelieving Israel to expand his outreach to a new group called the church. That he intended for his disciples to go beyond the boundaries of Israel with the good news of the cross and resurrection became clear in passages such as Matt 28:18–20 and Acts 1:8. Yet, neither of those passages says anything about Israel's promises being written off. That others have been drawn in to join a faithful remnant of Israel during the period of national rejection of Jesus as the Messiah cannot mean that God will not make good his promises to the nation as a whole when they repent. Then God will elevate Israel to her promised preeminence.

Occasion 3: James' Use of Amos 9:11–12 in Acts 15:16–18. "'After this I will return and rebuild David's fallen tent. Its ruins I will rebuild, and I will restore it, that the remnant of men may seek the Lord, and all the Gentiles who bear my name,' says the Lord, who does these things that have been known for ages"

---

[26] Ibid., 150. God's election of Abraham and his descendants is not necessarily a show of favoritism by God. That attribution assumes that God follows merely human standards.

(NIV). Sizer uses these words to demonstrate that James is "spiritualizing" the OT text to vindicate "the universality of the gospel and the results of the first-century mission."[27] In doing so, he denies that James refers to a predetermined and futuristic plan for national Israel, separate from the church.

On the contrary, James' use of Amos 9:11–12 in Acts 15:16–18 is not a spiritualizing of the OT text but points forward to the future reign of Christ on David's throne, a reign that will follow the present period, during which Israel, through unbelief, has been temporarily set aside. James begins his quotation with "after these things," words not found in the Amos text. After God finishes his dealings with all ethnic groups in this age of Israel's rejection, Christ will fulfill the promise made to David. That again will be a time of blessing for all nations but under different conditions. Then, the Son of David will occupy the throne, governing all peoples in righteousness and equity.

Occasion 4: Question about the Timing of the Kingdom. Sizer's explanation of Acts 1:6 is particularly weak. He approvingly cites John Calvin's comment on the disciples' question about Israel's coming kingdom: "There are as many mistakes in this question as there are words."[28] According to Sizer, over three years of learning from Jesus' teaching, the Lord's closest followers had missed the whole point of his teaching about Israel. He contends that Jesus' answer to the question "redefines the boundaries of the kingdom of God and thereby the meaning of chosenness. . . . They must turn their backs on Jerusalem and on their hopes of a materialistic kingdom."[29]

When the disciples asked Jesus, "Lord, are you at this time going to restore the kingdom to Israel?" that was the perfect occasion for Jesus to say, "There will be no future kingdom for Israel," but he did not. A careful reading of Jesus' answer reflects that he did not correct their expectation that a future kingdom for Israel was still in store. He simply told them that the time for it had not yet arrived. He gave the disciples a new task to undertake until the time of Israel's repentance, a task

---

[27] Ibid., 157.
[28] Ibid., 168–69.
[29] Ibid., 169.

of extending redemptive and pneumatological benefits to a new people (Acts 1:8), until his return to fulfill for the nation what God had promised Abraham and David. He reminded them of what he had so clearly taught earlier (Matt 24:36; Mark 13:32), that the time of the earthly kingdom's establishment was known only by the Father.

Two men in white clothing, who appeared in conjunction with Jesus' ascension (Acts 1:10–11), verified the legitimacy of the disciples' question about the restoration of Israel's kingdom. They pointed to his return to earth in the same manner as the disciples had seen him go, strongly implying that Jesus would return to Jerusalem and restore the kingdom promised to Israel.

Occasion 5: Peter's Sermon in Acts 2. Peter could have set the record straight once and for all, if the promises to Abraham and David were no longer valid, but he did not. He could have told an unbelieving Jewish crowd, "Israel has blown their chances at future blessing; God's promises to the fathers have been revoked," if that was true. But it was not.

Rather, he dwelt on the continuing hope of Israel for the future. In his Pentecostal sermon, Peter referred to David's words, "For it was not David who ascended into heaven, but he himself says: 'The LORD said to my Lord, "sit at My right hand, until I make Your enemies a footstool for Your feet"'" (Acts 2:34–35; cf. Ps 110:1). Pointing once again to Jesus' ascension into heaven, Peter noted the messianic connotations of David's words in Psalm 110. David did not ascend into heaven, but in fulfillment of that psalm, Jesus did. He will remain in heaven until his return to earth to sit on David's throne and establish the kingdom promised to David, when his enemies will become a footstool for his feet.[30]

Occasion #6: Paul's Soteriological Epistles. God's ongoing recognition of the distinctiveness of Israel among the world's population is evident in Paul's first letter to the Corinthians. He cautioned against causing a Christian brother or sister or anyone else to stumble, "Whether, then, you eat or drink or whatever you do, do all to the glory of God. Give no offense either to Jews

---

[30] See Bradley D. Klassen, "Peter's Use of Psalm 110:1 in Acts 2:33–36" (ThM thesis, The Master's Seminary, 2001).

or to Greeks or to the church of God" (1 Cor 10:31–32). Paul notes the three people groups that inhabit the earth. In doing so, he distinguishes unbelieving Israel from the church—the body of Christ—and from the rest of earth's peoples—here "the Greeks." Besides the church, earth's inhabitants include two other groups, the Jews and the Greeks. By distinguishing the Jews—i.e., non-Christian Jews, Christian Jews being included in the church—from the Greeks, Paul recognizes the ongoing distinctiveness of this ethnic group. Though not enjoying the OT promises to Abraham at the moment, they were still among God's elect people with hope of a promise-filled future if they would turn and accept Jesus as their Messiah.

In Romans, the same distinctiveness of Israel prevails. In Rom 1:16 Paul describes the priority of the Jews in receiving the gospel and in Rom 2:10 the priority of the Jews in responsibility. Romans 3:1–2 speaks of the advantage of the Jews as being entrusted with the oracles *(ta logia)* of God, a word that at least includes, and perhaps refers exclusively, to the promises made to them throughout the OT.[31] Paul specifically points out that Israel's unbelief through the centuries has not in any way canceled those promises whose fulfillment rests exclusively on the faithfulness of God: "If some did not believe, their unbelief will not nullify the faithfulness of God, will it? May it never be!" (Rom 3:3b–4a).[32] Romans 9:4–5 identifies Paul's kinsmen according to the flesh as those "who are Israelites, to whom belongs the

---

[31] C. E. B. Cranfield, *A Critical and Exegetical Commentary on the Epistle to the Romans: Introduction and Commentary on Romans I–VIII*, International Critical Commentary (Edinburgh: T&T Clark, 1975), 178–79. Douglas Moo writes, regarding the Greek word for oracles *(ta logia)*,

> "unmistakeably divine" utterances of the OT (Sanday Headlam); God's self revelation in both the OT and NT; the law, especially the Decalogue; the promises of the OT, or the OT as a whole, with special reference, perhaps, to the promises. Of these alternatives, the last suits best the general application of the word in the LXX and the NT. Paul sets out as the greatest of Jewish distinctions the fact that God has spoken to them and entered, with these words, into a special relationship with them. . . . That the promises of God are included in "the oracles" is, of course, obvious; and Paul has probably chosen to use this word rather than, for example, "the Scriptures," because he wants to highlight those sayings of the OT in which God committed himself to certain actions with reference to his people. *(The Epistle to the Romans*, The New International Commentary on the New Testament [Grand Rapids: Eerdmans, 1996], 182–83)

[32] Cranfield, *A Critical and Exegetical Commentary on the Epistle to the Romans: Introduction and Commentary on Romans I–VIII*, 176–77, 181–82.

adoption as sons, and the glory and the covenants and the giving of the Law and the temple service and the promises, whose are the fathers, and from whom is the Christ according to the flesh, who is over all, God blessed forever."[33] The promises to Abraham and David maintained their validity as late as AD 55, when Romans was written.

Furthermore, two chapters later, Paul explicitly rules out the idea that God has forsaken his promises to Israel: "I say then, God has not rejected His people, has He? May it never be! For I too am an Israelite, a descendant of Abraham, of the tribe of Benjamin. God has not rejected His people whom He foreknew" (Rom 11:1–2a). The apostle to the Gentiles is living proof of the continuing validity of God's promises to Abraham. As that apostle looks to the future, he sees the fulfillment of all those promises made to the fathers when he declares, "All Israel will be saved" (Rom 11:26a), referring, of course, to the time when "the deliverer will come from Zion" (Rom 11:26b). The Israelites who are alive on earth when Christ returns will experience the beginning of his kingdom reign on earth, as God promised to David. "Israel in this passage can hardly be any other than the physical descendants of Abraham, because Rom 11:28 speaks of a people who were enemies during Christ's time for the sake of the Gentiles, but who are nevertheless beloved 'because of the fathers.'"[34] "The

---

[33] Cranfield, commenting on the word translated "are" in 9:4, writes, "The presence of the present indicative of *einai* here (it is of course often left to be understood in Greek) is to be noted. It gives emphasis to the fact that the unbelieving Jews, of whom Paul is speaking, are *still* (even in their unbelief) Israelites." *A Critical and Exegetical Commentary on the Epistle to the Romans: Commentary on Romans IX–XVI*, International Critical Commentary (Edinburgh: T&T Clark, 1979), 460n5, emphasis in original.

[34] Matt Waymeyer, "The Dual Status of Israel in Romans 11:28," *The Master's Seminary Journal* 16, no. 1 (Spring 2005): 61–71. John Murray concurs in this identification of "Israel" in 11:26:

> It should be apparent from both the proximate and less proximate contexts in this portion of the epistle that it is exegetically impossible to give "Israel" in this verse any other denotation than that which belongs to the term throughout this chapter. There is the sustained contrast between Israel and the Gentiles, as has been demonstrated in the exposition preceding. What other denotation could be given to Israel in the preceding verse? It is ethnic Israel Paul is speaking and Israel could not possibly include Gentiles. In that event the preceding verse would be reduced to absurdity and since verse 26 is a parallel or correlative statement the denotation of "Israel" must therefore be the same as in verse 25. (*The Epistle to the Romans*, vol. 2, New International Commentary on the New Testament [Grand Rapids: Eerdmans, 1968], 96)

gifts and calling of God are irrevocable" (Rom 11:29), including God's election of Abraham and his descendants.[35] Unquestionably, Israel still maintained her special status with God when Paul wrote Romans. The descendants of Abraham were still God's elect people. But, what about their status at the time Paul wrote Galatians? Some have used Gal 6:16 as proof that the church is now the Israel of God, with the implication that ethnic Israel has been replaced by a spiritual people.[36] They use Gal 3:7 to point out that only those who believe the gospel are the sons of Abraham[37] and erroneously translate the second *kai* in 6:16 as an explicative "even," thus equating "the Israel of God" with "those who walk according to this rule," i.e., the church.[38] In so doing, they assign *kai* a near-impossible meaning. The conjunction can be used ascensively to mean "even" but not explicatively.[39] Furthermore, Paul never uses "Israel" to refer to the church.[40] In fact, no clear-cut example of the church being called "Israel" exists in the NT or in any church writings until AD 160.[41] Paul is wishing for peace and mercy for those who walk according to the rule of a new creation (Gal 6:15), a rule that excludes considerations of circumcision or uncircumcision.

That principle applies to the church, but in wishing for peace and mercy in the church, he remembers particularly those in the church "who have had to fight hard to break down those barriers that governed their lives for so long."[42] He singles out those

---

[35] Cranfield notes, "Paul's meaning in *agapētoi dia tous pateras* is rather that Israel is beloved because God is faithful to His own love, which in His sovereign freedom He bestowed upon the fathers on no other ground than His love, which knows no cause outside itself (cf. Deut 7:7f)." *A Critical and Exegetical Commentary on the Epistle to the Romans: Commentary on Romans IX–XVI*, 581.

[36] See Herman N. Ridderbos, *The Epistle of Paul to the Churches of Galatia* (Grand Rapids: Eerdmans, 1975), 227.

[37] Ibid., 119–20.

[38] The NIV typifies this error: "Peace and mercy to all who follow this rule, even to the Israel of God."

[39] For a good discussion of the meaning of *kai* in this connection, see S. Lewis Johnson Jr., "Paul and 'The Israel of God': An Exegetical and Eschatological Case-Study," in *Essays in Honor of J. Dwight Pentecost*, ed. Stanley D. Toussaint and Charles H. Dyer (Chicago: Moody, 1986), 187–88.

[40] Scot McKnight, *Galatians*, NIV Application Commentary (Grand Rapids: Zondervan, 1995), 302–4.

[41] Peter Richardson, *Israel in the Apostolic Church* (Cambridge: Cambridge University Press, 1969), 74–84, 206.

[42] Ibid.

Jews for special mention as he bestows his blessing. Those who have come to see themselves as part of a much broader body of people where ethnic distinctions do not pertain and understand their freedom from the law and freedom in the Spirit as taught in this epistle deserve the blessing in a special way. Another significant view sees an eschatological connotation in the Israel of God, looking forward to the future conversion of ethnic Israel at the return of Christ,[43] but whatever way one turns within the guidelines of exegetical soundness, "the Israel of God" in Gal 6:16 cannot refer to the church.

In discussing national Israel in his soteriological epistles, Paul had ample opportunity to exclude them from enjoying the promises made to the fathers by replacing the nation with the church. But, he did just the opposite. He kept a clear distinction between the two bodies of people, one being the physical descendants of Abraham awaiting fulfillment of Abraham's promises and the other being a body of Christ from all nations, established while the nation Israel remains in rejection.

Promises to Israel in the Apocalypse

Bruce Waltke is on record as finding no textual linkage to OT promises to Israel regarding a kingdom in Revelation 20. He writes,

> In the former essay I argued among other things that if there is any tension in one's interpretation between the Old Testament and the New, priority must be given to the New; that Revelation 20:1–10 cannot be linked textually with Israel's covenants and promises; that no New Testament passage clearly teaches a future Jewish millennium; and that the New Testament interprets the imagery of the Old Testament with reference to the present spiritual reign of Christ from his heavenly throne.[44]

---

[43] Johnson, "Paul and 'The Israel of God,'" in Toussaint and Dyer, *Essays in Honor of Pentecost*, 192–94.

[44] Bruce K. Waltke, "A Response," *Dispensationalism, Israel and the Church: The Search for Definition*, ed. Craig A. Blaising and Darrell L. Bock (Grand Rapids: Zondervan, 1992), 353. Waltke is referring to his earlier works "Kingdom Promises as Spiritual," in *Continuity and Discontinuity: Perspectives on the Relationship Between the Old and New Testaments: Essays in Honor of S. Lewis Johnson, Jr.*, ed. John S. Feinberg

In supporting this claim, Waltke professes allegiance to the grammatico-historical approach but adds certain rules of interpretation that "go beyond" that approach, rules such as the "priority of the Bible over other data," "the priority of New Testament interpretation over the interpretation of theologians," "the priority of clear texts over obscure ones," and "the priority of spiritual illumination over scientific exegesis."[45] He fails to notice, however, that in applying his rules beyond the grammatical-historical method, he violates time-honored principles of that method, such as interpreting a passage in its historical context[46] and the principle of single meaning.[47] Like others of a covenant theology persuasion, he interprets OT passages without adequate attention to their historical context, and in so doing, assigns them an additional meaning, one meaning being what the original author intended and the other being a meaning assigned by

---

(Westchester, IL: Crossway, 1988), 263–88; and "Theonomy in Relation to Dispensational and Covenant Theologies," in *Theonomy: A Reformed Critique* (Grand Rapids: Zondervan, 1990), 59–88.

[45] Waltke, "Kingdom Promises as Spiritual," in Feinberg, *Continuity and Discontinuity*, 263–65.

[46] M. S. Terry writes, "The interpreter should, therefore, endeavour to take himself from the present and to transport himself into the historical position of an author, look through his eyes, note his surroundings, feel with his heart, and catch his emotion. Herein we note the import of the term *grammatico-historical* interpretation," and "Subject and predicate and subordinate clauses must be closely analyzed, and the whole document, book, or epistle, should be viewed, as far as possible from the *author's historical* standpoint." *Biblical Hermeneutics: A Treatise on the Interpretation of the Old and New Testaments* (1885; repr., Grand Rapids: Zondervan, 1947), 231 (emphasis in the original), 205 (emphasis added). B. Ramm adds, "Some interaction with the culture and history of a book of Holy Scripture is mandatory" and "The interpreter must know *Biblical history*. . . . Every event has its historical referent in that all Biblical events occur in a stream of history." B. Ramm, *Protestant Biblical Interpretation: Textbook of Hermeneutics*, 3rd rev. ed. (Grand Rapids: Baker, 1970), 150, 154 (emphasis in original).

[47] "A fundamental principle in grammatico-historical exposition is that the words and sentences can have but one significance in one and the same connection. The moment we neglect this principle we drift out upon a sea of uncertainty and conjecture" (Terry, *Biblical Hermeneutics*, 205); "But here we must remember the old adage: 'Interpretation is one; application is many.' This means that there is only one meaning to a passage of Scripture which is determined by careful study" (Ramm, *Protestant Biblical Interpretation*, 113). Summit II of the International Council on Biblical Inerrancy concurred with this principle: "We affirm that the meaning expressed in each biblical text is single, definite and fixed. We deny that the recognition of this single meaning eliminates the variety of its application" (Article VII, "Articles of Affirmation and Denial," adopted by the International Council on Biblical Inerrancy, 10–13 November, 1982). For further discussion of the principle of single meaning, see chap. 6 in my *Evangelical Hermeneutics*.

a NT writer.[48] He fails to grant NT writers the prerogative of assigning additional meanings through use of their revelatory gifts of apostleship and prophesy.[49]

Waltke's view deserves a response in light of his inability to find any reference to Israel's covenants and promises in Revelation in general and in Rev 20:1–10 in particular. Since Rev 20:1–10 cannot be divorced from the remainder of the Apocalypse, that passage should be viewed through the eyes of the whole book.

As emphasized earlier, the OT describes four covenants that are most relevant to "perspectives on Israel and the church": the Abrahamic, the Palestinian or Land, the Davidic, and the new covenants. Some consider the Land covenant to be a part of the Abrahamic, so that covenant will be considered as part of the Abrahamic. The three major covenants of God with Israel are the Abrahamic, the Davidic, and the new covenants.

This study will examine the book of Revelation to see what kind of fulfillments of these covenants it records. Results yielded by differing hermeneutical approaches to the book will also come under scrutiny. The treatments selected for comparison will be three recent evangelical commentaries on Revelation by Greg Beale, David Aune, and Grant Osborne.

The Abrahamic Covenant

God promised Abraham a people, the land, and being a source of blessing to all families of the earth, as pointed out earlier in this chapter.

A People. Revelation depicts a number of times and a number of ways that God will fulfill his promises to Abraham. Abraham's descendants are in view several times in the book. Perhaps the most conspicuous instances are in 7:1–8 and 14:1–5, in which the 144,000 descended from the twelve sons of Abram's grandson Jacob are mentioned. These are not the total number of Abraham's descendants but are a select group from among that number who will in later times fulfill a special mission.[50]

---

[48] For an explanation of the NT use of the OT that does not violate either of these principles, see my discussion in chap. 9 of *Evangelical Hermeneutics*, 241–69.

[49] Ibid.

[50] Others who interpret the book literally may see a different role for the 144,000 (e.g., John F. Walvoord, *The Revelation of Jesus Christ* [Chicago: Moody, 1966], 140), but

Of course, covenantalists do not accept the literal meaning of the 144,000. Beale, in line with his eclectic hermeneutics, concludes that "the group of 7:4–8 represents a remnant from the visible church, which professes to be true Israel"[51] or "the totality of God's people throughout the ages, viewed as true Israelites."[52] He describes his eclecticism as a combination of the idealist and the futurist approaches to the book.[53] Eclectic hermeneutics allow a person to switch from literal to allegorical and vice versa in a passage in order to confirm a preferred theological persuasion. In Revelation, this most often happens by assuming that the book's apocalyptic genre allows for such vacillation. Eclecticism allows Beale to interpret idealistically in some places, as in chapters 7 and 14, and futuristically in others, as in chapter 19.

In contrast with Beale, Aune sees the 144,000 as future Christians, not believers of all ages.[54] He also differs from Beale when he differentiates the 144,000 from the innumerable multitude of 7:9–17.[55] A comparison of these two allegorists in their comments on this passage illustrates how varying interpretations of Revelation are uncontrolled when exegetes forsake the use of grammatical-historical principles. Aune reaches his conclusions after laboring hard to find a consensus definition of apocalyptic genre.[56] He eventually has to set down his own definitions of "genre" and "apocalypse,"[57] while admitting that some authorities disagree with his definitions.[58]

Hermeneutically, Osborne falls into the eclectic camp with Beale, but instead of combining just idealist and futurist approaches, he combines futurist with preterist and idealist.[59] He,

they all agree that the 144,000 are literal descendants of Abraham.
[51] G. K. Beale, *The Book of Revelation: A Commentary on the Greek Text*, The New International Greek Testament Commentary (Grand Rapids: Eerdmans, 1999), 423.
[52] Ibid., 733.
[53] Ibid., 48–49. After being criticized for his eclecticism, he described to me privately his approach as "realistic" hermeneutics, but realism for some can be just as subjective as eclecticism.
[54] David E. Aune, *Revelation 6–16*, Word Biblical Commentary, vol. 52B (Dallas: Word, 1998), 443–44.
[55] Ibid., 440.
[56] Ibid., lxxi–xc.
[57] Ibid., lxxxi–lxxxviii.
[58] Ibid., lxxxviii–lxxxix.
[59] Grant R. Osborne, *Revelation*, Baker Exegetical Commentary on the New Testament (Grand Rapids: Baker Academic, 2002), 21–22.

too, can vacillate to suit his own theological leanings. Yet, he advocates "hermeneutical humility" and caution, whatever principles of interpretation one adopts.[60]

He understands the 144,000 to be the church because of emphasis on the church throughout Revelation,[61] finding "no mention of Jewish believers apart from the Gentile church elsewhere in Revelation,"[62] a statement that will be shown to be fallacious below. Osborne's other supports for his conclusion draw upon other NT passages such as Gal 6:16, in which he wrongly claims that the church is called Israel.[63]

As I have discussed more fully elsewhere,[64] valid exegetical arguments for taking designations in Rev 7:4–8 in other than their literal meaning are nonexistent. The only arguments for understanding them otherwise are theologically, not hermeneutically, motivated. Suffice it to say that no clear-cut example of the church being called "Israel" exists in the NT or in ancient church writings until AD 160.[65] John Walvoord's point is also strong: "It would be rather ridiculous to carry the typology of Israel representing the church to the extent of dividing them up into twelve tribes as was done here, if it was the intent of the writer to describe the church."[66] Add to these the difference in number and nationality between the 144,000 and the innumerable multitude of Rev 7:9–17, and identification of the 144,000 as descendants of Abraham, Isaac, and Jacob becomes evident.

Another reference to the descendants of Abraham comes in Revelation 12, when the text tells of a great sign in heaven about a woman with child. The term *semeion* (12:1) is the contextual signal to understanding a figurative interpretation of the woman. The connection of the woman's description with Gen 37:9 identifies her as national Israel. God will in the future provide a place of refuge for the nation from the animosity of the dragon.

As part of a lengthy acknowledgment that the woman represents Israel, Beale makes the following exegetically

---

[60] Ibid., 16.
[61] Ibid., 311.
[62] Ibid.
[63] Ibid., 311–12.
[64] Thomas, *Revelation 1–7* (Chicago: Moody, 1992), 473–78.
[65] Richardson, *Israel in the Apostolic Church*, 74–84, 206.
[66] Walvoord, *The Revelation of Jesus Christ*, 143.

unsubstantiated statements: "This then is another example of the church being equated with the twelve tribes of Israel (see on 7:4–8). Chapter 12 presents the woman as incorporating the people of God living both before and after Christ's coming."[67] He does see references to the OT community of faith that brought forth the Messiah.[68] Yet, he notes, "It is too limiting to view the woman as representing only a remnant of Israelites living in trial at the last stage of history" and adds the conclusion that "the woman in 12:1–2 represents the community of faith in both the Old and New Testament ages."[69] Through some unexplained interpretive transition, he moves from a recognition that the woman is a symbol for Israel to making her a symbol for both believing Israel and the believing church.

Aune analyzes the words about the woman as probably derived from the Greek Leto- Apollo-Python myth. With only one passing mention of Gen 37:9–11,[70] he allows that the myth about the woman can be read as a reference to Mary and her child from a Christian perspective, or as a reference to Israel, the persecuted people of God, from a Jewish perspective.[71] Aune seems to pursue a reader-response type of hermeneutic in this instance.

Osborne correctly identifies the woman as Israel by referring to Gen 37:1–9, with the sun and the moon referring to Joseph's parents and the stars his brothers, but, inexplicably, he says that she represents the church in Rev 12:17.[72] He fails to explain how Jacob and Leah[73] are parents of the church as they are of Joseph. In Rev 12:6, he opts for a futurist explanation, identifying those persecuted during the "final terrible persecution" as the church.[74] How Israel, the people of God, suddenly becomes the church, the people of God, he does not explain. The transition appears to be quite arbitrary. Again, the radical disagreement of allegorists in their handling of Revelation 12 illustrates the subjective nature

---

[67] Beale, *Revelation*, 627.
[68] Ibid., 629.
[69] Ibid.
[70] Aune, *Revelation 6–16*, 680.
[71] Ibid., 712.
[72] Osborne, *Revelation*, 456.
[73] Osborne seemingly identifies Joseph's mother as Leah, but actually Joseph's mother was Rachel (Gen 30:22–24).
[74] Osborne, *Revelation*, 464.

of interpretation once the interpreter has forsaken grammatical-historical principles.

Cogent reasons exist for identifying the woman as the faithful remnant of Israel of the future and the dragon as the devil who attempts to destroy her.[75] Clearly, the sun and the moon in Gen 37:9–10 refer to Jacob and Rachel, the parents of Joseph. National Israel is the mother who begat the Messiah, a feat that cannot with any justification be attributed to the church. To claim that Revelation makes no distinction between the people of God in the OT and another redeemed people is without merit. Such a distinction has already been noted in comparing 7:1–8 with 7:9–17. Whatever the composition of the innumerable multitude in 7:9–17, they are explicitly distinct from the 144,000 in 7:1–8. This account in Revelation 12 furnishes another instance of God's faithfulness in fulfilling his promise to Abraham by raising up from him and preserving a people that become a nation.

Beale, Aune, and Osborne concur that Rev 2:9 and 3:9 are references to national Israel but reject any teaching of future national repentance, saying that the verses simply refer to vindication of the Philadelphian believers.[76] Yet submission and homage by Jews in 3:9 can hardly be rendered by anyone who does not repent and become Christ's follower.[77]

The Land. God also promised Abraham possession of the land to which he was to lead him, the land that came to be known as Israel, "the promised land." Rev 11:1–13 tells of measuring of the temple and two witnesses active in Jerusalem, a city in the heart of that promised land.

The following chart highlights differences between hermeneutical approaches to Rev 11:1–3. It reflects the results of the eclecticism of Beale and Osborne as compared with a literal or grammatical-historical approach to the book:

---

[75] See Thomas, *Revelation 8–22* (Chicago: Moody, 1995), 117–21, for a more extensive discussion.

[76] Beale, *Revelation*, 240–41, 286–88; Aune, *Revelation 6–16*, 162–65, 237–38; Osborne, *Revelation*, 190–91.

[77] See Thomas, *Revelation 1–7*, 282, for further discussion.

Three Views on Revelation 11:1–12

Of special interest for this study are rows 2, 3, 4, 5, 9, 11, and 13. All pertain to a geographical location within the land that God promised to Abraham. Following a futurist, literal approach to the book, one learns that these are part of the future fulfillment of his promise to Abraham.

Term or Expression	Beale	Osborne	Thomas
[1] "measure" (11:1)	"the infallible promise of God's future presence"; "the protection of God's eschatological community" (559) "until the parousia" (566)	"preservation of the saints spiritually in the coming great persecution" (410; cf. 411); "a 'prophetic anticipation' of the final victory of the church" (412)	"a mark of God's favor" (80-81)
[2] "the temple (naon)" (11:1)	"the temple of the church" (561); "Christians" (562); "the whole covenant community" (562); "the community of believers undergoing persecution yet protected by God" (566)	heavenly temple depicting "the church, primarily the saints of this final period but secondarily the church of all ages" (410)	"a future temple in Jerusalem during the period just before Christ returns" (81-82)
[3] "the altar" (11:1)	"the suffering covenant community" (563)	"the [heavenly] altar of incense" (410)	"the brazen altar of sacrifice in the court outside the sanctuary" (82)
[4] "the worshipers" (11:1)	"believers worshiping together in the temple community" (564)	"individual believers" (411)	"a future godly remnant in Israel" (82)
[5] "in it" (11:1)	"it" referring to the temple or the altar (571)	"in the church" (411)	"in the rebuilt temple" (82)
[6] "the court that is outside the temple (naou)" (11:2)	"God's true people," including Gentiles (560)	"the saints who are persecuted" (412)	"the wicked without God" (83)

continued next page

(Note: page numbers in parentheses refer to Beale's commentary, Osborne's commentary, and Thomas's commentary.* On the chart, the shaded blocks show Beale and Osborne essentially agreeing with each other. Elsewhere they substantially disagree with one another. They disagree with a literal understanding in all fourteen areas.)

* Thomas, *Revelation 8–22*.

Term or Expression	Beale	Osborne	Thomas
[7] "cast outside" (11:2)	"not protected from various forms of earthly harm (physical, economic, social, etc.)" (569)	not protected from the Gentiles/nations (412); God delivers his followers into the hands of sinners (413)	"exclusion from God's favor" (83)
[8] "the Gentiles" (11:2)	"unbelieving Gentiles and Jews" (569)	"the church handed over to the Gentiles/nations for a time" (412)	"a group [of non-Jews] in rebellion against God who will oppress the Jewish remnant" (83-84)
[9] "the holy city" (11:2)	"the initial form of the heavenly city, part of which is identified with believers living on earth" (568)	"the people of God" (413)	"the literal city of Jerusalem on earth" (84)
[10] "forty-two months" (11:2)	"figurative for the eschatological period of tribulation" (565);"attack on the community of faith throughout the church age" (566)	"a limited period that is strictly under God's control"; "a time of martyrdom but also a time of preservation and witness" (415)	"the last half of Daniel's seventieth week" (85)
[11] "they will trample on" (11:2)	persecution of the church from Christ's resurrection until His final coming (567)	"the saints will suffer incredibly" in a physical sense (413)	"future defilement and domination of Jerusalem" (86)
[12] "the two witnesses" (11:3)	the church; "the whole community of faith" (573)	"two major eschatological figures . . . [and a symbol for] the witnessing church" (418)	two future prophets, probably Moses and Elijah (87-89)
[13] "the great city" (11:8)	"Babylon" = "Rome" = "the ungodly world" (591-592)	Jerusalem and Rome; secondarily, all cities that oppose God (426-27)	Jerusalem (93-94)
[14] the resurrection and ascension of the two witnesses (11:11-12)	"divine legitimation of a prophetic call" (599)	"A proleptic anticipation of the 'rapture' of the church" (432)	the resurrection of the two witnesses (97)

Turning attention to Aune, one sees that he agrees with Osborne that the temple refers to the heavenly temple, not the earthly one, but he does so under the assumption that the earthly temple will not be rebuilt.[78] Yet, he later acknowledges that the temple described in 11:1–2 is most definitely the earthly temple

---

[78] Aune, *Revelation 6–16*, 596–97.

in Jerusalem.[79] He also believes that "the holy city" is a clear reference to the earthly city Jerusalem that is referred to again in 11:8.[80] Yet, he agrees with Osborne that the worshipers are a divinely protected remnant of Christians who will survive until the arrival of the eschaton.[81]

For those whose hermeneutical principles accord with literal interpretation, the land promises to Abraham are resounding through the Apocalypse. Other references to the land promised to Abraham include Rev 16:16 and 20:9. The former refers to a place called Harmagedon or Armageddon, where a future battle will be fought. The "*Har-*" prefix probably refers to the hill country around a town called Megiddo. Megiddo was a city on the Great Road linking Gaza and Damascus, connecting the coastal plain and the plain of Esdraelon or Megiddo. That the kings from the east must cross the Euphrates River to get to the land of Israel and Megiddo is another indication of the geographical connotation of Armageddon and of the fulfillment of the land promise to Abraham (Rev 16:12).[82] The reference in 20:9 speaks of "the camp of the saints and the beloved city," most clearly a reference to the city of Jerusalem.

In Beale's system, "Armageddon" is a figurative reference to the place where the final battle against the saints and Christ will be fought. He sees that as a name for the whole world.[83] Similarly, he opts for another allegorical interpretation when he sees "the camp of the saints and the beloved city" as the church.[84]

Aune calls Armageddon "the mythical apocalyptic-world mountain where the forces hostile to God, assembled by demonic spirits, will gather for a final battle against God and his people."[85] Regarding "the beloved city," he comments, "Since the heavenly Jerusalem does not make its appearance until 21:10 (aside from 3:12), 'the beloved city' cannot be the New Jerusalem but

---

[79] Ibid., 605.
[80] Ibid., 608–9.
[81] Ibid., 630.
[82] Thomas, *Revelation 8–22*, 261–62.
[83] Beale, *Revelation*, 838–39.
[84] Ibid., 1027.
[85] Aune, *Revelation 6–16*, 898.

must be the earthly Jerusalem."[86] Yet, one should not conclude that Aune handles Revelation's prophecies as a futurist. Because of his source and redaction critical assumptions, he simply assumes that the final editor of the Apocalypse incorporated earlier traditions and/or myths into the passage.

After briefly examining eight possible meanings, Osborne understands "Armageddon" to be a broadening of apostate Israel to depict all nations in their final war against God.[87] This too is allegorical. After acknowledging the term's geographical connotation,[88] he opts for a symbolic meaning. From OT times, the plain and the hill country around Megiddo were a well-known battleground and are a suitable location for Christ's final victory over his enemies. The plain of Megiddo is not large enough to contain armies from all over the world but furnishes an assembly area for a larger deployment that covers two hundred miles from north to south and the width of Palestine from east to west (see Rev 14:20).[89]

In agreement with literal interpretation, Osborne reverts to his literal-futurist mode in identifying "the beloved city" of Rev 20:9 with Jerusalem, which will have been reinstated as the capital of Christ's kingdom during the millennium.[90] That refreshing conclusion supports the land promise to Abraham by locating activities of the millennium geographically within the boundaries of territory promised to Abraham. This will be the location of Israel's Messiah in ruling his world kingdom on earth.[91]

Among Abraham's descendants, will be the "King of kings, and Lord of lords" (19:16), whose conquest will free the righteous of the earth from the deceptions, tyranny, and injustice of the beast and the false prophet (19:20). This great battle will eventuate in the imprisonment of the deceiver of the nations (20:3), a great blessing to all the families of the earth.

---

[86] Aune, *Revelation 17–22*, Word Biblical Commentary, vol. 52C (Dallas: Word, 1998), 1098–99.
[87] Osborne, *Revelation*, 596.
[88] Ibid., 594.
[89] Thomas, *Revelation 8–22*, 270–71.
[90] Osborne, *Revelation*, 714.
[91] See Thomas, *Revelation 8–22*, 425.

The Davidic Covenant

God's promises to David included the following: "When your days are complete and you lie down with your fathers, I will raise up your descendant after you, who will come forth from you, and I will establish his kingdom. . . . *I will establish the throne of his kingdom forever.* . . . *Your house and your kingdom shall endure before Me forever; your throne shall be established forever"* (2 Sam 7:12–13, 16; emphasis added).

Fulfillment of the Davidic covenant is a major theme of Revelation, from beginning to end. In Rev 1:5, the titles chosen for Christ come from Psalm 89, an inspired commentary on the Davidic covenant. Those titles are "the faithful witness, the first-born of the dead, and the ruler of the kings of the earth." "The firstborn of the dead" comes from "My firstborn" in Ps 89:27, "the ruler of the kings of the earth" from "the highest of the kings of the earth" in Ps 89:27, and "the faithful witness" from "the witness in the sky is faithful" in Ps 89:37.

David is prominent at the book's end, too. Revelation 22:16 reads, "I, Jesus, have sent My angel to testify to you these things for the churches. I am the root and the descendant of David, the bright morning star." Jesus is both the ancestor (the root) and the descendant (the offspring) of David. He is the beginning and end of the economy associated with David's family. In the words of 2 Sam 7:12, he is the descendant whom God promised to raise up after David. He will inaugurate the kingdom promised to David. Paul refers to Jesus similarly in Rom 15:12, calling him "the root of Jesse."

In Rev 5:5, one of the twenty-four elders assures John that "the lion who is of the tribe of Judah, the root of David" has conquered and will open the seven-sealed book. "Root" has the sense of "offspring" here and points to Christ's headship in the final Davidic kingdom. The title alludes to the messianic prophecy of Isa 11:1, 10.

Beale agrees in connecting these titles of Rev 1:5 with Psalm 89, but concludes that John views David as "the ideal Davidic king on an escalated eschatological level."[92] In other words, he sees an allegorical fulfillment of the promise to David,

---

[92] Beale, *Revelation*, 190–91.

not a literal understanding, as the promise would have been understood by David. He says that Christ assumed his sovereign position over the cosmos and is fulfilling his reign during the present, not in the future.

As for Rev 22:16, Beale does the same. Here he sees David's kingdom as both already inaugurated and future.[93] A literal understanding of the Davidic covenant, however, limits that kingdom to the future only. Note Beale's combination of idealist and futurist hermeneutics in this instance, allegorical in seeing a present fulfillment and literal in seeing a future fulfillment, in another violation of the principle of single meaning. At Rev 5:5, Beale has little to say about Jesus' connection to David. Concerning the two titles, he notes that "both concern the prophecy of a messianic figure who will overcome his enemy through judgment."[94] Those words fall into an idealist mold, which allegedly could be fulfilled at any time.

Aune notes the connection of Rev 1:5 with Ps 89:27, 37 [95] but fails to connect the psalm with the Davidic covenant on which the psalm furnishes a commentary. In Rev 22:16, he notes the messianic connotation of the title but again does not mention the Davidic covenant and its fulfillment in Revelation. He correctly ties the titles of Rev 5:5 with OT prophecies of the Messiah who was coming to reign but does not take the next step and tie them to fulfillment of the Davidic covenant of 2 Samuel 7. He does refer to the reign of David's house in that passage in connection with Rev 11:15, "He shall reign forever and ever," but that is the only place in his three volumes on Revelation that he does so.

Osborne prefers not to connect "the faithful witness" of Rev 1:5 with Ps 89:27, but he does connect the other two titles of 1:5 with Psalm 89.[96] Yet, he makes no direct connection with the fulfillment of Israel's Davidic covenant.[97] Concerning Rev 22:16, he relates "the Root and Offspring of David" to "the fulfillment of the

---

[93] Ibid., 1146–47.
[94] Ibid., 349.
[95] David E. Aune, *Revelation 1–5*, Word Biblical Commentary, vol. 52A (Dallas: Word, 1997), 37–40.
[96] Osborne, *Revelation*, 62–63.
[97] Ibid., 63.

Davidic messianic hope" and calls Jesus "the Davidic Messiah."[98] Still, he refrains from noting how such a fulfillment contributes to the hope of national Israel. Regarding 5:5, Osborne notes the connection of "the root of David" with Isa 11:1, a military passage, and admits that the military side of the Davidic imagery predominates in Revelation.[99] Yet, he fails to see him as the Christ returning to accomplish his victory. Rather, he identifies Jesus' cross as the major weapon in warfare with God's enemies.[100] That hardly does justice to a literal interpretation of Revelation and to fulfillment of Israel's Davidic covenant in the future.

In Rev 3:7, addressing the church at Philadelphia, Jesus refers to himself as the One who holds "the key of David." Possession of that key means that he has the right to admit to or exclude from the city of David, Jerusalem both old and new. That key pertains to the prerogative of determining who will have a part in the kingdom of David, over which he as the Messiah will rule. Again, this remark would be impossible without his fulfillment of the promise made to David.

Regarding "the key of David" (Rev 3:7), Aune concludes, "The phrase refers to the key *to* the Davidic or messianic kingdom, i.e., to the true Israel," but Aune erroneously equates "the true Israel with the church," not with a future kingdom promised to David and Israel in 2 Samuel 7.[101]

For Beale, "the key of David" is an amplification of a similar phrase in Rev 1:18 and equates to Jesus' power over salvation and judgment.[102] He correctly notes the stress of the Lord's sovereignty over those entering the kingdom, but he defines the kingdom as the church in the present era and consistently spiritualizes references to Israel in the OT. He does the same in Revelation, a book that so clearly points to a kingdom in the future, not a present one.[103]

Osborne equates "the key of David" in Rev 3:7 with "the keys of the kingdom" in Matt 16:18–19, keys which Christ holds and

---

[98] Ibid., 792–93.
[99] Ibid., 254.
[100] Ibid.
[101] Aune, *Revelation 1–5*, 235.
[102] Beale, *Revelation*, 284.
[103] See Robert L. Thomas, "The Kingdom of Christ in the Apocalypse," *The Master's Seminary Journal* 3, no. 2 (Fall 1992): 117–40.

passes on to his followers.[104] In the Revelation context, he sees a reference to Jesus as the Davidic Messiah, "who controls entrance to God's kingdom, the 'New Jerusalem' (3:12)."[105] Why Osborne speaks of access to the eternal kingdom rather than the millennial kingdom remains a mystery. The millennial kingdom pertains most specifically to the present earth, where Israel's hopes will be fulfilled. The "key" promise to the Philadelphian church shows that the resurrected church will share in the blessings of that future kingdom in which mortal Israelites will be most prominent.

In addition to specific references to David in the Apocalypse are a number of references to David's kingdom. In fulfillment of the Davidic covenant, Revelation speaks often of a future kingdom on the present earth, prophecies that correspond to OT prophecies about that kingdom. Revelation 11:15 records, "Then the seventh angel sounded; and there were loud voices in heaven, saying, 'The kingdom of the world has become the kingdom of our Lord and of His Christ; and He will reign forever and ever.'" What other kingdom could that be than the Messiah's future kingdom? The language of this proleptic song by the heavenly voices echoes Ps 2:2, a psalm that speaks of the transference of power from heathen nations to God and his Messiah.

Elsewhere, I have pointed out in numerous instances the dominant focus of Revelation on the futurity of the kingdom.[106] Discussion about the kingdom should not be limited to Rev 19:11–20:10. The teaching of the book as a whole needs to be taken into consideration. Anticipation of the future kingdom is an integral part of motivation for present Christian experience.[107] Whatever meaning "kingdom" may have for the corporate Christian church of today, that meaning does not eradicate the fact that a future kingdom on earth is still ahead; Revelation connects that future kingdom with God's covenants with David and Abraham.[108] Proleptic songs about the initiation of the kingdom also occur in Rev 12:10 and 19:6.

---

[104] Osborne, *Revelation*, 187.
[105] Ibid.
[106] Thomas, *Revelation 8–22*, 546–50.
[107] Ibid., 546.
[108] Ibid., 550–58.

Beale, in commenting on Rev 11:15, says, "God now takes to himself the rule that formerly he permitted Satan to have over the world."[109] Yet, two paragraphs later he comments,

> Vv. 16–17 show that it is the Lord whose eternal reign is focused on here. . . . The consummated fulfillment of the long-awaited messianic kingdom prophesied in the OT finally has come to pass. . . . It is difficult to say how Christ's delivering up the kingdom to the Father and subjecting himself to the Father at the consummation in 1 Cor. 15:24–28 relates to the present text. Perhaps Christ gives up the redemptive historical phase of his rule and then assumes an eternal rule alongside but in subjection to his Father.[110]

Beale has at least two difficulties with Rev 11:15: (1) At one point he says the verse looks forward to a change of rulership over *the world*, but in the next two verses he contradicts himself by changing the kingdom's domain from *this world* to the new heavens and the new earth in the eternal state. (2) His second difficulty, which he admits, is in understanding how Christ could at the time of the consummation deliver up the kingdom to the Father as 1 Corinthians 15 requires, since Christ will only be starting his rule over the kingdoms of this world at that time.

The response to both of Beale's dilemmas is an acknowledgment that the future kingdom will have a temporal phase relating to the present earth, followed by an eternal kingdom in the new heavens and the new earth. From its own statement, Rev 11:15 speaks of a future temporal kingdom on this earth, a transference of power from heathen nations to God and his Messiah. At the end of that future temporal kingdom the Messiah will deliver up that kingdom to the Father as 1 Corinthians 15 describes.

Aune creates for himself the same dilemma as Beale in first defining "the kingdom of the world" of Rev 11:15b as either the totality of creation or the human world in opposition to God and in conflict with his purposes, and then identifying the eternal

---

109 Beale, *Revelation*, 611.
110 Ibid.

reign of 11:15c as the eternal reign of God.[111] In so doing, he anticipates a future kingdom *on this earth* that will be eternal in duration, leaving no room for a new heaven and a new earth that he allows for elsewhere.

Osborne locates the replacement of the kingdom of the world with the kingdom of our Lord and his Messiah at the second coming of Christ and sees it as the fulfillment of Jewish and NT expectations.[112] He has the same dilemma as Beale and Aune, however, because he sees this as the beginning of Christ's eternal kingdom,[113] even though Rev 11:15 specifically locates this kingdom in *this world*, not in the new creation. He makes no allowance for the millennial kingdom whose location will be the present earth.[114]

Of course, at this point neither Beale, Aune, nor Osborne says anything about a fulfillment of the Davidic covenant. That is because Rev 11:15 creates an impossible situation for those who interpret the book nonliterally, but for those who interpret it literally, it marks the fulfillment by God of the promises he made to David, and ultimately to Abraham, too.

The Apocalypse has much more to say about the fulfillment of the Davidic covenant and the prominent role of Israel in the kingdom, but it has much to say about the new covenant also.

The New Covenant

Jeremiah 31:31–34 records God's new covenant with Israel. Among its other provisions are two relevant to the present discussion. When God said, "I will forgive their iniquity, and their sin I will remember no more" (v. 34), that was partly how Abraham would be a source of blessing to all people, and when he said, "I will be their God, and they shall be My people" (v. 33), he provided for Israel and all other peoples a new relationship with himself, another source of universal blessing.

Forgiveness of sins. Much in Revelation deals with the forgiveness of sins. In Rev 12:11, a heavenly voice sings about the blood

---

[111] Aune, *Revelation 6–16*, 638–39.
[112] Osborne, *Revelation*, 440–41.
[113] Ibid., 441.
[114] For further verification on the location of the millennial kingdom, see Thomas, *Revelation 8–22*, 550–52.

of the Lamb: "They [referring to the martyrs among the Israelites] overcame him [referring to the devil] by the blood of the Lamb" (KJV). Anywhere the book refers to the blood of the Lamb, or simply to the Lamb, it alludes to Christ's death at Calvary to provide forgiveness of sins (see 5:6; 7:14; 13:8). Revelation refers to the Lamb twenty-five times. The Lamb did not die sacrificially for Israel alone, of course—redemption is among the benefits extended to the body of Christ, as pointed out above[115]—but his death happened for Israel's sins especially, as the Servant Song of Isa 52:13–53:12 emphasizes. The 144,000 special servants from among Israel were "redeemed from the earth" according to Rev 14:3 (ESV). They are seen on Mount Zion standing with the Lamb in 14:1. Their redemption must be provided by the suffering Messiah. According to 5:9, the redemption came through the blood of the Lamb. Since Beale, Aune, and Osborne do not connect the woman of chapter 12 with Israel specifically, the fact that they do not connect the blood of the Lamb in 12:11 with God's new covenant promise to Israel is no surprise. Beale identifies the woman as "all believers, past, present and future."[116] Aune says, "The passage deals with the proleptic victory of Christian martyrs."[117] Osborne identifies the overcomers in 12:11 with overcomers in the seven churches in Revelation 2–3.[118]

Part of God's promise to Abraham was that he would be a source of worldwide blessing. Obviously, forgiveness of sins was part of a fulfillment of that promise, but the new covenant spoke of more than that. Jeremiah 31:33b–34a promises, "I will put My law within them and on their heart I will write it; and I will be their God, and they shall be My people. They will not teach again, each man his neighbor and each man his brother, saying, 'Know the LORD,' for they will all know Me, from the least of them to the greatest of them." Such a condition as this can exist only after the binding of Satan spoken of in Rev 20:1–3. Satan will no longer have freedom to deceive the nations (20:3). Until that time,

---

[115] Because of Israel's rejection of her Messiah at his first advent, Jesus extended the benefit of forgiveness of sins beyond the boundaries of Israel (Matt 26:28; see Mark 14:24). This is why Revelation also speaks of forgiveness when the objects are not limited to Israel (see Rev 1:5; 7:9, 14, 17).

[116] Beale, *Revelation*, 663.

[117] Aune, *Revelation 6–16*, 702–3.

[118] Osborne, *Revelation*, 475–76.

he will continue his leadership as "the prince of the power of the air, of the spirit that is now working in the sons of disobedience" (Eph 2:2b) and as "the ruler of this world" (John 12:31). He has been judged already in a potential sense through the crucifixion of Christ, but the implementation of that judgment awaits the future kingdom on earth and the complete fulfillment of the covenant that God made with Abraham.

Control of the world in that future day will be in the hands of the descendant of David—the King of kings and Lord of lords (Rev 19:16)—and those who rule with him (Rev 20:4). He will raise the dead, including those who have been martyred during Daniel's seventieth week, immediately before the millennial kingdom, and they will rule with him. It will be a rule of righteousness and equity, and thus Abraham and his descendants will be a source of blessing to all people.

A New Relationship with God. Clearly, in the New Jerusalem phase of David's future kingdom, Israel and all others who have received the forgiveness benefit of the new covenant will enjoy an unparalleled relationship with God. John writes in Rev 21:3, "Behold, the tabernacle of God is among men, and He will dwell among them, and they shall be His people, and God Himself will be among them." This promise comes in conjunction with the descent of the holy city, the New Jerusalem, from heaven (21:2). It recalls God's new covenant promise to Israel, "I will be their God, and they shall be My people" (Jer 31:33d; see Jer 32:38; Ezek 37:27).

Aune recognizes the covenant formula, "I will be their God, and they shall be my people (Jer 31:33 [LXX 38:33])," in Rev 21:3c, but sees it here as referring to *all* people. He recognizes that it is limited to the righteous in Israel throughout the OT.[119] He, of course, would not recognize God's dealings with Israel in particular in Revelation 7, 12, and 14 in order to bring them to this point. Beale sees fulfillment of Jer 31:33 by all people who trust in Jesus, "the true seed of Abraham and the only authentic Israelite, who died and rose for both Jew and Gentile."[120] He writes, "Everyone represented by Jesus, the ideal king and

[119] Aune, *Revelation 17–22*, 1123.
[120] Beale, *Revelation*, 1047. See also 1048, where Jer 31:33 appears.

Israelite, is considered part of true Israel and therefore shares in the blessings that he receives."[121] Thereby, he shuns the literal fulfillment of the new covenant with national Israel in the future kingdom. Osborne connects Rev 21:3 with the promise of Ezek 37:27 as well as Jer 31:33b but interprets the verses not as pointing to a fulfillment spiritually by Christians today but by all people in the new heaven and new earth.[122] He omits any reference to the original recipients of the promises in Ezekiel and Jeremiah and their unique role. Ethnic Israel is the reason for this previously nonexistent, close relationship between God and not only Israel but all peoples. All the families of the earth will be blessed through God's promise to Abraham.

The promise of Rev 21:3 does extend beyond the boundaries of Israel, but to deny its special relevance to Israel and her new covenant is to ignore the clearly distinctive role of national Israel through earlier portions of the Revelation and even in producing this new closeness to God. Revelation 21:12, 14 shows that Israel will have a role distinct from the church even in the new Jerusalem, the eternal state. As the special object of God's choice, she will ever be distinctive.

Summary of Israel in the Apocalypse

The book of Revelation is full of references to God's faithfulness in fulfilling his promises to national Israel, specifically the Abrahamic, the Davidic, and the new covenants. For him to turn away from Israel to fulfill them with other peoples, as those who interpret the book in an eclectic, nonliteral, or allegorical manner suggest, would violate his faithfulness to his promises.

The means used by Beale, Aune, and Osborne to avoid finding references to Israel in the Apocalypse vary. Beale and Osborne generally resort to an eclectic hermeneutic, choosing an idealist or allegorical meaning whenever the text refers to Israel. Any reference to Israel for them becomes a reference to the church, which they call the "New Israel." Aune does not describe his hermeneutics as "eclectic," but his method of interpreting the

---

[121] Ibid.
[122] Osborne, *Revelation*, 734–35.

Apocalypse easily falls into that category. He labors to find definitions for "apocalyptic" and for "genre," ending with his own definition that he admits will not be acceptable to some. He then uses apocalyptic genre as justification for combining a literal-futuristic-mystical method in some passages with an allegorical-idealist-historical method in others. He and Osborne nibble at literal fulfillment here and there but explain it away by a species of genre principles used to override normal grammatical-historical principles, by reader-response hermeneutics, or by historical criticism.

All three men take negative references to Jewish people literally in Rev 2:9 and 3:9 but revert to figurative meanings for Israel and the sons of Israel in chapters 7 and 14. The frequent disagreements between the three graphically portray how uncontrolled interpretation can be when one forsakes a literal method of understanding Revelation. With a literal approach to the book, references to Israel are plain and plentiful.

With this characteristic of the book as a whole in mind, for someone to say "that Revelation 20:1–10 cannot be linked textually with Israel's covenants and promises; that no New Testament passage clearly teaches a future Jewish millennium; and that the New Testament interprets the imagery of the Old Testament with reference to the present spiritual reign of Christ from his heavenly throne"[123] is a denial of what is obvious through adopting meanings other than what words have in their normal usage. It is to view those verses as completely divorced from their context, an exegetically unacceptable decision. God will fulfill in a literal manner all the promises he made to national Israel and will retain his eternal attribute of faithfulness. Along with the rest of the Old and New Testaments, the Apocalypse interpreted literally verifies his compliance with his promises to the nation.

Response by Robert L. Reymond

Thomas references and cites numerous verses that he says teach that all of God's promises to Abraham and to his

---

[123] Waltke, "A Response," in Blaising and Bock, *Dispensationalism, Israel and the Church*, 353.

descendants, including his land promise, remain intact, and that national Israel has in the past, still does, and will in the future occupy a prominent place in God's plan for the ages, culminating in a Jewish millennium with the glorified Christ sitting on the throne of David in Jerusalem. On the other hand, the church is a separate and distinct entity from national Israel, a mystery unknown to the Old Testament prophets that is not fulfilling the promises made to Israel. Because he raises so many dispensational "curiosities," I cannot deal with all of them in a short response, so I will respond to only two.

Thomas's Understanding of Israel

Thomas, as I have said, maintains that the land promise to Israel continues in its validity throughout the Old and New Testaments, from Genesis to Revelation. Never does Jesus or any of the apostles say otherwise. But is this so? In his parable of the wicked farmers (Matt 21:33–45; Mark 12:1–12; Luke 20:9–19), which I have treated elsewhere, Jesus tells the story of a landowner who leased his vineyard to some farmers and then went into another country. When the time came for him to receive his rental fee in the form of the fruit of the vineyard, the landowner sent servant after servant to his tenants only to have them beaten or stoned or killed. Last of all, he sent his son and said, "They will respect my son." But when the tenants saw the landowner's son they said: "This is the heir; come, let's kill him and take his inheritance." This they did, throwing his body out of the vineyard. When the landowner came, he destroyed those tenants and leased his vineyard to others. The intention of the parable is obvious: The landowner is God the Father, the vineyard is the nation of Israel (see Isa 5:7), the farmers are Israel's leaders, the servants are the prophets of the Old Testament theocracy (Matt 23:37a), and the son is Jesus himself. The central teaching of the parable is also obvious, as it was to its original audience (Matt 21:45): after having sent his servants the prophets repeatedly in Old Testament times to the nation of Israel to call the nation back to him from sin and unbelief, only to have the prophets rebuffed, persecuted, and often killed, God, the owner of Israel, had, in sending Jesus Christ, moved beyond sending another mere servant. Matt 21:37 reports: "Then *last of all* he sent his son" and Mark 12:6: ". . . having one son, his *beloved*, he also sent him to them *last*" (NKJV). Here Jesus represented himself as God's *final* ambassador, after whose sending none higher can come. The Son of God is the highest conceivable messenger of God. And the rejection of his Son, unlike the rejection of the prophets sent before him, was to *entail neither God's continuance of dealing with the nation of Israel in mercy, nor a mere change in politico-religious administration*. Rather, Jesus taught that his rejection by Israel's national leaders would *eventuate in the complete overthrow of the theocracy and the rearing from the foundation up of another structure (Christ's church), in which the Son would receive full vindication and supreme honor by Spirit-filled believers*. As A. T. Robertson comments, "[The truth in this parable] was the death-knell of the Jewish nation with their hopes of political and world leadership."[124] Jesus' exact words are as follows: "I tell you, the kingdom of God will be taken away from you and given to a people producing its fruits" (Matt 21:43 ESV; see also Mark 12:9 and Luke 20:16). National Israel, except for its elect seed, would be judged, and the special standing it had enjoyed during the old dispensation was to be given to the already emerging *international* church of Jesus Christ, comprised of the elect Jewish remnant and the elect Gentiles. And as Jesus had predicted, Israel's rulers rejected him and incited Rome to execute him by crucifixion, the temple and the city of Jerusalem were soon destroyed (see Matt 24:1–35), the Jewish people dispersed, and Israel ceased to exist as a political entity, as Moses had predicted in Deut 28:15–68 and 31:24–29.

Then Paul declared in 1 Thess 2:15–16 that the Jews who "killed both the Lord Jesus and the prophets, and drove us out, and displease God and oppose all mankind by hindering us from speaking to the Gentiles that they might be saved—so as always to fill up the measure of their sins. But [God's] wrath has come upon them at last!" (ESV). This divine rejection came to expression in God's hardening the mass of Israel save for the elect

---

[124] A. T. Robertson, *The Gospel according to Matthew, The Gospel according to Mark*, vol. 1 in *Word Pictures in the New Testament* (Nashville: Sunday School Board of the Southern Baptist Convention, 1930–32), 172.

Jewish remnant. Once again we are told that Israel as an ethnic entity has become *lo-ammi* ("not my people"), with a finality about it, save for the elect remnant (Rom 9:27–29; 11:7–10). But, because God has by no means rejected every single Jew, choosing in grace a Jewish remnant (Rom 11:1–5), throughout this age elect Jews continue to be saved by being "provoked to jealousy" (Rom 11:11, 14) by the multitudes of saved Gentiles enjoying the spiritual blessings originally offered to their fathers, and who accordingly, through faith in Jesus Christ, are being grafted into the cultivated "olive tree" (Rom 11:23–24). The salvation of Gentiles is then the primary avenue to the salvation of the Jewish elect; indeed, in this way "all Israel" will be saved (Rom 11:26).

In light of these biblical data the church should affirm the following four propositions: (1) The modern Jewish state is not part of the messianic kingdom of Jesus Christ. To put it bluntly, modern Israel is the spiritual son of Hagar (Gal 4:24–25) and thus is "Ishmaelitish" due to its lack of Abrahamic faith in Jesus Christ. It has accordingly forsaken any biblical claim to the land of ancient Israel. (2) The land promise of the Old Testament served as a type of the realization of the purposes of God for his redeemed people that encompasses all the nations (Gen 12:3) and the entire cosmos (Rom 4:13). Christians are the true heirs, along with Abraham, of the land promise in its antitypical, consummated character. (3) The Old Testament predictions about the return of Israel to the land in terms of a geopolitical reestablishment of the state of Israel are better understood as having fulfillment at the "restoration of all things" that will accompany the resurrection of believers at the return of Christ (Acts 3:21; Rom 8:22–23). To interpret these predictions literally would be a retrograde elevation of type over antitype. (4) The future messianic kingdom will embrace the whole of the recreated cosmos and will not experience a special manifestation that could be regarded as "Jewish" in the "Holy Land" or anywhere else.

Thomas's Understanding of the Church

Thomas, also in a traditional dispensational manner, views the church and the present church age as a mystery form of the kingdom of heaven that has been inserted into history but is still overshadowed by the nation of Israel. Nor is it fulfilling any Old Testament promises given to the nation of Israel. But is this so?

I would urge that the church should recognize anew that Jesus Christ is not only its Savior and Lord but also its chief prophetic scholar. It is from his "eschatological dualism"—the kingdom has come in grace and is yet to come in judgment—that the church should and must derive the programmatic paradigm within which the rest of Old and New Testament eschatology should be placed. What the Old Testament had not clearly distinguished chronologically—but had represented more as a single, though complex, unit—Jesus distinguished, by speaking of the kingdom's arrival first in grace and only later breaking into history in judgment with cataclysmic fury and great glory.

The distinctions Jesus made clearly teach that the present age is the consummating period of God's saving activity and is therefore "eschatological" in the salvific sense. Moreover, Christ's present reign is not simply one reign alongside others. Distinct in its nature from all other kingly reigns—as distinct as a man is from beasts (Dan 7:2–14)—his kingdom of grace is, as Carl F. H. Henry states,

> the only kingdom that decisively attests that life is more ultimate than death, that mercy can outreach the arenas of sin and guilt, and that the sphere of God is greater than the realms of hell. It signals the satisfaction of all legitimate human need, the triumph of divine mercy, humanity living life fit for eternity, the homecoming of the renewed community of God. It is the kingdom that cannot be frustrated by the puppet kingdoms of Satan but that explains them for what they really are. It is the enduring kingdom amid others that rise only to have their half day and then perish. . . . [T]he coming of Jesus of Nazareth advances the prophetic promise of the eschatological kingdom into the sphere of fulfillment—if not total fulfillment, yet nonetheless realization in a crucially significant way. . . . Jesus in his own person is the embodied sovereignty of God. He lives out that sovereignty in the flesh. He manifests the kingdom of God

by enthroning the creation-will of God and demonstrating his lordship over Satan. Jesus conducts himself as Lord and true King, ruling over human hearts, ruling over demons, ruling over nature at its fiercest, ruling over sickness, conquering death itself. With the coming of Jesus the kingdom is not merely imminent; it gains the larger scope of incursion and invasion. Jesus points to his release of the victims of Satan, and to his own devastation of demons and the demonic, as meaning that "the kingdom of God has come upon you" (Mark 12:28). He reveals God's royal power in the salvific sense.[125]

The age to come, witnessing as it will God's consummating judgment activity and the ushering in of the new heaven and new earth, is "eschatological" in the final, eternal sense. That age will be ushered in by the King at his coming in power and great glory:

He shall come with [his raptured glorified church and with] a retinue of heavenly beings, an entourage of angels, which he refused to summon when he was impaled on the cross but who as God's servants remain at Christ's disposal in this final vindication of the godly and punishment of the wicked.

To this eschatological climax we are directed not only by the Old Testament prophets but by Jesus of Nazareth as well. The past New Testament fulfillment does not exhaust either the predictions of the prophets or the promises of Jesus on earth or the apostolic teaching. In the present age the Church . . . at her best . . . only approximates [the kingdom], and at her worst she can even do violence to it. Jesus Christ himself, and the apostles in agreement, and the Old Testament writers in anticipation, speak in principle and in fact of Christ's second coming and of the kingdom's coming . . . in its complete and consummate manifestation, a kingdom coming on

---

[125] Carl F. H. Henry, "Reflections on the Kingdom of God," *Journal of the Evangelical Theological Society* 35, no. 1 (1992), 42.

earth as well as existing in heaven, a kingdom temporal and historical. . . . that dwarfs all world empires.[126]

We may summarize Jesus' eschatology in this way:

(1) He envisioned two ages—this present (evil) age and the age to come of the new heaven and new earth—as comprehending the remainder of time as we know it. He said nothing about a third, intermediate period or millennial age following this age.

(2) He envisioned these two ages as consecutive—that is, they neither overlap, nor is there any indication of a gap between them, but the age to come follows immediately upon this present age.

(3) The great epochal event that terminates this age and ushers in the age to come is the glorious, visible return of Christ and its concomitant circumstances.

When Christ returns, he will resurrect the Christian dead, transform the Christian living, and catch both groups up in one body "to meet the Lord in the air" (1 Thess 4:13–18; see also 1 Cor 15:23; Phil 3:20–21; 2 Thess 1:5–10, especially v. 7); these saints then return immediately with him to earth to participate in the judgment of the resurrected and transformed wicked (1 Cor 6:2). The return of Christ, with its entailments for the church—namely, the resurrection of the dead, the last judgment, and the final state—is the focal point of New Testament eschatology, and it must be every Christian's as well. *No other problems, queries, doubts, disagreements, diversities of viewpoint, unresolved questions, or controversies respecting the relationship of other events to the advent of Christ in glory can be permitted to set this one great fact aside or blur its significance and centrality for the eschaton.* Christ is coming! And Christians will be raised from the dead or transformed (if living) to imperishability, honor, power, and immortality (1 Cor 15:42–43). Those who have this hope within them purify themselves even as they are pure (1 John 3:2–3). Such is always the byproduct of the resurrection hope!

---

[126] Ibid., 42–43.

Response by Robert L. Saucy

As an adherent of progressive dispensationalism (PD), and thus part of what is generally deemed dispensationalism, I find myself in general agreement with the basic thesis of Thomas's essay, namely that the Old Testament identity of Israel and promises given to that nation remain valid throughout the Scriptures. Thus, the church is not Israel. However, some of the distinctions between Israel and the church and the supporting biblical interpretations do raise problems.

To consider first the agreements, Thomas rightly insists and provides good biblical evidence that the promises related to the nation of Israel, beginning with God's promise to Abraham that "I will make you a great nation" and give it a land, have never been canceled or "spiritualized . . . into something else" (p. 94). His claim that PD "for the most part" denies this because of belief "in only one people of God" (p. 94), I believe, is based on a misunderstanding.[127]

Thomas's tactic of demonstrating that the New Testament does not cancel Israel's promises—by looking at all of the significant texts that might suggest that Israel's promises have been cancelled (and are often so used)—is strong. In some instances, however, especially because of his denial of a present aspect of the Davidic kingdom, the interpretation of the text cannot be followed (e.g., Acts 2 and 15). Nevertheless, overall his case is well made that the unbelieving Israel as represented by its leaders was rejected, but the promises were still valid for a future believing Israel that would come about according to the promises.

In general, the basic grammatical-historical hermeneutical principle that leads to a literal understanding, unless the context makes it obvious that the biblical writer intended to use the language metaphorically, is to be commended. However, it is difficult to follow his rejection of the general principle of Poythress that predictions in the Old Testament can be enriched in meaning by later revelation. Thomas himself states that the

---

[127] Thomas's citation from *Progressive Dispensationalism* by Blaising and Bock speaks of Gentiles sharing in "the same *blessings of the Spirit*" with Jews (that is, spiritual blessings of new covenant salvation), but it also recognizes the continued "national differences," which suggests national territories.

Abrahamic covenant "became more specific as time passed" (p. 88), which, it might be added, seems a bit contradictory to the statement that "the single grammatical-historical meaning is set by the historical context in which words are spoken, never to be changed or added to" (p. 91).

Turning to problems or disagreements, many of them are related to the denial that the present kingdom to which believers in the church are related and through which they are blessed in Christ is the promised messianic or Davidic kingdom. While the kingdom to which the church is related is not clearly stated, several comments seemed to indicate that the present church was not participating in the messianic Davidic kingdom.

To state, for example, that "after these things" (Acts 15:16) refers to after the church age, and that James uses his citation from Amos 9 to point to the future reign of Christ following this present period, is to ignore the issue of the Jerusalem council, which was not about Israel's future but the question of the present salvation of Gentiles. James uses Amos to indicate that the prophecies foretold Gentile salvation in messianic times, which had begun with the rebuilding of the house (lineage) of David, that is, the coming of Christ the Son of David.

Similarly, to understand that Peter's discussion of Christ sitting at the right hand of God in fulfillment of Ps 110:1 (Acts 2:30–36) was to assure his hearers of "a future kingdom for Israel" is again a failure to see it in context. Clearly Peter's statement about the resurrection and exaltation of Jesus was to explain the source of the amazing outpouring of the Spirit on that day. It came as a result of the exaltation of Jesus to the place of messianic authority. This does not deny a future reign of Christ in Jerusalem, but it does suggest that our relation to Christ and the blessings that we receive are from him as the Messiah of the prophesied Davidic kingdom—"the holy and sure blessings of David" (Acts 13:34).

The denial that the kingdom presently at work is the prophesied messianic kingdom is difficult to sustain biblically. Although Thomas does not explicitly identify the kingdom of the "mysteries" (Matthew 13; Mark 4; Luke 8), his discussion suggests that Jesus is no longer referring to the same prophesied messianic kingdom that he has previously proclaimed. To be sure, the mysteries point to a new revelation. But there is no evidence that Jesus is changing the identity of the kingdom to which the mysteries relate. The kingdom that operates on earth in the form of the mysteries prior to its overt manifestation in the reign of Christ from Jerusalem—the kingdom to which the present church is related—is the first phase of the Davidic messianic kingdom.

The same reality is seen in the parable of the nobleman who went to a distant country to receive a kingdom for himself (Luke 19:11–27). Clearly, the expectation of the appearance of the kingdom, which initiated Jesus' parable of the nobleman (Luke 19:11), was a reference to the prophesied messianic kingdom. Jesus' story of a nobleman going to a far county to receive a kingdom was, therefore, obviously a reference to himself going away to receive the kingship of this kingdom even as taught by Peter in Acts 2. The servants who wait for his return to execute his kingly authority on earth cannot be other than the believers of the church, who are thus related to Jesus as the messianic King of prophesied kingdom. The various references that indicate a present relationship of believers to kingdom realities (see Rom 14:17; 1 Cor 4:20; Col 1:13) must all refer to the Davidic messianic kingdom.

Another problematic issue, which seems corollary to the problem just noted, is the perspective of the nature of the messianic kingdom throughout the essay. Several comments suggest that the Davidic kingdom is essentially a theocracy, that is, a literal political reign of Christ from Jerusalem having to do primarily with Israel but extending to all nations. The disciples are said to be unable to grasp Jesus' teaching concerning his suffering because they "still expected the Davidic kingdom to be next on the agenda" (p. 100). "A literal understanding of the Davidic covenant . . . limits that kingdom to the future only" (p. 128). The Messiah "would bring worldwide blessing by some day sitting on David's throne, ruling from Jerusalem" (p. 96). No doubt this future "worldwide blessing" includes spiritual blessings similar to those enjoyed in the church today. But apparently the present spiritual blessings in the church are unrelated to the

Davidic kingdom, which seemingly demands Christ literally ruling on earth from Jerusalem.

But Scripture associates the present spiritual blessings in the
church with Jesus as the Son of David, and thus with the Davidic
covenant and kingdom. Zacharias prophesied that forgiveness of
sins that would come as a result of the "horn of salvation" raised
up "in the house of David" (Luke 1:69; see also 72). The apostles
proclaimed the salvation that came through Jesus, the descendant of David, as the promised "holy and sure blessings of David"
(Acts 13:23, 34, citing Isa 55:3). In Isa 55:3, these "sure blessings
of David" are explicitly connected to the promised new covenant,
which Thomas acknowledges is the source of the present spiritual blessings in the church. All of this suggests that blessings
of the promised Davidic kingdom are presently enjoyed in the
church.

The failure to recognize the present blessings of the church
as related to the prophesied messianic Davidic kingdom leads to
a final concern, namely, the relation of Israel and the church.
Although this is not explicitly elaborated in the essay, the emphasis on Israel as distinct from the church, and most significantly the rejection of Israel and the church as finally constituting the "one people of God," implies an exaggerated distinction
and suggests a failure to recognize the biblical mission of Israel
as a witness and light to bring God's salvation to Gentiles.

As noted above, Thomas excludes the church from participating in any fulfillment of the Davidic covenant, which focuses
on Jesus as the Davidic king. Equally telling are the comments
concerning the new covenant. The church is said to be receiving "special benefits" of the promised new covenant. But, "the
church does not represent the fulfillment of national Israel's new
covenant. . . . Only believing Israelites . . . in the future [i.e. the
millennium] can enjoy the full benefits of that covenant of which
the church has *only a taste*" (emphasis added).[128]

---

[128] Thomas appears to support his thesis that the church is not really fulfilling the
promised new covenant on the ground that that the provision of Jer 31:33b–34a concerning the law being written on the heart and the people no longer needing teachers can
only be fulfilled when Satan is bound during the 1,000-year reign. To be sure, these provisions are not presently perfect. But the citation of this passage from Jeremiah in Hebrews
8 and 10, as well as 2 Cor 3:3, suggest that the provision of writing God's *torah* on the
heart is presently true, although not yet fully manifest. Similarly, John declares that we

The New Testament manifestly teaches that Christ has inaugurated the new covenant and that the old covenant is now obsolete (Hebrews 8, 10). Moreover, Jesus declared that he would give his life for "many," which included Gentiles, and the blood of that sacrifice was the blood of the new covenant (Luke 22:20), which the church celebrates in the sacrament of the Lord's Supper (1 Cor 11:25). Paul ministered as a servant "of the new covenant" (2 Cor 3:6 NKJV).

Beyond this evidence, excluding the church from participating in promises made to Israel contradicts Paul's teaching in Eph 3:6 that Gentiles are "fellow partakers of the promise in Christ Jesus through the gospel." The "promise" mentioned is clearly a reference to "the covenants of promise," which includes the new covenant given to Israel, to which Gentiles previously were "strangers" (Eph 2:12).

This, of course, does not mean that the church is fulfilling these promised covenants in place of Israel, to whom they were promised. Nor does it mean that everything in the promises is applicable to the church. The church, for example, has no particular land as was promised to the nation of Israel. But the blessings that the church enjoys in Christ—which are essentially spiritual according to the New Testament, flow from partaking in the fulfillment of the Old Testament covenants Christ has inaugurated.

The New Testament teaching of Gentile participation in the new covenant promised to Israel is in a very real sense the teaching of the Old Testament as well. Justification by faith, which surely includes the new covenant provision of forgiveness of sins, was in the promised blessing to Abraham that all the families of the earth would be blessed in him (Gal 3:8–14; see also Rom 4:9–25). This fulfillment of the Abrahamic covenant is thus also the fulfillment of the new covenant.

The promised salvation of the nations likewise can only be understood as participation in the new covenant along with Israel.

---

have an anointing of the Spirit, who teaches us, and therefore have no need for anyone else (1 John 2:27). Again, this is not fully perfected—gifted teachers are still given to the church, but the provision has been inaugurated. Far from simply getting benefits from the new covenant or only a taste, the Christian Gentiles as well as Jews in Christ today are full participants in the salvation of the covenant.

God's salvation would go to "the ends of the earth" (Isa 49:6; see also Ps 7:2). As a result, the nations will recognize Israel's God (Ezek 36:23). They will "fear" and "worship" Yahweh (see Pss 86:9; 102:15, 22; Isa 11:10). Gentiles and Israel will worship together in Zion (Isa 2:2–3; 56:7; Jer 3:17). All of this suggests that the same salvation promised to Israel in the new covenant addressed to them was intended to go to the Gentiles as well. It might be noted in passing that the fact that it was addressed to Israel (e.g., Jer 31:31) does not mean that others were excluded from participating in it. Israel was to be the channel of God's salvation to the world, the same new covenant salvation that they received (see John 4:22: "salvation is from the Jews").

Thomas's denial of the present participation of the church in Israel's covenant promises in a partial fulfillment of those promises no doubt is connected with his rejection of the church and believing Israel of the Old Testament and the future restored Israel as being "one people of God." If the idea of "the people of God" signifies a people with whom God has established a special relation expressed through a covenant between the people and God (which I take to be the biblical meaning), then I believe there is good evidence to see all believers finally as "one people of God" through the new covenant in Christ.

The reality of Israel and Gentile believers being one as "the people of God" is manifest in Isaiah's prophecy of the messianic days when Egypt and Assyria will become "the third party" with Israel, and God will say, "Blessed be Egypt my people, Assyria my handiwork, and Israel my inheritance" (19:24–25 NIV). In addition, God's promise that through the new covenant, people would be "My people" is asserted not only in relation to Israel but also to believers in the church (2 Cor 6:16). And, finally, in the eternal state, *all people* among whom he will dwell are "His people" (Rev 21:3).

To be sure, Israel as a nation was created to serve a special purpose in God's historical plan of salvation. But the distinction of purpose does not make different peoples of God. Church elders have a different ministry than non-elders, but they are all equally the people of God.

In sum, Thomas aptly demonstrates that the concept of Israel retains its meaning throughout the Scriptures and that the promises related to that nation also remain valid and will be fulfilled. In affirming this, however, I believe that the essay errs in not realizing the union of Israel and the church in God's salvation. It fails to see that Israel was called to be a channel of salvation for the nations or Gentiles through their participation in the salvation promised in the covenants originally made with Israel (Abrahamic, Davidic, and new) and thus our present participation in the "already" aspects of those covenants as we await the "not yet" with the return of our Lord.

Response by Chad O. Brand and Tom Pratt Jr.

Robert Thomas has written an essay on the topic of Israel and the church that presents the traditional dispensational position with great clarity and without compromise. He has long been a faithful evangelical scholar who has contributed much to the church and its understanding of Scripture, and for that we are grateful. We do have several major concerns about his exposition, however.

Having first detailed the land promise to Israel in various OT texts, Thomas proceeds to what is the heart of his essay: occasions when Jesus and the apostles might have canceled out the land promise to Israel but did not. First, what should we say about the fact that Jesus did not cancel out the land promise? We actually think it would have been odd for him to have done so, even if it was clear to him that such would be the case. Though his words and actions in the early days of his ministry often did cause offense and occasionally even a riot (Luke 4:14–30; Mark 2:1–12; Mark 3:23–28), he was also careful on several occasions to instruct those who were healed not to tell anyone (Mark 1:40–44), and on other occasions he stayed out of the towns in order not to arouse opposition too early in his work (Mark 1:45). In the few months leading up to the crucifixion, he was less concerned to disguise what he was doing, especially beginning with the resurrection of Lazarus (John 11:1–44), a miracle that incited the Jews to plot his demise (John 11:45–57). Presenting a deposition on the land promise would not likely have been part of the message that burdened him in his three years or so of ministry.

Recall as well that Jesus makes few explicit claims to deity (John 8:58 being a notable exception), though he implies it in many texts (Matt 11:25–28; 21:37–38; John 3:13; 5:17–29; 6:35, 38, 46, 62; 8:12, 38; 10:7, 11, 30; 11:25; 14:6; 15:1; 16:28, etc.).[129] Many explicit statements as to his deity come in Acts, the Epistles, and Revelation (Acts 20:28; Titus 2:13; Heb 1:8; 2 Pet 1:1; 1 John 5:20; Revelation 1), and in editorial comments by John in his Gospel and from the lips of others (John 1:1, 18; 20:28). There are many other texts, of course, in various parts of the NT that imply his deity or state it in so many words. But it would be difficult to make a *certain* case for his deity if we had only his words to go by. So, the fact that Jesus had "occasions" to make some repudiation of the land claim but failed to do so does not render Thomas's point certain.

Thomas next zeroes in on the testimony of the apostles, noting the opportunities they had to repudiate the land claim but did not, citing several passages (Acts 1:6; 2:34–35; 3:23; 10:34–35; 15:16–18; Rom 1:16; 3:1–2; 9:4–5; 11:1–2, 28; 1 Cor 10:31–32; Gal 6:16). We would disagree with his interpretation of several of these texts, such as Acts 15:16–18. There James refers to the prophecy of Amos (9:14–15) where the prophet states, "I will restore the fortunes of my people Israel, and they shall rebuild the ruined cities and inhabit them; they shall plant vineyards and drink their wine, and they shall make gardens and eat their fruit. I will plant them on their land, and they shall never again be plucked up out of the land which I have given them, says the LORD your God" (RSV). Thomas interprets this, writing, "James refers to a predetermined and futuristic plan for national Israel, separate from the church." He then identifies that as the millennial kingdom, which in his view includes only Israel with Christ in the Holy Land. But why? Anthony Hoekema queries, "Why, now, should the meaning of these words be restricted to the millennium? The passage speaks of a residence of Israel in the land

---

[129] Several of his acts point to this reality, especially his healing of the blind (Mark 8:22–25; 10:46–52; John 9), as no one beside him in all Scripture ever healed a blind person.

which will last not just for a thousand years but forever."[130] We anticipate that Thomas would reply that promises made to Israel could only be fulfilled in national Israel. But that begs the question, especially in Acts 15. It sure seems as though James is applying the prophecy to the Gentile situation. James prefaces his quotation by saying, "the words of the prophets are in agreement with this" (NIV), and the "this" is that God is taking for himself people from among the Gentiles. Perhaps Richard Longenecker gets it right. First he notes that the LXX adds "the remnant of men" in this text. Then he comments, "In the end times, James is saying, God's people will consist of two concentric groups. At their core will be restored Israel (i.e., David's rebuilt tent); gathered around them will be a group of Gentiles (i.e., 'the remnant of men') who will share in the messianic blessings but will persist as Gentiles without necessarily becoming Jewish proselytes."[131] Amos, then, foresaw this inclusion of Gentiles into the covenant. We do not wish to concede Thomas's interpretation of the other texts, but we need to move quickly to our primary response.

It is curious that Thomas avoids at least one very significant text, as well as a few others. In 1 Pet 2:9, Peter states, "But you are a chosen race, a holy priesthood, a holy nation, a people for His possession, so that you may proclaim the praises of the One who called you out of darkness into His marvelous light" (HCSB). The first four phrases are quotes from Exod 19:6, the text that opens the covenant-making section of the book. It is the preamble to the Ten Commandments, and it states God's attitude toward his covenant people, Israel. But now, here, these words are spoken to a congregation, and even to the church in general. Here are words that addressed Israel originally, that now describe the Lord's churches. God had intended for all Israel to be a kind of royal priesthood, but they failed. Later, Isaiah would predict that the Servant of the Lord would complete that task: "Wake up, wake up; put on your strength, Zion! Put on your beautiful garments, Jerusalem, the Holy City! For the uncircumcised and

---

[130] Anthony Hoekema, *The Bible and the Future* (Grand Rapids: Eerdmans, 1979), 208. We do not endorse Hoekema's amillennialism but concede that he may well be correct in this assessment.

[131] Richard N. Longenecker, "The Acts of the Apostles," *The Expositor's Bible Commentary*, vol. 9, ed. Frank E. Gaebelein (Grand Rapids: Zondervan, 1981), 446.

the unclean will no longer enter you. Stand up, shake the dust off yourself! Take your seat, Jerusalem. Remove the bonds from your neck, captive Daughter of Zion" (Isa 52:1–2 HCSB). The "beautiful garments" here are priestly garments (see Lev 28:2).[132] Isaiah was looking to the postexilic condition of Judah, but as we know, they did not live up to this. The Servant who would bring about this transformation is the Lord, and that transformation is already-but-not-yet and will be finalized either in the millennium, the eternal state, or both. Peter applies this language to the church, some of the most precious language of all spoken to Israel.

Thomas argues that his approach takes Scripture literally, while other approaches do not. All evangelicals wish to take Scripture literally, but that commitment is not enough, left to itself, since taking the Bible literally can mean a variety of different things. Classical dispensationalists such as Thomas see the new covenant of Jeremiah 31 as applying to Israel and Israel only, since it is made "with the house of Israel and with the house of Judah" (Jer 31:31 HCSB). But, Luke 22:20 and Heb 8:7–12 clarify that the new covenant has been established with the church. What seems clear to us is that later covenants in Scripture take the elements of earlier covenants and rework them in terms of promise and fulfillment. This is especially the case with the new covenant in Christ. Redemption is an unfolding phenomenon in Scripture. Dispensationalists are fond of pointing out that the church era is a "parenthesis" in God's overall plan, but it would be more correct to affirm that "in God's overall plan the Mosaic law-covenant should be viewed as more of a parenthesis or something temporary, leading us to what the old covenant was ultimately pointing toward, namely the dawning of the new covenant in Christ."[133] In other words, everything in the OT points toward its fulfillment in Christ. It is not so much that the church has replaced Israel, as it is that Christ has fulfilled Israel. He is the antitype of both Adam and Israel.[134] Thomas, on the other

---

[132] J. Alec Motyer, *Isaiah: An Introduction and Commentary*, Tyndale Old Testament Commentaries, vol. 18, ed. D. J. Wiseman (Downers Grove: InterVarsity, 1999), 328.

[133] Peter J. Gentry and Stephen J. Wellum, *Kingdom through Covenant: A Biblical-Theological Understanding of the Covenants* (Wheaton: Crossway, 2012), 99.

[134] E. Earle Ellis, *Paul's Use of the Old Testament* (Grand Rapids: Baker, 1981), 134.

hand, represents what might be called a "flat" hermeneutic that does not allow for progressive revelation. What this means is that the NT interpretation of the OT supervenes on the OT itself. It has nothing to do with whether or not the OT was correct, but it has everything to do with progressive revelation in terms of the *canonical horizon* of Scripture. Richard Lints has pointed out that Scripture has three horizons: the textual, and epochal, and the canonical.[135] We begin our exploration of a text with its local and historical context. Then we proceed to examine and understand that text in its redemptive-historical epoch. But interpretation is not completed until we see the text in terms of the overall canonical situation. When we examine something like the new covenant, we have to look at it in terms of all three contexts. When we do, it becomes clear that both believing Israel and the believing church are included in this covenant. Herman Ridderbos has stated it like this: "It is on account of this fulfillment of the prophecy of the New Covenant in the Christian church that all the privileges of the Old Testament people of God in this spiritual sense pass over to the church."[136] We might state it slightly differently, since we believe that God still loves Israel, but the basic idea remains.

One final issue—Thomas makes this comment toward the end of his essay: "Revelation 21:12, 14 shows that Israel will have a role distinct from the church even in the new Jerusalem, the eternal state. As the special object of God's choice, she will ever be distinctive" (p. 135). This may be our point of greatest dispute with the form of dispensationalism represented by Thomas. We are convinced that texts such as Eph 2:14–15 obviate such notions: "For He is our peace, who made both groups one and tore down the dividing wall of hostility. In His flesh, He made of no effect the law consisting of commandments and expressed in regulations, so that He might create in Himself one new man from the two, resulting in peace" (HCSB). At this point, we think we are taking the Bible more literally than even Thomas.

---

[135] Richard Lints, *The Fabric of Theology: A Prolegomenon to Evangelical Theology* (Grand Rapids: Eerdmans, 1993), 259–311.

[136] Herman Ridderbos, *Paul: An Outline of His Theology*, trans. John Richard De Witt (Grand Rapids: Eerdmans, 1975), 336.

CHAPTER 3

The Progressive
Dispensational View

BY ROBERT L. SAUCY

The relationship of Israel and the church in progressive dispensationalism, as in other systems of theology, flows out of an understanding of the broad plan and development of God's saving activity as revealed in Scripture. With all dispensationalism, progressive dispensationalism sees a distinction between Israel and the church. But, contrary to other dispensational views, progressive dispensationalism views this distinction within the unified historical program of the *messianic* kingdom of Old Testament prophecy. That is, progressive dispensationalism sees God's present activity in and through the church as the *already* of an already-not-yet working out of messianic kingdom salvation. The *not yet* of messianic salvation will come only with the return of Christ and his righteous reign on earth, when his salvation will encompass all structures of human society and the will of God will be done on earth as it is in heaven.[1]

Specifically with regard to the relationship of Israel and the church, the position of progressive dispensationalism that will

---

[1] The completion of messianic salvation will bring the end of the salvific work of the messianic kingdom, and Christ then "hands over the kingdom to the God and Father, when He has abolished all rule and all authority and power" and "all things are subjected to Him" (1 Cor 15:24, 28). Unless noted otherwise, Scripture quotations are from the New American Standard Bible.

be briefly elaborated in this essay is broadly encapsulated in the following points: (1) Israel is to be understood throughout Scripture in its original Old Testament meaning, and its prophesied mission as a special nation in the service of God's salvation program for the world will be fulfilled in accord with the Old Testament prophecies; (2) the church represents the inauguration of the prophesied messianic salvation in which Gentiles share in God's new covenant salvation together with Jews as the people of God and the new eschatological humanity; and (3) the church as the fruit of the message of the inaugurated kingdom is essentially a spiritual community destined to live in a hostile world until the return of Christ. It continues a mission similar to Israel's as witness to God's glory in the world as ambassadors of Christ and his coming kingdom. But, it does not fulfill Israel's calling as a national witness that will be fulfilled with the coming of the Messiah, his judgment of the nations and restoration of the nation of Israel, and his kingdom reign on earth.

Hermeneutical Principles Underlying Progressive Dispensationalism[2]

Progressive dispensationalism affirms traditional historical-grammatical hermeneutics as its starting point. God gave his revelation through normal human language that is to be interpreted according to the plain meaning derived from its grammatical construction, historical context, and literary genre. As with normal human language use, the literal definition of a word is to be taken unless there is indication—usually evident—that it is intended to be understood figuratively. Whether words are understood literally or figuratively—and figurative language must convey literal meaning in order to be understood—there is one sense intended. No deeper or second meaning, such as

---

[2] For more on hermeneutics of progressive dispensationalism, see Darrell L. Bock, "Hermeneutics of Progressive Dispensationalism," in *Three Central Issues in Contemporary Dispensationalism: A Comparison of Traditional and Progressive Views*, gen. ed. Herbert W. Bateman IV (Grand Rapids: Kregel, 1999), 85–118; Paul D. Feinberg, "Hermeneutics of Discontinuity," in *Continuity and Discontinuity: Perspectives on the Relationship between the Old and New Testaments*, ed. John S. Feinberg (Westchester, IL: Crossway, 1988), 109–28.

allegorical or mystical meanings asserted by some of the Jewish and early Christian interpreters, is to be sought.

The application of normal historical-grammatical hermeneutics in relation to Scripture, however, is more complicated than with other books. For to speak of the "historical" meaning raises the question of whether the meaning in the mind of the human writer is the same as that of the divine author; if not, whose meaning is sought? There is also the question of typology that, because of the brevity of human life, does not arise in books authored solely by humans. The interpretation of Scripture, therefore, calls for further elaboration of basic grammatical-historical hermeneutics.

The Full Meaning Is Canonical

Because the Scripture is God's Word conveyed through a human author (2 Pet 1:21), a text may have a more limited meaning to the human author in his historical context than it does to the divine author. This is particularly true in the area of prediction, where the human author may know only the rudimentary meaning of a prophecy.[3] For example, the prediction that the seed of the woman would bruise the serpent on the head (Gen 3:15) no doubt meant more to the human writer and those to whom he wrote than simply the physical triumph of man over the snake. We cannot, of course, know for certain what was in the writer's mind as he was writing under the inspiration of the Spirit, but there is no evidence that he understood the full reality of his words as depicted in the New Testament picture of Christ's defeat of Satan (see Col 2:15; Rom 16:20; Heb 2:14; 1 John 3:8; Rev 12:7–9). Similarly, it is difficult to believe that the "seed" and "blessing" promised in the covenant with Abraham were understood by Abraham and his contemporaries as they are elaborated later in the Old Testament prophets and the New Testament.

In acknowledging that the meaning of the original writer was not as full or complete as later revelation, we are in a sense moving beyond the usual understanding of "historical"

---

[3] Commenting on 1 Pet 1:10–11, Peter Davids writes, "The prophets could speak about this time which they did not understand because it was 'the Spirit of Christ' who was in them giving testimony." *The First Epistle of Peter*, New International Commentary on the New Testament (Grand Rapids: Eerdmans, 1990), 61.

in historical-grammatical hermeneutics—i.e., the understanding of the human writer and his contemporaries. We could, of course, state that the full meaning was in the historical context in the mind of the divine author. But, this would surely be using *historical* in a different sense.[4]

The truth that later revelation can enrich the meaning of an earlier revelation, however, does not mean that later revelation changes or reinterprets the earlier revelation. The meaning of the early revelation may be developed by elaboration such as the fuller description of the "blessing" that would come to all the nations through Abraham's seed mentioned above. Or, later Scripture may add additional referents to the original prediction, such as the fact that Jesus of Nazareth is the seed of the woman who would defeat the serpent, Satan. In some instances, there may be multiple referents, such as the prophecies concerning the Davidic kings culminating in the Messiah, or fulfillments, as in the case of the prophecies that referred both to Israel's return from Babylon and a final future fulfillment from exile.[5] Later revelation may add details that are not even mentioned in the original prediction.

In all such instances where later revelation enlarges the meaning of the original statement, the essential meaning of the original is retained in the fuller meaning. There is an organic relationship between them. As a bud develops into a blossom and then fruit, so the meaning of the original prediction develops a fuller meaning in the later revelation. In other words, the fruit is the expression of the original genetic information of the DNA of the bud.

This is not to say that one should read the fuller New Testament revelation back into the Old Testament as if one were to attribute the full meaning of a fruit to its bud. The bud is still the bud, but even as the bud takes on greater meaning after we have seen the fruit, so the original prediction takes on fuller meaning in light of its blossom and fruit in the fulfillment of the

---

[4] On the limitation of the historical-grammatical interpretation of Scripture in light of the divine author, see Vern S. Poythress, "The Presence of God Qualifying our Notions of Grammatical-Historical Interpretation: Genesis 3:15 as a Test Case," *Journal of the Evangelical Theological Society* 50, no. 1 (March 2007): 87–103.

[5] See Jer 24:4–7; 29:10–14; Ezek 36:8–15.

New Testament. As the parts are better understood in relation to the whole, so the resultant meaning of the grammatical-historical exegesis of a text that is limited to a particular historical context is enriched by understanding it in relation to the whole of its later development in the canonical Scripture.[6] The meaning of "Jesus Loves Me," when sung as a young child, surely grows richer as the singer matures and continues to learn about God's redemptive grace through the sacrificial system of the Old Testament and Christ's ultimate sacrificial death for us.[7]

This same principle of a fuller meaning applies to type and antitype, which are analogous to promise and fulfillment.[8] Although the type retains its historical meaning, the greater reality or antitype enriches the meaning of the original type. For example, the statement of Hosea in 11:1 that "out of Egypt I called My son" (HCSB) retains its meaning as a reference to the exodus of Israel even though Matthew sees this text as *fulfilled* in Jesus' stay in Egypt (Matt 2:15). But surely the meaning of sonship and the rescue of historical Israel from Egypt gain meaning from the

---

[6] What I am espousing here is similar to the "Canonical Process Approach" of Bruce Waltke, "A Canonical Process Approach to the Psalms," in *Tradition and Testament: Essays in Honor of Charles Lee Feinberg*, ed. John S. Feinberg and Paul D. Feinberg (Chicago: Moody, 1981), 3–18; the *Sensus Plenior* understanding of Douglas Moo, "The Problem of *Sensus Plenior*," in *Hermeneutics, Authority, and Canon*, ed. D. A. Carson and John D. Woodbridge (Grand Rapids: Zondervan, 1986), 179–211; Poythress, "The Divine Meaning of Scripture," in *The Right Doctrine from the Wrong Texts?*, ed. G. K. Beale (Grand Rapids: Baker, 1994); and the "Complementary" approach of Bock, "Hermeneutics of Progressive Dispensationalism," in Bateman, *Three Central Issues*, 85–118.

[7] This example is from Poythress, "The Divine Meaning of Scripture," in Beale, *The Right Doctrine*, 101.

[8] Moo notes that one of the "basic assumptions" of typology is "that God so ordered Old Testament history that it prefigures and anticipates His climactic redemptive acts and that the New Testament is the inspired record of those redemptive acts" ("The Problem of *Sensus Plenior*," in Carson and Woodbridge, *Hermeneutics*, 198); see D. A. Carson, "Mystery and Fulfillment: Toward a More Comprehensive Paradigm of Paul's Understanding of the Old and New Testament," in *Justification and Variegated Nomism*, vol. 2, ed. D. A. Carson, Peter T. O'Brien, and Mark A. Seifrid (Grand Rapids: Baker, 2004), 404–10.

Typology had its roots already within the Old Testament as the writers recognized the repetition of divine acts and looked to similar new and ultimate acts. Thus the writers of the Old Testament could have known that some things in their writings were types. See Francis Foulkes, "The Acts of God: A Study of the Basis of Typology in the Old Testament," in Beale, *The Right Doctrine from the Wrong Texts?*, 342–71; see also Gerhard von Rad who notes that the prophets utilized the old traditions in looking for "a new David, a new Exodus, a new covenant, a new city of God: the old had thus become a type of the new and important as pointing forward to it." Gerhard von Rad, *Old Testament Theology*, vol. 2 (New York: Harper and Row, 1965), 323–24.

history of the greater Son and his divine protection in this inci-
dent. Similarly, the historical meaning of David's kingship is enhanced when we see its full meaning in the kingship of Christ.

In sum, it should be evident that the hermeneutical principle
espoused here is essentially the same as that set forth by many
other biblical interpreters. The difference in our understanding
of the relation of Israel and the church thus rests not primarily
on hermeneutical procedure but rather on our interpretation of
the New Testament explanation of the meaning of the earlier Old
Testament revelation.

Proper Interpretation Begins with the Old Testament

The Bible is the record of God's *historical* saving actions—the
story of the progressive outworking of cosmic salvation. As any
history or story is best understood by starting from the beginning,
so the Scriptures are best understood by starting with the Old
Testament. Later events and words find their meaning not only
from their contemporary context but also from the context of prior
history. As David Baker says in his summary of recent studies on
the New Testament interpretation of the Old Testament, "The historical and theological basis for the writing of the New Testament
was the Old Testament."[9] Proper interpretation thus requires that
we stand in the interpretive shoes of the New Testament writers,
who knew and believed the Old Testament.

Along with the history of people living under the old covenant, the Old Testament also contained prophetic material that
transcended the old covenant—promises of a new covenant, and
the salvation for Israel and the world that would flow from it. In
fact, the prophecies of the Old Testament extended to the same
ultimate goal of God's salvation seen in the New Testament—a
new creation including a new heavens and a new earth. When
we interpret the New Testament writings, we need to have all of
these Old Testament prophecies in mind, even as they were in
the mind of the writers of the New.

The fact that the Old Testament predictions are not all reiterated with the same prominence in the New Testament should

---

[9] David L. Baker, *Two Testaments, One Bible*, rev. ed. (Downers Grove: InterVarsity, 1991), 29.

not be taken to mean that they are no longer valid and their fulfillment is no longer to be expected. There is no reason to believe that the New Testament writers, whose hope rested on these eschatological promises, saw them as no longer valid, unless they clearly indicate that they are no longer in force or that they have been reinterpreted. In short, the Old Testament predictions of the future times of the Messiah on to the total cosmic recreation should be understood as still valid unless the New Testament positively indicates otherwise. Rather than doing so, we will see that the New Testament writers, in broad strokes, give positive evidence of their belief in the continuing validity of the Old Testament predictions.

Typology in Relation to Israel and the Church

The relation of Israel and the church often involves biblical typology,[10] which in its general meaning refers to the correspondence between an event, a person, or a thing with other events, persons, or things in biblical history.[11] As we have noted earlier, this correspondence is seen by many as a form of prophecy in which the type is divinely intended to prefigure its antitype.

Whether one thinks of Israel as a type—for Scripture never explicitly makes that identification—depends on one's concept of the relationship between a type and its antitype. If a type is understood as a *shadow* pointing forward to the *reality* of its antitype, then Israel is not a type. For it would mean, as with the sacrifices of the old covenant, that the coming of the reality in the antitype brings the type to an end.

On the other hand, if a type is more loosely defined simply as a general historical and theological correspondence, then the many analogies between Old Testament Israel and the New Testament people of God may well be explained by seeing Israel as a type without necessitating its cessation as a nation and the

---

[10] See, for example, Feinberg, "Hermeneutics of Discontinuity," in Feinberg, *Continuity and Discontinuity*, 120–23; Leonhard Goppelt, *Typos: The Typological Interpretation of the Old Testament in the New* (Grand Rapids: Eerdmans, 1982), 136–51; Mark W. Karlberg, "The Significance of Israel in Biblical Typology," *Journal of the Evangelical Theological Society* 31, no. 3 (1988): 257–69; Vern Poythress, *Understanding Dispensationalists* (Grand Rapids: Zondervan, 1987), 97–117.

[11] Feinberg, "Hermeneutics of Discontinuity," Feinberg, *Continuity and Discontinuity*, 121.

fulfillment of the promises related to its future. It would simply be saying that many things about God's activity with his Old Testament people correspond to his activity with the church (see 1 Cor 10:11). The real question is whether the Scriptures actually teach the end of Old Testament national Israel with the coming of the church.

As we will see later, a further problem with seeing the "Israel" of the prophecies as typical of the church in messianic days is that the picture of the type in the prophecies does not correspond to the antitype: the reality of Israel in the prophecies does not fit the reality of the church.

Partial Fulfillment of a Prediction Does Not Change the Meaning

Progressive dispensationalism holds, with many interpreters, that the present stage in the historical outworking of God's salvation program involves the partial fulfillment of the Old Testament messianic kingdom promises. However, the truth that the fulfillment is only partial—that is, divided between an already-not-yet time frame—does not alter the meaning of the original promise. For example, Jesus cited only part of Isaiah's prophecy of the Messiah's role (Isa 61:1–2) as fulfilled in him at the beginning of his earthly ministry. Ending with the ministry of proclaiming "the favorable year of the LORD" (Luke 4:17–19) he did not continue to cite as fulfilled the words that declared that the Messiah would also proclaim "the day of vengeance of our God" (Isa 61:2). Scripture goes on to associate the primary fulfillment of "the day of vengeance of our God" with the future coming of the Messiah, thus rendering a partial present fulfillment of Isaiah's prophecy with the complete fulfillment awaiting the future. Despite this separation that was not explicit in the original prophecy, the prophecy is fulfilled in its original meaning. (Compare also John the Baptist's prediction that the One coming would "baptize you with the Holy Spirit and fire" [Matt 3:11] which many interpreters separate as references to the soon coming of the Spirit at Pentecost and the later eschatological judgment.)

Few would dispute these examples, especially the prophecy of Isaiah. But what about prophecies that are cited as an interpretation of New Testament events when it is difficult to see how the events do, in fact, fulfill the prophecies—or at least everything mentioned in the citations, or in their original contextual meaning? An example of such is Peter's use of Joel 2:28–32 to explain the phenomena of the day of Pentecost in Acts 2:17–21. Peter's statement that "this is what was spoken of through the prophet Joel" (v. 16) clearly indicates that he understood what had just happened as a fulfillment of Joel's prophecy of the eschatological outpouring of the Spirit. But, the original prophecy of Joel is set within the broader context of Israel's restoration to the land and the eschatological judgment of the nations that oppressed Israel (see Joel 3:1–21), a context which is considerably different than that of Peter, where the nation of Israel has yet to receive its Messiah and is under the heel of a foreign nation.

A natural interpretation of both the prophecies and the events of Pentecost leads easily to the conclusion that the first part of the prophecies concerning the eschatological outpouring of the Spirit had been inaugurated (Acts 2:17–18)—messianic days had arrived. But it is difficult to see the great cosmic events described in verses 19–20 connected to the coming of the day of the Lord as fulfilled by the phenomena on Pentecost. Moreover, these same cosmic phenomena are several times associated with the return of Christ in glory with effects of dismay and fear upon the people, which are not seen at Pentecost (see Matt 24:29; Mark 13:24–25; Luke 21:25–26).

On the basis of these two facts, derived through natural interpretation, namely, that (1) the language of the prophecy is not in accord with the reality of Pentecost, and (2) the Scriptures clearly apply the same prophecy to a different situation, we conclude that these cosmic phenomena were not fulfilled at Pentecost but rather describe the awesome events associated with the future Day of the Lord, which was always impending, thus making calling on the name of the Lord for salvation urgent.

These principles utilized in the interpretation of Joel's prophecy provide the paradigm for the interpretation of all prophecies for which the New Testament gives some indication of fulfillment.

The interpreter needs to ask two questions: (1) What does the New Testament context of the prophecy clearly indicate as the fulfillment of the prophecy? Does the language explicitly state that the prophecy is completely fulfilled, or could it be understood as only a partial fulfillment? The answer to these questions is often influenced by the following question. (2) Does Scripture, including the Old Testament and the New, give clear indication of a greater future fulfillment of the same prophecy? If, in response to the first question, there is no compelling reason to insist that a prediction has been completely fulfilled, and the answer to the second question is positive—i.e., there is indication of a greater future fulfillment of the prediction—then the prophecy should be understood as presently partially fulfilled with a final fulfillment yet to come, an already-not-yet fulfillment.

The possibility of a partial fulfillment of many messianic prophecies should be expected, in that the Old Testament prophecies are generally associated simply with the coming of the Messiah, whereas their fulfillment in the New Testament clearly involves two advents. The different positions on the relationship of the church and Israel as well as many other differences in eschatology essentially relate to how the Old Testament prophecies are understood in connection with the two comings of Christ.

Progressive dispensationalism thus agrees with many others that a partial fulfillment of the messianic prophecies began with the ministry of Christ at his first coming. But, it insists that the partial fulfillment is a partial fulfillment of the normal meaning of the original prophecy. The future completion of the fulfillment is also understood to be in accord with the original meaning of the prophecy so that ultimately the prophecy is fulfilled according to its original meaning.[12]

---

[12] This is not to say that some aspects of the original prophecy may be described in terms appropriate for the understanding of the hearers of its time—e.g., wars involving horses and swords, rather than future weapons totally unknown at the time of writing. Such adaptations to the understanding of the original hearers, however, do not change the essential meaning of the original prophecy. In the case of warfare, without indication that the writer is speaking symbolically, but is rather speaking in terms of concrete realities—such as people, nations, and geographical places—the prophecy is to be understood as real warfare even though the actual weapons may be different in the future fulfillment.

Conclusion

The fundamental principle of hermeneutics underlying progressive dispensationalism's interpretation of Scripture is that all of Scripture is to be understood according to its plain meaning, derived from historical-grammatical interpretation done in consideration of its literary genre and both the divine and human authors. God intended the prophecies to convey understandable truth, even though in some instances, such as the suffering of the Messiah, the full understanding was not fully grasped until its fulfillment. Our distance from the historical context, especially the Old Testament, raises difficulty at times in discerning whether the language is to be understood literally or figuratively, or whether future scenarios are described in terms understandable to those hearing the prophecy (e.g., implements of war). But, progressive dispensationalism believes that, when interpreted on the basis of the principles above, the plain meaning of the Old Testament prophecies is retained in their New Testament fulfillments.

The Relationship of Israel and the Church in Old Testament Salvation History

The Bible is essentially the inspired record of God's salvation history in which both Israel and the church are prominent. We will, therefore, seek to understand their meaning and relationship by considering their place and significance in the historical outworking of God's saving activity.

Salvation Is Channeled through Israel

Although salvation was promised in the *protoevangelium* (Gen 3:15), and God's saving grace was active all through the time from the entrance of sin until Abraham, no plan of salvation was actually inaugurated until the call of Abraham and the covenant promises given to him. In the covenant with Abraham, God, for the first time, gave promises designed to bring salvation blessing for all mankind: "I will make you a great nation, and I will bless you, and make your name great; and so you shall be a blessing; . . . And in you all the families of the earth will be blessed" (Gen 12:2–3). Beginning with these foundational promises as elaborated in subsequent reiterations to Abraham, and his descendants, Isaac and Jacob,[13] and throughout the further revelation of God's program of salvation, we see that Israel is to serve as the channel of God's salvation to the world.

Israel's role in the Abrahamic covenant. The Abrahamic promises, including their later explications, contain three essential elements: (1) Abraham would have numerous seed (descendants), (2) these descendants would constitute a nation, and (3) blessing (salvation) would come for all the peoples of the earth. The Hebrew structure of the original promise in Gen 12:1–3 reveals that the blessings of verses 2 and 3—personal blessing for Abraham and the "great nation"—all lead to the final goal of verse 3, the blessing of all peoples.[14] In the words of William Dumbrell, "The Kingdom of God established in global terms is the goal of the Abrahamic covenant."[15] The Abrahamic covenant promise is thus the seedbed of all the remaining covenants and the kingdom program of salvation.

For our purposes, two important things should be noted in the Abraham promises. First, Abraham is going to have a seed (descendants) that will constitute a "great nation," later identified as the nation of Israel. The initial promise refers only to the "great nation" (Gen 12:2), but the term "seed" takes precedence in subsequent statements to the patriarchs, beginning with the promise of a land for Abraham's "seed" in Gen 12:7.[16] Gentiles are later included as a spiritual "seed" through their relationship with Christ, but this does not preclude the literal, physical dimension present in the promise. In the initial fulfillment, God affirms to Abraham that his seed would "come forth from [his] own body" (Gen 15:3–4). From Isaac, the descendants of Abraham are traced by physical descent through Jacob and his sons until the Seed, Jesus Christ, appears and the Gentiles are

---

[13] For reiterations and elaboration of the Abrahamic promise to Abraham, see, Gen 12:7; 13:14–17; 15:5, 12–21; 17:1–8; 22:15–18; to Isaac, Gen 26:3–5; and to Jacob, Gen 28:13–14.

[14] For the explanation of the Hebrew text, see William J. Dumbrell, *Covenant and Creation* (Nashville: Nelson, 1984), 65.

[15] Ibid., 78.

[16] References to posterity (most of which include the term *seed*) include Gen 12:7; 13:15–16; 15:5; 17:2, 5–10, 13, 16, 19–20; 18:18; 21:12; 22:17–18; 26:3–4, 24; 28:13–14; 32:12; 35:11–12; 46:3; 48:4, 16.

included in him. It is therefore impossible to ignore this physical dimension and identify Abraham's seed merely as *anyone of faith*.

This promised seed was to become a "nation," which in the Old Testament involved "the three major aspects of race, government, and territory."[17] Thus, the seed would not only be distinct physically as the literal descendants of Abraham; they would also be a nation distinct from other nations. Moreover, they would constitute a "great" nation, referring to their might and reputation in the world. In this promise that Abraham's literal descendants would become a great nation, we find the original meaning of biblical Israel. Thus, on the basis of the promise to Abraham, *Israel is an ethnic people who constitute a nation among nations that bears a unique relationship to God*—a nation created by God in fulfillment of his salvation promise.[18]

The second truth of the Abrahamic promises important to this discussion is the fact that this great nation would bring blessing to all peoples. Originally, God told Abraham, "And in you all the families of the earth will be blessed" (Gen 12:3). Later repetitions of the same universal promise to Abraham, Isaac, and Jacob, indicate that the blessing was also to come through Abraham's seed, e.g., "In your seed all the nations of the earth shall be blessed" (Gen 22:18; see 26:4; 28:14). Scripture clearly reveals that this "blessing" is nothing less than God's all-encompassing historical salvation. The seed of Abraham, i.e., the nation Israel, would somehow be a channel of that blessing to all peoples.

Israel's role in the Mosaic covenant. The mission of Abraham's seed in the service of divine salvation is further specified in God's covenant made with them at Sinai. They would be "a kingdom of priests and a holy nation" (Exod 19:6). Explaining "kingdom of priests," Martin Noth says, "Israel is to have the role of the priestly member in the number of earthly states. Israel

---

[17] Ronald E. Clements, *"gôy,"* in *Theological Dictionary of the Old Testament*, ed. G. Johannes Botterweck and Helmer Ringgren (Grand Rapids: Eerdmans, 1975), 2:428. See A. R. Hulst, *"am/gôy people,"* in *Theological Lexicon of the Old Testament* (Peabody, MA: Hendrickson, 1997), 2:910.

[18] For other evidence indicating that Israel was a "nation" or a "people" set apart from other nations, see Exod 33:13; Num 14:12; 23:9; Lev 20:26; Deut 4:34; 10:15. See also Ronald E. Clements, *Old Testament Theology: A Fresh Approach* (Atlanta: John Knox, 1978), 89; *"gôy,"* TDOT 2:427.

is to do 'service' for all the world (cf. also Isa 65:5f.); this is the purpose for which Israel has been chosen."[19]

Israel would also no longer be simply a community of people but a "holy nation," set apart from the other nations to display to the world the glory of God in a society. In the words of Dumbrell, Israel "has now been elevated into a distinct entity and endowed with special privileges. Probably then we are here . . . thinking of Israel as offering in her constitution a societary model for the world. She will provide, under the direct divine rule which the covenant contemplates, the paradigm of the theocratic rule which is to be the biblical aim for the whole world."[20]

Israel's greatness or renown among the nations would come solely because God had chosen her and brought her into covenant relationship with him. Challenging the people to obey God's instructions just prior to their entrance into the promised land, Moses declared,

> "See, I have taught you statutes and judgments just as the LORD my God commanded me, that you should do thus in the land where you are entering to possess it. So keep and do them, for that is your wisdom and your understanding in the sight of the peoples who will hear all these statutes and say, 'Surely this great nation is a wise and understanding people.' For what great nation is there that has a god so near to it as is the LORD our God whenever we call on Him? Or what great nation is there that has statutes and judgments as righteous as this whole law which I am setting before you today?" (Deut 4:5–8)

The greatness of the nation would come from their display of wisdom and understanding in life, which comes from obedience to the law. In sum, Israel is destined to be a "great nation" in

---

[19] Martin Noth, *Exodus* (Philadelphia: Westminster, 1962), 157. Similarly, Brevard Childs says, "Israel as a people is also dedicated to God's service among the nations as priests function with a society." Childs, *The Book of Exodus* (Philadelphia: Westminster, 1974), 367.

[20] Dumbrell, *Covenant and Creation*, 87. John I. Durham similarly says, "As a 'holy people' . . . they are to be a people set apart, different from all other people by what they are and are becoming—a display-people, a showcase to the world of how being in covenant with Yahweh changes a people." Durham, *Exodus*, Word Biblical Commentary, vol. 3 (Waco, TX: Word, 1987), 263.

comparison to all the other nations of the world because Yahweh is Israel's God and he intends to reveal his greatness to the world through her.

The constituting of the seed of Abraham into a great nation through the Mosaic covenant confirms what was previously said concerning the meaning and identity of Israel. The name "Israel" first appears in Scripture as a renaming of Jacob (Gen 32:28). At the establishing of the covenant, the people of the "holy nation" are identified as "the house of Jacob" or "the sons of Israel" (Exod 19:1, 3), clearly linking them physically to Abraham through Jacob.

Although with the division of the kingdom, Israel became the designation of the northern kingdom of the ten tribes in distinction from the southern kingdom of "Judah" (which included Benjamin), the majority of the references to "Israel" in the Old Testament refer to the comprehensive people of God, "identified by that name since their sojourn in Egypt."[21] It was possible for someone who was not in the physical lineage of Abraham through Jacob to become part of Israel as a proselyte. But, the physical element is never lost in favor of a purely religious definition of Israel. Jakob Jocz accurately expresses the evidence of the Old Testament: "What divides Israel from the rest of humanity is not entirely physical, and is not entirely spiritual, but a combination of both. The physical and the spiritual are never separate entities."[22]

The concept of Israel as a national entity also involved territory or a land. This is evident immediately with the promise to Abraham of a land for his descendants (Gen 12:7; 15:18–21). The importance of a land to the concept of Israel is expressed by Walther Zimmerli: "The land in Old Testament faith is not something indifferent that could just as well be as not be. It is something that belongs to the complete relation of God to Israel. . . . It is the sign of the confirmation of God's love for Israel and of Israel's belonging to God."[23]

---

[21] H. J. Zobel, "*yiśrā'ēl*," in *Theological Dictionary of the Old Testament*, 6:404.

[22] Jakob Jocz, *A Theology of Election* (New York: Macmillan, 1958), 65.

[23] Walther Zimmerli, *The Old Testament and the World* (Atlanta: John Knox, 1976), 77; see Magnus Ottosson, "*erets*," in *Theological Dictionary of the Old Testament*, 1:403.

The full meaning of "Israel" in the Old Testament thus includes: (1) a people who are physically descended from Abraham
through Jacob, (2) who form a national entity set apart from the
other nations of the world, (3) who occupy a territory as other
nations, and (4) whose total existence is determined by their covenantal relationship to God.

With the demise of Israel's kingdom or nationhood that began with the fall of the northern kingdom, Israel became more
of an "ideal entity"—i.e., Israel conceived in its perfection—that
was instantiated in Judah and then in the exilic and postexilic
Jewish communities. But, this should not be understood as elim-
inating the concept of nationhood and its accompanying territorial dimension from the meaning of "Israel." When the people of
Israel no longer exist as a nation, or are scattered among other
nations, they are no longer fully Israel, but their hope, fed by past
promises and prophecies of Israel's future, is for ideal Israel to
again be fully instantiated in a restored national existence.

Israel's future role according to Old Testament prophecy. It
should not be surprising that the role of Israel as the channel of
God's salvation to the world is most prominent in the prophecies of the time of the Messiah—the day of salvation, which all
Scripture anticipates.[24] Interestingly, these prophecies, for the
most part, were written during the time of Israel's failure to live
up to her covenant obligations with the resultant demise of her
theocratic kingdom and status as a "great nation" (eight to fifth
centuries BC).

Israel's mission to the nations is especially conspicuous in
Isaiah's prophecies related to the Servant of the Lord. While the
identity of the servant is a fluid concept, sometimes referring to
the nation of Israel or a godly remnant of it and sometimes to an
individual who is best seen as the Messiah, Isaiah makes it clear
that the nation is involved in the mission of the Servant. The first
mention of "servant" clearly applies to the nation—"But you,
Israel, My servant" (Isa 41:8)—as do many other references (see
42:19; 43:10; 44:1–2; 45:4; 48:20; see also Ps 137:22; Jer 30:10).
In the passages where the Servant is the Savior who brings salvation to all, including the nation of Israel through his atoning

---

[24] See Gen 49:18; Isa 25:9; 49:8; 61:2; Luke 1:68–77; 2:30; 2 Cor 6:2.

work, the reference is obviously to a special individual distinct from the nation of Israel, i.e., the Messiah (see Isa 42:1–9; 49:1–9a; 50:4–11; 52:13–53:12). But, in these passages, there are also descriptions of the servant's ministry, in which Israel shares as a nation. Twice the servant is assigned the task of being "a light to the nations" (42:6; 49:6). While the reference in both passages is probably to an individual messianic Servant, in 49:3 the Lord addresses him with the words, "You are My Servant, Israel." Instead of understanding this as an indication that the Messiah would replace the nation of Israel in its mission of service to the world, the reference is to a Person who would be, in a sense, the ideal Israel who would enable Israel to fulfill its mission.[25]

Thus, while certain saving functions of the Servant can only be properly applied to the individual messianic Servant, there is an interrelationship between the mission of the messianic Servant and Israel as the servant in terms of being a light to the nations. As H. H. Rowley explains, "While the mission will be peculiarly fulfilled in one, it is nevertheless the mission to which all are called, and all should enter in some measure into it."[26]

Isaiah's affirmation of the ministry of Israel following the servant passages confirms the participation of the nation in the Servant's ministry. In the context of Israel's restoration (Isa 51:1–3), God calls out, "Listen to me, my people; hear me, my nation: The law will go out from me; my justice will become a light to the nations . . . my arm will bring justice to the nations. The islands will look to me and wait in hope for my arm" (vv. 4–5 NIV). The agent of this action is the Lord himself. But, the close connection to the restoration of Israel and the description of Israel as "you who know righteousness, a people in whose heart is My law" (v. 7), together with Isaiah's earlier statement that "the law will go out from Zion" (2:3 NIV), shows that Israel is involved as God's minister in bringing salvation to the nations.

---

[25] John N. Oswalt, *The Book of Isaiah: Chapters 40–66* (Grand Rapids: Eerdmans, 1998), 291.

[26] H. H. Rowley, "The Meaning of Sacrifice in the Old Testament," *Bulletin of the John Rylands Library*, XXXIII (September 1950), 108–9; see also John Bright, "Faith and Destiny," *Interpretation* 5, no. 1 (January 1951): 24.

Again, after telling a restored Israel that the glory of the Lord "will appear upon you," Isaiah declares, "Nations will come to your light, and kings to the brightness of your rising" (Isa 60:1–3; see also 55:4–5). Similarly, referring to the redemption of Israel, the prophet declares, "The LORD has bared His holy arm in the sight of all the nations, that all the ends of the earth may see the salvation of our God" (Isa 52:10). Far from giving up on sinful Israel and seeing the individual messianic Servant fulfill the nation's role as the channel of salvation to the nations, Isaiah's prophecies declare that Israel, once redeemed through the work of the messianic Servant, will finally fulfill her original calling as a nation.[27]

This final eschatological salvation of the nations will come with the manifestation of God's glory for all the earth to see. This radiation of God's glory to the nations is destined to be displayed particularly through Israel. As Christopher North says, commenting on God's declaration, "I have created [them] for My glory" (Isa 43:7), "Israel, ransomed and restored, is the final evidence of the majesty which all mankind is to see . . . and acclaim."[28] The prophet Zechariah declares of eschatological Jerusalem, "I will be the glory in her midst. . . . Sing for joy and be glad, O daughter of Zion; for behold I am coming and I will dwell in your midst . . . . Many nations will join themselves to the LORD in that day and will become My people" (Zech 2:5, 10–11).

Israel as the channel of God's salvation to the nations is also significant in the book of Psalms: "God be gracious to us and bless us, And cause His face to shine upon us—that Your way may be known on the earth, Your salvation among all nations. . . . God blesses us, that all the ends of the earth may fear Him" (Ps 67:1–2, 7 NASB; see also Pss 98:1–3; 102:13–16). As one Jewish commentator explains, "Israel's blessing is to be a blessing for all men. . . . if Israel has the light of God's face, the world cannot remain in darkness."[29]

---

[27] John Oswalt, *The Book of Isaiah: Chapters 1–39* (Grand Rapids: Eerdmans, 1986), 52.

[28] Christopher R. North, *The Second Isaiah* (Oxford: Clarendon Press, 1964), 121.

[29] I. Abrahams, *Annotations to the Hebrew Prayer Book, Pharisaism and the Gospels,* cited in A. Cohen, *The Psalms: Hebrew Text, English Translation and Commentary* (Hindhead, UK: Soncino, 1945), 2–7.

Israel was called to function as a channel of God's salvation to the nations by being a lighthouse of divine revelation through the special revelation in the Scriptures (Ps 147:19–20; see Rom 3:2) and life as a "holy nation," but also through God's revelation of himself in his historical activity with that nation, both in judgment and blessing, as he has done in the past. Above all, the regathering of the people of Israel and their restoration to the land as a blessed and prosperous nation—a regathering that entails God's judgment against the nations who have scorned and persecuted Israel's people—will be an undeniable manifestation of God, both to Israel (Ezek 34:30; 36:38; 37:14; 39:22, 28–29) and to the nations of the world (20:41; 28:25; 36:22–23, 36; 37:28; 39:21–23, 27–28). The psalmist expresses the same truth in his anticipation of the day when God will "have compassion on Zion . . . [and] be gracious to her," and as a result "the nations will fear the name of the LORD and all the kings of the earth Your glory" (102:13, 15).[30]

This theme of the Old Testament prophetic tradition—for which many other texts could be adduced—is well summed up in the words of H.–J. Kraus: "*God reveals his sovereignty, which brings salvation, through the act of bringing Israel back from its captivity and gathering his people together.* In this final act of liberation the saving might of God is manifest to all the world."[31]

The nature of the promised salvation channeled through Israel. An important factor in the question of whether the church fulfills Israel's prophesied role is the nature of the promised salvation. For the Old Testament prophets and in fact all of Scripture, biblical salvation is more than the gift of eternal life and the deliverance of the individual from the effects of sin. It is the holistic salvation of history—a salvation that restores the order of creation. Specifically related to humanity, salvation

---

[30] The restoration of Israel is not only a manifestation before the world of God's saving power but also an event necessary to preserve his holy nature as the God of Israel (cf. Ezek 36:20–22).

[31] H.-J. Kraus, *The People of God in the Old Testament* (New York: Association Press, 1958), 77. Robert Martin-Achard similarly says, "The final result of the restoration of Israel is the encounter between Yahweh and the nations. . . . *It is by granting life to His People that Yahweh makes it the light of the world.*" *A Light to the Nations: A Study of the Old Testament Conception of Israel's Mission to the World* (Edinburgh: Oliver and Boyd, 1962), 30–31.

meant the restoration (or recreation) of true human community, in which all of life, including all of the structures of society, was lived totally under the beneficent rule of God. Israel, through its covenant relationship with God, was called to be the vanguard of this salvation for all nations. Commenting on God's exhortation to his Old Testament people in Amos—"Let justice roll down like waters and righteousness like an ever-flowing stream" (5:24)—Kraus explains, "Justice and righteousness . . . are the foundations, the basic ordinances for the life of Israel. . . . Israel has been chosen to live according to the law of God, that is to say, to live under the sovereignty of God, as sovereignty that is *intended to cover every aspect of the whole of life.*"[32]

The salvation of the coming messianic days thus entailed the inward transformation of the individual, which would result from a promised making of a "new covenant" (see also "covenant of peace" and "everlasting covenant," Ezek 37:26), through which the people would receive a new heart and spirit in order to live out God's instructions (Jer 31:31–33; Ezek 36:25–29; 37:12–14, 20–27). But, it also included, as a result of this inward salvation, an outward salvation of humanity's social structures—socio-economic-political righteousness and international peace. This fullness of the promised salvation awaits the return of the Messiah, when the governments of this world will be replaced with his righteous reign.

Salvation includes the nations (Gentiles). The salvation of the nations is especially prominent in the promises related to the future messianic times. But, how is this Gentile salvation related to the nation of Israel and the promises of her own salvation? And, when is the salvation of the Gentiles to take place according to the Old Testament prophecies?

The salvation of the Gentiles in relation to Israel. God's salvation program is carried out through history on the basis of covenants with his people. But, no salvation covenant is ever expressly made with Gentiles—the covenant with Noah was preservative but contained no provision for bringing about final salvation. The apostle Paul confirms this in the New Testament, declaring that the covenants and promises belong to Israelites,

---

[32] Kraus, *The People of God in the Old Testament*, 170 (emphasis added).

his "kinsmen according to the flesh" (Rom 9:3), and that Gentiles, prior to their salvation in Christ, were "strangers to the covenants of promise" (Eph 2:12).

Nevertheless, the prophecies concerning Gentile salvation make it clear that the same salvation that Israel knows will be known among the nations (e.g., Pss 67:2; 117). The nations will "fear" and "worship" Yahweh, Israel's God, who has now made himself the God of the nations as well (e.g., Pss 86:9; 102:15, 22; Isa 11:10; Jer 3:17; Ezek 36:23; Zeph 2:9; 3:9). They will do so together at Jerusalem (Isa 56:7; Jer 3:17). "Justice" and "peace," the fruit of salvation, will be brought to the nations (Zech 9:9; see Isa 2:2–4; Mic 4:1–3). Both Israel and the nations will have a relationship with the same God.

As a result, the nations will be called by the same special names that were previously reserved for God's chosen covenant people Israel (see Isa 19:25, "Blessed is Egypt My people, and Assyria the work of My hands, and Israel My inheritance"; see also Zech 2:10). The hope of Old Testament prophecy is expressed in Solomon's prayer "that all the peoples of the earth may know Your name, to fear You, as do Your people Israel" (1 Kgs 8:43; see Ps 145:7, 11–13; Isa 45:18–25; 55:4–7; Jer 16:19).

The Old Testament never speaks of God making the "new covenant" with the Gentiles as he does with Israel (see Jer 31:31; 32:36–40). But, the above evidence of Gentile salvation clearly suggests that, already in the Old Testament, the Gentiles are promised participation along with Israel in the eschatological salvation of the new covenant. This reality is buttressed by the fact that the new covenant is simply the culmination of the salvation promises to Abraham and David,[33] both of which contained explicit reference to the "blessing" of the nations through their descendants (see Gen 12:3; 22:18; Ps 72:17). Moreover, the final goal of the new covenant to bring the people into a familial relationship with God—"I will be their God, and they shall be My people" (Jer 31:33)—is enjoyed by Gentile nations as well as by the nation of Israel.

---

[33] Walter Kaiser, *Toward an Old Testament Theology* (Grand Rapids: Zondervan, 1978), 234. See also George N. H. Peters, *The Theocratic Kingdom*, 3 vols. (Grand Rapids: Kregel, 1957), 1:322.

There is no evidence, however, that in participating in the salvation covenants of Israel the nations become part of Israel or a "new Israel" composed of Jews and Gentiles. In the covenant with Abraham, all the families of the earth are to be blessed, with no indication that this blessing came through becoming part of the "great nation," i.e., Israel. Throughout all of the Old Testament, Israel is referred to as a nation (see Gen 12:2; 17:5; 18:18; Exod 19:6; 33:13; Deut 4:34; 10:15; 26:5; Ps 33:12; Jer 31:36; Ezek 37:22), and even as a nation preeminent among the nations (Deut 26:19; 28:12–13; Jer 31:7: Zeph 3:20). All of this makes it impossible to see "Israel" as simply the people of God from all nations. This conclusion is further confirmed by the reference mentioned earlier, in which Egypt and Assyria are called God's people and yet remain distinct from the nation of Israel, as Isaiah's words indicate: "In that day Israel will be the third party with Egypt and Assyria" (Isa 19:24).

That some texts speak of Gentiles joining themselves to Israel as aliens and participating in the worship of God at Jerusalem should not be surprising, given the fact that a glorious restored Jerusalem in Israel is the center of the prophesied messianic kingdom (e.g., Isa 14:1; 65:3–7). But, there is nothing in these references that indicates that such joining to the nation of Israel is the way of all Gentile salvation.

In sum, the Old Testament teaches that the Gentiles participate in the salvation covenants made with Israel and thus become related to God as his people, even as Israel. But, they do so as Gentiles alongside Israel, not by becoming Israel. There is simply no teaching in the Old Testament that all of God's people are finally "Israel."

The time of Gentile salvation. The primary teaching of Old Testament prophecy is that God's salvation is extended to the nations through his historical manifestation in the restoration of Israel. But, there is also a picture—minor in comparison—of salvation going to the nations when Israel is in rebellion against God. In Deut 32:1–43, which is traditionally taken as a summary of Israel's history from inception until the end of days, God predicts the final salvation of Israel and the nations rejoicing in it along with Israel (vv. 36–43). Prior to that, however, there is another scenario in which Israel is unfaithful and God responds by turning to the Gentiles: "They have made Me jealous with what is not God; They have provoked Me to anger with their idols. So I will make them jealous with those who are not a people; I will provoke them to anger with a foolish nation" (v. 21).[34] According to Paul's use of this text, this would involve the jealously of anger over seeing God bestow blessing on those other than themselves, as illustrated in the jealous anger over the success of the apostle's ministry among the Gentiles in Pisidian Antioch and Thessalonica (Acts 13:45; 17:5).[35] But, the blessing of Gentiles would also lead to a jealousy of emulation on the part of some of Israel as they saw the blessing of their own covenants experienced by the Gentiles apart from them (Rom 11:11, 14).

God's words through the prophet Isaiah also look to the extension of God's salvation to the Gentiles while Israel is in disobedience: "I was ready to be sought by those who did not ask for me; I was ready to be found by those who did not seek me. I said, 'Here am I, here am I,' to a nation that was not called by my name" (Isa 65:1 ESV). Most modern commentators understand this verse to refer to God's gracious manifestation of himself to a rebellious Israel. But, some, along with the older interpreters including Luther[36] and Calvin,[37] see it as a reference to God extending his salvation to Gentiles.

In support of this latter view, Derek Kidner and others note that the Hebrew construction of the verbs translated "ready to be sought" and "ready to be found" refer to actual events. That is, God's *permitting himself to be sought and found* by the people does not simply refer to an attitude of grace on God's part but also the result of his action in *the people actually seeking*

---

[34] For the view that this refers to eschatological times and not some historical enemies of Israel God would use to judge Israel, see Eugene H. Merrill, *Deuteronomy*, The New American Commentary, vol. 4 (Nashville: B&H, 1994), 418n25.

[35] This same jealousy is expressed against Jesus (Mark 15:10) and the apostles ministering among Jewish people (Acts 5:17). It was, therefore, in essence, a jealousy of God's blessing going to those whom the Jewish religious leaders felt were undeserving compared to them.

[36] Martin Luther, *Luther's Works*, vol. 17: *Lectures on Isaiah chs. 40–66* (St. Louis: Concordia, 1972), 375–77.

[37] John Calvin, *Commentary on the Book of the Prophet Isaiah* (Grand Rapids: Eerdmans, 1948), 4:377–80.

and finding God[38]—thus the translation in the recent Holman Christian Standard Bible: "I *was sought* by those who did not ask; I *was found* by those who did not seek Me" (emphasis added). Moreover, the description of those to whom God presented himself according to the Hebrew text is "a nation that was not called by my name" (ASV, ESV, HCSB, KJV, NKJV) rather than "a nation that did not call on my name"—the reading of the ancient versions followed by most modern versions (see 63:19). Nowhere else is Israel said to be a nation not known as God's people. The description is thus best applied to Gentile nations to whom God would extend his salvation blessings when Israel was in rebellion.[39]

If we are correct in seeing this as a reference to Gentile salvation, then this takes place while Israel is in rebellion, as the context immediately following suggests (see vv. 2–3, "I have spread out My hands all day long to a rebellious people . . . a people who continually provoke Me to My face"), and as the apostle Paul clearly applies Isaiah's text to his own time, when the majority of Israel is in disbelief and salvation is going to the Gentiles (Rom 10:20–21).

Finally, we might note Mal 1:11, where, in the midst of expressing his displeasure with the impure and hypocritical offerings of Israel's present priests, God says, "For from the rising of the sun even to its setting, My name will be great among the nations, and in every place incense is going to be offered to My name, and a grain offering that is pure; for My name will be great among the nations." As Malachi later predicts the restoration of Israel (see 3:1–4:6), this earlier reference to God's name becoming great among the nations probably refers to God's salvation going to the Gentiles while Israel represented by her priests is in disobedience—i.e., a future "reception of the heathen into the

---

[38] Derek Kidner, "Isaiah," in *New Bible Commentary*, 3rd ed., ed. Donald Guthrie and J. A. Motyer (Leicester, UK: InterVarsity, 1970), 624.

[39] For similar understanding of the reference as referring to Gentiles, see Geoffrey W. Grogan, "Isaiah," in *The Expositor's Bible Commentary*, vol. 6, ed. Frank E. Gaebelein (Grand Rapids: Zondervan, 1986), 349; Edward J. Young, *The Book of Isaiah*, vol. 3 (Grand Rapids: Eerdmans, 1972), 502; Carl Wilhelm Eduard Nägelsbach, "The Prophet Isaiah," in *Lange's Commentary on the Holy Scriptures*, vol. 11 (repr., Grand Rapids: Zondervan, 1960), 689; Joseph Addison Alexander, *Isaiah, Translated and Explained*, abr. ed. (1867; repr., Minneapolis: Klock & Klock, 1981), 413.

kingdom of God in the place of Israel which would be rejected for a time."[40] Since Israel's restoration is always final according to the prophecies, this salvation of the Gentiles during Israel's disobedience must precede the dominant picture of Gentile salvation subsequent to Israel's restoration. This is also the understanding of the apostle Paul, as he sees his Gentile mission, foretold in the Deuteronomy and Isaiah Scriptures noted above, as taking place before the restoration of Israel (see Rom 10:19–21; 11:11, 14).

Summary characteristics of the Old Testament prophetic hope. In summary it will be helpful to briefly note several important characteristics of the Old Testament hope. First, the salvation covenant promises depict a comprehensive holistic salvation encompassing all things spiritual and material. All aspects of human life—the personal, inward, and individualistic, as well as the social, communal, and international—are part of the prophetic picture. It is difficult to conceive of any aspect of God's salvation portrayed in the New Testament that is not already seen in the Old Testament hope.

Second, there is no final fulfillment of any of the salvation covenant promises. The promise of a holy nation, Israel's possession of the land, the righteous rule of the seed of David, and the worldwide blessing of salvation for Israel and the nations, all remain an unfilled hope in Old Testament history. Third, the prophetic hope looked forward to a real historical fulfillment of the covenant promises, or as Walther Eichrodt puts it, the prophets made "*a real entry of God into history* the centre of their belief" so that "the hoped-for consummation and the national community in its concrete earthly actuality" were related and the "Israelite hope remained loyal to this earth."[41]

While we look to the New Testament for the authoritative understanding of the fulfillment of this Old Testament hope, we

---

[40] Carl Friedrich Keil, *Biblical Commentary on the Old Testament: The Twelve Minor Prophets* (Grand Rapids: Eerdmans, 1949), 2:437. See also E. Ray Clendenen, "Malachi," in Richard A. Taylor and E. Ray Clendenen, *Haggai, Malachi*, The New American Commentary, vol. 21A (Nashville: Broadman & Holman, 2004), 277–78); and Peter A. Verhoef, *The Books of Haggai and Malachi* (Grand Rapids: Eerdmans, 1987), 231.

[41] Walther Eichrodt, *Theology of the Old Testament*, vol. 1 (Philadelphia: Westminster, 1961), 490–91.

cannot set aside this picture of the Old Testament prophecies and their prior understanding by God's people as irrelevant.

The Relation of Israel and the Gentiles in the New Testament Salvation History

The New Testament writers saw the coming of Christ and his work as the fulfillment of the Old Testament covenant promises. They consistently supported their teaching by reference to the Old Testament. The question of the relationship of Israel and the church thus rests on how one understands the New Testament use of the Old Testament prophecies. Do the New Testament writers see the fulfillment in Christ as entailing a reinterpretation of the Old Testament promises and hope? Or, do they see the relationship of Israel and the church as the fulfillment of the Old Testament prophecies concerning Israel and the salvation of the Gentiles fundamentally as these prophecies were understood by the Old Testament people of God?

The Fulfillment of the Salvation Promises "in Christ"

It is acknowledged at the outset that all of the Old Testament salvation covenants are fulfilled in Christ. He is the ultimate promised "seed," in which all salvation is accomplished. With Christ, we have reached the "last days" of history. In him, we have come to the heavenly Jerusalem (Heb 12:22), the eternal "new Jerusalem" (Rev 21:2, 10). These truths, however, do not dissolve the meaning of the salvation promises into the person of Christ, nor preclude all other human ministry in salvation history.

Even as Christ's fulfillment of the salvation covenants does not negate the present priestly ministry of the church in the service of God's salvation, so his fulfillment of the promises does not deny a future ministry of Israel in that same service. Moreover, it should be noted that our coming to God's final eschatological salvation in Christ did not yet bring either the end of history or our personal perfection. As the final salvation of Christ is progressively being fulfilled in the case of our individual salvation, so it is progressively fulfilled in salvation history. Thus the fulfillment of the prophecies in Christ does not deny a place or time for Israel's participation in that fulfillment in Christ.

The Inauguration of Messianic Salvation

The New Testament opens with the announcement that the time of fulfillment of the salvation covenant promises is at hand. The proclamation of the drawing near of the prophesied kingdom by John the Baptist and Jesus (Matt 3:2; 4:17) was made without elaboration, no doubt on the assumption that the hearers would recognize it as the fulfillment of the messianic prophecies contained in their Scriptures. This is evident also in prophetic messages surrounding these new events. Zacharias declares that God "has visited us and accomplished redemption for His people, and has raised up a horn of salvation for us in the house of David His servant—as He spoke by the mouth of His holy prophets from of old" (Luke 1:68–70; see 1:46–55). In accord with the Old Testament, this salvation is comprehensive involving outward political freedom from the yoke of enemies and inner spiritual transformation (see Luke 1:71–79).

Also in agreement with the Old Testament, this messianic salvation would entail both the restoration of Israel and the salvation of the Gentiles. In a virtual repetition of the promise to David, the angel announced to Mary concerning her son, "the Lord God will give Him the throne of His father David; and He will reign over the house of Jacob forever, and His kingdom will have no end" (Luke 1:32–33; see 2 Sam 7:16). Later, Mary proclaimed that God "has given help to Israel His servant, in remembrance of His mercy, as He spoke to our fathers, to Abraham and his descendants forever" (Luke 1:54).

Jesus would also bring salvation for the nations or Gentiles. The aged Simeon, addressing God while holding the infant Jesus, declares, "my eyes have seen Your salvation, which You have prepared in the presence of all peoples, a light of revelation to the Gentiles, and the glory of Your people Israel" (Luke 2:30–32). Isaiah's prophecy that "all flesh will see the salvation of God" is now being fulfilled with the coming of the Messiah (Luke 3:6; Isa 40:5; on the salvation for Gentiles, see also Matt 12:18, 21).

Jesus' ministry focused on the people of Israel in accord with the prominent picture of Old Testament prophecy—the salvation of the Messiah would come first to restore Israel and then go out to the nations (see Matt 10:5–7; 15:24). But, the rejection of Jesus as the Messiah by the Jewish leaders representing the nation resulted in the failure of the prophesied restoration and brought judgment instead. Jesus' lament over Jerusalem epitomizes this tragic turn of events: "Jerusalem, Jerusalem. . . . How often I wanted to gather your children together, the way a hen gathers her chicks under her wings, and you were unwilling. Behold, your house is being left to you desolate! For I say to you, from now on you will not see Me until you say, 'Blessed is He who comes in the name of the LORD!'" (Matt 23:37–39; see 21:33–43). But, as implied in the last part of this Scripture, this situation of judgment for Israel would be temporary even as the Old Testament consistently predicted.[42] This is confirmed by other New Testament Scriptures, which we will look at later.

The rejection of Christ by his people Israel, and in reality also by the Gentiles (Acts 4:27), did not thwart God's plan of salvation. Instead, the cross and resurrection of Christ were the climactic saving activity of God that brought to reality the promised eschatological salvation. Through his obedient death as our substitute/representative, Jesus accomplished salvation and was exalted as Lord over all, installed at the right hand of God as the Messiah (Acts 2:30–36; see Phil 2:8–11). In Christ, the salvation of the prophesied new covenant that would ultimately make all things new was inaugurated.

The Present Salvation for Jew and Gentile

The beginning era of eschatological salvation is characterized by salvation going to only a remnant of Israel, along with Gentiles, while the nation continues under domination of Gentile powers. As we saw previously, this scenario of God's salvation going to the Gentiles when Israel as a nation was in disobedience was predicted in the Old Testament. In the face of his rejection by Israel, Jesus also increasingly foretold the same message: Israel

---

[42] G. R. Beasley-Murray, *Jesus and the Kingdom of God* (Grand Rapids: Eerdmans, 1986), 306–7. Jesus' prediction that his disciples would, in the future, exercise rulership over the tribes of Israel also supports Israel's future restoration (Matt 19:28; Luke 22:30).

would experience God's judgment while his salvation would go out to the Gentiles (see Matt 8:11–12=Luke 13:28–29; Matt 22:1–14=Luke 14:16–24; Matt 21:33–43; 24:2; Luke 21:24). *Salvation goes to a Jewish remnant.* Despite the rejection of Jesus by Israel as a nation, the new covenant eschatological salvation went first to the people of Israel. Following the plan set by Jesus, the witness of the disciples began in Jerusalem and from there extended to all Judea, Samaria, and the remotest parts of the earth. Like Jesus during the last week of his ministry, the apostles proclaimed salvation at the temple mount in Jerusalem, the center of Jewish religious authority (Acts 3:11–26; 5:12, 21–26, 42). For as many as ten years[43] the followers of Jesus proclaimed the new messianic salvation among the Jews only. While Israel as a nation represented by its leaders rejected the message, thousands of Jews in Jerusalem and surrounding Jewish areas welcomed it. Thus, the new eschatological community of God's people, Christ's *ekklēsia* (Matt 16:18) began with Jewish people and, for a considerable time, was essentially constituted by Jews.

The new community of Jewish believers, with its foundation of the twelve apostles, represents a connection with the Old Testament people of God. But, they did not constitute the promised eschatological restoration of Israel as a nation, or a "new Israel." Rather, these Jewish participants in the new messianic salvation represent the believing remnant of Israel, or the Israel that continues to experience the "rich root" of God's salvation in Paul's metaphor of the olive tree, while the majority of Israel is presently cut off (see Rom 11:5, 17). They are the remnant Israel that has transitioned into the new age of the messianic salvation. The twelve apostles are central in this transition. Even as Jesus ministered especially to Israel, seeking its restoration, so his authoritative delegates minister especially to Israel. Centered in Jerusalem, they play the leading role in the beginning of the new community of the new covenant salvation. At least as far as

---

[43] See dating in Harold W. Hoehner, *Chronology of the Apostolic Age* (ThD diss., Dallas Theological Seminary, 1965), 381; and, F. F. Bruce, *The Acts of the Apostles*, 3rd ed. (Grand Rapids: Eerdmans, 1990), 92, 252.

the historical record of Acts, as soon as the Gentile mission is established, the Twelve largely fade from the scene.[44]

But, Scripture makes it clear that this believing remnant of Israel, including the Twelve, is not now the only Israel. The apostle Paul anticipates the day when the "natural branches," representing the Israel that is now experiencing the hardening judgment of God, will one day be grafted back into what he calls *"their own* olive tree" (Rom 11:24, emphasis added). Then "all Israel," or Israel as a whole in distinction from the present remnant, will experience God's salvation and consequent restoration in fulfillment of the historic covenants and promises given to them (Rom 11:25–31; cf. 9:4–5).

Salvation extends to the Gentiles. Through the immediate intervention of divine revelation to the Roman centurion Cornelius and to the Jewish apostle Peter, the new messianic salvation expanded beyond the initial Jewish community. This was initially perplexing for many Jewish believers. The disconcerting element was not that Gentles could be saved, but that God had given the same new covenant salvation to the Gentiles as Gentiles and not through becoming in some way part of Israel. There was no difference in status before God. As if this was something of a new realization to him, Peter's first words to the gathering in the house of Cornelius were, "I most certainly understand now that God is not one to show partiality, but in every nation the man who fears Him and does what is right is welcome to Him" (Acts 10:34–35; see Acts 11:17–18).

There is no indication in the historical record of this extension of salvation, including the discussion that surrounded it (e.g., the Jerusalem conference, Acts 15), that the Gentiles who had received salvation were now conceived as part of Israel or the believing remnant of which the apostle Paul saw himself as a member (Rom 11:5). Nor are they referred to as spiritual Jews.

The present era of salvation is fulfillment of Old Testament prophecy. The present era of salvation of a Jewish remnant and Gentiles from all nations is the beginning fulfillment of the

---

[44] See Andrew C. Clark, "The Role of the Apostles," in *Witness to the Gospel: The Theology of Acts*, ed. I. Howard Marshall and David Peterson (Grand Rapids: Eerdmans, 1998), 173–81; Ben Witherington III, *The Acts of the Apostles: A Socio-Rhetorical Commentary* (Grand Rapids: Eerdmans, 1998), 126–27.

prophesied messianic salvation. We will consider this more fully in the following section, and simply note here that the New Testament messengers of this salvation saw themselves as fulfilling Old Testament prophecy.

Their mission is grounded in their Christology. According to Peter on the day of Pentecost, through his sacrificial death, resurrection, and ascension, Jesus had been exalted to the right hand of God—the place of messianic authority, all in accord with Old Testament prophecy (see Ps 110:1).[45] He was now "both Lord and Christ"—enthroned as the messianic King (Acts 2:36), although his actual reign over this kingdom awaits his return to earth (Luke 19:11; 21:31; 22:30; Acts 1:6–7).[46]

His new messianic authority has, however, ushered in the promised new covenant salvation of the messianic era—eschatological forgiveness of sins and the gift of the Spirit (Acts 2:33–39). Peter supports the early apostolic ministry of this new gospel by citing a messianic text from Ps 118:22: "He [Jesus] is the stone which was rejected by you, the builders, but which became the chief corner stone" (Acts 4:11). Despite his rejection, the exalted Jesus had become the cornerstone of God's building, which was being built through the ministry of the apostles.

The early believers thus saw their mission of the proclamation of salvation to Israel and the nations as the fulfillment of Scripture. In line with the fundamental principle of the earlier salvation covenant promises (Gen 12:3; 22:18) and Jesus' teaching that God's salvation was channeled through Israel, the witnesses went first to Israel. As Peter said to "the men of Israel," "It is you who are the sons of the prophets and of the covenant which God made with your fathers, saying to Abraham, 'And in your seed all the families of the earth shall be blessed.' For you *first*, God raised up His Servant and sent Him to bless you by turning every one of you from your wicked ways" (Acts 3:25–26, emphasis added). As the intended channel of God's saving revelation for the

---

[45] See Bock, "The Use of the Old Testament in Luke-Acts: Christology and Mission," in *Society of Biblical Literature 1990 Seminar Papers Series* (Atlanta, GA: Scholars, 1990), 503–5.

[46] For a fuller discussion of Acts 2:34–36 and the time of the kingdom, see Robert Saucy, *The Case for Progressive Dispensationalism* (Grand Rapids: Zondervan, 1993), 69–76, 94–110.

world and the ones to whom the promises originally belonged (Rom 9:4), the message must logically go first to the Jews (see Acts 13:46; Rom 1:16). Even after the salvation had gone out to the Gentiles, this priority is acknowledged in the apostle Paul's custom of going first to the synagogues (e.g., Acts 17:1–2).[47]

But, messianic salvation was also for the Gentiles. This is implied in Peter's statement that it was "first" for Israel—it was also for others. Later, Paul asserts in his defense that everything he says was predicted by "the prophets and Moses," namely, "that the Christ must suffer and that, by being the first to rise from the dead, he would proclaim light both to our people and to the Gentiles" (Acts 26:23 ESV). In fulfillment of Isaiah's prophecies concerning the messianic Servant, Christ, through his death and resurrection, brought light both to Jews ("our people") and Gentiles (see Isa 42:6; 49:6; 60:3). The apostle understands his own mission as a participation in this messianic ministry, declaring, "For so the Lord has commanded us, 'I have placed you as a light for the Gentiles, that you may bring salvation to the end of the earth'" (Acts 13:47).

It is important to note in these statements that salvation for the Gentiles was not *simply* the result of the Jewish rejection. In truth, not all Jews rejected Jesus, and the apostles continued to minister to Jews as well as Gentiles (Acts 20:21; 28:17). Rather, the reality of Gentile salvation was seen as the fulfillment of the prophecies of messianic salvation, which included all nations.

The Jerusalem Council concluded, with James, that the salvation of Gentiles agrees with the prophecy of Amos. The re-building of the fallen tabernacle (or, "tent," "hut") of David, i.e., the Davidic dynasty or "house" rebuilt in Christ, signals the time of Gentile salvation (Acts 15:13–19; Amos 9:11–12). Like many others, Amos's prophecy simply looked forward to the events of the days of the Messiah as one movement, without dividing them into the *already-not-yet* phases of fulfillment that comes with the New Testament and the two comings of the Messiah. The original context of Amos's words therefore includes the resto-ration of Israel and the Davidic kingdom (see Amos 9:13–15). However, the emphasis of the words cited in Acts 15 is on the

---

[47] See also, Acts 13: 5, 14; 14:1; 17:10, 17; 18:4, 19, 26; 19:8; 28:17; 2 Cor 11:24.

restoration of the Davidic kingship and its encompassing of the Gentiles ("I will rebuild its [David's tent's] ruins, . . . I will restore it [David's tent]," Acts 15:16).

James is therefore not using the Amos 9 prophecy to assert that the phenomenon of Gentile salvation signifies the restoration of the promised kingdom. Jesus had already indicated that this would not take place soon (Acts 1:6–7), and Peter had taught that the restoration would await the repentance of Israel and the return of Christ (Acts 3:19–21). Rather, James and the others of the council simply recognized that the prophesied messianic era had begun with Christ and included salvation for the Gentiles.[48]

In a similar manner, Paul uses several prophecies of messianic times when both restored Israel and Gentiles rejoice together in the salvation of God in support of his present ministry of the gospel that has brought Jew and Gentile together in Christ (Rom 15:7–12). For the apostle, these prophecies are applicable to the present time of the church in that the Messiah has come and inaugurated his saving work, which was prophesied to encompass both Jew and Gentile. Christ "has become a servant to the circumcision on behalf of the truth of God to confirm the promises given to the fathers, and for the Gentiles to glorify God for His mercy" (Rom 15:8–9). As a result, there is something of the phenomena foreseen in the prophecies that has become reality, e.g.: "Rejoice, O Gentiles, with His people" (Rom 15:10 [Deut 32:43]); "Praise the Lord all you Gentiles, and let all the peoples praise Him" (v. 11 [Ps 117:1]).

But, the apostle's use of these messianic prophecies in relation to the present salvation does not mean that he intends to say that they are completely fulfilled during this age before the return of Christ. In the first place, the use of these prophecies must be harmonized with his earlier teaching in chapters 9–11, where he continues to affirm Israel's covenants and promises (Rom 9:4–5), assert a future salvation for "all Israel" (11:25–27),

---

[48] On the use of Amos 9 in Acts 15, see Walter C. Kaiser Jr., *The Use of the Old Testament in the New* (Chicago: Moody, 1985), 177–94; see also Ernst Haenchen, *The Acts of the Apostles* (Philadelphia: Westminster, 1971), 448.

and foresee a time of even greater blessing for the Gentiles as a result of Israel's redemption (11:12, 15).

Furthermore, the cited prophecies are not presently fully fulfilled. In addition to their original messianic kingdom context of a restored Israel, which is not yet present, the citation of Isa 11:10—"There shall come the root of Jesse, and He who arises to rule over the Gentiles, in Him shall the Gentiles hope" (Rom 15:12)—is clearly not completely fulfilled now. The context of Isaiah's words is that of universal peace among nations under the reign of the Messiah (see Isa 11:6–10). Such peace is not present today, nor does the New Testament hold out hope for it before the return of the Messiah.

Without any evidence that the apostle is radically reinterpreting these Old Testament messianic prophecies, it is best to understand his citations similar to James's use of Amos 9 in Acts 15. What was viewed in the Old Testament as taking place in connection with the coming of the Messiah is now apportioned with two comings. The Old Testament predicted that in the messianic age, the Gentiles would be included in the salvation of God. Therefore, Gentiles are being saved along with Jews. But, the present evangelization of the nations is not the complete fulfillment of the Old Testament hope. That the apostles saw their messianic citations as only partially fulfilled in the present time is evident when we consider Paul's more specific description of his ministry as "an apostle of Gentiles" to "move to jealousy my fellow countrymen and save some of them," which would ultimately lead to the salvation of all Israel and even greater blessing for the world (Rom 11:11–15).

In sum, the present age of the church in which messianic salvation is going to a Jewish remnant and the Gentiles is a fulfillment of Old Testament prophecy—albeit partial. It is the "already" of an "already-not-yet" fulfillment of the messianic salvation promises.

The Relation of the Church and Israel

From what has been said thus far in this essay concerning God's plan of salvation history, the reader may begin to surmise the basic relationship between Israel and the church in our interpretation of the biblical revelation. The church is the initial phase of the prophesied messianic salvation involving the creation of a new humanity in which both Jews and Gentiles share a new relationship with God as his people through the new covenant initiated by Christ's saving work. It is not a new Israel replacing the Israel of the Old Testament prophecies and thus fulfilling the role of that nation in the as yet unfulfilled historic plan of salvation. In this section, we will consider the further understanding and elaboration by the New Testament writers on the nature of the church and its relationship to the nation of Israel.

Salvation of the church channeled through Israel. Consideration of the relation of the church and Israel includes the truth of Jesus' words: "Salvation is from the Jews" (John 4:22). As we have seen previously, from the beginning the church was essentially Jewish, centered in Jerusalem. More importantly, the church was founded on the apostles who, although not representative of the *restored* nation of Israel, were nevertheless connected with Israel as part of the believing remnant of that nation in the church today. The prophecy of Jesus that the Twelve would rule over the twelve tribes of Israel in the future also connects them to Israel (Matt 19:28).

The Twelve—and perhaps a few others, such as Paul, who had been commissioned by the risen Lord—as the representatives of Christ became the foundation of the church, through their authoritative divine revelation of the message of messianic salvation (Eph 2:20; see Matt 16:18, Peter as representative of all apostles). To carry the matter one step further, the Jews played the primary role of doctrinal teachers in the early postapostolic churches composed of both Jews and Gentiles. As Oskar Skarsaune says of the writings of the Apostolic Fathers, "These documents are best understood against the background of mixed communities, in which a minority of Jewish believers acted as the teachers and theological experts for the greater Gentile majority."[49]

The apostle Paul notes this relationship of the church and Israel in his caution to the Gentiles at Rome: "do not be arrogant toward the branches [i.e., the Jews]; but if you are arrogant,

---

[49] Oskar Skarsaune, *In the Shadow of the Temple: Jewish Influences on Early Christianity* (Downers Grove: InterVarsity, 2002), 222.

remember that it is not you who supports the root, but the root supports you" (Rom 11:18). The present tense of the Greek verb translated "supports" in the citation indicates that this relationship of the church to its Jewish heritage continues unbroken[50] (see also Rom 15:27).

The church is the eschatological people of God, encompassing Jews and Gentiles. The time when Gentiles would be the people of God alongside Israel became reality with the coming of the Messiah and the inauguration of his salvation in the eschatological new covenant. The concept of the people of God, previously used only in reference to Israel and still applied to them (see Rom 11:1–2), now also encompassed believing Gentiles. God was "taking from among the Gentiles a people for His name" (Acts 15:14; see 18:10). Terminology applied to Israel as the people of God is now applied to the church, which includes both Jews and Gentiles (Titus 2:14; see Exod 19:5; see also Rom 9:25–26; 2 Cor 6:16; and 1 Pet 2:9–10). As we will see below, the new usage of this terminology does not mean that the church is assuming the place of Old Testament Israel. But, it does clearly indicate that the "people of God" has been enlarged to include Gentiles along with Israel, as the prophecies predicted would take place in messianic times.

As the eschatological people of God, the church is the fruit of the promised new covenant salvation, which would bring all redeemed humanity into their final intimate relationship with God. United together to form one body "in Christ," the members of the church—both Jew and Gentile—are sons and daughters in the one family of God (2 Cor 6:16–18; see Rev 21:3, 7). They constitute the beginning of the "one new man" (Eph 2:15) whose head is Christ, the "last Adam" (1 Cor 15:45).

The explanation of the new union of Jew and Gentile in Christ provided by the apostle in Ephesians is crucial for our understanding of the relationship of Israel and the church. In 2:11–22 Paul explains the effect that the coming of the Messiah had on both Gentile and Jew. In fundamentally negative statements, he sets forth the spiritual status of the Gentiles compared to that of the people of Israel (v. 12). Gentiles had no relationship to Christ, i.e., no messianic hope and ministry of the preincarnate Christ in their midst, as was the case of Israel (see 1 Cor 10:4). They were not part of Israel and therefore had no covenants of promise as they had none of their own. All of this left them with "no [true] hope and without [the true] God in the world" (Eph 2:12). The emphasis in all of this is that prior to the coming of Christ, the Gentiles did not share in the spiritual privileges of God's elect people, Israel.

The saving work of Christ brought a radical new situation. Through his death, the Gentiles who had been far off are now, in Christ, brought near to God. The law, which had functioned as a dividing wall that created enmity between Gentile and Jew, was abolished. All of this resulted in the establishment of peace for Jew and Gentile in Christ.

In all of this, the apostle does not say that the Gentiles were made part of Israel, or that Gentile and Jew together have become a new Israel. Rather, through his saving work, Christ creates "in Himself . . . the two [i.e., Jew and Gentile] into *one new man*" (v. 15, emphasis added). Both Jew and Gentile are now reconciled to God "in one body [i.e., the church, cf. 4:4]" (v. 16). The salvation that came with Christ did more than reverse the previous status of the Gentiles in relation to Israel, i.e. making the Gentiles citizens of Israel whereas formerly they were "excluded from the commonwealth of Israel" (Eph 2:12). Christ's saving work brought about creation of a *new humanity*, in which Jew and Gentile are joined together as one in their relationship with God.

As a result, believing Gentiles and Jews in the church are "fellow citizens," not just with Israel but "with the saints"—all the believers of all ages, including those prior to the existence of Israel (v. 20). The commonwealth of their citizenship is not stated, but in Phil 3:20, the apostle identifies believers as being citizens of a heavenly commonwealth (see also the believers' relationship to the heavenly Jerusalem, Heb 12:22–23). In addition, Gentiles, along with Jews, now share an intimate relationship with God as members of his family—"God's household"—and are being built together into a new spiritual temple for the dwelling of God (vv. 20–22).

All of this new reality is described in Ephesians 3 as the revelation of "the mystery of Christ" (v. 4), the full scope of which is earlier revealed in 1:9–10 as "the summing up of all things in Christ"—i.e., "the summing up and bringing together of the diverse elements of the cosmos in Christ as the focal point."[51] The unity of Jew and Gentile in the church is thus a beginning fulfillment of God's comprehensive plan for the cosmos. The content of this phase of the mystery is summed up in 3:6: "that the Gentiles are fellow heirs and fellow members of the body, and fellow partakers of the promise in Christ Jesus through the gospel." The essence of Paul's explanation of this mystery is that Gentiles share together with Jews in the eschatological salvation that has come in Christ, i.e., the inheritance of all the blessings promised to Abraham and his descendants, the spiritual blessing of union with the Messiah, and the promise that encompasses all of the blessings of the prophetic promises related to eschatological salvation.

This new unity of Jew and Gentile in Christ is the fulfillment of the eschatological salvation promised for messianic time. It was the result of the apostle's ministry of proclaiming "light both to the Jewish people and to the Gentiles" as a fulfillment of the Prophets and Moses (Acts 26:22–23; see also Rom 16:25–26).

Although the Old Testament prophecies contain no explicit teaching concerning the body of Christ and its related concepts of believers being "in Christ" and being indwelt by Christ, there are truths in the previous Scriptures that point in the direction of these new realities. As Russell Shedd says, "the doctrine of the Body of Christ is . . . an explicit application of the Hebraic conception of corporate personality"—often noted in relation to Israel as the servant of the Lord and the messianic Servant in Isaiah and the Son of Man and the saints in Daniel 7. Thus, it does not seem too much to say also, with Shedd, that, while the corporate personality does not entail the spiritual union found in Christ, it is nevertheless a type of "the unity of the Church."[52]

---

[51] Andrew T. Lincoln, *Ephesians*, Word Biblical Commentary, vol. 42 (Dallas: Word, 1990), 33.

[52] Russell Phillip Shedd, *Man in Community* (Grand Rapids: Eerdmans, 1964), 165, 169; see also E. Earle Ellis, *The Old Testament in Early Christianity* (Tübingen: J. C. B. Mohr [Paul Siebeck], 1991), 110–12. Ernest Best similarly concludes that the "concept

Furthermore, the indwelling of the Spirit—which results in the indwelling of Christ (see Rom 8:9–10) and the formation of the body of Christ (see 1 Cor 12:13)—is explicit in the prophesied new covenant (see Ezek 36:27; 37:14). The New Testament revelation concerning the body of Christ surely adds to these foundational prophecies, but it is going too far to say that there is nothing concerning this truth in the previous prophecies.[53]

In sum, the church is the beginning fulfillment of the promised eschatological messianic salvation, in which Gentiles would share along with Israel in God's salvation. They do so by being incorporated into the salvation covenant promises that belong to Israel (see Rom 9:4–5).

The church is not eschatological Israel. Although many throughout church history have identified the church made up of Jew and Gentile as the new Israel, the New Testament does not bear this out. In the first instance, one never finds the New Testament writers using the term "Israel"—or similar language commonly used, such as "new Israel" or "spiritual Israel"—for the church. Secondly, the New Testament does not reveal the church as fulfilling the prophesied mission of Israel's salvation history.

The church is never called "Israel." The term "Israel" occurs sixty-eight times in the New Testament, and except for a few disputed texts, all of the others clearly refer to the national covenant people of the Old Testament. In his scholarly study, *Israel in the Apostolic Church*, Peter Richardson argues that the first explicit use of "Israel" for the church is made by Justin Martyr in the mid-second century.[54]

---

of Christ as a corporate or inclusive personality" lies behind the metaphor of the body of Christ. Best, *One Body in Christ* (London: S.P.C.K, 1955), 94; see also 203–14.

[53] Hiddenness or being unknown thus not only means that the mystery is not present in previous prophecy; it can also refer to something that was in the prophecy but had not yet become known in the sense of being actualized or experienced. Something of the mystery of Christ and the gospel of salvation was surely part of Old Testament prophecy (see Rom 16:25–26; 1 Cor 2:1; 2:7; Eph 3:4; 6:19; Col 2:2, 4:3; 1 Tim 3:16). For a fuller discussion of the relationship of the church to Old Testament prophecy, particularly in connection with the concept of *mystery*, see Saucy, "The Church as the Mystery of God," in *Dispensationalism, Israel and the Church: The Search for Definition*, ed. Craig A. Blaising and Darrell L. Bock (Grand Rapids: Zondervan, 1992), 127–55; see also D. A. Carson, "Mystery and Fulfillment: Toward a More Comprehensive Paradigm of Paul's Understanding of the Old and New Testament" in the same volume, 412–25.

[54] Peter Richardson, *Israel in the Apostolic Church* (Cambridge: Cambridge University Press, 1969), 9–14.

Although used less frequently by modern interpreters, one text that has historically been cited in support of the church as a new Israel is Romans 9:6: "But it is not as though the word of God has failed. For they are not all Israel who are descended from Israel." By itself, this might appear to extend the meaning of Israel to include Gentile believers outside the historic Jewish Israel. Consideration of the context, however, indicates that the apostle is not referring to Gentiles but rather to a division *within* Israel. Having introduced the major section by declaring his concern for "my brethren, my kinsmen according to the flesh, who are Israelites" (Rom 9:3–4), the apostle goes on to elaborate God's elective purpose *within* the physical descendants of Abraham (see 9:7–13). The point of the entire section is that while the promises of God to Israel may appear to have failed when one looks at the totality of Israel, which is predominantly unbelieving, there is a faithful remnant within Israel—what John Murray aptly calls "an 'Israel' within ethnic Israel."[55]

The text most frequently used for the church as "new Israel" is Gal 6:16: "And those who will walk by this rule, peace and mercy be upon them, and upon the Israel of God" (Gal 6:16). The Greek word (*kai*), translated "and" in the phrase "*and* upon the Israel of God" (NASB) is sometimes understood to have an explicative or explanatory sense, leading to the translation, "And those who walk by this rule, peace and mercy be upon them, *even* upon the Israel of God" making "those who walk by this rule"— all believers or the church—the equivalent of "the Israel of God." Aside from the fact that the vast majority of versions[56] retain the meaning "and" in this text, there are several factors that militate against equating the church with Israel here.

Most importantly, if Paul uses "the Israel of God" for the church in this text, it would be the only instance.[57] Moreover, since Galatians is probably the first of his extant writings, why do we not find evidence of this meaning in his many subsequent

---

[55] Murray, *The Epistle to the Romans*, vol. 2 (Grand Rapids: Eerdmans, 1965), 9.

[56] E.g., ASV, ESV, HCSB, KJV, JB, NASB, NEB, NKJV.

[57] Ernest DeWitt Burton, *A Critical and Exegetical Commentary on the Epistle to the Galatians* (Edinburgh: T&T Clark, 1921), 358.

uses of the term "Israel," especially in Romans 9–11, where he deals extensively with Israel?[58]

The message of Galatians also militates against referring to the church as "the Israel of God." In this letter, the apostle is not only defending justification by faith but also his ministry of salvation to Gentiles as Gentiles—i.e., the new messianic salvation encompassed the Gentiles as well as the Jews (see 3:8, 14). This makes it extremely unlikely that he would conclude his argument by calling Gentiles "the Israel of God." In all probability, Paul used these words in 6:16 to encourage the faithful Jews— the true Israel—who recognized and lived by the truth of Paul's message, and also to prevent the Gentiles from an attitude of pride in relation to Israel (see Rom 11:17–18).[59]

Paul's description of the true "Jew" in Rom 2:28–29 as one who is "circumcised in heart" has also led many to see him referring to all believers as "Jews" and therefore the "Israel of God."[60] But, again, the context is concerned with ethnic Jews and not believers in general (see v. 17). As in Rom 9:6, Paul's concern here is with the distinction between Jews who bear the name merely by ethnicity and those who bear it also in spiritual reality. Linking both texts together, Walter Gutbrod concludes,

> The distinction at R. 9:6 does not go beyond what is presupposed at Jn. 1:47 [Andrew, "a true Israelite," NIV], and it corresponds to the distinction between *Ioudaios en tō kruptō* [a Jew inwardly] and *Ioudaios en tō phanerō* [a Jew outwardly] at R. 2:28f., which does not imply that Paul is calling Gentiles true Jews.[61]

There are simply no clear instances in the New Testament— and thus in all of Scripture—where the terms "Israel" or "Jew" are used for other than the historic ethnic descendants of Abraham. Nor is there any explicit teaching using other terminology that

---

[58] W. D. Davies, "Paul and the People of Israel," *New Testament Studies* 24 (1978): 10–11.

[59] Richardson, *Israel in the Apostolic Church*, 84.

[60] Dunn, *Romans 9–16*, 125.

[61] Walter Gutbrod, "*Israēl*," in *Theological Dictionary of the New Testament*, ed. Gerhard Kittel (Grand Rapids: Eerdmans, 1964), 3:387.

Gentiles are now "spiritual Israel" or "spiritual Jews," or that the church is "new Israel."

To be sure, the New Testament writers apply many descriptions of the people of God in Old Testament Israel to the church. Believers are "Abraham's seed" (Gal 3:29 NIV), "like Isaac, children of promise" (Gal 4:28), and "the true circumcision" (Phil 3:3). The Christian community is "a chosen race, a royal priesthood, a holy nation, a people for God's own possession" (1 Pet 2:9)—all appellations of Israel.

Space permits only a few thoughts in response to the application of these statements to the church. That the church is the "seed of Abraham" and "children of promise" harmonizes well with the truth of both Old and New Testaments that all the families of the earth were to be blessed in Abraham (Gen 12:3). It is significant that the apostle cites only this aspect of the Abrahamic covenant—the blessing for "all the families of the earth"—in relation to the application of the gospel to the Gentiles, and that they are Abraham's seed (Gal 3:14, 29). Nowhere does he make reference to the "great nation," as if the Gentiles, as the seed of Abraham, were now that nation or a part of it. In addition, Abraham, as the recipient of the foundational salvation promise and the exemplar of salvation by faith, is explicitly said to be the father of both Jews and Gentiles (Rom 4:12, 16), indicating that a Gentile does not have to be thought of as a spiritual Jew in order to have Abraham as his father.

In general, it should not be surprising that expressions used for Israel as the people of God should be applied to others who are also the people of God. The prophets had predicted the time when Gentiles would become the people of God alongside Israel. Terminology appropriate for the people of God—including circumcision of the heart, which spoke of the "righteousness of the faith" (see Rom 4:11)—is therefore applicable to both Israel and Gentiles without demanding that all believers are Israel.[62] The evidence of Scripture in this regard is aptly summed by Richardson, when he states, "In spite of the many attributes, characteristics,

---

[62] For a fuller discussion of terminology previously related to Israel also applying to the church, see Saucy, *The Case for Progressive Dispensationalism*, 202–6; see also W. Edward Glenny, "The Israelite Imagery of 1 Peter 2," in Blaising and Bock, *Dispensationalism, Israel and the Church*, 156–87.

privileges and prerogatives of . . . [Israel] which are applied to the
. . . [church], the Church is not called Israel in the NT."[63]
What the New Testament writers did not do—namely, identify the church as "Israel"—the postapostolic church, on the basis
of historical, sociological, and theological factors, unfortunately
did do not long afterward.[64]

The church does not fulfill the prophesied mission of Israel.
A further indication that the church is not the eschatological
Israel is seen in the fact that the church does not fulfill the
prophesied mission of Israel. To be sure, as Israel was called as a
nation to be a light of God's salvation to the nations, the church
has a similar mission: to "proclaim the excellencies" of God and
be his witness to all nations (1 Pet 2:9; Matt 28:18–20; Acts 1:8).
However, the avenues through which Israel and the church fulfill their function as God's witnesses to the world, and also the
result of their missions, are considerably different.

The church is commissioned to go to the nations, glorify-
ing God through the proclamation of the gospel in word and
life as the community of God's people living *within* the nations.
However, as we have seen, in the case of Israel Scripture declares
that God reveals his glory to the world through his historical
dealings with her as a nation—both in judgment and blessing—
visibly and openly before the eyes of the nations of the world.[65]
The climactic revelation of his glory to the nations is to take
place, according to the prophets, when God manifests his power
and grace in redeeming and restoring Israel for all to see (see
Ezek 36:23; 39:27).[66]

Not only do the church and Israel fulfill their mission
through different avenues, but the result of their mission is
also dissimilar. The church is destined to bring the light of the
gospel to all the nations during this age (Matt 24:14). But, the

---

[63] Richardson, *Israel in the Apostolic Church*, 7.

[64] For further discussion of the factors involved in the early tendency to usurp the
prerogative of Israel for the church, see Richardson, *Israel in the Apostolic Church*;
Jeffrey S. Siker, *Disinheriting the Jews: Abraham in Early Christian Controversy* (Louisville: WJK, 1991); Marvin R. Wilson, *Our Father Abraham* (Grand Rapids: Eerdmans, and
Dayton, Ohio: Center for Judaic Christian Studies, 1989).

[65] See earlier discussion in section, "Israel's future role according to Old Testament
prophecy."

[66] For a fuller discussion of the revelation of God through Israel, see Saucy, *The Case
for Progressive Dispensationalism*, 311–16.

New Testament gives no evidence that the nations as such will be transformed through the witness of the church. Instead, this age will be characterized by ungodliness, which will reach its climax under the sway of a world ruler in opposition to God and his people (Matt 24:3–14; 2 Thess 2:3–10; 1 Tim 4:1; 2; Tim 3:1–5; 1 John 2:18). Accordingly, the church will endure suffering and tribulation among the nations to the end of the age, resulting in defections from the faith (Matt 5:10–12; 24:9–10). Thus, while the witness of the church will bring spiritual blessing to many, it is not destined to bring about the transformation of the nations. In contrast, as seen earlier, the revelation of God's glory through his activity with Israel is destined to bring the nations to the acknowledgement of God. This distinction between the "already" aspect of kingdom salvation through the mission of the church, and the "not yet" dimension of salvation associated with the prophesied mission of Israel demonstrate that the church is not "new Israel" fulfilling Israel's prophetic role.

The restoration of Israel and the completion of messianic salvation. The completion of messianic salvation awaits the return of the Messiah to establish his kingdom reign over the earth in fulfillment of the church's prayer, "Your kingdom come. Your will be done, on earth as it is in heaven" (Matt 6:10). According to the Old Testament prophecies we saw earlier, Israel is to play a central role in the revelation of God's glory before the nations that will result in their salvation. Thus, there are numerous prophecies, both before and after the Babylonian exile, that predict God would display his love and power in redeeming Israel, rescuing her from her enemies, and restoring the nation in the promised land.[67]

The writers of the New Testament do not reiterate these promises to the same extent, for they were already in their Scriptures. Rather, their primary focus was on the explanation and significance of the new climactic saving act of God in Christ and its application in the new community. They do, however, give clear indication of the continuation of this hope for Israel.

---

[67] See also Isa 11:11–16; 14:1; 27:12–13; 43:5–6; 49:8–12; Jer 16:14–15; 23:3–8; 31:8; Ezek 11:17–21; 20:33–44; 36–37; 39:25–29; Joel 3:17–21; Amos 9:11–15; Micah 4:6–7; Zeph 3:14–20; Zech 10:6–12; 12.

Jesus' statement, mentioned earlier, suggesting that Israel would someday say, "Blessed is He who comes in the name of the LORD!" (Matt 23:39), along with the implication of a reversal of fortune for the nation, when Jerusalem would no longer be "trampled under foot by the Gentiles" (Luke 21:24), both indicate a restoration of that nation.[68] The promise that the twelve disciples would sit on thrones judging the twelve tribes of Israel in the kingdom (Matt 19:28; Luke 22:30) also "confirms the view that Jesus looked for the restoration of Israel."[69]

Peter's reference to a future "restoration of all things," promised through the ancient prophets, likewise indicated Israel's restoration. For the term "restoration" had specific, national implication for his Jewish audience, including both physical restoration to the land (e.g., Jer 16:15; 24:6; 50:19) and spiritual restoration (see Mal 4:6; Matt 17:11; Mark 9:12).[70]

The fullest New Testament discussion of Israel's eschatological hope is provided by Paul in Romans 9–11. A full discussion of his teaching on this theme is beyond the scope of this essay.[71] But, several things point to his continued belief in the fulfillment of the Old Testament promises related to Israel. He directly counters any thought that God has rejected his people: "God has not rejected His people, has He? May it never be" (Rom 11:1–2). He asserts that the unbelief of some cannot "nullify the faithfulness of God" (Rom 3:3), which C. E. B. Cranfield rightly sees as the affirmation that God's purpose for Israel still stands.[72]

The "covenants" and "promises" still belong to "Israelites," who are Paul's "kinsmen according to the flesh" (Rom 9:3–4).

---

[68] John Koenig, *Jews and Christians in Dialogue: New Testament Foundations* (Philadelphia: Westminster, 1979), 11–12; G. R. Beasley-Murray, *Jesus and the Kingdom of God* (Grand Rapids: Eerdmans, 1986), 304–6; Eduard Lohse, *"Siōn,"* in *Theological Dictionary of the New Testament*, 7:329; David L. Turner, *Matthew*, Baker Exegetical Commentary of the New Testament (Grand Rapids: Baker, 2008), 562.

[69] E. P. Sanders, *Jesus and Judaism* (Philadelphia: Fortress, 1985), 103; see also Karl Ludwig Schmidt, *"basileia,"* in *Theological Dictionary of the New Testament*, 1:586.

[70] For a discussion of the entire restoration concept, see Arthur Wainwright, "Luke and the Restoration of the Kingdom to Israel," *Expository Times* 89 (December 1977), 76–79; see also Albrecht Oepke, *"apokathistēmi,"* in *Theological Dictionary of the New Testament*, 1:388–89.

[71] For a fuller discussion of Pauline prophecies concerning Israel, see Saucy, *The Case for Progressive Dispensationalism*, 246–63.

[72] C. E. B. Cranfield, *The Epistle to the Romans*, vol. 1 (Edinburgh: T&T Clark, 1975), 181.

This confidence of the apostle in Israel's hope rests in the sovereign, elective purpose of God. Israel is still "beloved for the sake of the fathers," despite her disobedience, and therefore the "gifts and the calling of God"—the covenant promises mentioned in 9:4 and Israel's functional call to ministry[73]—are "irrevocable" (Rom 11:28–29). The essence of the apostle's words here is aptly stated by nondispensationalist John Murray: "the adoption, the covenants, and the promises in their application to Israel have not been abrogated."[74]

Because of Israel's rejection of their Messiah, Paul sees only a remnant of Israel presently being saved—the rest are under the judgment of partial hardening during this age (Rom 11:5, 25). However, the day is coming, after the judgment is lifted and the present ministry to the Gentiles is fulfilled, that "all Israel [i.e., Israel as a whole in distinction to the present remnant] will be saved" (Rom 11:26). In the metaphor of the olive tree, the natural branches will again "be grafted into their own olive tree" (11:24)—into the rich root of the blessing of the salvation covenant made with Israel's patriarchs, from which some have now been cut off (v. 17).

The explanation of this "salvation" in terms of the spiritual blessing of removing ungodliness and taking away their sin (11:26–27) does not deny the further elements of a restoration of the nation in the promised land in accord with the Old Testament prophecies. The salvation is the fulfillment of "My [i.e., God's] covenant with them" (v. 27), referring to the new covenant, in which the underlying basis of all promises is the spiritual blessing of forgiveness of sins (see Jer 31:34). But, the spiritual blessings of the new covenant are also associated in the Prophets with the material blessings including the restoration of Israel to the land, as O. Palmer Robertson explains: "The return of Israel to the land, the rebuilding of the devastated cities, the reconstitution of the nation—even resurrection from the dead—play a vital role in the prophetical formulation of new covenant expectations."[75]

---

[73] Ibid., 181; see also Dunn, *Romans 9–16*, 694.

[74] Murray, *The Epistle to the Romans*, vol. 2 (Grand Rapids: Eerdmans, 1965), 101.

[75] O. Palmer Robertson, *The Christ of the Covenants* (Phillipsburg, NJ: P&R, 1980), 297; see Walter C. Kaiser Jr., "The Old Covenant Promise and the New Covenant," *Journal*

Given the apostle's clear affirmation of the continuation of Israel's covenant promises, and no clear evidence to the contrary, there is no compelling reason to see the apostle's emphasis on the central aspect of spiritual transformation in the salvation of Israel as the denial of the other elements of the new covenant, including the prophesied picture of the restoration of Israel to the land.

In accord with the Old Testament prophecies that the nations would be blessed as a result of God displaying his glory and righteousness in Israel, Paul sees the future salvation of Israel bringing even greater blessing to the world than that occurring presently through the church's evangelization. He writes, "Now if their transgression is riches for the world and their failure is riches for the Gentiles, how much more will their fulfillment [or, "full number," HCSB] be!" (Rom 11:12). And again, "If their rejection is the reconciliation of the world, what will their acceptance be but life from the dead?" (11:15).

Although not all agree, the natural interpretation of these statements seems to be in harmony with Murray, who sees in verse 12 a "gospel blessing [for Gentiles] far surpassing anything experienced during the period of Israel's apostasy . . . occasioned by the conversion of Israel on a scale commensurate with that of their earlier disobedience," and in verse 15 "an unprecedented quickening for the world in the expansion and success of the gospel."[76]

Thus, contrary to many interpreters, Paul does not see the present evangelization of the nations and the coming of "fullness of the Gentiles" (11:25) prior to the salvation of all Israel as the reversal of the Old Testament prophecies that depicted the nations being blessed through the restoration of Israel. Rather, in harmony with the Old Testament prophecies, there is a present salvation of Gentiles during this age that will be used in some

---

of the Evangelical Theological Society 15, no. 1 (Winter 1972): 15.

[76] Murray, *The Epistle to the Romans*, 2:79, 84; see also John Stott, *Romans: God's Good News for the World* (Downers Grove: InterVarsity, 1994), 299. If "life from the dead" is a reference to a resurrection, it would be "the first resurrection," inaugurating the millennial kingdom and the blessings of life for the world as a result of Christ's kingdom reign (see Rev 20:4–5). Such a view of a double resurrection, according to Oepke, was predominant in Jewish tradition at the time of the writing of the New Testament (Albrecht Oepke, "*anistēmi*," in *Theological Dictionary of the New Testament*, 1:371).

sense to bring about the salvation of Israel, which in turn will bring even richer blessing of salvation to the world. This richer blessing includes not only richer spiritual blessings but the completion of the promised messianic blessing of natural fruitfulness, justice, righteousness, and peace in all of the structures of human communal life.

Some Theological and Practical Implications of the Progressive Dispensational Understanding of Israel and the Church in Salvation History

While progressive dispensationalism shares with all conservative evangelicals the central doctrines of the historic Christian faith, the understanding of salvation as progressively worked out in historical actions on the basis of the biblical covenants, including the distinction between Israel and the church, does carry certain implications in theology and church practice. These are not all unique to progressive dispensationalism, but their logical entailment in this interpretation is perhaps more obvious than in some of the other positions. Several of these will be briefly noted.

Theological Implications

A progression of salvation activity and experience. The historical development of salvation on the basis of the biblical covenants, involving progressive revelation and saving activity, leads to distinctions in the economies of salvation. While all systems of theological interpretation recognize some distinctions between the dispensations or economies of salvation, especially between the old and new covenants, progressive dispensationalism's distinction between Israel and the church logically entails distinctions that are not all as clearly recognized in other theological systems.[77]

Progressive dispensationalism, along with all dispensationalism, tends to see more of a real development in salvation and its

---

[77] Bernard Ramm acknowledges the contribution of dispensational distinctions to a greater awareness of the progressive nature of God's revelation and historical development. Ramm, *Protestant Biblical Interpretation*, 3rd ed. (Grand Rapids: Baker, 1970), 177.

experience in the transition from the old covenant to the new. On the basis of the sacrifice of Christ, which brought an ultimate forgiveness of sins, the new covenant brought the believer into an immediate relationship with God not yet enjoyed under the sacrificial system of the old covenant. Also, the Spirit had not yet been "given" to take up residence in the human heart (cf. John 7:39). This change of relationship was symbolized by the tearing of the sanctuary curtain, which formerly barred the believer from direct fellowship with God (see Matt 27:51).

The experience of being "regenerated," "born again," or becoming a "new creation," which is never said of anyone under the old covenant, along with the indwelling of the Holy Spirit promised in the new covenant, provide a more powerful transforming principle of life planted deep within their heart than that enjoyed under the old covenant. In short, the believer could never be made "perfect" under the old covenant (Heb 7:19) but waited for the perfection in Christ through the new covenant (Heb 11:40).

Progressive dispensationalism also recognizes a progression of revelation between the old and new covenant in relation to God's rule for the believer's life. The inauguration of the new covenant rendered the old covenant obsolete (Heb 8:13). The commands, statutes, and laws of the old Mosaic covenant are no longer the regulations for God's people, both Jew and Gentile, who now live together under the new covenant. Since the old covenant was made with Israel and never with Gentiles, and the church is not some kind of restored or true Israel, there is no question of which stipulations of the Mosaic covenant are carried over for the believer in the church. The new covenant believer lives by the commands and instructions addressed to new covenant believers in the New Testament, as well as any instructions given to mankind as a whole, which have never been revealed to be obsolete (e.g., the death penalty, Gen 9:6).

This is not to say that the old covenant revelation and the historical record of God's dealing with his people living under that covenant have no pertinence for the present-day believer. The stipulations of the covenant were expressions of God's *eternal righteousness*, contextualized for his people Israel at that time in the history of salvation. Thus, despite the fact that they no longer serve as explicit directives for the believer's life under the new covenant, they do serve as illustrations of God's righteous principles for his people of all times. Paul refers to the old covenant as a "guardian" (Gal 3:24–25 HCSB), who was a person (usually a slave) who conducted a youth to and from school and generally superintended his conduct but was no longer needed when the boy became of age. Because of the redeeming work of Christ and the gift of the indwelling Spirit, new covenant believers are adult sons and daughters and no longer under the "guardian" of the law (see Gal 3:25–4:11).

Politics and the "already" presence of the kingdom in the church. The interpretation of the prophetic Scriptures according to their natural sense, including the distinction between Israel and the church, also logically entails a premillennial position—namely, that Christ's kingdom will only be established on earth when Christ returns (see Luke 19:11; Rev 11:15). Thus, as mentioned earlier, we find nothing in the New Testament that suggests that the present mission of the church is the transformation of society and bringing the nations to the prophesied millennial conditions of peace and prosperity under the rule of Christ. The political realm during this age has been committed by God to civil government and not the church (Rom 13:7). Thus the apostle, representing the church, does not see his ministry as having any direct function in the realm of politics (1 Cor 5:12).[78]

While the kingdom of Christ is not yet here in its political form, it is already present in spiritual power through the word of the gospel (Matt 13:19) and the Spirit (Matt 12:28). Working primarily through the church, the goal of this kingdom power focuses on witness to the nations of Jesus as the exalted messianic King and the salvation of the kingdom that he has inaugurated.[79] This witness in the power of the kingdom, although not now entailing a political mission as the church, nevertheless can have political impact. The transforming power of the gospel of the kingdom changes lives, including politically. Even unbelievers

---

[78] See E. Earle Ellis, *Pauline Theology: Ministry and Society* (Grand Rapids: Eerdmans, 1989), 17–25, 151–59.

[79] See the summary descriptions of the proclamation of the early church in Acts 8:12; 19:8; 20:25; 28:23, 31. The proclamation of Christ's kingdom also included his coming as Judge to reign in righteous government over the earth (see Acts 10:42; 17:31).

can be influenced for good through the proclamation of the truth of God pertaining to the realm of human government and society in general—e.g., justice and personal morality.

Most importantly, living life together in the church, as the eschatological community of love (Acts 2:44–47) and as individuals in the various sectors of society, demonstrates the power of the kingdom and influences society as salt and light (Matt 5:16; 1 Pet 2:12). In love for others, through speech and deed, believers are to pursue righteousness, justice, and peace through every possible avenue—personally, in relation with neighbors, and collectively, through the structures of society, including involvement in the political process.

In all of this, the church is never commanded to become directly involved in politics or political administration. The individual believer, of course, does participate in the various spheres of this life (e.g., business, labor, art, etc.), including politics. As members of these spheres, believers witness as Christian participants of the particular sphere but not as a ministers of the church.

In sum, with regard to the political implication of the presence of Christ's kingdom, the church does not yet manifest the kingdom with the *power of coercive force*, which is finally the power of the political realm, with its armies and police to enforce its laws. (Such power will be present with the future righteous reign of Christ.) The spiritual power of the *already* aspect of the kingdom manifest through the church today is essentially the same power that Christ displayed when here on earth—the *power of God's persuasive love* manifest in weakness which is the only truly transforming power.

The perspective on present-day Israel. Believing that God will yet display his glory to the nations through his saving activity with Israel, the progressive dispensationalist seeks to understand the present situation of Israel in relation to this biblical teaching. The present state of Israel is not yet the fulfillment of that prophesied restoration, as that is to be the result of spiritual renewal (Zechariah 12–14; Acts 3:19–21). But, Scripture's picture of Israel in the land enduring suffering at the hands of the nations through which they will turn to God suggests the reestablishment of Israel's existence as a national entity prior to conversion.[80] Ezekiel's two stage restoration—first the gathering of dry bones to form a lifeless body, and then infusing it with life (Ezek 37:1–14)—can also be understood to support this scenario (see also 36:24–31).[81]

Not certain whether the present Israel represents the fulfillment of this prophecy, although it probably does, the progressive dispensational believer works and prays for Israel's conversion so that the time of restoration under the reign of the Messiah may come. Recognizing the validity of a present homeland for the Jewish people on the basis of the world's political action and the biblical promises, the believer supports the present existence of Israel and opposes those that would abolish it.

This does not mean unqualified support for all of Israel's actions. It is not yet the "holy nation" of her destiny and is capable of sinful actions, as are all nations. Even as God declares that he shows no favoritism among the nations, but has concern for the people of every nation, so his people must do likewise (cf. Amos 9:7; Acts 10:34–35; Rom 2:11). Called to proclaim and live God's righteousness in the world, the believer, like Israel's prophets of old who surely supported Israel as God's chosen nation, must today condemn injustices done by Israel as well as injustices practiced by the other nations of the world.

Implications for Church Practice

The distinction between Israel and the church—i.e., that the church is not new Israel—provides help in understanding the relationship of the practices of Israel as the people of God living under the old covenant and the new people living in the church. History demonstrates that the early belief in a replacement or supersession theology influenced the church to appropriate to itself practices—along with their theology—from the Old Testament covenant made with Israel that were inconsistent

---

[80] On the basis of scriptural prophecies, the return of Israel in unbelief was expressed by many premillennialists long before the establishment of the present state of Israel (Hendrikus Berkhof, *Christ the Meaning of History* [rep. ed., Wipt & Stock, 2004], 152).

[81] Ralph H. Alexander, "Ezekiel," *The Expositor's Bible Commentary*, vol. 6 (Grand Rapids: Zondervan, 1986), 925–26; see also Hos 3:5, on which Hans Walter Wolff notes that, "the return to Yahweh begins with the political and cultic nadir." Wolff, *Hosea: A Commentary on the Book of the Prophet Hosea* (Philadelphia: Fortress, 1974), 62.

with the new realities of the church under the new covenant.[82] Some of the most significant of these relate to church ministry and the sacraments. As Dunn states, Christianity reverted *"to OT categories of sacrifice and priesthood*, at first in a spiritual or allegorical way, as a means to expressing continuity with the ideal of OT spirituality, but then in an increasingly literal way."[83]

The three levels of ministry—bishop, priest, and deacon—developed in the early apostolic church from the Levitical pattern of high priest, other priests, and Levites, all of which were distinct from the laity. This development of the priesthood, with its special powers, also led to understanding the Eucharist as a sacrifice in place of the unworthy sacrifices of Israel. These early trends in ecclesiology, which were developed with the aid of a replacement theology,[84] continue to shape the church today—primarily the Roman Catholic and Orthodox churches but also much of Protestantism, at least in practice (e.g., clergy-laity hierarchicalism), if not in theological theory.

The issue of the relationship of Israel and the church also has implications bearing on the question of the subjects of church baptism. For many advocates of infant baptism, the most significant basis for this practice is the continuity of God's covenant of grace throughout the Scriptures. Summarizing Calvin's position, which he also held, Murray explains that "infants are baptized because the covenant belongs to them as to the infants of the Jews under the Old Testament."[85]

To be sure, circumcision and baptism have many analogies. Most importantly, they are both initiatory rites symbolizing entrance into a covenantal relationship. But, the distinction between Israel as a nation and the church leads to a clear distinction with regard to entrance into the covenantal communities. Because God's covenant with Israel was with a nation, one

---

[82] See Ronald E. Diprose, *Israel and the Church: The Origin and Effects of Replacement Theology* (Waynesboro, GA: Authentic Media, 2000).

[83] James Dunn, *The Parting of the Ways* (London: SCM Press, 1991), 255, emphasis in original. See also, Jaroslav Pelikan, *The Christian Tradition*, vol. 1 (Chicago: University of Chicago Press, 1971), 25–26.

[84] Diprose, *Israel and the Church*, 136.

[85] John Murray, *Christian Baptism* (Philadelphia: P&R, 1962), 48, see also 57–58n30; John Calvin, *The Institutes of the Christian Religion*, ed. John T. McNeill (Philadelphia: Westminster, 1960), IV, xvi, 5–11, 24.

entered into the covenant through *physical birth*, marked by infant circumcision. In contrast, under the new covenant one also enters the covenantal relationship through birth, but it is the *new birth* of regeneration. This distinction from the old covenant is evident in that the Scripture nowhere refers to a remnant of the faithful within the new covenant as there was within the old covenant with its physical hereditary relationship. All in the new covenant are believers.[86]

Thus the recognition of Israel as a national entity with national covenant promises in distinction from the church as a new covenant community, and not new Israel, leads to a distinction in covenantal membership between the church and historic Israel, and thus the persons who are to receive the covenantal signs.

Conclusion

Progressive dispensationalism seeks to understand the Scriptures not only as the source of truth regarding creation, mankind, and God, and their relationship, but also as the divine record of God's saving activity in *history*. It may be described as systematic theology derived from a biblical theology, which looks at the diverse Scriptures in their historical context. The progression of salvation in the historical salvation covenants of Scripture reveals God's election of Israel as a nation and a role for that nation distinct from the present church. Rather than detracting from the spiritual unity of God's saving program present in the church, the fulfillment of Israel's role as a particular nation, in which God is yet to display his glory, will expand the present spiritual salvation to bring about that holistic salvation of individual and society promised by the prophets, in which all people are united in their diversity as the one people of God.

---

[86] Although it was recognized that there could be professing believers who were not genuine (e.g., 1 John 2:18–19), the Scripture gives no indication that these unbelievers are actually in the covenant. Nor is there any theological statement suggesting that there is a church within the church comparable to the apostle's statement concerning an Israel within ethnic Israel: "For they are not all Israel who are descended from Israel" (Rom 9:6).

Response by Robert L. Reymond

Saucy espouses what he calls "progressive dispensation-alism"—progressive in the sense that his view allows the New Testament church to fulfill some Old Testament prophecies without displacing national Israel as their primary referent, with their more primary fulfillment to be fulfilled in a future millennium ushered in by the return of Christ. Thus, progressive dispensationalism continues to be dispensational premillennialism, which view, in my opinion, is not very "progressive." And their premillennialism is their bugbear, as I shall now show.

I argued in my response to Thomas that Christ should be enthroned as the church's "chief prophetic scholar" and that his "eschatological dualism" should be accordingly given first place in any hermeneutical system.

1. Jesus envisioned two ages—this present (evil) age and the age to come—as comprehending the remainder of human existence. He said nothing about a third, intermediate period or millennial age. I find no millennial reign in Jesus' eschatology.
2. He envisioned these two ages as consecutive, that is, they neither overlap, nor is there any indication of a gap between them, but the age to come follows immediately upon this present age.
3. The great epochal event which terminates this age and ushers in the age to come is the glorious return of Christ and its concomitants.

When Jesus began his public ministry, he declared, in the same vein as John, his forerunner, but in even sharper terms, "The time *has been fulfilled*. The kingdom of God *has drawn near*. Repent and believe the gospel" (Mark 1:15; see also Luke 4:21). Later, Jesus would declare, "From the days of John the Baptist *until now*, the kingdom of heaven *has been forcefully advancing*, and *violent men* are trying to subvert it" (Matt 11:12; Luke 16:16). To the Pharisees—some of those "violent men"—he declared, ". . . if I drive out demons by the Spirit of God, then the kingdom of God *has come* upon you" (Matt 12:28 NIV, emphasis added; Luke 11:20). To the chief priests and elders of the nation who opposed him, Jesus declared, "I tell you that the kingdom of God will be taken away from you [suggesting that it was present] and given to a people who will produce its fruit" (Matt 21:43 NIV). Finally, at the last Passover meal, Jesus declared to his disciples, "I confer on [that is, "give by covenant to"] you a kingdom, just as my Father *conferred* one on me" (Luke 22:29 NIV, emphasis added). Clearly, with the coming of Jesus to the nation of Israel, the kingdom or "rule" of God had broken into history and into the lives of Christ's generation in his own coming.

And yet Jesus also spoke of the kingdom of God as something future, which awaited his coming in glory when the full manifestation of his power would make actual the divine rule throughout the world. For example, he taught his disciples that they should pray, "May your kingdom come" (Matt 6:10). He then declared,

> Not everyone who says to me, "Lord, Lord," will enter *the [future] kingdom of heaven*, but only he who does the will of my Father who is in heaven. Many will say to me *on that day*, "Lord, Lord, did we not prophesy in your name, and in your name drive out demons and perform many miracles?" Then I will tell them plainly, "I never knew you. Away from me, you evildoers!" (Matt 7:21–23 NIV, emphasis added)[87]

Finally, at his last Passover meal, on the night of his betrayal, Jesus informed his disciples, "I will not drink of this fruit of the vine from now on until that day when I drink it anew with you in my Father's kingdom" (Matt 26:29 NIV). Clearly, for Jesus the final manifestation of the kingdom of God lay in the future.

In this tension between the "already" and the "not yet," we are faced with what quite properly has been referred to by biblical theologians as the New Testament paradigm—traceable to Jesus as its originator—of "eschatological dualism," that is to say, in the grace sense the kingdom of God *has* come; in the judgment sense the kingdom of God is *yet* to come.

---

[87] Similarly, see Jesus' remarks in his Olivet Discourse (Matt 25:31–34).

Paul's Eschatology

For Paul, as for all of the biblical writers, the beginning point for the future complex of events that brings world history to a close is the bodily, visible, public return of Christ (1 Thess 4:13–18; 2 Thess 1:5–10, esp. v. 7; Phil 3:20–21; 1 Cor 15:23). Paul speaks of "the appearing of the glory of our great God and Savior Jesus Christ" as the Christian's "blessed hope" (Titus 2:13 ESV). The concept of a millennial reign per se is found only in Revelation 20, a book with extensive symbolism. Most likely, this Johannine "millennium" should be understood as symbolizing either the present *spiritual* reign of Christians with Christ (20:4a; see John 5:24–25; Rom 5:17; 14:17; Eph 2:6; Col 1:13) or the present reign of the martyred saints in the intermediate state (20:4b), or perhaps both together, rather than literally as an aspect of the *eschaton*. *Whatever John intended by his teaching, it is beyond dispute that there is no clearly delineated millennial period in Paul's eschatology.*

The most appropriate place where Paul might have spoken about it if, in fact, he had advocated a millennial reign of Christ is the pericope in 1 Cor 15:20–26, but he makes no mention of it there. Premillennialists claim that Paul alludes to the millennial kingdom in 1 Cor 15:24 by his reference to "the kingdom" and in 15:25 by his phrase, "He must reign." That is, they insist that a gap of one thousand years must be inserted *between* verses 23 and 24.

Geerhardus Vos responds to such an interpretation:

> Much is made of the argument that [the "then"] at the beginning of vs. 24 proves a *substantial* interval between the parousia [Christ's appearance] and "the end." But . . . that ["then"] is [not] out of place on the [Amillennial] view, . . . if Paul meant to affirm *mere succession without any protracted interval.* ["Then"] can be used . . . to express *momentary sequence of events.* . . . Of course, a brief interval in logical conception . . . must be assumed: [the end] comes, speaking in terms of strict chronology, after the rising of [the ones in Christ]. But

that by no means opens the door to the intercalation of a rounded-off chiliad of years.[88]

To those premillennialists who still insist that the "kingdom" referred to in 1 Cor 15:24 is the millennial kingdom, to be inserted between verses 24 and 25, I would observe that according to 15:51–55, Christ destroys death, his *last* enemy, *at* his coming, by effecting the resurrection. This means that the reign in question in 15:25 occurs *before* his coming. Paul's statement is explicit: "He must reign *until* He has put all His enemies [including his last enemy, death] under His feet" (emphasis added) and history reaches its consummation *with* his coming and the occurring resurrection and the eschatological judgment, which immediately ensue. He then delivers up his messianic reign to the Father, that the triune God might be all in all. Careful reflection will show that this representation of the relationships of the referred-to events can and will bear the stringency of syllogism. The reign of Christ that Paul envisions here is a reign of conquest in the sense that it is and will be a spiritual triumph over the forces of evil as it saves and subdues the elect to God and eventually raises them from the dead.

Some premillennialists, acknowledging that the millennium cannot be found anywhere else in the New Testament outside of Revelation 20, apply the biblical/theological principle of progressive revelation to this situation and propose that this important bit of revelation was made to John alone as the last living apostle. But, it is not likely that such a major feature in the eschatological complex would have been kept from all of the apostles save John, the last to die. What would have been God's purpose behind the keeping of this feature of the *eschaton* from the majority of first-century Christians? Furthermore, such an approach requires that the much larger "amillennial" stance of the rest of New Testament eschatological teaching be forced into the narrower, pictorial mold of the highly symbolic vision of the

---

[88] Geerhardus Vos, *The Pauline Eschatology* (Princeton, NJ: Princeton University Press, 1930), 243 (emphasis added). BAGD also states that "in enumerations [*eita*, "then"] often serves to put things in juxtaposition without reference to chronological sequence," thus becoming "in general a transition word" (e.g., "next"). Accordingly, the "order" words as such cannot bear the weight that the premillennialist wishes to place upon them.

Apocalypse, more specifically, into *one* ten-verse pericope in *one* chapter of that apocalyptic vision. Finally, the proclamation of eschatological matters was a vital, integral aspect of Paul's "gospel"; his eschatologically oriented message was also preached by the other apostles (1 Cor 15:11). These correlative facts suggest that all of the apostles preached essentially the same eschatological vision. For John to proclaim later a millennial reign of Christ that would precede the eternal "new heaven and new earth" state, a period that these premillennialists acknowledge none of the other apostles taught, could be construed to mean that the other apostles had proclaimed error when they taught that the resurrection of men and the destruction of "the world which is present" will immediately usher in, not an intervening kingdom age, but the "new heaven and new earth" state.

Peter's Eschatology

Peter's eschatology is beyond question the eschatological dualism of his Lord. The "already" aspect of his eschatology is evident in the fact that Christ has been revealed in "the end of the times" (1 Pet 1:20 HCSB), and most important, *his messianic reign has already begun* (1 Pet 3:22). The "not yet" aspect of Peter's eschatological vision is apparent from the fact that he can speak of God sending "the Christ . . . [who] must remain in heaven *until the time comes for God to restore everything*" (Acts 3:20–21 NIV, emphasis added). So, there is both an "already" and a "not yet" aspect to the kingdom in Peter's eschatology.

Does Peter endorse a millennial reign anywhere in his writings? In the third chapter of 2 Peter, in which he deals with future things, Peter divides the whole of cosmic history into three periods: (1) the first period—"the world of that time"—extended from the beginning of the creation to the Genesis flood (3:5–6 HCSB); (2) the second period—"the present heavens and earth"— extends from the flood to the *eschaton* (3:7 HCSB); and (3) the third period—"the *eternal* kingdom of our Lord and Savior Jesus Christ" in "the new heavens and a new earth, where righteousness will dwell"—will extend from the *eschaton* on throughout eternity (1:11; 3:13 HCSB, emphasis added). Therefore, his readers are to make every effort to make their calling and election sure, for they have yet to enter that "*eternal* kingdom of our Lord and Savior Jesus Christ" (2 Pet 1:11 NIV, emphasis added). The "day of judgment and destruction of ungodly men" yet awaits the unrighteous (2 Pet 3:7; see also 2:9 NIV). The "day of the Lord [or, "of God"] will come like a thief" (2 Pet 3:10a, 12 NIV), at which time "the heavens will disappear with a roar; the elements will be destroyed by fire, and the earth and everything in it will be laid bare" (2 Pet 3:10 NIV). Peter even declares that a major responsibility of his teaching ministry was to make known "the power and [second] coming of our Lord Jesus Christ" (2 Pet 1:16 NIV), the very coming that the false teachers among them had been scoffingly rejecting, saying, "Where is this 'coming' he promised?" (2 Pet 3:4 NIV).

As Paul did before him (2 Pet 3:15–16a; see Rom 2:4), Peter explains Christ's "delay" in coming is actually evidence of the divine patience toward sinners extending to them time to repent and be saved (2 Pet 3:9, 15). But, Peter makes no reference or allusion to an intermediate millennial period between this age and the age to come. If he had believed in a millennial kingdom following this age, the perfect place where he should have referred to it is in 2 Peter 3, but as we have just seen, he makes no mention of it.

John's Eschatology

Premillennialists admit that John makes no mention of a millennium in his Gospel or in his three general letters. But, they say, he refers to the millennium in Revelation 20. This issue deserves a straightforward response.

The book of Revelation is addressed to seven particular churches in the Roman province of Asia (1:4, 11; chaps. 2–3). There were more churches than these seven, of course, but the number seven suggests the representative idea of completeness or totality. The book is distinguished from the other New Testament books by its plethora of symbols—mystifying numbers, strange beasts, cryptic descriptions—all marking the book as apocalyptic in nature, and its apocalyptic character has made it a difficult book to interpret. But the key to understanding John's Revelation is really quite simple. A careful reading of the book will disclose that the end of the world (depicted either by the second coming of Christ, by cataclysmic cosmic upheaval, by the final judgment, or by a combination of these) does not occur just one time in the book, namely in Revelation 19–20, as dispensationalists contend. To the contrary, it is clearly and strikingly depicted in each of the seven visions of the Revelation. Again and again, not just once, the book brings us to the end of this age in striking ways.

The following Scripture references verify this fact: The *first* vision—the letters to the seven churches in chapters 2 and 3—speaks prophetically and brings the reader by these letters seven times to a contemplation of the final judgment to come and the eternal state (Rev 2:7, 11, 17, 25–27; 3:3–5, 10–12, 14, 21). The *second* vision pertains to the seals. Here we read in 6:17, "For the great day of their wrath *has come*, and who can stand?"(NIV, emphasis added). The *third* vision pertains to the trumpets. Here we read in 10:7, "But in the days when the seventh angel is about to sound his trumpet, the mystery of God *will be accomplished*" (NIV, emphasis added see 11:15, 18–19). The *fourth* vision pertains to the woman, the dragon (Satan), and his helpers. In 14:14–20, especially verse 15, we read, ". . . the time to reap *has come*, for the harvest of the earth is ripe," and in 14:16, ". . . the earth *was harvested*"; in 14:19 we read, "The angel swung his sickle on the earth, gathered its grapes and threw them into the great winepress of God's wrath" (NIV, emphasis added). The *fifth* vision pertains to the seven last plagues. We read in 15:1 they were "last, because with them God's wrath *is completed*"; in 16:15–21, especially verse 17, we read, "The seventh angel poured out his bowl into the air, and out of the temple came a loud voice from the throne, saying, '*It is done!*'" (NIV, emphasis added). The *sixth* vision pertains to the fall of Babylon. We read in 19:11–21, especially verse 15, "Out of his mouth comes a sharp sword with which to strike down the nations. 'He will rule them with an iron scepter.' He treads the winepress of the fury of the wrath of God Almighty" (NIV). Premillennialists interpret this reference to Christ's "ruling" the nations as an oblique allusion to his millennial reign. However, the verb says nothing about "ruling" but means rather "He will shepherd," the intended idea being that

Christ will "act as a shepherd" who deals with the enemy nations by dashing "them to pieces" (Ps 2:9 NIV; Rev 2:27). The *seventh* and final vision pertains to the dragon's doom, with Christ and his church the final victors (20:1–15).

Since this is so, it follows that the Apocalypse should be read as a series of recurring *parallel* or *recapitulating* visions depicting the terrible judgments awaiting the ungodly, and *not* as a series of visions with each one following its predecessor chronologically. Only in the seventh vision of the Revelation is found the millennium pericope, which begins with Satan's binding that occurred during our Lord's ministry here on earth (see Matt 12:29) and ends with the saints in the new heaven and new earth (21:1). Premillennialists chide amillennialists for suggesting that Satan is "bound" today. But we interpret Satan's binding to mean only that he is unable in this age to "deceive the nations" as he was able to do in the ancient dispensation. In other words, today his binding, while real, is a *relative* and *not* an absolute binding as it will be someday. If this interpretation seems to play fast and loose with the words of the text, those who disagree with it must acknowledge that it accords, *first*, with Jesus' earlier declared binding of Satan (Matt 12:29), which was not absolute either but was a binding only in the sense that Satan's "goods" may now be plundered; *second*, with Jesus' assurance that, by his cross, the prince of the world would be "driven out" (John 12:31), not immediately but eventually, as evidenced by the fact that Gentiles were then desiring to "see him"; and *third*, with the declaration of the author of Hebrews that Christ "destroyed" him who held the power of death (Heb 2:14–15), not absolutely as yet but in the sense that he cannot hold subject those whom Christ saves.

In this seventh vision John is shown what happens to Satan. Throughout this age the church militant (Rev 20:4a) and the martyred church triumphant (20:4b), being united with him, reign with Christ, having been regenerated by him, which regeneration is the "first resurrection" of 20:5 (see John 5:24–25; Eph 2:4–6). Though Satan tries to mount a final effort to overthrow the kingdom of Christ through the great apostasy and the man of lawlessness (see 2 Thess 2), he fails and is cast into the lake of fire and brimstone. There he will be tormented day and night forever and ever (Rev 20:1–10). Then John sees a great white throne. *Christ* will be seated upon that throne as King of kings and Lord of lords. And John sees Christ, the glorified Lamb, sitting upon that great, white throne. What a wondrous sight that will be! And John sees the earth and the heaven flee away from his face. What must he be, before whose face earth and heaven retreat as in dismay! What power, what majesty will be his! Then John sees the dead, small and great, brought before him, and he shall judge them and cast them into the lake of fire (20:11–15), the theme with which he began his prophecy in Rev 1:7.

John then sees in a new heaven and a new earth the holy city, new Jerusalem (the completed church triumphant), coming down from God and prepared as a bride adorned for her husband, in whose midst dwells the enthroned triune God (21:1–27), and from whose throne flows the river of the water of life for the "healing" of all who live in her. The redeemed "will see his face, . . And they will reign for ever and ever" (22:4–5).

In the epilogue, Rev 22:6–21, the angel who showed John these things testifies that what John had seen is true (22:6). The Spirit and the bride (the church) now issue the invitation to come and drink of the water of life (22:17). Jesus promises a third time to come (22:20), to which John responds with a simple "Amen. Come, Lord Jesus" (22:20 NIV).

Following this age will appear, as the final entailment of our Lord's second coming, not a millennial age but the new heaven and new earth. If dispensationalists would give up their premillennialism, they would give up their dispensationalism. If they would give up their dispensationalism, they would give up their premillennialism.

Response by Robert L. Thomas

Saucy, in blazing a trail for progressive dispensationalism (PD for short), sought a mediating position between dispensationalism and nondispensational systems.[89] Unfortunately, in seeking a

---

[89] Saucy, *The Case for Progressive Dispensationalism*, 29.

midpoint, he derived some of his hermeneutical principles from systems other than dispensationalism—principles reflected in his article for this perspective volume. In response, I will point out some of these with their implications.

NT Use of the OT

At one point Saucy writes, "The difference in our understanding of the relation of Israel and the church thus rests not primarily on hermeneutical procedure but rests on our interpretation of the New Testament explanation of the meaning of the earlier Old Testament revelation." This statement comes just after he has criticized the systems that read the NT back into the OT. He acknowledges that traditional historical-grammatical hermeneutics do not allow that, but he tries to eliminate hermeneutical principles by distinguishing between meanings that God intended and those that humans understand. In the same general context, he criticizes a system that finds OT meanings only in the NT. Yet, in practice, that is exactly what PD does.

By allowing NT passages to provide meaning for the OT, one is doing the same as other nondispensational systems. Hermeneutics is a human discipline and should not allow a combining of separate passages to determine any meaning. Each passage should stand on its own grammatical-historical phenomena. By reading the NT meaning into the Abrahamic covenant, if it differs from the historical-grammatical OT meaning, one has breached another hermeneutical principle: the principle of single meaning. It amounts to finding a literal and a spiritual meaning in Gen 12:1–3, 7, the same error committed by systems that disdain any dispensational implications.

Saucy's statement, "proper interpretation begins with the Old Testament," should be refined to read, "proper interpretation of the Old Testament begins and ends with the Old Testament before going to the New Testament." As he notes, the issue of the NT use of the OT is crucial. In his perspective essay, he apparently does not see the NT "as entailing a reinterpretation of the Old Testament promises and hope." Yet, elsewhere he has written that the NT passage is sometimes only an application, not an interpretation, of the OT meaning.[90]

He affirms historical-grammatical principles of hermeneutics as a starting point but indicates, as stated above, that the principles will not work in interpreting the Bible because it is a divine-human book. Rather, he advocates that the full meaning of a passage is canonical and favorably cites, among others, Vern S. Poythress, an avowed covenant theologian, as holding the same. The assumption is that the NT, in citing the OT, is always right because of its inspiration: "The difference in our understanding of the relation of Israel and the church thus rests not primarily on hermeneutical procedure but rests on our interpretation of the New Testament explanation of the meaning of the earlier Old Testament revelation." This reviewer finds his position regarding hermeneutical procedure disappointing because any theological system that ignores hermeneutics is necessarily flawed.

Admittedly, the NT writers were always right in their use of the OT, but did they always follow historical-grammatical principles when they cited the OT? My investigations indicate that sometimes they did and sometimes they did not. Saucy's present essay cites an example of the latter. That is in Acts 13:47, a case in which a NT use of the OT does not do hermeneutical justice to the OT passage it cites. Granted the rightness of NT use because of NT inspiration, in that passage Paul, in his ministry to Gentiles, identifies himself as the person spoken of in Isa 42:6 and 49:6. In the OT context, that person is the promised Messiah of Israel, as Saucy says in another part of his essay. This is certainly right because of NT inspiration but cannot qualify as a proper use of historical-grammatical principles. That is not a correct interpretation of the OT. It is right because as an apostle, Paul gave an authoritative meaning to an OT passage, a meaning not found in the OT. The two OT verses never refer to Paul.

Elsewhere I have cited a few NT passages which assign what I call "nonliteral" uses of various OT passages.[91] Clearly, in its context, Isa 65:1 uses words to refer to Israel's repentance in

---

[90] Ibid., 56, 206.
[91] Robert L. Thomas, "The Use of the Old Testament in the New Testament," in *Evangelical Hermeneutics: The New Versus the Old* (Grand Rapids: Kregel, 2002), 247–51.

conjunction with Christ's second coming. Paul was not wrong in Rom 10:20 by citing the Isaiah passage in relation to the church. As a writer of inspired Scripture, he was not mistaken; it was merely an application, however, as he was writing about the church in a historical context different from Isaiah's. Isaiah was looking forward to the future kingdom after the return of Christ, but Paul's usage of the text was not.

The historical context of Isa 8:14–15 refers the verses to the stumbling of Israel and consequent captivity in Babylon of those who opposed Isaiah's message; but, quoting Jesus, Luke 20:17–18 applies the same words to the stumbling of the contemporaries of Jesus who rejected him as Messiah at his first advent. Paul and Peter (Rom 9:32–33; 1 Pet 2:8) do the same with Isa 8:14–15. Luke, Paul, and Peter, as NT writers, were not wrong in what they penned, since they were applying the words to their contemporaries, not interpreting the OT each time. By divine revelation, they gave new meanings to an OT passage that could not have arisen through sound principles of interpretation of the OT, the authority for these new meanings being the NT passages themselves, not the OT.

Someone may ask, How were the Jewish and other early Christians to realize the authority of nonliteral citations of the OT? or Was Christ's authority for such nonliteral citations of the OT recognizable in the early church? Early Christians could have thought of the gospel as conflicting with what they had learned about the OT. But they did not think that. The authority of the NT was recognizable because the early church knew that Christ had authorized apostles to represent him in receiving new revelations appropriate to new situations once the church began at Pentecost.

As a verification of apostolic authority, Christ's authorized representatives gave literal understandings to OT passages at times. Of course, there are many such instances. Typical examples of these include Matt 1:23 and its citing of Isa 7:14. The latter passage could not have referred to Isaiah's own son in Isa 8:3 because the prophet gave him the name "Immanuel."

Another literal fulfillment in a NT use of the OT is Matt 21:5, citing Zech 9:9: "Shout in triumph, O daughter of Jerusalem!

Behold, your king is coming to you; He is just and endowed with salvation, humble, and mounted on a donkey, even on a colt, the foal of a donkey." Such examples are plentiful.

Authority of the Apostles and Prophets

As Saucy puts it, the apostles were Christ's "authoritative delegates," but not just to Israel especially, as he says, but to the whole body of Christ. When Christ gave gifts to the church as a whole, he included gifts of apostleship and prophecy (see 1 Cor 12:28; Rom 12:6; Eph 4:11). As Harris asserts, "The test of canonicity applied by the early church was apostolic authorship."[92] Apostleship was clearly a gift that, on occasion, allowed the gifted ones "to receive input from the Spirit in their inner consciousness and through the Spirit to transform that input into inspired words they communicated to others."[93] The gift of prophecy's close association with apostleship in a number of NT contexts indicates that it too was a revelatory gift.

Another broad context in which the two gifts appear is Eph 2:19–3:10. Contextually, the foundational role of the two includes the reception and transmission of previously undisclosed "revelation" (Eph 3:3, 5) regarding the fellow heirship and joint membership of Jews and others in the body of Christ (Eph 3:6). Paul described information "which in other generations was not made known to the sons of men, as it has now been revealed to His holy *apostles and prophets* in the Spirit" (Eph 3:5, emphasis added). In the broad context, technical vocabulary related to divine revelatory activity appears: *apokalypsin* ("revelation") in 3:3, *mysterion* ("mystery") in 3:3 and *mysterio* ("mystery") in 3:4, *apekalyphthē* ("has been revealed") in 3:5, *mysteriou* ("mystery") in 3:9, and *apokekrymmenou* ("hidden") in 3:9. When used with each other, the words portray God's activity in making known to his special servants hitherto unrevealed information on the outworking of his program in the world.[94]

---

[92] R. Laird Harris, *Inspiration and Canonicity of the Scriptures* (Greenville, SC: A Press, 1995), 285.

[93] Robert L. Thomas, "Appendix D: Spiritual Gifts and New Testament Canonicity," in *Understanding Spiritual Gifts*, rev. ed. (Grand Rapids: Kregel, 1999), 157.

[94] For further discussion, see ibid., 156–57.

The Ephesians citations above call for comments on Saucy's special definitions of technical words in the NT. He has worked hard to come up with definitions of "mystery" and "type" that would fit his system. The effort is reflected at various points in his essay, but his definition distorts the meaning that Paul gives to the revelatory activity spoken about in the Ephesians passages just cited. Paul makes quite clear that the church was not a subject of divine revelation in the OT:

> That by revelation there was made known to me the mystery, as I wrote before in brief. By referring to this, when you read you can understand my insight into the mystery of Christ, which in other generations was not made known to the sons of men, as it has now been revealed to His holy apostles and prophets in the Spirit. (Eph 3:3–5)

Recognized lexicographers agree with Paul that what he discusses in the Ephesian passages is "the unmanifested or private counsel of God . . . (God's) *secret, . . . a secret or mystery, too profound for human ingenuity.*"[95]

In the writings of Peter, Paul, and John, the revelatory nature and divine authority of apostleship and prophecy was recognized early in the Christian era. The earliest church fathers did the same, for example in the Muratorian Canon and the *Shepherd of Hermas*. In commenting on a statement from the Muratorian compiler, Bruce has written,

> This making Paul follow the precedent of John is chronologically preposterous; it probably indicates, however, that for the compiler the primary criterion of inclusion in the list was prophetic inspiration. In the early church as a whole the predominant criterion appears to have been apostolic authority, if not apostolic authorship; for this writer, however, even apostolic authorship evidently takes second place to prophetic inspiration.[96]

---

[95] BDAG, 662 (emphasis original).

[96] F. F. Bruce, *The Canon of Scripture* (Downers Grove: InterVarsity, 1988), 164.

The two revelatory gifts, then, were God's way of launching a new work in the world, a church that had its own revelation built partially on the OT, but in some instances requiring a different understanding of the OT. The historical and theocratic situation of the church was and is quite different from that of Israel. That the church's representatives at times attached new meanings to OT passages should not be surprising.

The Hazards of Preunderstanding

Elsewhere I have elaborated on shipwrecks caused by recent trends in evangelical hermeneutics. One of those is the proclivity of interpreting a passage in accord with an interpreter's preconceived idea of what the passage should teach.[97] This appears to have happened in the development of progressive dispensationalism. Saucy began his interpretive process under the assumption that he had found a midpoint between traditional dispensationalism and nondispensationalism, somewhere close to his dispensational roots. He then proposed a system to match that preunderstanding. What he failed to heed, however, was the danger of violating significant hermeneutical principles. I have sought to point out some of those with their implications.

Saucy's Position on the Future

The position of PD regarding the rapture of the church is somewhat tentative, as Saucy has written elsewhere. His work on *The Case for Progressive Dispensationalism* offers no defense of the pretribulational rapture of the church because dispensationalism "does not ultimately stand or fall on the time of the rapture."[98] That uncertainty is a possible explanation for why he sees the nineteenth-century establishment of the nation Israel as probable fulfilled prophecy. For him, allowing that the church is already fulfilling OT prophecy about the Gentile nations leaves very little unfulfilled in PD. Traditional dispensationalism, however, sees no future fulfillment of biblical prophecy until after the rapture of the church. The rapture is imminent.

---

[97] Thomas, "The Hermeneutical Landscape," in *Evangelical Hermeneutics*, 13–37.
[98] Saucy, *The Case for Progressive Dispensationalism*, 8–9.

The Best Perspective

In choosing the best option to explain the relationship between Israel and the church, I have landed solidly on dispensationalism, not progressive dispensationalism, as the obvious choice, in my essay. Saucy has presented some valid points, such as declaring the absence of any NT use of "Israel" to refer to the church, but he has violated some grammatical-historical hermeneutical practices, such as advocating a reading of the NT back into the OT. Those violations deprive him of a clear-cut understanding of the relationship between Israel and the church.

Response by Chad O. Brand and Tom Pratt Jr.

According to Saucy,

> Progressive dispensationalism seeks to understand the Scriptures not only as the source of truth regarding creation, mankind, and God, and their relationship, but also as the divine record of God's saving activity in *history*. It may be described as systematic theology derived from a biblical theology, which looks at the diverse Scriptures in their historical context. The progression of salvation in the historical salvation covenants of Scripture reveals God's election of Israel as a nation and a role for that nation distinct from the present church. Rather than detracting from the spiritual unity of God's saving program present in the church, the fulfillment of Israel's role as a particular nation, in which God is yet to display his glory, will expand the present spiritual salvation to bring about that holistic salvation of individual and society promised by the prophets, in which all people are united in their diversity as the one people of God (p. 208).

This succinct conclusion from his fine essay fairly states the obvious burden and direction of his position. It has much to commend it and is mostly convincing in its exegetical conclusions and theological derivatives, if one accepts at face value certain presuppositions we will discuss below.

Progressive dispensationalism is to be commended for pointing to the holistic nature of a true biblical salvation program and
its gradual unfolding in history and on into suprahistory. Saucy
is most convincing when he is arguing that the national hopes
founded on promises to Abraham and nurtured through the history of Israel have not yet seen their full fruition. He is correct
to point us to a day when God's entire program of salvation will
be in full view and dominate the universe, especially this "earth"
(land), as it does the heavenlies already. And he is most certainly
correct to tie this hope and anticipation to the aspirations of
Israel for the restored kingdom of the Davidic king to hold sway
on this planet. Finally, he is right to point out that "the church"
has not been given the task of accomplishing what in the end
must finally be imposed from above by the sovereign King of the
Lord's own choosing and exaltation.

However, Saucy goes astray when he contends for what
amounts to a temporarily suspended plan of holistic salvation
that at once somehow preserves, as he puts it above, "the spiritual unity of God's saving program present in the church," and
"the fulfillment of Israel's role as a particular nation," so as to
"*expand* (our emphasis) the present spiritual salvation to bring
about that holistic salvation of individual and society promised
by the prophets, in which all people are united in their diversity
as the one people of God." In our opinion, the ability to accept
this conclusion depends on three presuppositions: (1) First is
the use of terminology that defines what constitutes a biblical
understanding of "the people of God" *vis a vis* the designators
"Israel" and "the church." (2) Second is the theological construct
that assumes the present "spiritual salvation" must be somehow
"expanded" to reach its goal, the "not yet" of biblical prophetic
anticipation. (3) The necessary alternative to this scenario is
to be found in what is commonly referred to as "replacement"
theology. We will take these up separately as we proceed.

Are we to assume that "the people of God" is synonymous
with "Israel" (the political entity Saucy calls "nation," especially
the focus of the Old Testament) and "the church" (that visible
entity made up of ethnic Jews and Gentiles in the present age of
"eschatological salvation")? If we accept this proposition, then

most of the exegesis and theological reflection in the essay hold up under examination. If, however, "the people of God" are not now and have never been synonymous with these visible designations, we are faced with sorting out the various ways in which Scripture points us to this reality. We contend in our contribution to this volume that the people of God have always been in some sense "hidden" from view (think Abel) and characterized by a walk with God (think Enoch) that he defines and commends and urges upon the merely visible religious world, whether it is Israel or the church or the Gentile world, including both ethnic Jews (think the "7,000 in Israel" of Elijah's day) and Gentiles (think all those before Abraham circumcised his family, and then Rahab, Ruth, the widow of Zarephath, etc.). To take up the central subject of this book is to seek to discover what "Israel" and "church" really mean in the context of Scripture and salvation history. We would concede that the salvation of God is spiritual, physical, political, socio/cultural, intellectual, and universal. We would not, however, limit the biblical message to a simple either-or distinction of mission and plan to two visible historical entities, for at best both are generally finding themselves in Scripture under censure and being urged to higher (spiritual?) realities. As Paul would say, both must "seek those things which are above" (Col 3:1 KJV). This conception of the true "people of God" appears to us to be the heart of John's prophetic message in the Apocalypse. Just who are the "conquerors," and how shall they weather the storm that rages around them inside and outside the churches?

The second presupposition is in some ways more troubling than the first, for it strikes at the very nature of the biblical narrative. Are we to believe and teach that the current "eschatological salvation" (Saucy's terminology) is not the goal and *sine qua non* of biblical truth about literally everything there is to know and experience of the Christ of Israel and the church?[99] Must this present manifestation of his glory in the church be "expanded" by a return to a failed paradigm? Is the principle of "progressive"

---

[99] Can it be successfully denied that Paul's contention that Christ, as "head of the church," is the One who has and will have and has always had "preeminence" in all things (Col 1:9–23) implies and requires a unity of those things past and present and future and in heaven and upon earth?

revelation and "dispensational" governance of the universe to be reversed at the end of the age and stood on its head? Shall we return to Sinai (as did Elijah)—more literally to a fallen hero (David and the beloved Israel) and a truncated "land" in the Middle East—or shall we expect things we have never imagined to be the actual fulfillment of the promises made to the fathers of old? Nothing, in our opinion, is clearer in the records of the OT than that the experiment with national Israel has fallen in the street by the time of Malachi, not because the promise of God has failed, but because Israel simply cannot keep its end of the covenantal bargain.[100] Four hundred years would elapse, much like the period from the Patriarchs to Moses, awaiting the arrival of Yahweh's Servant to pull all the strands of promise and prophecy and failure and rejection and exile together into one great moment of redemption. The faith of Israel is to be focused on the Lamb of God, not the aspiration for nation-state dominance. The rule of the Davidic King has been established on high, and the evidence of it is the outpouring of the Holy Spirit on all believers. When the current iteration of the visible and supposed "people of God" has run its course, the King shall descend and make "manifest" the true "Sons of God" (Rom 8:18–25) who have been hidden in Christ so they might be "found in Him," as Paul would say (Phil 3:9). Many of these will be ethnic Jews and may constitute a massive proportion of Jews living at that time, but they do not need the existence of a nation-state to give glory to the God of their salvation, just as the Gentiles who have all along been "grafted in" (Rom 11:17–24) with the true branches won't need a visible church to identify them. The identity of both is not a matter of the "flesh" but of the "Spirit." We contend that the progressive revelation of Scripture does not turn back on itself but proceeds toward the heavenly goal and will eventually arrive in the New Jerusalem.

Finally, there is no necessity for a theology of "replacement," for the church does not replace Israel. Rather, the church extends Israel's scope to include all those being grafted into the

---

[100] Like Adam and Eve before them, national Israel failed the test and has been expelled from the Lord's "garden," the land that flows with good things.

original olive tree. Jeremiah is clearly teaching this when he reports Yahweh's word:

> Thus says the LORD concerning all my evil neighbors who touch the heritage that I have given my people Israel to inherit: "Behold, I will pluck them up from their land, and I will pluck up the house of Judah from among them. And after I have plucked them up, I will again have compassion on them, and I will bring them again each to his heritage and each to his land. And it shall come to pass, if they will diligently learn the ways of my people, to swear by my name, 'As the LORD lives,' even as they taught my people to swear by Baal, then they shall be built up in the midst of my people. But if any nation will not listen, then I will utterly pluck it up and destroy it, declares the LORD." (Jer 12:14–17, ESV)

Neither Paul nor Jeremiah envision a replacement of Israel by the church, but they do consistently see the joining of Gentile converts and Jewish "returnees" (we take this to mean, theologically, those who repent of their apostasy) together in complete peace and fellowship around the one "name," that is, "As the LORD lives." References to "land" in this Jeremiah passage clearly cannot imply that all the converted nations will somehow be shoehorned into the strip of land we know as Israel/Palestine. The expansiveness of the gospel of salvation is that Israel, though having failed to carry out the provisions of the Sinai covenant, has now become the messenger of worldwide salvation and redemption, calling on the nations to join them in one worldwide glorification of the King who is coming to rule and reign. Jeremiah and Paul envision the dichotomy between those who are being "built up in the midst of my people" and those whom the King will "utterly pluck . . . up and destroy." Such a people (those "built up") from all the ages will "inherit the earth (land)," or more to the point, "the cosmos" (Rom 4:13). This is consistent with the transformational theology of Paul and the remainder of the New Testament (as well as passages such as Ezekiel 37)—Israel is not replaced; it is transformed (John 3:1–14 and Rom 12:1, 2 being primary in this teaching,

with the same implications elsewhere in passages such as 2 Cor
5:16–21; Eph 4:23; Col 3:10 and Titus 3:3–7) by the new covenant
through the Spirit poured out.
The reader is finally directed to our discussion of the promised "seed" as it is traced through Scripture. Saucy is convinced
that there must be a distinction made between the "seed" as
Christ and the "seed" as a "great nation." We will not attempt
to retrace the discussion in each essay here but refer you to
the original materials. In closing, however, it is appropriate to
make the point that Paul makes in Galatians and Romans particularly. In both Gal 3:16–29 and Rom 4:13–25, he is attaching
major theological significance to the certainty that the "seed"
is in fact Christ because the law has in effect condemned those
to whom it came originally and saddled them with a "curse."
Furthermore, the original promise(s) iterated to Abraham, including those concerning a "nation" and "many nations," were
made when he was uncircumcised and could only exercise
faith, for which he was "counted" as righteous. That same faith
saves Jew and Gentile alike, apart from the law, and joins them
as "heirs" of the promise(s). We think it entirely inappropriate,
therefore, to refer to this weighty theology, central to all historical orthodoxy, as somehow diminishing the aspect of physical
descent in favor of designating the people of God, "Abraham's
seed merely *as anyone of faith*" (Saucy's emphasis). The use
of "merely" seems particularly infelicitous, since it diminishes
such a salient point for Paul in both epistles and underlies so
much of his presuppositional theology elsewhere. Moreover,
both John the Baptist (Matt 3:7–10) and Jesus (John 8:39–47)
question the descent of national Israel represented in their
leaders and the crowds that came out to them. The point of all
three was that "Israel" was being redefined and transformed by
the call to faith in Christ. No more important issue confronts
the church than this distinction—who is the one who is "of the
faith of Christ"? Who is it that will be clothed with the "new
man" in Christ? It is not *merely* those who have faith but *only*
they who have faith in him. It seems to us that if we fail to
identify such a fundamental as bearing upon our identification

of the "Israel of God" and the church that withstands even the "gates of Hell," we have pulled the theological rug from under our own feet. How shall we then stand?

CHAPTER 4

The Progressive Covenantal View

BY CHAD O. BRAND AND TOM PRATT JR.

This essay will explore what it means to be the people of God, and it will do that over against three other perspectives. Two of the chapters in this book of essays travel paths that have been established for some time: the covenantal and dispensational approaches to eschatology and ecclesiology. Arguably, covenantal theology arose during (or in the immediate aftermath of) the Reformed tradition on the continent and then spread to certain elements within the Anglican faith. It developed its themes in the debates between Reformed and Lutheran Christians in the seventeenth century. Its ecclesiology, somewhat borrowed from Augustine, held to a close continuity between the two testaments, with circumcision and baptism being analogous to one another. Its eschatology, pursued with a similar hermeneutic, also held to testamental continuity. The classical dispensational position is of more recent origin (basically nineteenth century) and takes a quite different tack, arguing for a large discontinuity between the two testaments.[1] The two positions "in the middle" are the progressive dispensational view and ours. They share

---

[1] See the excellent series of essays in John S. Feinberg, ed., *Continuity and Discontinuity: Perspectives on the Relationship between the Old and New Testaments* (Wheaton: Crossway, 1988).

many similarities but also dissimilarities, both hermeneutical and ecclesiological, as we hope to show.

In the story of the first hinge-point of human and cosmic history, God spoke to man these fateful words: "cursed is the ground because of you; . . . thorns and thistles it shall bring forth for you; and you shall eat the plants of the field. By the sweat of your face you shall eat bread, till you return to the ground, for out of it you were taken; for you are dust, and to dust you shall return" (Gen 3:17–19).[2] In typical biblical fashion, of course, the remedy to this situation had already been stated when God said, "I will put enmity between you and the woman, and between your offspring and her offspring; he shall bruise your head, and you shall bruise his heel" (v. 15). The promise to "crush" the head of the serpent by means of the "seed" of the woman is the "promise" of the over-riding plan of redemption that shall soon overtake the cosmos.[3] It is the promise to bring true justice to the whole creation through the sacrifice of the one "seed" for the sins of "the many" (Rom 5:18–19). The ordered and "good" relationship of all things to the Creator, which has been so disrupted because of Adam's sin, will one day be returned to its rightful order and "the man" (and woman included in him)[4] will have dominion through the one man Christ Jesus, who is finally united with his bride in glorious marriage. The comprehensive nature of this "new creation" of all things is contained in what the Bible means by "righteousness," with its concomitant overtones of justice and uprightness in all relationships established in the creation week and the individual justification of Adam's race through personal faith in Jesus Christ. It is this "righteousness" that is now "being revealed," according to the apostle Paul (Rom 1:17), "by faith from first to last" (NIV) through the gospel. For the creation was "subjected to futility" (Rom 8:20 ESV) on account of man's

---

[2] Unless noted otherwise, Scripture quotations are from the English Standard Version.

[3] See W. J. Beecher, *The Prophets and the Promise* (New York: Cornell University Press, 1905).

[4] We would suggest here that this is a harbinger of the manner in which God's good creation contains within itself ahead of time the "seed" that remedies an ensuing problem—in this case, the man's need for differentiation to satisfy his "alone"-ness and to fulfill the mandate from the Creator to "be fruitful." The "rest" into which God enters before the story of differentiation commences suggests from the outset a settled provision of all that will ultimately be needed to complete the final picture.

THE PROGRESSIVE COVENANTAL VIEW — **233**

severing of relationship with God, and all cannot be "good" again until "the freedom of the glory of the children of God" has been brought to full fruition (Rom 8:21 ESV). This chapter will follow a basic procedure. First, we will examine the nature of biblical righteousness, what it means for the people of God to be in right relationship with the Lord. We will then examine both the success and the failure in Israel's own experience of that righteousness in her worship of the Lord, with a view to ascertaining what it means to be the people of God. We will then examine future eschatology to see how Israel and the church relate to one another in the unfolding plan of God. We will attempt to establish the position that Jesus came as the fulfillment of all Old Testament expectations. He established a community of the Spirit that will endure through the ages, a community in whom his righteousness will be manifested through all eternity.

Righteousness, the Church, and the Plan of God

The ongoing debate of the last several decades on the so-called New Perspective on Paul has resolved itself in many circles into a struggle over whether there is any "gospel" in an approach that sees Paul, in the book of Romans particularly (but elsewhere at least implicitly), emphasizing the "climax" of the history of the people of Israel as revealing salvation through the fulfillment of covenant promise(s)[5] in the life, death, and resurrection of Jesus. This emphasis is often made to stand against a traditional "Roman road" reading of the quest for personal salvation through the first eight chapters of Romans especially. In fairness, both sides tend to make sweeping statements that attempt to discredit

---

[5] We will refer to "the promise" in the singular as encompassing all the promises made to Abraham's descendants in the manner of Paul at Gal 3:29. In the context, he is making the case that all the elect from among Gentiles are "heirs," thus making them recipients through the one promise of all the benefits unpacked in the ensuing promises. Its fundamental oneness is implied in the maker and recipient—that is, the maker is one God (Gal 3:20) and the recipient is one people. For a full exegetical discussion of this material, see Bruce W. Longenecker, *The Triumph of Abraham's God* (Edinburgh: T&T Clark, 1998), esp. 55–58, and N. T. Wright, *The Climax of the Covenant: Christ and the Law in Pauline Theology* (Minneapolis: Fortress, 1992), 157–64.

or devalue the insights of the other side without making room for a fuller reading from both directions. It seems to us that the old evangelism tool, "the Roman road to salvation," is a bit simplistic and does not do justice to all that the apostle Paul is trying to do in Romans (and elsewhere).[6] On the other hand, it is surely futile to read Paul in such a way as to exclude or diminish his clear interest in and dedication to the salvation of individuals for the greater glory of God among both Jews (first) and Gentiles.[7] Therefore, for many "soul-winners," little is to be accomplished by delving into Paul's larger concerns in writing Romans and other letters, since the eternal destinies of persons individually trumps the grand "plan of salvation" for the cosmos. On the other hand, many advocates of the New Perspective seem to gain great intellectual satisfaction and theological comfort in ferreting out the intricacies of Paul's thought without thereby strengthening the actual experience of salvation by individual believers, though they do not intend that to be the case.

Obviously, this is an oversimplification of the debates over the "New Perspective"[8] (particularly such issues as the "imputation," or lack thereof, of the sin of Adam to all and of the righteousness of Christ to believers, the substitutionary atonement of Christ for the sins of the ungodly, the wrath of God poured out upon the Son, and the differences between strictly covenantal and forensic views of justification). Still it highlights the areas of particular concern to this book and this essay specifically. For it is of little value to discern either the future of Israel as a nation

---

[6] See especially the ongoing work of N. T. Wright and most clearly his commentary on Romans. N. T. Wright, "Romans," in *The New Interpreter's Bible: Acts-1 Corinthians*, ed. Robert W. Hall (Minneapolis: Abingdon, 2002).

[7] In presenting the counterpoint to Wright, John Piper has cogently commented that unless there is a way of personal salvation being described in Romans, there is no "good news" to balance the bad news about what has happened to God's Son in the hands of sinful men and the wrath to come upon men. John Piper, *The Future of Justification: A Response to N. T. Wright* (Wheaton: Crossway, 2007), 20.

[8] We do not mean to imply here that there is a clearly delineated single perspective, since the literature has burgeoned into many nuanced perspectives. We also recognize that the New Perspective itself is not acceptable in all of its claims, but we do affirm that the debate has helped interpreters clarify some issues that had previously remained somewhat murky. We will expand on this in the pages that follow.

or the institutional church today unless it impacts the experience of salvation among believers individually.

Thus, a particular concern of the New Perspective debates to this essay is the matter of whether or not the "salvation" (or "redemption," as Paul emphasizes in Galatians particularly) of Israel as a people and/or persons impacts the "salvation" of Gentile believers in any way that is eternally significant for saving faith. This issue most often confronts those attempting to do justice to the full Pauline doctrine of justification.[9] Surely the most pertinent question is, *who exactly comprise the "congregation" of the justified in the sight of God, and what is their "place" in the present age and the one to come?*[10] More to the point, who or what is "the Israel of God" (Gal 6:16; see Romans 9–11), and how does this terminology fit in the schema of salvation present and future with proper relation to the eternal plan for the kingdom of God?[11] Finally, is the God of Abraham, Isaac, and Jacob to be trusted with the preservation of those now joined to Christ in an ongoing process of salvation, especially if there is any doubt about how he has or will preserve his integrity (righteousness) in handling the preservation and salvation of Abraham's ethnic offspring?

Here, then, we offer our suggested framework for the resolution of several key issues addressed in this book. Our proposal is that the entire debate over the significance of Israel and the church in eschatological perspective is bound up in the *history of salvation* as it is revealed in the metanarrative of Scripture. Further, how one reads that "story" clearly impacts one's view of the "way" of personal salvation, which must answer the question,

---

[9] That is, does justification entail in its biblical fullness the "setting to rights" (as N. T. Wright so often puts it) of *everything*, or is it primarily or *exclusively* about individual forensic "right-ness" before God?

[10] With reference to the institutional church, the discussion concerns, as far back as Augustine, the visible vs. the invisible church or congregation. In more recent times, since the Reformation, the various groupings broadly denominated "Puritans" had ongoing struggles over the exact nature of the church as true or apostate or simply false. See Edmund S. Morgan, *Visible Saints: The History of a Puritan Idea* (New York: Cornell University Press, 1963) for an overview and Richard F. Lovelace, *The American Pietism of Cotton Mather: Origins of American Evangelicalism* (Grand Rapids: Eerdmans, 1979), for a concentrated look at the most influential of American Puritans in this quest.

[11] For our purposes here, the answers to these questions must address the promises to Israel concerning land and rule and prosperity within the covenant.

"Who or what are the *genuine* people of God?" The dispensational approach virtually requires multiple pathways to this salvation,[12] and the traditional covenantal approach requires some form of halfway inclusion of those still unjustified in the visible people of God. Consequently, we think both approaches are amiss.

One of the most significant issues in this debate is the question of how entry is gained into this "people," since it is not contemplated anywhere in Scripture that individuals will experience salvation without incorporation within a grouping of other persons in a relationship of love and service. Again, that question hinges on the identity of this group/congregation. Failure to resolve this issue in a thoroughgoing biblical manner, in our opinion, is what leads to several wrong conclusions. The following discussion seeks to highlight these areas of contention and propose a solution.

As the title of this volume shows, the dialogue has resolved itself into an apparent dichotomy between two entities, "Israel" (perceived as a national and political entity among the visible "nations" of the natural world) and "the church" (perceived as an eschatological community [warranting a time-designated expression, "Church Age"] marked out by certain disputed structures and practices and a mission to spread the "gospel" among the nations). While these terms for designating a "people of God" are obviously nuanced and fleshed out in the literature, it seems to us that this dichotomy is the essence of the intended

---

[12] We believe that a careful reading of the literature of both traditional (more explicitly) and, in some cases, progressive dispensationalism (more implicitly and ambiguously) will verify this conclusion, if only in the failure to state unequivocally that personal salvation has always and only been achieved by grace through faith. We contend with Paul that the law was "added" and has as its only positive goal the retaining of the original land and the material prosperity that went with it. It could not by its nature and that of man provide a way of "salvation." For statements by a progressive dispensationalist to the effect that the law might be seen as salvific, consider the following: "If the law is to be understood as that which defined righteousness in one era in the history of salvation, as Paul seems to describe it in [Romans] 5:14, it can similarly be said to be 'salvifically obsolete' in view of Christ's coming and the ministry he carried out." David K. Lowery, "Christ, the End of the Law in Romans 10:4," in *Dispensationalism, Israel and the Church: The Search for Definition*, ed. Craig A. Blaising and Darrell L. Bock (Grand Rapids: Zondervan, 1992), 236. Nothing else in the essay clarifies this statement satisfactorily. On the other hand, another essay in the same volume seems clearly to deny that the law had salvific properties (Kenneth L. Barker, "The Scope and Center of Old and New Testament Theology and Hope," in Blaising and Bock, *Dispensationalism, Israel and the Church*, 293–328). Perhaps more clarity will be forthcoming as the debate continues.

differentiation. We are concerned, however, that such a dichotomy is artificial and, in the end, unbiblical.

We will discuss this assertion within the following framework: (1) The oneness[13] of the God of the Bible demands that there be but one people that are "his" out of all the "nations" (or tribes or peoples) of the earth. (2) This people, because of sin, are not his by natural birth into any entity (nation, tribe, family) but must be born into his people "from above," both implicitly and explicitly demanding an action by God himself for its efficacy. (3) This one people has not changed in its dynamic nature since Yahweh set out to create it through the lineage of Abraham. It is growing out of one stock, and that is, Jewish stock.[14] (4) The marker for this people is not external, i.e., ceremonial, sacramental, or "carnal" in Paul's terminology, in any way but is internal and dynamic within the individual and the "congregation" of people. That marker is the presence and power of the Holy Spirit, manifested in outward activity of many kinds. The externals can only be symbolic and testimonial of greater realities. (5) The designation "body of Christ" to describe the congregation of believers is both a fulfillment of Jewish aspiration and an all-encompassing summation of the true nature of the new creation.

1. The Oneness of God Demands One People

The oneness of God is assumed and argued to be the basis of a single people throughout Scripture (Deut 6:3; Rom 3:29–30; Gal 3:20; see Zech 14:9; Mark 12:29; John 17:3; 1 Cor 8:4–6). Stated succinctly, "There is one God, and there is one mediator between

---

[13] We take our cue here from the *Shema* of Israel and do not intend to enter discussion of the nature of the Trinity, which we take to be distinctiveness-in-unity.

[14] We will be using this terminology in the manner Paul does in Rom 2:28–29. Though he will at times use this term pejoratively, it is clear he understands that the "true Jew" who has "true circumcision" (Phil 3:3) of the heart is the elect person for the purpose of inheriting the promise(s).

God and [all][15] men, the man Christ Jesus" (1 Tim 2:5 ESV).[16] Thus, there is one body, one flock, one family, one building, one tree/vine, one inheritance (one "land"),[17] one promise, one city, one temple, one bride, one priesthood, one Lord/faith/baptism, and ultimately one "seed," one Son, one Christ, who is pleasing to the one Father of us all. Paul makes this point clearly in his argument against the Judaizers, who would make the one *sperma* (seed) have multiple meanings and actually pervert the gospel he had preached to the Galatians.[18] The "Son" is one and the same as the chosen son (Israel, originally only Jacob, as opposed to Esau) and the "natural" son (Adam), to which Luke carefully testifies with his genealogical passage following the ascription of Sonship to Jesus from the heavenly voice. His obedience and sacrifice are sufficient to make all acceptable in the one just Person (Acts 7:52), who is both Son of Man and Son of God. His "followers" (just like Israel in the desert) constitute a "new" (really renewed or reconstituted and transformed) Israel, originally chosen from the ethnic Jewish people.[19] Consequently, when Jesus tells the woman at the well (John 4) that salvation is "of the Jews," he cannot mean that only ethnic Israel is "saved," but that, in the

---

[15] The context of this statement is a call to prayer for "all people," whether authority figures or the mass of humanity who need to come to Christ for salvation. This one mediator contrasts with the reference in the Galatian letter to a mediator of the law (implying two mediators or two covenantal relationships), but as Paul concludes, "God is one" (Gal 3:20), so Moses cannot be the final mediator to whom the promise is given.

[16] The most extensive discussion of the issues briefly stated here is in James D. G. Dunn, *The Partings of the Ways: Between Christianity and Judaism and Their Significance for the Character of Christianity*, 2nd ed. (London: SCM, 2006).

[17] The God of the Bible does not own only a small piece of land in the Middle East any more than he can fit into an earthly temple. The land is all his and the actual land "of promise" is "the cosmos," as Paul says in Romans 4 about the inheritance of Abraham. Heaven is his throne and the earth is his footstool. This "land" is to be the possession of the redeemed race, all of those "in Christ," to whom it is now in the process of being subjected (1 Cor 15:25–28 and many others that take their cue from Ps 110:1), until the final revealing of the adopted sons of God (Rom 8:19–25).

[18] Gal 3:15–18. On the significance of the Pauline usage of *sperma* in the singular, see Longenecker, *The Triumph of Abraham's God*, 128–34. The one "seed" is Christ and the one people caught up and "found in him" (Phil 3:9).

[19] This decision on the part of the earthly Jesus was preceded by an all-night prayer time that surely clarified the will of the Father in the mind of the human Son so that he began to traverse the land with a symbolic twelve followers (Luke 6:12–16), and, in the context of Mark's story, makes it plain that those who follow him are his true kinfolk (Mark 3:31–35)—in contrast to the unbelieving mass of Israel (including apparently unbelieving portions of his natural family at this point; see John 7:3–8) and their recalcitrant leaders.

history of salvation framework, all peoples must *come to the God of Israel* and the Son who sacrificed for sinners outside the gates of Jerusalem, but they come as worshipers "in spirit and in truth."[20] When all the cosmos is "drawn" to him (John 12:32; see 3:18; 8:28), they must enter the "land" where he was slain (figuratively, as his disciples) and take up his death-stake and walk with him up and down in the land as "followers." But this land is not a "holy" land, and there is no longer a "holy" place (temple) or a "holy" city, for these are all subsumed in Christ to whom the true worshipers come.[21] For he is himself the salvation that is "of the Jews"—that is, he is the "true Jew" (see Rom 2:28–29; see Exod 4:22–23).[22]

There is also one Spirit into whom this one people is "baptized." This is the one Spirit who was with Israel in the wilderness but was "grieved" (Isa 63:10; see Eph 4:30) by her apostasy. It is the same Spirit that filled John and Jesus and "rushed upon" the prophets of old. David feared it might be taken from him as it was from Saul (Ps 51:11–12). It is the Spirit who hovered over the chaos in creation and filled the artisans building the tabernacle with wisdom. And, it is clearly the Spirit of Pentecost returning to animate and fill the entire people of God,[23] first in Judea and eventually, according to Acts and the apostles in their writings, the people of God all over the Mediterranean world. Together they constitute "one new man in place of the two" (Eph 2:15 ESV; see Gal 3:28). Our concern here is that, contrary to (at least) traditional dispensationalist thinking, this unity is the fundamental characteristic of the relationship between God and his

---

[20] Surely this is the ultimate meaning of the kingly rule of Israel among the nations. When all people are drawn to Jesus and worship Israel's true King and Lord, Israel has achieved its destiny. The Spirit is seen here as authenticating the preaching of the true Word by bringing faith and salvation to the hearers.

[21] See, on this point, Graeme Goldsworthy, *Prayer and the Knowledge of God: What the Whole Bible Teaches* (Downers Grove: InterVarsity, 2003), 132. The purpose of a "land" in biblical perception is to provide space for man and God to have fellowship. This need is met in Christ himself first and then in the new creation—a place of *shalom* and Sabbath rest. The shadow (in the parlance of Hebrews) is Canaan, but the reality is Christ filling the cosmos.

[22] We will be developing this point as we go along. See below for additional explanation.

[23] This event and its immediate aftermath beg to be compared to the dedication of the temple (2 Chron 7:1–10), and the three thousand converts as a replacement of those killed in the rebellion at Sinai.

people throughout Scripture, and the apparent disjunction is resolved clearly in Christ as the one representative of the natural "man" in Adam (1 Cor 15:45–49; see Rom 5:12–21; Heb 2:5–18) and the "elect" man in Israel (Exod 4:22; see Ps 2:7; Isa 42:1; Matt 17:5; Eph 1:6; Col 1:13; 2 Pet 1:17; 1 John 5:9).[24] Further, we are concerned that most "covenantal" theologizing on the subject of the elect manifested in the visible church does not do justice to the biblical emphasis on the real versus the visible in defining the nature of the current congregation, the true people of God—those who have come "to Mount Zion and to the city of the living God, the heavenly Jerusalem, and to innumerable angels in festal gathering, and to the assembly [lit., *ekklēsia*] of the firstborn who are enrolled in heaven" (Heb 12:22–23 ESV). This "church" is assembling and has truly already arrived "in Christ" (Eph 1:3), the new Adam and Israel(ite).

2. The People of God Are His by Divine Election and Spiritual Birth

The people of God are elect and chosen out of the world, and according to Jesus, the ones he is receiving into his "church" are the ones "given to (him)" by this one God and Father of the Lord, Jesus Messiah. They are clearly not coincident with the entire nation of Israel. This people of God is not born into that relationship naturally (Gal 4:26–31). They are born "from above" (John 3; see Ezekiel 36–38; Ps 87:4–6; Isa 4:3; Phil 3:18–20; Col 3:1–4) and go through life "seeking the city" (Heb 11:10, 13–16; 12:22–24) that is above because their citizenship (i.e., political affiliation) is in this city above, where their names are "written" in the book of life, a register of true citizens.[25] That city is Jerusalem and there is no other, though it is called Zion in places when it is presumed to be separated from the earthly city of the same name. For that city has lost its designation as the true "city of the great king" (Ps 48:2) and is called, in its apostasy, "Sodom and Egypt" (Rev 11:8) and is spoken of as "enslaved" (Neh 9:36;

---

[24] Note also the "love" of Yahweh for this Son on the plains of Moab (Deut 7:8). This is surely the root passage of the declaration of the heavenly voice at Jesus' baptism and the repeated Pauline use of the terminology associated with "beloved."

[25] Exod 32:32; Ps 69:28; Isa 4:3; Ezek 13:9; Dan 12:1; Luke 10:17–20; Phil 4:3; Heb 12:23; Rev 3:5; 13:8; 17:8; 21:27.

Ezra 9:9; Gal 4:25) in its own land even up to Paul's discussion in Galatians.[26] Its destruction is predicted clearly by Jesus in his prophetic discourse (Matt 24:15–28) and is treated as the end of a certain "generation" (Matt 23:29–39; see 1 Thess 2:19), a designation that implies more than simply a time-delimited grouping.[27]

John the baptizer makes it plain that his baptism is establishing a "new" people when he rebukes those coming to him with the assertion that God is able to make stones into "children of Abraham."[28] This "restoration" (Mal 4:5–6; Luke 2:12) is, at least implicitly, a reconstitution of Israel harkening back to the crossing of the sea and the Jordan, with implications also from Noah's passage through the flood (1 Cor 10:1–4; 1 Pet 3:20–22). Jesus is quite insistent that it is necessary for John to pass Jesus physically through this same water "to fulfill all righteousness," a statement that, in our thinking, can only refer to the ultimate "setting to rights" (Matt 3:15) of all things in the new creation, beginning with a *new exodus* experience.[29] Further, the parable of the Tenants (Matt 21:33–44 and parallels) is quite explicit in the pronouncement that another *"ethnos"*[30] will be given the kingdom because it is being taken away from those originally entrusted with it. As A. T. Robertson comments, "It was the death-knell of the Jewish nation with their hopes of political and religious world leadership."[31] The New Jerusalem is that which

---

[26] There is wide diversity of scholarly opinion as to whether it was commonly believed in first-century Judaism(s) that the promises of return from exile had already been fulfilled. The primary sources tend to indicate a division among the various sects and parties, but few were satisfied that the contemporary situation in Israel met the criteria of prophetic hopes. Many were, in fact, calculating the seventy weeks of Daniel for clues.

[27] A simple and accessible review of this NT perspective on the fate of Jerusalem can be found in David E. Holwerda, *Jesus and Israel: One Covenant or Two?* (Grand Rapids: Eerdmans, 1995), 106–12.

[28] Matt 3:9; cf. John 8:39. The implication of this exchange is clear that John is implicitly charging these naysayers with being Gentiles, those outside the actual people of God and in the parlance of the day outside the covenant.

[29] Of particular value for this view is the work of Rikki E. Watts, *Isaiah's New Exodus in Mark* (Grand Rapids: Baker Academic, 2001). David Pao's work on the Lukan materials is cited later in this essay.

[30] For the purposes of our discussion, it matters not whether one expects this "nation" to be a converted and believing Israel in the millennium, for our contention is that the Israel of God springs from this root and is its true consummation "in Christ."

[31] A. T. Robertson, *Word Pictures in the New Testament* (Nashville: Sunday School Board of the Southern Baptist Convention, 1930–32), in loc. It is notable also that "the stone" that will smash any it falls on likely is an echo of Dan 2 where the stone strikes the

"comes down" (Rev 22:9–27) and is the one that the Lord "builds" (Psalm 127; Isa 62:6–8; Heb 11:10; 13–16). In Christ's person, it is the "house" Yahweh promised to build for David (2 Samuel 7, a passage filled with enigmatic nuances). Its gates are named for the tribes of Israel, but the foundation is the apostles of the Lamb, thus joining the apparently divided people of the current discussion. It is the "prepared place" of John 14. In its final form, "coming down," it is the "bride" and the city conflated as one social unit to contrast with the great harlot of Babylon, Satan's counterfeit.

3. The People of God Arise from the Supporting Root of Historic Israel

The people of God are "planted" in the "land" (earth, ground), and there is only one vine, Christ (Isaiah 5; see Ps 52:8; Isaiah 61; Hos 14:6; John 15), a clear designation of Christ Jesus as the Israel of Isa 5:1–7 (see Jer 11:15–16). Paul notes about this vine/plant that those who have been "broken off" from the "cultivated" plant are grafted *back* into the same plant, and those who simply grew up "wild" (Gentiles) are grafted into that plant, a Jewish plant (Romans 11). The historical Israel is considered to be the supporting root and the original "lump," into which Gentiles have been placed, and into which any future ethnic Israelite will be returned through faith in Christ (Rom 11:23) and no other means.[32] The stump ("root of Jesse," Isa 11:1–10; see 6:13[33]) is not removed and replaced, but made to sprout again. Therefore, the "all Israel"[34] of Romans 11 is coincident with the "Israel of

---

great statue. Israel seems to be identified now with the beastly nations of Daniel. See also John 19:15, "We have no king but Caesar."

[32] The strange idea that somehow the final "conversion" of Israel will happen at the *parousia* is almost an offensive concept, for it implies that there will be a generation of "believers" who will be allowed to by-pass the "offense of the cross" in favor of a "sign from heaven" (see Matt 12:38–41). Not only is it offensive to the Pauline preaching (1 Cor 1:18–25; see Rom 9:30–33); it partakes of the original satanic temptation to the "Son of God" that he should float down from the temple wing in a grand arrival, thus avoiding the necessity of the cross, a temptation repeated by Simon Peter personifying Satan (Matt 16:22–23). We find the careful exegesis and exposition of Romans 9–11 in Wright, "Romans," in Hall, *The New Interpreter's Bible*, 620–99, to be quite compelling on the issues we address in this essay relating to the Pauline teaching.

[33] Here the "holy seed" (in Paul's parlance, Christ) is the remnant.

[34] This is a reference, we contend, to the regular promise of the prophets from the "God of Israel," after the northern kingdom has in effect disappeared into the Diaspora,

God" of Galatians 6 and includes the Gentiles who have been grafted into the plant (that is, Christ) during the time of visible ethnic Israel's apostasy and hardening.[35] It is all the elect of God from all the nations and the tribes of the "Israel of the flesh," for the implication in both Paul's metaphor and Jesus' discourse on the vine and the branches is that the branches removed were inauthentic and those put in (and pruned for fruit-bearing) are lively from connection to Christ. It is this very liveliness that makes them candidates for the ever-trying and painful experience of "pruning."[36]

The pruning-for-fruit-bearing motif is regularly apparent in the biblical narrative of Israel's history (and prior to it in the story of Noah and his family) as repeatedly a representative remnant passes through judgmental experiences to pave the way for salvation for others. Abram and Lot arrive in the "promised land" and must separate so God can continue to deal with Abram alone. Lot finds himself embroiled and entangled in Sodom, having apparently lost the family he loves to pagan enticements,[37] and Abraham must plead for his rescue with Yahweh (a clear "set-up" on the Lord's part). Jacob is separated out from Esau and goes into exile, only to return in great wealth and power to face his apparently angry brother bent on revenge. At Jabbok it is

---

to gather Israel, not just Judah and Benjamin, in the coming "new exodus" anticipated in Isaiah and discussed during the transfiguration. Note especially the calling of Ezekiel to be a watchman for "the house of Israel," Ezek 3:1–17 (the referent here obviously to the Babylonian exile group), and continuing references in his prophecy to this mission. Zephaniah, in the days of Josiah (when attempts were made to join the kingdoms in worship), looks forward to this time (Zeph 3:9–20) and obviously includes people(s) from among the nations in the great ingathering to be "my worshipers" (vv. 9–10), who "call upon the name of the LORD" and "bring my offering." Micah 4 and 5 partake of this flavor also, especially in discussing the "remnant of Jacob," which is likened to "a lion among the beasts" (Mic 5:7–9: see Gen 49:9; Rev 5:5) as it is "among the nations, in the midst of many peoples" (ESV). See our further discussion on the gathering in at Pentecost.

[35] See Wright, "Romans," in loc., for a full discussion of this position. We contend with Wright that if this is not the proper interpretation of Paul's teaching at this point, "he would done better to have put the preceding eleven chapters [of Romans] on the fire" (689), for everything he has been saying leads to this conclusion.

[36] For thorough treatments of the primary materials on the remnant, see Mark Adam Elliot, *The Survivors of Israel: A Reconsideration of the Theology of Pre-Christian Israel* (Grand Rapids: Eerdmans, 2000), and Gerhard Hasel, *The Remnant: The History and Theology of the Remnant Idea from Genesis to Isaiah* (Berrien Springs, MI: Andrews University Press, 1980).

[37] This despite Lot being "righteous" (2 Pet 2:7) and "vexed" (KJV) in the place he chose for himself and his family.

Jacob alone who wrestles until he is "blessed" with the new name that will characterize his people for millennia and the courage to present himself to Esau as a savior protecting his family. Joseph is sent out alone from an increasingly debauched and decadent family that by and large wishes his death. His story reads like the type of Christ in becoming the righteous remnant that "many people should be kept alive" because "God meant it for good" (Gen 50:20). The theme continues at Sinai with Moses pleading for the entire nation (even at his own expense) and setting up the "tent of meeting" for any who "sought the LORD" (Exod 33:7–11). It continues in the prophets, beginning most notably with the seven thousand whom Yahweh tells Elijah will survive the coming judgment.[38] As bookends to the prophetic period from the eighth to the fifth centuries BC, Isaiah has his "disciples" (8:16) and "witnesses" (43:10–12) and Malachi his "jewels" who "spoke with one another," whom the Lord "remembers" by writing their names "in a book" so that "once more you shall see the distinction between the righteous and the wicked, between one who serves God and one who does not serve him" (Mal 3:16–18).

Jesus is clear that his followers must take up their own crosses and bear them as he has done (Matt 16:24; Luke 9:23), denying themselves. They must proceed through the "narrow gate" and walk along the "hard way" (the *thlipsis* way of tribulation; Matt 7:14), a word confirmed by Paul to the believers at Derbe and Lystra and Iconium (Acts 14:22).[39] This dual congregation of pruned fruit-bearers, the true vine of Israel, appears as "sealed" in Revelation 7, first the elect of the tribes of Israel and then the elect multitudes from among Gentiles.[40] Notice how Paul refers

---

[38] The Sinai event finds further use by the author of Hebrews when he updates the central thought to refer to Jerusalem and the sufferings of Christ and his followers (Heb 13:12–13). See on this last point P. W. L. Walker, *Jesus and the Holy City: New Testament Perspectives on Jerusalem* (Grand Rapids: Eerdmans, 1996), 216–21. Hasel makes this point about Elijah's experience at Horeb (*Remnant*, 159–172). Elliot and Hasel are in substantial agreement that the key for our purposes here is not that the size of the group is small but that they "survive" judgmental times.

[39] This way of "tribulation" is confirmed consistently throughout the NT: Mark 10:30; Luke 22:28–29; John 15:20; 16:33; Acts 9:16; Rom 8:17; Phil 1:20; 1 Thess 3:3; 2 Thess 1:5; 2 Tim 2:12; 3:12; 1 Pet 5:10; Rev 1:9.

[40] Several commentators agree with this designation of the two entities in the passage, and others do not. Regardless, there are not two peoples in the heavenly vision of John

to everyone outside this people of God in Corinth as "Gentiles" (1 Cor 12:2 NKJV) and to the congregation as "brothers" related to "our fathers" in the wilderness experience (1 Cor 10:1). In the second Corinthian letter in our canon, Paul goes further by linking the fulfillment of promises made to ethnic Israel to an exhortation to holy living, as the "temple of the living God," by a predominantly Gentile congregation (2 Cor 6:16–7:1).[41] This is parallel to his designation of Gentiles (prior to their believing unto salvation) as "separated from Christ, alienated from the commonwealth of Israel and strangers to the covenants of promise" (Eph 2:12), clearly implying that this condition has now been remedied in Christ. In the exercise of church discipline, Jesus, being quoted by Matthew to a congregation he designates as "church," directs (with Matthew's obvious approval) that those who will not be reconciled to the brothers and sisters are to be considered "Gentile," a characterization that must have as its underlying conviction that the "church" of the Lord is "Jew-ish" in its essential nature. This must, of course, point to a greater reality, a heavenly and eschatological one that Paul has urged upon the Corinthians, the Galatians, the Ephesians (and the others to whom the letter of that name was delivered), and the Romans. Peter concurs with this vision of the church as the extension of the true Israel when he uses the Old Testament language of election and calling of Israel to designate those now called out from the "futile ways" of their forefathers, who were "not a people" and had "not received mercy," and urges them to "keep your conduct among the Gentiles honorable" (ESV).[42] Third John (v. 7) also treats "Gentiles" as outsiders to a group that is at least mixed and perhaps predominantly not of ethnic Jewish origin.

National Israel, of course, came under the same curse as Adam and was ultimately rejected as "not my people" (Hos 1:10; 6:7; see Rom 9:26–27; 1 Thess 2:14–16), putting them in

---

but one comprising all those preserved in the "great tribulation."

[41] Note especially the sources of his quotations (Exod 6:7; Lev 26:12; Isa 52:11; Jer 31:33; Ezek 11:20), which he transfers to the Corinthians with the phrase "since we have these promises" (7:1).

[42] First Peter 1:13–2:12. Peter seems clearly to be implying a dual understanding of "Gentile" here. The "Gentiles" who have now joined the congregation designated by the language of calling to Israel are now distinct from the "Gentiles" in the world from which they came.

246 - PERSPECTIVES ON ISRAEL AND THE CHURCH

solidarity with the Gentiles even in premessianic times. In effect, they have become uncircumcised (Phil 3:3; Col 2:11), with all the deleterious effects that entails. This was also the condition of the generation that died in the wilderness, so that a new ceremony of circumcision was required before entry to the land of promise (Josh 5:2–9). Nevertheless, this does not mean that to be a Jew is to be forever outside the mercy of the one God, but it does mean that no hope for salvation exists in any ethnic or legalistic clinging to the covenant of Abraham or Sinai or of Torah (Rom 10:4; see 4:13–25). Jesus, in his cross, alone "redeemed" Israel from the "curse" (explicit in the covenant) when he died "under the law" as the One identified (through baptism at the Jordan) with sinful Israel. When he died, Israel died, or as Paul would say, "I died."[43]

Those in Israel who had been looking to God for a Messiah who would first rescue the nation from its political bondage before the ingathering of the Gentiles could commence were shocked and dismayed like Saul of Tarsus. The apostle to the Gentiles, however, came to see that only after the rejection of Messiah by ethnic Israel as a whole could the Gentile mission proceed with a view to making the nation "jealous" (Rom 11:11).[44] In reality, the nation, through Christ, had died and risen again to the new reality and was now being "sent" on a new mission (John 20:21). In a great reversal, to be matched at the consummation of the age, "to the Jew first" became "and also the Greek" for the glory of the God who saves those in the act of disobedience and rebellion. Paul, in our opinion and that of many others, holds out the conviction that the final outcome will see a great ingathering, a

---

[43] See on this Paul's discussion in Galatians. His argument undoubtedly stems from the historical reality that the curses of the law found in Deuteronomy 28 fell upon Israel and were only finally expunged when Christ died "under the law." This will lead him to assert here and elsewhere (Gal 2:19; Rom 7:4) that "through the law died to the law" and make it universal for all those "under the law." This can only be accomplished through the imputation of Christ's death to others, especially those raised under the law's pedagogical thumb.

[44] The context of this idea clearly comes from Hosea's prophecy and appears to be implied by the eschatological passage in Hosea 3, especially vv. 3–4. Paul is apparently reflecting on this prophecy as his hope for a final ingathering of Israelites. See also Longenecker, *The Triumph of Abraham's God*, 94–95. This historical situation is surely implied in the famous Isaianic problem of "the Servant" who is mysteriously seen as Israel/Jacob and another personage (Isa 49:1–7; 52:13–53:12), the one unable to complete the mission and the other doing so through sufferings, but both at times conflated.

"fullness," of Israelites "according to the flesh" that will match the "fullness" of the Gentiles in the matchless grace and wisdom of God (Rom 11:11–36).[45] Therefore, Paul can ultimately say, "But God's firm foundation stands, bearing this seal: 'The Lord knows those who are his,' and, 'Let everyone who names the name of the Lord depart from iniquity'" (2 Tim 2:19 ESV).[46] This is clearly the one people of God.[47]

4. The Marker of the People Is the Internal Presence of the Holy Spirit

The one tangible, and in many senses visible, mark that sets apart the true, single people of God in this age is the presence and power of the Holy Spirit. Lamented for his grieving in the desert (Isa 63:10) and anticipated in his return to be "poured out" (Joel 2:28–30; see Isa 32:15; 44:3) universally "on all flesh," he is the true builder of the city and temple according to Zechariah (Zech 4:1–10; 6:12–15), for Israel's disobedience has occasioned the necessity for the building work of the Branch.[48] His descent upon the Son is seen as a dove (Matt 3:16; Luke 3:22) and the

---

[45] See, for instance, covenantal theologian John Murray's discussion of this in Romans. John Murray, *The Epistle to the Romans: Volume II, Chapters 9 to 16*, New International Commentary on the New Testament, ed. F. F. Bruce (Grand Rapids: Eerdmans, 1963), 75–103.

[46] See Num 16:5; Nah 1:7; John 10:14, 27; Luke 13:27; 1 Cor 8:3.

[47] Near the time of publication deadline for this volume, G. K. Beale published his magisterial study, *A New Testament Biblical Theology: The Unfolding of the Old Testament in the New* (Grand Rapids: Baker Academic, 2011). Space does not permit careful interaction with it here. His chaps. 20–22 address the subject matter of this section, and we are in substantial agreement with his analysis. Our material was already written when we were able to spend some time in Beale's volume. We think it appropriate to cite his own conclusion reflecting on Paul's discussion of the *mysterion* in Eph 3:3–6: "Some commentators have seen the mystery as consisting of complete equality [between Israel and the church], but as far as I can determine, none have apparently underscored the basis for such equality lying in the one person 'Christ Jesus' as the true Israel, since there can be no distinguishing marks in him but only unity," 654. We had reached this conclusion for ourselves prior to finding this passage. We clearly concur with Beale. Additionally, see Graeme Goldsworthy, *The Goldsworthy Trilogy: Gospel and Kingdom* (UK: Paternoster, 2000), 108–22, which takes substantially the same position we advocate here.

[48] Notice here again the implication that Christ is the remnant that is truly faithful to build the Lord's house. On the building as the work of Spirit and Branch, see Beale, *The Temple and the Church's Mission: A Biblical Theology of the Dwelling Place of God* (Downers Grove: InterVarsity, 2004), 321–24. This exposition does not deny that the immediate need for Spirit assistance in the time of Zechariah is real and anticipated. However, as is true throughout the Prophets in particular, the present crisis calls forth the future prospect in its fullness. More will be said on this below.

"rending" of the heavens (Mark 1:10) in answer to the prayer of Isa 64:1. Here is the first "member" of the household of faith, the head of the house/body (Eph 1:22–23; Col 1:11), even the firstfruits—all perfectly wonderful metaphors for the Person in which the gospel of the kingdom resides incarnate—indeed, he is the "heir of all things" (Heb 1:2; see Ps 2:8–9; Matt 28:18).

The visible mark of belonging to the people of God is not circumcision (all would agree), but neither is it an external symbol or sacrament.[49] Calvin argued that baptism is "the sign of initiation by which we are received into the society of the church, in order that, engrafted in Christ, we may be reckoned among God's children."[50] We do not believe that Scripture teaches this. Thus, Paul can conflate the spiritual with the physical of baptism (Romans 6) and be rather glad that he had not baptized many of the Corinthians (1 Corinthians 1).[51] It is the reality of the Holy Spirit, first poured out according to the promise of Joel as the power and proof of the arrival of the kingdom (and the "day of the LORD"), that is the mark of the New Testament believer.[52] It is the long-awaited "circumcision" of the heart, urged upon and promised to Israel by Moses and the prophets (Deut 10:16; 30:6; Jer 4:4; 31:33; 32:39–40; Ezek 11:19; 36:26–27), now coming to remnant Israelites "from every nation under heaven" (Acts 2:5),[53] and decried for its absence in the masses and leadership of Israel by the "filled-with-the-Spirit" Stephen (Acts 7:51). In this spiritual sense, circumcision is still the mark of the people of God (Phil 3:3). It can only be pictured ("portrayed," Gal 3:1) through

---

[49] Our position, as advocates of the Free Church tradition, is that neither baptism nor the Lord's Supper are technically the visible marks of the church. See the discussion in David L. Smith, *All God's People: A Theology of the Church* (Wheaton, IL: Victor, 1996), 130–33.

[50] John Calvin, *Institutes of the Christian Religion*, ed. John T. McNeil, trans. Ford Lewis Battles, The Library of Christian Classics (Louisville: WJK, 1960), 4.15.1.

[51] Paul is clear that his sense of being "sent" is not to baptize but to preach. This does not diminish the command to baptize, but it clarifies the true mission, lest we become enamored with visible symbols that do not save or justify.

[52] For a discussion of the implications of this fulfillment of the Jewish expectation of the arrival of the "Day of the Lord," see Goldsworthy, *The Goldsworthy Trilogy: The Gospel in Revelation*, 200–228.

[53] This is a clear indication of prophetic fulfillment in the gathering together of "all Israel" from its exile to be infused with the promised new covenant blessing. Note, however, that Jeremiah receives his prophetic insight after relating the prayer of 31:7, "O LORD, save your people, the remnant of Israel." The new covenant blessing appears to be an answer to this prayer (see Rom 11:2–5).

preaching and in symbolic death and burial in immersion in water and "proclaiming" in the Supper the Lord's death till he comes (1 Cor 11:26).

The repeated experience of the Spirit is everywhere the identifier of the people of God in the early church and the mark of the fulfillment of the promise(s) of God to Israel (Acts 2:30–31; 13:32–33), especially as the gospel spread to those considered "unclean" (Samaritans and Gentiles) by pious Jews such as the Jerusalem Council and Paul the persecutor. The "unclean" have their hearts "cleansed" by faith (Acts 15:9) so as to be proper receptacles for the "Holy" Spirit.[54] The promised "blessing" that comes from covenantal relationship is called the "inheritance" (Acts 20:32),[55] and those who are to receive it are called "heirs of God and joint heirs with Christ" (Rom 8:15–17 NKJV). The writer of Hebrews assures us that the promise(s) could not be "completed" (or, perfected) until the current generation of faith came into being and received its reward for endurance (Heb 11:39–40). The seal and down payment that assures this eventuality for all is the presence of the Holy Spirit (Eph 1:13–14; 4:30). No one without this "assurance" has any right to assume a participation in the final issue of the "inheritance" (Rom 8:9–11).[56]

To the believer, the presence of the Spirit creates a palpable confidence and faith that manifests as increasing assurance of salvation and love for God and the neighbor (Rom 5:5; Gal 4:6;

---

[54] See Peter's testimony to the Council in Acts 11 and 15 concerning his entire experience in the conversion of the house of Cornelius. James speaks to this issue also when he points to the ingathering of Gentiles as a restoration of the Davidic kingdom so that Gentiles "who are called by my name" (v. 17) may become subjects (Acts 15:15–18).

[55] On the significance of "the word of His grace" (emphasized by Paul in this passage) as a possession of the Lukan churches, and them only, see David W. Pao, *Acts and the Isaianic New Exodus* (Grand Rapids: Baker Academic, 2000), 147–79. We see the mission of the Spirit to endow the messianic community with the authentic "Word" (written upon the heart as well as proclaimed), which in Luke's accounting grows and triumphs throughout Acts. The rider on the white horse of Revelation 19 images the kingly triumph of the Word incarnate.

[56] We are not here referring to psychological and emotional factors alone characterizing "assurance." The essence of biblical assurance is firm conviction about the truth of the gospel (God has already acted in Christ through the resurrection) and the faithfulness of God in Jesus Christ to perform what he has promised—this is the essence of "faith" (Heb 11:1). However, over time the believer is clearly expected to experience as living reality the overflow from within of love, joy, and praise that characterizes true worship. Certainly the congregation is expected to model it as a real and living experience in its corporate worship and service.

Eph 1:15; 5:18–20; Heb 11:1) and the "fruit of the Spirit" (Gal 5:22). To the observer from without, it may show itself as an uncommon and unearthly kind of love for others and for God (John 15:13) and faithful witness (Acts 1:8; Rev 12:11). These Christ promised when he said all people would know that the people of God are the disciples of Christ "if you have love for one another" (John 13:35; 15:26–27). Paul called this manifestation of the Holy Spirit a "pouring forth" among and in believers (see Rom 5:5; Titus 3:6) and the *"par excellence"* way (see 1 Cor 12:31, referring to what follows in chap. 13). It[57] is unmistakable in its manifestation, such that it settles disputes (Acts 15:8; Gal 3:2), gives guidance (Acts 13:1–4; 15:28; 16:6–10), gifts believers individually and the church corporately with supernatural service abilities and wisdom (Romans 12; 1 Corinthians 12; Ephesians 4), and, most tellingly, causes people to ask for explanations that lead to the preaching of the gospel and evangelistic "success" (Acts 2) through the convicting and convincing work Jesus promised (John 16:8–11) and that which he urged his disciples to seek through prayer (Luke 11:13), a prayer that was answered at Pentecost.[58] Likewise, its absence is cause for questioning the genuineness/nature of the discipleship/salvation one has entered (Acts 19:1–7; Rom 8:9) and the gospel one has believed. It was the answer to the uppermost question after the resurrection: "Lord, will you at this time restore the kingdom to Israel?" (Acts 1:6–8), for the restoration of power in the world is at the root of their questioning. More could be said here,[59] but it is in this factor alone that we find the kind of spiritual

---

[57] "It" through this section does not imply lack of personality by the Spirit, but rather the tangible manifestation of his work. Our take on this issue is substantially different from that of the descriptions given by Morgan regarding Puritan piety and its attempts to isolate carefully the inner fact of saving faith by various questionings and tests, what Morgan calls the "morphology of conversion" (*Visible Saints*, 66–73, 90–92). Nevertheless, the issue of visibility of Christian character and faith in those accepted for membership in local churches remains a valid practical outworking of the biblical concept of "church."

[58] This is likely to be understood in terms of the kingdom "coming" as the Lord's Prayer stipulates in the context. It is certainly what the apostles were seeking before Pentecost (Acts 1:6–8). On this point see David Seccombe, "Luke's Vision for the Church," in *A Vision for the Church: Studies in Early Christian Ecclesiology*, ed. Markus Bockmuehl and Michael B. Thompson (Edinburgh: T&T Clark, 1997), 50.

[59] Especially in the area of many statements by Jesus akin to "My sheep hear my voice" (John 10:27), indicating that genuine believers hear the Word and receive and practice it when it is preached.

authority Jesus gave to his congregation and described as "keys of the kingdom" (Matt 16:19; see John 20:23). Where the keys are used in the Spirit-empowered preaching of the Word (1 Cor 2:4–5; 1 Thess 1:5) the door of salvation is both opened and shut by the faithful steward. Paul sees this as the "aroma" of life in one direction and death in the other (2 Cor 2:14–16).

The Free Church tradition (Baptists and others) has long contended that all of this entails that only those who have made a voluntary commitment to Christ and to the church are eligible for membership, since, ideally, membership in the church is coincident with membership in Christ's body (1 Cor 12:12–13; Eph 4:1–6). This conviction developed over a period of years in the context of Anabaptist, Puritan, Separatist, and Baptist struggles over the question of what qualifies one to be considered a "member" of a church. Is it a theological confession, a reputation of moral living, a profession of justifying grace, or all of the above?[60] Generally, the Anglican Puritans (the "stay-inners") accepted the Augustinian view that all are baptized into the church, all partake of the sacraments and are "members" of the church, but that only some among this membership are elect. Calvin and the Reformed tradition have generally followed this approach as well. The Separatist tradition (along with some later Congregationalists) baptized all but expected some kind of actual profession of faith in order for persons to be accepted to full membership.[61] The Baptists (and Anabaptists), as their name implies, baptized only those who made a credible profession of faith and admitted only them to church membership.[62] They alone were admitted to the ordinances (sacraments) of the church. This is the position we find to be consistent with the teachings of Scripture.[63]

---

[60] Morgan, *Visible Saints*, 1–112; Chad Owen Brand and David E. Hankins, *One Sacred Effort: The Cooperative Program of Southern Baptists* (Nashville: B&H, 2005), 5–27.

[61] In New England this resulted in considerable confusion that led to several modifications, such as the Half-way Covenant. See, for instance, Francis J. Bremer, *The Puritan Experiment: New England Society from Bradford to Edwards*, rev. ed. (Lebanon, NH: University Press of New England, 1995), 161–65.

[62] This is based on numerous biblical texts, such as Matt 28:18–20, with this sequence: make disciples, baptize them, and teach them. The book of Acts follows this sequence, not the sequence promoted in paedobaptist theology.

[63] The dilemma faced eventually by the New England Puritans and their coreligionists was succinctly stated by Morgan in *Visible Saints*, 125–29, when he noted that

5. The People of God Are the Body of Christ

Though there may be many localized congregations, organically there is only one "body," and that is the Messiah. All who identify with him by faith (not sacraments) are "baptized" by him in the Spirit (1 Cor 12:12–13)[64] and become one body, with no "middle wall" separating the entities or the individuals (see Eph 2:11–3:20 for the most detailed and lengthy Pauline explanation). Christ is the "head" (surely meaning a fulfillment of the promise to Israel that they would be "the head and not the tail" [Deut 28:13]) over all things, and as such is over his body "the church" (Eph 1:22–23; Col 1:18). Thus, Paul can say, "If any one is in Christ he is a new creation" (2 Cor 5:17; see Ps 104:30 for a possible "echo," as the *ruach* blows). Emphasis should be placed on "any" and the designation of more than just the individual as "new creation." In the Colossian letter, he can speak of this summation of all things within the body of Christ as being a new creational entity (for he is "the firstborn of all creation") and anticipate the time when "the church" (not simply one local congregation) will reach maturity "in Christ" (Col 1:15–29). He uses the same kind of language in speaking to the Galatian churches collectively as he wrestles with their immaturity, even experiencing "anguish of childbirth" (4:19; see Isa 54:1) over their formation into Christ. Individual, local congregations are not complete in themselves and do not coincide directly with the entire body of Christ.[65] The sufferings of Paul (and, by implication, others) are experienced in

---

generational overlaps eventually overtook the system of baptizing the children of believers. For those who grew to maturity and had children themselves before ever they could meet the standard of actual "saving faith" in its various formulations by church authorities, the issue of what to do about baptism of their children thrust itself upon the ideal of the church as "a company of the faithful." Without a resolution, the church was destined to become "a genealogical society of the descendants of the faithful" (128). Given the conundrum of infant baptism and the desire for "the restriction of church membership to visible saints," disagreements and dissatisfaction with the ongoing conflict over this issue would consume much of the history of these churches in the seventeenth and eighteenth centuries (Morgan, *Visible Saints*, 129).

[64] This is not the place to enter the debate about the "baptism in/of the Spirit." What is clear in this context and the current discussion is that there is one body and not two or more. But, see further, Walter C. Kaiser Jr., "The Baptism in the Holy Spirit as the Promise of the Father: A Reformed Perspective," in *Perspectives on Spirit Baptism: Five Views*, ed. Chad Owen Brand (Nashville: B&H, 2004), 15–46.

[65] This is not to diminish the role of local congregations, for they bring the body into its visible and tangible form, but each localized group is not the whole. The whole *ekklēsia* is the one gathered before the throne of God as Israel was at Sinai. This is our

his thinking as participatory with the sufferings of Christ for "his body . . . the church" (Col 1:24; see 2 Cor 4:11–12).[66] Paul uses this same language to exhort the elders at Ephesus to pay attention to their duties to "shepherd the church of God, which He purchased with His own blood" (Acts 20:28 HCSB), a reference that cannot be limited to Ephesus alone.

Given this understanding of the eschatological,[67] organic unity of the people of God, demonstrated biblically in each of the areas above, it is not a stretch at all to see the underlying theology of John's Apocalypse and prophecy as it relates to these matters. Goldsworthy's insights on this subject are telling in his discussion of the Day of the Lord.[68] The devout in Israel had come to see, through the prophets, that a day of reckoning would come for them and their enemies, but with differing outcomes for the two parties. Israel would indeed face the need to repent and get in right relationship with their God in order that he might deal with the Gentiles through the Davidic kingdom.[69] It is this underlying theme that animated all who looked in Jesus' day for a salvation in political terms, but they had at least some understanding that the people of God would need to repent to avoid judgment and receive the blessing of the coming age.[70] Many of these faithful form the remnant that would have responded positively to the preaching of John and would have been drawn to Jesus.[71] Nevertheless, they were unaware at first and unclear

---

conviction, but see also Seccombe, "Luke's Vision for the Church," in Bockmuehl and Thompson, *A Vision for the Church*, 56–57.

[66] Equivalent terminology to Paul's conception of the unity of believers in one body are the familial references to sisters and brothers in the Lord that are used universally by NT writers and the conception of fellowship (*koinonia*), all of which transcend mere localized visibility.

[67] This conception takes into account that "mystery" has shrouded the arrival of the time for bringing all things together in Messiah, especially as Paul conceives of it in Ephesians 3.

[68] Goldsworthy, "The Great Day of God Almighty," *Trilogy*, 210–28.

[69] For discussion of the Isaianic anticipation of Israel's supremacy to the Gentiles and its implications, see Pao, *Acts and the Isaianic New Exodus*, 217–45. Isaiah does not see Israel in defeat but victorious through the Servant. In our analysis, this victory is one of bringing about Gentile subservience to the Davidic King and the God of Israel through the gospel.

[70] The idea of a need to prepare through some form of repentance for the coming of Messiah animates the factionalism of Second Temple Judaism manifested in the parties who encountered Jesus and those who seceded at Qumran.

[71] Those like Saul of Tarsus would have thought themselves "ready" for Messiah

even after the resurrection that the kingdom would "come" only through the preaching of the gospel.

So, as they were taught by the risen Savior after the resurrection and before his ascension, they asked about the "restoration" of the kingdom of David. Jesus made it clear they would not know the nature or timing of the final consummation, but they would experience the power necessary to complete the task of bearing witness to the arrival of the kingdom among all the nations of earth. This empowerment arrived in the events of the Pentecost festival a few days later, as they and exiles from all over the Mediterranean world received the promised Spirit.[72] Peter announced for the first time that the "day of the Lord" anticipated in Joel had arrived and the time of repentance and restoration was now here (Acts 2:16–21). As we noted above, Paul also is reported to have preached this same message in the synagogues of Pisidia (Acts 13:32–35), and we presume everywhere he went, as this is surely only a sampling of his preaching.

These excerpts from the preaching of the apostles illustrate the use made by the New Testament "witnesses" (Acts 1:8)[73] of the fulfillment events recorded about Jesus and previously anticipated by the preaching of the prophets. A call to repentance (seen first in John, and then in Jesus, and then in Peter) is announced in light of the events being portrayed through prophetic preaching that partakes of both predictive and apocalyptic elements. In John's final "revelation," these culminating events of the "day of the Lord" are preached to seven churches in Asia by the Spirit and resound with the same words Jesus used repeatedly in his earthly ministry: "He who has ears to hear, let him hear!"[74] This

---

through their own rigorous practice of the law. Thus, they needed "no repentance," as the famous parables in Luke 15 suggest.

[72] See Acts 2:5–13 for Luke's emphasis on the gathering of the exiles as prophesied especially in Isa 11:11.

[73] The language Jesus uses here suggests the fulfillment of Isa 32:15; 43:10, 12; 44:8; 49:6. The significance of this fulfillment is enhanced by the Lukan narrative of the election, by OT lot, of Matthias to fill out the "twelve," made complete now after the defection of Judas. See Pao, *Acts and the Isaianic New Exodus*, 123–29, for documentation of the significance of the Twelve as a "reconstitution" of Israel from the remnant as fulfillment of prophecy at this point.

[74] See Beale's analysis of this phenomenon in "The Hearing Formula in Revelation," in Bockmuehl and Thompson, *Vision for the Church*, 167–80. He concludes, "The hearing formula functions as the Spirit's witness to Christ's (the King's) new covenant . . . to exhort the true Israel to faithfulness to her acknowledged Lord" (172).

is not a localized message but a universal one to the congregations and individuals in them wherever they may be in time and space.[75] With two exceptions (Smyrna and Philadelphia), they are called to repentance. All must endure and join the cosmic battle in varying ways. As they follow the One "who overcomes" (Rev 3:21),[76] they will "overcome" (and it is individuals who are challenged in the third-person singular)[77] those things portrayed under the heading of seals, trumpets, and bowls, the machinations of beast and false prophet, and the allure of the seductive city, if they repent and endure as those who stand by the blood of the Lamb, the word of their testimony, and do not love their lives in the face of death (Rev 12:11; see 13:9–10; 14:12–13). This is not the place for a full study of the themes in Revelation, but it is clear that the churches of Asia and the ages of earth are being warned not to become earth-bound in their thinking and living, for judgment is coming upon everyone "who dwell[s] on the earth" (Rev 6:10; 13:14; 14:6; 17:8; see 1 Kgs 8:27). This theme coincides with Paul's affirmations about the "heavenlies" and the "above things" in Ephesians and Colossians.[78]

A clear warning to the visible church is surely intended in the two bookends, Ephesus and Laodicea—the one threatened with loss of its place and the other with the displeasure of its Savior. All is not well with these entities in the eyes of the Lord and the discernment of the Spirit: "The Christian Church *as a whole* is perceived as being in poor condition."[79] Indeed, the churches are being addressed as unbelieving and rebellious as Israel was in the Prophets and the earthly ministry of Jesus. The "hearing" formula harks back to the days of Isaiah, Jeremiah, and

---

[75] Ibid., 170.

[76] Note that here and at 2:26 the reward for conquering is rule with the messianic Ruler, not just for ethnic or national Israel but for all those in the churches who follow the conquering One.

[77] It is significant that the localized "churches" do not appear again in the bulk of John's visions but are subsumed in the call to individuals to be faithful and the various gatherings of great throngs of saints for praise and "following" the Lamb. Eventually these conquerors appear as ruling and judging in the millennium. Finally, it is "the churches" who are urged to say "Come!" as the composite "bride" (Revelation 16–17).

[78] Can it be denied that the model prayer given to us by Jesus presupposes that it is the perfection of the "heavenlies" that is the object of our praying for the will of God to be done on earth?

[79] Beale, "Hearing," in Bockmuehl and Thompson, *Vision for the Church*, 170 (emphasis in original).

Ezekiel, and the parabolic communication they and Jesus used.[80] As Beale points out, "The parables throughout the book not only have a judicial effect on the unbelieving but are meant also to shock believers caught up in the compromising complacency by revealing to them the horrific, beastly nature of idolatrous institutions with which they are beginning to associate."[81] This is the means of calling out the remnant "conquerors" from within the visible churches.

Clearly, of course, none will overcome without the enabling of the Spirit who is speaking to the churches and the preservation implied in the "sealing" of the "servants of our God" (Rev 7:3). This sealing is the same as that spoken of by Paul in Eph 1:13, as the same word group is in use both places. It is the presence and power of the Holy Spirit, the true mark of the people of God, who marks them out from those who receive the mark of the beast. As we have noted above, the perfect number from among ethnic Jews[82] and the Gentile nations are so marked and prepared for what is to come. This figure again is used to mark them out as "virginal" in their character as joined to Christ (Rev 14:1–5; see 2 Cor 11:2) in his righteousness and the "firstfruits" of the new creation (see Jas 1:18). They are shown later as those "made ready" and dressed in white for the marriage supper of the Lamb (Rev 19:7–8) and finally appear as the New Jerusalem coming down from God. The woman who gave birth to the child (Rev 12:1–6) begs to be seen as the remnant of the faithful in ethnic Israel (perhaps echoed in the numerous "daughter of Zion" references in the Prophets) who are hidden in the wilderness, most likely now transformed into the people of God thrust out of the synagogues (John 9:22; 12:42; 16:2) and meeting as the true

---

[80] Isa 6:9–11; Jer 5:21; 17:23; Ezek 3:22–27; 12:2; Matt 13:9–17.

[81] Beale, "Hearing," in Bockmuehl and Thompson, *Vision for the Church*, 175.

[82] This interpretation is supported and denied among the commentators, but it commends itself to us particularly in light of the fact that nowhere else in Scripture is the tribal listing for Israel matched with this one. The most useful interpretation seems to be that Yahweh has always known and marked out those that were his out of the physical descendants of Jacob as well as from among the Gentiles. We would have no objection to bringing the two together into one entity as the elect seen preserved on earth and rejoicing in the heavenlies.

Israel.[83] This experience had been foreshadowed in Jesus' own experience (Luke 4:20–29).

Given the foregoing discussion, we conclude that the idea of "replacement" of Israel by "the church" with a resultant "church age" is not only a misnomer but a misreading of the history of salvation as well. Richard Bauckham remarks, in commenting on Rev 7:4, that the picture there presented "indicates not so much the replacement of the national people of God as the abolition of its national limits."[84] In Goldsworthy's characterization, it is the glorious result of the mission to the Gentiles carried out by the saved remnant of ethnic Israelites. Therefore, the current stage is more adequately denominated the age of transformation or new creation, for "in Messiah" nothing matters but "new creation" (Gal 6:15), which for Paul and others has already begun, though it has not yet been consummated. Another possible designation, of course, is the "age of the Spirit,"[85] as it is the time when the Son, having purified the elect by his blood and having received the heavenly kingdom with all its blessings, has poured out his Spirit (see Peter's preaching at Pentecost) as the creative power that hovers in birth pangs (the book of Revelation is recording these writhings of both the dragon and the Spirit) over the new creation as he did in the original creation (Gen 1:2) and at the conception of the Son in Mary's womb (Matt 1:16; Luke 1:35) and in the resurrection from the tomb, which lies empty (Rom 1:4).

---

[83] Note the reference twice to the contrast between this group and the "synagogue of Satan" at Smyrna and Philadelphia (see John 8:43–44), and in this last case specifically those who "say that they are Jews and are not, but lie" (Rev 3:9 ESV). Pointedly, the word that follows makes this church the Israel of God: "Behold, I will make them come and bow down before your feet and they will learn that I have loved you" (an apparent reference to the designation of both Israel in the wilderness and Jesus at his baptism as "beloved"). Is this a barely veiled reference to Satan's attempt to subvert the mission of the cross in the days of Jesus' incarnation? Now the members of the people of God in the churches "conquer" through faithfulness in bearing its reproach. More will be said on this subject later.

[84] Cited in N. T. Wright, *The Climax of Prophecy: Studies of the Book of Revelation* (Edinburgh: T&T Clark, 1993), 224–35. Most appealing is Goldsworthy's idea that the tribal numbering of Israel implies the faithful remnant of ethnic Jews who have succeeded in their mission to bring in the innumerable multitude of the Gentiles. Graeme Goldsworthy, *Christ-Centered Biblical Theology: Hermeneutical Foundations and Principles* (Downers Grove: IVP Academic, 2012), 164–65. We previously noted in Pao the term "reconstitution" as a possibility also.

[85] This terminology is in fact used by Seccombe, "Luke's Vision for the Church," in Bockmuehl and Thompson, 49. We discovered his usage after having our own thoughts on it.

This is the often mischaracterized "spiritualization" of the promises, as if they are now in some ethereal and intellectually disembodied state. On the contrary, they are spiritual in the sense that Paul describes them in several places (most vividly in his "all spiritual blessings in the heavenly places" [Eph 1:3]), but especially in the Corinthian correspondence. They are spiritual and not carnal or "after/of the flesh" (Rom 8:5–11; 2 Cor 5:16), and cannot be known without the renewal of heart and mind through the presence and work of the Holy Spirit (1 Cor 2:10–16).[86] Like the body of Messiah (as Paul describes the resurrection in 1 Corinthians 15 and the Gospels portray the risen Christ), they have taken on immortality instead of temporality and incorruption in place of corruptibility. These promises were sowed in the earthly and raised now in the heavenly (Eph 1:3, 20; 2:6; 3:10);[87] they await the consummation of the age to be realized in full flower and fruitfulness. They once spoke of a strip of land in the Middle East, but now they envelop the cosmos (Rom 4:13). This is what W. D. Davies has called "the cosmic awareness of primitive Christianity," encompassing a cosmic view of Christ, church, and salvation, seen through the lens of new creation and a new eschatological age.[88]

The people of God are destined in the millennial reign and the new creation to have "dominion" over all things promised to Adam and his descendants, a dominion never completed by the Davidic line, due to apostasy, but clearly exercised by Christ when the kingdom came near (Luke 10:8–18; see Matt 3:2), both in his Person and in the authority given to his disciples and the seventy, and, by implication, to his people throughout the eschatological era.[89] In the meantime, the whole creation and believers

---

[86] A simple concordance survey will demonstrate that "spiritual" in the Corinthian correspondence simply means "of the Holy Spirit."

[87] John's "revelation" appears to be unpacking what Paul says here. See below.

[88] W. D. Davies, *The Gospel and the Land: Early Christianity and Jewish Territorial Doctrine* (Berkeley: University of California Press, 1974), 370. This is a magisterial treatment of the entire subject of the land as it bears on the discussion in this volume.

[89] Note also Pao's discussion of Luke's emphasis on the reuniting of the Palestinian kingdom in the triumph of the gospel in Judea and Samaria, specifically prior to its advance to Gentile regions (*Acts and the Isaianic New Exodus*, 127–29). Note also that Luke specifies in a clear OT idiom that, following the conversion of Saul, "the church throughout all Judea, Galilee, and Samaria had *peace*, being built up and walking in the fear of the Lord and in the encouragement of the Holy Spirit, and it increased in numbers" (Acts

"groan" with the Spirit (Rom 8:18–23) and experience the "lusting" of the flesh against the Spirit (Gal 5:16–18; Rom 7:15, 18–19; Jas 4:5) and the reciprocal return pressure of the Spirit. That Spirit, who grew weary (was actually filled with anguish and pain) of striving and contention with depraved humankind (Gen 6:3), will "conquer" in the new humankind bearing the unblemished image of its Lord. Here is the destiny of the one people of God "fulfilling" the promise(s). Surely this is "literal" enough to satisfy our attempts to conceive of all there might be in the mind of God, spoken by the prophets and apostles, though we be "slow of heart to believe" all that they have to say (Luke 24:25). As Paul says, all the promises are "Yes in him" (2 Cor 1:20). With Abraham we are called to "Arise, walk through the length and the breadth of the land, for I will give it to you" (Gen 13:17; see Matt 28:19–20).

Israel's Worship, the Temple and the Synagogue

Given the foregoing, it remains to give explanation to the historical reality that ethnic Israel experienced irreparable separation from the messianic community established by the Spirit in Jerusalem and worshiping in the temple and synagogues of Jerusalem, and thenceforth carrying the message of Israel's fulfilled hopes into the Mediterranean world. It is notable that Luke is careful to refrain from using the term "church" as a marker for the infant fellowship of believers until a clear separation began to arise (Acts 5:11) surrounding the deaths of Ananias and Sapphira. At this point, the community is marked out with its own brand of spiritual discipline from "above," and "the rest" (5:13) take notice with fear but also with apparent admiring awe.[90] This separation in conception and terminology is further emphasized after the martyrdom of Stephen (who pointedly used the "church" terminology to refer to Israel in the wilderness [7:38]) as persecution arises instigated by Saul of Tarsus. Only then, having established the ancient roots of "church" terminology, does Luke refer regularly to this group by that technical term. By contrast, those

9:31 HCSB, emphasis added). This approximates the Davidic reign (2 Sam 7:1; see Josh 11:23) and the age of Solomon (1 Kgs 8:54–61).

[90] The best manuscript evidence does not support the use of *ekklēsia* in Acts 2:47.

who accuse Paul before the Romans refer to his group as *hairesis* ("sect" or "party," Acts 24:5; 28:22), implying some continuity.[91] As Seccombe states, "Though the Church [*sic*] was undoubtedly new in form, Luke contends that properly understood it is an ancient foundation. Were it not so, it would hardly have been taken seriously by first-century inquirers as a divine entity."[92] This is a point of continuity between old and new covenants.

Since the Judean Christian community remained temple- and synagogue-oriented[93] for an extended period, and the Pauline mission to the Gentiles assumed the rule, "To the Jew first and also to the Greek," how and why did a schism eventuate and remain apparent throughout subsequent history? James Dunn[94] carefully and meticulously lays out the conflict between the early messianic community and ethnic Jews steeped in Second Temple Judaism(s). The truth of the gospel, revealed in the life, death, and resurrection of Jesus, impacted most heavily four fundamentals of that Judaism: (1) monotheism—"God is One"; (2) election—the people of God; (3) covenant—a relationship governed by Torah; and (4) the temple—the remaining concrete expression of the land.

We can only summarize and comment briefly on this history as analyzed from Dunn's schema and the studies of other scholars. The temple was early on the focus of conflict. Jesus himself had found it lacking in its mission to be the "house of prayer for all nations" (see Matt 21:12–13 and parallels). As it was originally constituted, the temple was the summit of the development of the Davidic kingship extended into the reign of his son Solomon and was the subject of the most profound and far-reaching prayer and answer of the OT (2 Chronicles 6–7; see 1 Kings 8–9) as the divine Presence descended as in the wilderness he had upon the tabernacle.[95] This was what made Jerusalem so important to Israel. "Jerusalem was precious to Old Testament believers

[91] This is the same terminology used to describe the Pharisees and Sadducees (Acts 5:17; 15:5).
[92] Seccombe, "Luke's Vision for the Church," in Bockmuehl and Thompson, *A Vision for the Church*, 56.
[93] Note particularly James's usage of this terminology for the groups he writes (Jas 2:2).
[94] Dunn, *The Partings of the Ways*.
[95] James M. Hamilton Jr., *God's Indwelling Presence: The Holy Spirit in the Old and New Testaments*, NAC Studies in Bible & Theology (Nashville: B&H, 2006), 25–55.

because the temple was there, and the temple was precious to them because God was there."[96] From this pinnacle, the history of Israel had been all downhill into exile (despite brief attempts at reformation and renewal) and a disappointing return of small groups (the remnant[s]) attempting to reestablish former glories. By fits and starts, a smaller and less ornate worship center was established during rough times (see Ezra, Nehemiah, Haggai, and Zechariah), with minimal protection from the walls and city that surrounded it. Israel remained "enslaved" in her own land, as we noted above, but more ominously, the presence of Yahweh that left in Ezekiel's vision never returned to the second temple. The ministries of Ezra and Nehemiah appear to be aimed at remedying this situation,[97] but the canon of the OT closes with a call from Yahweh to "shut the doors" (Mal 1:10) because of the unworthiness of the worship being conducted there, and the promise that "the LORD whom you seek" will come to the temple, preceded by one who prepares the way of repentance (Mal 3:1).

All is not hopeless, however, for during the prior building period encompassed in the prophecy of Zechariah, a glorious prospect and promise is revealed. The Lord promises through his prophet, "Thus says the LORD, I have returned to Jerusalem with mercy; my house shall be built in it, declares the LORD of hosts, and the measuring line shall be stretched out over Jerusalem. Cry out again, 'Thus says the LORD of hosts: My cities shall again overflow with prosperity, and the LORD will again comfort Zion and again choose Jerusalem'" (Zech 1:16, 17 ESV). This prospect is clearly more than meets the naked eye in the years of Zechariah and Haggai, or even of Ezra and Nehemiah. Zechariah's further vision is even more profound: "Run, say to that young man, 'Jerusalem shall be inhabited as villages without walls, because of the multitude of people and livestock in it. And I will be to her a wall of fire all around, declares the LORD, and I will be the glory in her midst'" (Zech 2:4–5 ESV). The sequence of visions closes with the promise we iterated above that it is "by my Spirit, says the LORD" (Zech 4:6 ESV) that the temple will ultimately be built.

---

[96] Ibid., 38.

[97] Their repeated attempts to purify the people and the priesthood and encircle the temple grounds with protective walls did not lead to a return of the fiery-cloud presence of Yahweh as it had been in the case of the original tabernacle and the temple of Solomon.

Now, while it is clear that Zerubbabel is intended to take courage for his immediate task, the process there begun will eventually issue in a work of the Spirit of God that goes beyond mere material construction projects and anticipates the "fire and glory" manifested previously in Israel's history.[98] Daniel had anticipated just such a "building" that starts with a "stone [that] was cut out by no human hand" (Dan 2:34 ESV), a direct contrast to idols and the earthly temple, which are made with men's hands.

The ensuing centuries saw the rise and fall of Greek rule and the establishment of Roman hegemony, with the puppet Edomite family of Herod most prominent in the "land," backed by the might of Roman procurators and legions. Only briefly did the Hasmonean Jewish family succeed in any degree of independence from outside political domination of this period and succeeding generations. Central to this attempt was the emphasis on the need for divine deliverance, which could not be expected unless the temple worship, mediated through the proper priesthood, could be established. The factionalism that developed in this period over just how to accomplish this return to supposed pristine worship that is acceptable to Israel's God is the reality that confronts one who comes to the New Testament as the "day of the Lord" dawns.

Wright documents the state of affairs founded upon the hope that the new age foreseen by the prophets would soon dawn. All had pointed to the restoration of the temple by a Davidic and/or priestly figure who would usher in the "end time." But, it was clear that this time had not arrived, "or else why would the Romans still be ruling the land, and why had Messiah not come?" It was widely assumed that the temple that was contemporary to the time could not be the eschatological temple. Wright explains, "There was therefore a residual ambiguity about the second Temple in its various forms. Many Jews regarded it with suspicion and distrust. It nevertheless remained, *de facto* at least,

---

[98] See Beale, *Temple and the Church's Mission*, 142–44, for further discussion. His analysis had been previously proposed in Meredith G. Kline, *Glory in Our Midst* (Overland Park, KS: Two Age, 2001), 71–94.

the focal point of national, cultural and religious life."[99] But, the prophecies of glory still awaited fulfillment.

By this time the temple worship under the leadership of the Sadducean party of priests and the machinations of the ambitious Herod(s) had succeeded in making Jerusalem and the Judean region "a Temple state or Temple land" within the Roman Empire.[100] According to the Roman administration of the time, the temple warranted enough territory to support its various functions and cultic duties within the culture of ethnic Judaism throughout the Mediterranean world. By having Galileans circumcised, the Hasmoneans were able to claim that territory also as part of the temple land. This is the apparent origin of the term "judaizing," to make people into Judeans for political purposes in the empire.[101] Needless to say, in the tense atmosphere of the first century in Palestine, such political clout led to economic power and religious supreme significance that bordered on the mythological. The temple itself no longer resembled the "day of small things" seen in the early return from Babylonian exile. Its magnificence could truly be seen and felt as one of the wonders of building and architecture and wealth of the ancient world. Some contemporaries saw past the façade. For them,

> the Pharisees in particular, in conjunction with the burgeoning synagogue movement, developed the theory that study and practice of Torah could take the place of Temple worship. Where two of three gathered to study Torah, the Shekinah rests upon them. The presence of the covenant God was not, after all, confined to the Temple in Jerusalem, which was both a long way off and in the hands of corrupt aristocrats. It had been democratized, made available to all who would study and practice Torah.[102]

---

[99] N. T. Wright, *The New Testament and the People of God* (Minneapolis: Fortress, 1992), 226. His discussion on this topic is widespread throughout his book.

[100] See on this paragraph Dunn and his various sources in *The Partings of the Ways*, 42–47. Also see Wright, *People of God*, 226–67. Wright develops further the idea that Torah itself had become a symbol and means of experiencing the land promise: "For millions of ordinary Jews, Torah became a portable Land, a moveable Temple" (228).

[101] Dunn, *The Partings of the Ways*, 43.

[102] Wright, *People of God*, 228. Wright cites other Second Temple primary sources throughout this section. For further discussion of Jesus' relationship to the Jerusalem

Jesus was not impressed either (Matt 24:1; Luke 19:44), and he appears to be mirroring this Jewish conviction when he promises that he personally will be "in the midst" of them (Matt 18:20) when two or three of them gather.[103] The heavenly Father punctuated this situation when the veil of the temple was torn (Matt 27:51) in at least a double *entendre*—for there is no divine presence behind the veil of holy separation, and now the way into the "holiest" has been penetrated by none other than the beloved Son, "through the veil, that is, His flesh" (Heb 10:19–20 NASB; see 9:8). In him alone, the Shekinah has returned to transform the temple in his own body.

Despite having heard their Master speak of himself as the only proper dwelling place/temple for the majesty of God (John 2:14–22), the apostles and the growing community of Spirit-filled believers did not abandon worshiping and praying in the temple and local synagogues of Jerusalem and Judea, as Luke points out in Acts on several occasions, and the later mission strategy was constantly initiated in new areas with the Jewish synagogues. However, the conflict surrounding their early preaching and the tension inherent in declaring the local leadership and people guilty of the death of Messiah came to a head with the arrest of the Hellenist Stephen. His sermon at his "trial" was not calculated to soothe hurt feelings or calm troubled water, for he ultimately declared the temple to be idolatrous—"made with hands," code-wording for the making of idols.[104] This most egregious of charges against the religious establishment and its shrine would never be expunged from the relationship of ethnic Jews and messianic community until the temple itself was destroyed and Judaism became in a sense homeless at Jamnia, but the synagogue assumed the role of prayer-house and place of Torah-reading, as we have noted above. Hostility prevailed throughout the Mediterranean world everywhere the gospel of the crucified and risen Messiah was preached, first within the

---

temple, see Wright, *Jesus and the Victory of God* (Minneapolis: Fortress, 1996), 413–28, 490–93.

[103] This passage is freighted with heavy significance, as it is preceded by the pronouncement about the keys of spiritual authority and followed by a reference to full and overarching forgiveness achieved in the seventy times seven of Daniel's vision.

[104] The full treatment of this subject is most enlightening in Beale, *We Become What We Worship: A Biblical Theology of Idolatry* (Downers Grove: IVP Academic, 2008).

synagogue and then alongside and outside of it, as Luke attests repeatedly.

It is not difficult to trace the trajectory of separation: first, the temple above all focusing as it did upon place/land and worship; then Torah and its force as a socializing culture that gave Israel a peculiar identity even in the surrounding Gentile world of the Dispersion; then disputes over the actual identity of the people of God who inherit the promises made to Abraham; and finally the Person of Jesus, Messiah, unique Son of God, and incarnate Word and Creator. In many ways the Gospels of the New Testament record are attempts to reconcile the Jewish masses and leadership to the claims of what one sect of Judaism declared had happened in the unique event(s) surrounding Jesus of Nazareth. Coming as they do primarily after the ministries of Paul and Peter were completed (or at least well along), they bid the *qahal* of Israel to see in the *ekklēsia* (mentioned only by Matthew among the Gospel writers) of Jesus the true "congregation" or "synagogue" of Israelites. But, as Dunn shows so well, they are arguing for this from within the Judaisms of the day, especially before AD 70 and its tragic events. Only John appears to write with the destruction of temple and city in the past and the eschatological prospect fully in view. By that time, his Christology has developed fully into an area of faith that stands outside any hope of reconciliation with traditional Judaism's ongoing disputes within the accepted norms of the day.

Elsewhere in the New Testament, Paul's struggles with "Judaizers" in the churches lead him to argue for reconciliation along the lines of a single covenant of faith through Abraham and his "seed." He clearly argues for the congregations he establishes to be seen as extensions of Israel (only separated by the hostility of Jewish envy), seeks to redefine Jewishness in terms of Old Testament categories and promises related to the Holy Spirit, and contends for Torah as "fulfilled" in them by means of the Spirit working through faith and love. He repeatedly affirms the oneness of God consistent with the *Shema* of Israelite veneration. James appears to be addressing the "twelve tribes in the Dispersion" (Jas 1:1) to be inclusive of any who hold to messianic faith through Jesus, regardless of where they find themselves situated outside the Judean framework, but appears to be emphasizing a specifically Jewish audience he expects to comport themselves as the "nucleus of the messianic renewal of the people of Israel."[105] Peter addresses the "elect exiles of the dispersion" (1 Pet 1:1) as an apparently mostly Gentile group using the *diaspora* as a "potent theological interpretation of the facts of Gentile Christian existence."[106] All this is to note that through the first century no sharp dichotomy appears between the messianic community and that of the pious Israelite community, except the one fostered by those who came to be polemicized in places in the New Testament as "the Jews," a designation Dunn points out as used by those with an "outside" perspective. The separation was a thrusting out, not a running away, except in clear cases where Paul saw threats to the gospel itself (Gal 1:6–9; 2:11–14).[107] To the end of the life we have recorded in Scripture, the apostle to the Gentiles stated that his career ending in the Roman imprisonment was "for the sake of the hope of Israel" (Acts 28:20 NASB; see 24:15). Sadly, he suffered greatly in his love and intercession for his "kinsmen according to the flesh" (v. 3 in Rom 9:1–5) and held out the hope and conviction that large numbers of the mass of ethnic Israel would turn at last to Christ (Rom 11:25–32), but only if they "do not continue in their unbelief" (11:23).

Rabbinical Judaism took up the burden of the failed political and geographical nation of Israel after the tragedy of AD 70 and solidified its claims to represent the authentic tradition of Moses and the prophets after the transfer of Palestinian rabbinical leadership to Jamnia. The gradual progress to full separation of Judaism from messianic congregations and of ordinary "Christians" (as opposed to leadership) from the synagogues continued at least until the final Jewish revolt against Rome was put down in AD 135. Dunn suggests the full separation with official sanction and definite "parting" sociologically, politically, and theologically did not occur until the time of Constantine.

---

[105] Richard Bauckham in Bockmuehl and Thompson, *Vision for the Church*, 154.

[106] Ibid., 160.

[107] But even in this, the point is that both laid claim to being the authentic expression of the people of God—one now oriented to Torah and the other toward "faith in Jesus Christ" (Rom 3:22; Gal 2:16).

He notes that both Christian and Jewish sources show exhortations from leadership to ordinary religious practitioners urging them to avoid one another—that is, do not go to synagogue or attend a "church."[108] We cite this phenomenon to contrast it with the premise of this volume. "Israel and the Church" in relationship have a long and varied history from the first century to the twenty-first, encompassing genuine compassion and dialogue on one hand leading to conversion and fulfillment of hope, cast against the Holocaust and its legacy of hate and guilt and Middle Eastern turmoil on the other. Would that Paul's urging "to the Jew first" had been the norm throughout two thousand years!

The Present State of Israel

Given the foregoing discussion, can it be argued effectively that the political entity in the Middle East of today is somehow the recipient of the promise(s) made to Abraham? We cannot conceive of and have not seen such an argument in our treatment. We are disposed to view benevolently the attempt of world bodies going back to the Balfour Declaration to provide a secure homeland to embattled Jews from hostile cultures around the world. We repudiate all attempts in the history of the church to treat Jews contemptuously, whether intemperate remarks by second-century church Fathers, Constantine's attempts to treat Jews harshly, Luther's disparaging remarks, or Nazism's horrific treatment of the Jewish people. Particularly in view of the events that led to the Holocaust and the revival of anti-Semitic attitudes in the Muslim world (wherever it has a foothold) and in Europe and other areas, we view as positive the general direction of those nations that seek to protect Israeli freedom and self-determination. This we would support without resort to any biblical warrant other than the need for justice and protection of the innocent.

However, just as the United States suffers from its ability to stand on its own among nations and is envied and hated for that,[109] no matter how just and benevolent its policies, we

---

[108] Dunn, *The Partings of the Ways*, xviii–xxiv.
[109] Witness how quickly world opinion turned upon the US after the overwhelming sympathy and outpouring of support immediately after the 9/11 attacks. As soon as we

recognize that the current state of Israel's resolve to protect its citizenry in the face of overwhelming hostility from its neighbors is used as justification for condemning its policies in world bodies and the media. The United States government should recognize this phenomenon and maintain credible assurance to Israel and the world that it will stand with her in the hour of threats to her national survival. We believe that it is only such assurance of our nation's willingness to lend sustained assistance guaranteeing survival and the opportunity to prosper that will avoid a tragic clash that threatens all of the world with severe repercussions. Without that assurance, Israel's neighbors will surely seek to fulfill their dream and promise to throw the Jews of that nation into the sea and eliminate them from the earth. A nuclear *denouement* is likely for at least six million Jews and countless others if American deterrence does not assure stability in the region. The only alternative is an Israeli preemptive strike to assure its survival.

Israel has a legal right to national and ethnic survival of its people. We wish for them that they will someday soon turn to Christ for salvation in huge numbers. For it is only in this that true peace and inheritance of the promises will come. We will now turn to an assessment of the *denouement* of history, the events related to the Second Advent of Christ.

The Second Advent, Israel, and the Church

We are not capable, in a short treatment such as this, to cover future eschatology[110] in any detail, but we will summarize the biblical teaching in a short manner, mainly discussing the issues relevant to Israel and the church and their relationship so as to position our understanding relative to the other views in this volume. We would recommend that readers consult standard

---

ceased to be the victim and became an aggressive defender of our national security, we once again were the objects of scorn and polemics.

[110] "Eschatology," or "last things," needs to be seen rightly as beginning with Christ's first advent, and we would be comfortable with seeing that as beginning with his baptism, at which the eschatological Spirit descended on him. Graham A. Cole, *He Who Gives Life: The Doctrine of the Holy Spirit*, Foundations of Evangelical Theology, ed. John S. Feinberg (Wheaton, IL: Crossway, 2007), 174.

treatments of future eschatology to fill in the details, several of which we will cite.

Future eschatology for the believer begins at death: "man is destined to die once, and after that to face judgment" (Heb 9:27 NIV). What follows death is disputed among students of the Bible. Since the time of Augustine, many Christian teachers have affirmed the continued conscious existence of the believer in some form of intermediate state.[111] Generally, interpreters of the Bible have held this to be a nonembodied (or, nonextended) conscious existence.[112] Some, such as Martin Luther, have doubted the consciousness of this post-death condition, and others have followed him in this, particularly Adventists but also in recent years some evangelicals.[113] In the late Middle Ages, the doctrine of Purgatory became a standard teaching in Roman Catholic circles, but this doctrine was abandoned by the Protestant Reformers, who contended that it had no biblical basis. Generally speaking, the majority of evangelical interpreters have held to the continuity of the spiritual and conscious existence of believers beyond death, a teaching which Paul presents in 2 Cor 5:1–10 and in Phil 1:21–23 and which is supported by Jesus' comment to the thief on the cross, "Truly I tell you, today you will be with me in paradise" (Luke 23:43 NIV).[114]

The next event on the eschatological calendar, in our view, would be the great tribulation that Jesus mentions in Matt 24:21 (and parallels). The two great questions that divide interpreters on this issue are, first, the relationship of the church (and even of Israel) to it, and second, whether it is future, relative to us, or past. To take the second question first, most evangelicals through the centuries have seen the great tribulation as a literal

---

[111] Anthony A. Hoekema, *The Bible and the Future* (Grand Rapids: Eerdmans, 1979), 92.

[112] See John Calvin, *Tracts and Treatises of the Reformed Faith*, trans. Henry Beveridge (Grand Rapids: Eerdmans, 1958), 3.413–90.

[113] Hoekema, *Bible and the Future*, 92; among evangelicals who have taken this position, see Philip Edgecumbe Hughes, *Paul's Second Epistle to the Corinthians*, New International Commentary on the New Testament, ed. F. F. Bruce (Grand Rapids: Eerdmans, 1962), in loc. (2 Cor 5:1–10), and Murray Harris, "Paul's View of Death in 2 Corinthians 5:1–10," in *New Dimensions in New Testament Study*, ed. R. N. Longenecker and Merrill C. Tenney (Grand Rapids: Zondervan, 1974), 317–28.

[114] Wayne Grudem, *Systematic Theology: An Introduction to Biblical Doctrine* (Grand Rapids: Zondervan, 1994), 593.

historical period (seven years, or perhaps less) that lies in the future and that will be the precursor to the Second Advent.[115] From time to time, however, popular teachers and writers have advocated the view that this event has already occurred with reference to us, though it was still in the future when Jesus gave the Olivet Discourse, that is, that it was fulfilled in AD 70 at the fall of Jerusalem.[116] We are unable in the scope of this work to engage these ideas in any kind of real discussion, but others have already done so to our satisfaction. The other issue related to the tribulation has been more divisive among conservative evangelicals—whether or not believers in this current age will enter the tribulation alongside unbelievers, and whether they will remain in such a state until the time of the Second Advent.[117] This has some relevance for our treatment of Israel and the church, so we need to spend a little more time on this matter.

The doctrine of the pretribulational rapture of the church was formulated among evangelicals in the early nineteenth century.[118] Though it took some time to gain momentum in English and American theological circles, by the early twentieth century it had become the most "popular" view among conservative Bible readers, largely because it was the schema used in the widely

[115] George Eldon Ladd, *The Blessed Hope: A Biblical Study of the Second Advent and the Rapture* (Grand Rapids: Eerdmans, 1956), 19–34.

[116] James Stuart Russell, *The Parousia: The New Testament Doctrine of Christ's Second Coming* (1887; repr., Bradford, PA: International Preterist Association, 2003), 66–114; R. C. Sproul, *The Last Days according to Jesus* (Grand Rapids: Baker, 2000), 111–28. There is a major difference between Russell and Sproul, since Russell believes that all events of future eschatology were fulfilled in AD 70, while Sproul believes that both the resurrection of the dead and the new heavens and new earth are still to come.

[117] Alan Hultberg, ed., *The Rapture: Pretribulation, Prewrath, or Posttribulation*, 2nd ed., Counterpoints (Grand Rapids: Zondervan, 2010).

[118] Dave MacPherson, *The Rapture Plot* (Simpsonville, SC: Millennium III, 1995), 1–120. Though this book is sometimes sensationalistic, it provides good historical data not found in most treatments. For a brief but cogent essay on the history of the debate over the timing of the rapture, see Richard R. Reiter, "A History of the Development of the Rapture positions," in *Three Views on the Rapture: Pre-, Mid-, or Post-Tribulational*, ed. Gleason Archer (Grand Rapids: Zondervan, 1984), 1–44. This is actually the first edition of the work by Hultberg cited in the previous note, though the newer book is mostly rewritten with (mostly) new authors. A more extensive treatment of the historical material can be found in Timothy P. Weber, *Living in the Shadow of the Second Coming: American Premillennialism, 1875–1982*, enlarged ed. (Chicago: University of Chicago Press, 1987), esp. 13–104.

read *Scofield Reference Bible* that was published in 1909.[119] In "classical" and "revised" dispensationalism[120] the period of the tribulation was seen as a resumption of the covenant with Israel, and the 144,000 of Revelation 7 were seen to be literally Jews saved under the covenant of works in the tribulation period.[121] This was required in that system since Scofield and others argued that the "church age" was a parenthesis in God's overall plan of a history-long covenant with Israel that would resume in the tribulation and continue into the millennium. In addition, some traditional dispensationalists (as opposed to progressive dispensationalists) go so far as to say that "the Tribulation is part of God's program for Israel and not the Church," and that through this Tribulation ". . . Israel's national salvation" will occur.[122] Perhaps the most significant dictum of dispensationalism before the 1980s is Ryrie's statement, "What then is the *sine qua non* of dispensationalism? . . . A dispensationalist keeps Israel and the Church distinct."[123] If you have read the earlier portions of our discussion here, you will already discern that we consider that interpretation to be invalid. A more acceptable interpretation has been offered by progressive dispensationalists, at least one of whom argues that the twelve tribes of Revelation 7 can be seen as "the twelve tribes of Israel, and the twelve apostles

---

[119] Craig A. Blaising, "Dispensationalism: The Search for a Definition," in *Blaising and Bock, Dispensationalism, Israel and the Church*, 21.

[120] The nomenclature for distinguishing these positions has become somewhat tortuous in our day. There was an older form (or forms) of the movement that predated the Scofield Bible, then "Scofieldism" saw a crystallizing of a classical set of views. The publication of various works by John Walvoord in the 1950s and then of *Dispensationalism Today* (Chicago: Moody, 1965) by Charles Ryrie, and the publication of the *New Scofield Reference Bible* in 1967, witnessed various transitions from classical positions to what might be termed "revised dispensationalism" in light of new scholarship within the movement. Progressive dispensationalism appeared in the 1980s with the work of Robert Saucy, Craig Blaising, and others. For this terminology and its applications, see Craig A. Blaising and Darrell L. Bock, *Progressive Dispensationalism* (Grand Rapids: Baker, 1993), 9–56.

[121] See the *Scofield Reference Bible* notes for this.

[122] Arnold Fruchtenbaum, "The Role of Israel in Dispensational Theology," in *Dispensationalism Tomorrow and Beyond: A Theological Collection in Honor of Charles C. Ryrie*, ed. Christopher Cone (Ft. Worth: Tyndale Seminary Press, 2008), 140.

[123] Ryrie, *Dispensationalism Today*, 44–45. The recent attempt to modify this dictum by progressive dispensationalists has caused a storm of controversy within dispensationalism. One volume representing a traditional dispensationalist response is Wesley R. Willis and John R. Master, eds., *Issues in Dispensationalism* (Chicago: Moody, 1994).

of the 'new Israel,' the church."[124] Whether that interpretation is acceptable in our hermeneutical system is not entirely clear from just that comment. Other progressive dispensationalists hold something closer to the classic view of that particular text, while still eschewing Ryrie's famous dictum.[125]

Defenders of the pretribulational view (such as Paul Feinberg) contend that divine wrath will be poured out during Daniel's seventieth week, and that since the wrath extends through the entire week, believers must be protected. They argue that Rev 3:10 promises exemption from this wrath and that this exemption also includes removal from the earth before the "week" begins. They also contend that the biblical requirement that "nonglorified believers" enter the millennial kingdom at the end of the tribulation requires a time space for such persons to be saved, and that the seven-year gap works well for that, whereas a posttribulational view would not. Then, in view of such scholars, there appears to be a distinction between texts that anticipate the rapture and those that anticipate the Second Advent, so that 1 Thess 4:13–18 describes the rapture, while 1 Thess 5:1–11 pictures the Second Coming.[126] Generally, such scholars also argue that texts that anticipate the imminent return of the Lord demand a pretribulational interpretation, since, presumably, we are not in the tribulation today.[127] The main point for our purpose, though, is that traditional pretribulationism (not the progressive dispensational interpretation) sees the tribulation as a return to the covenant with Israel.

The midtribulational rapture view has never had a great number of advocates. Gleason Archer defended this position by arguing many of the same points that Feinberg did in the same volume (Alan Hultberg, ed., *Three Views on the Rapture: Pre-, Mid-, or Post-Tribulation*), but distinguished himself from the pretribulational position by maintaining that the divine wrath was not executed during the entire seventieth week of Daniel

---

[124] Daniel L. Turner, "The New Jerusalem in Revelation 21:1–22:5," in Blaising and Bock, *Dispensationalism, Israel and the Church*, 288.

[125] Blaising holds that the 144,000 are a "remnant of Jewish believers during the tribulation." Hultberg, *The Rapture*, 281. He is one of the key figures, though, in modifying the hard line distinction between Israel and the church.

[126] This is a summary of Feinberg's position in the 1984 edition of *The Rapture*, 45–86.

[127] John Walvoord, *The Rapture Question* (Findlay, OH: Dunham, 1957), 75–82.

but only in the later part of the week.[128] He also identified what he considered to be shortcomings in the other two positions and tried to make a case that his position "fixed" those problems. Since that book came out, midtribulationism has been generally replaced by the prewrath rapture view. The first significant book defending this view appeared in 1990,[129] and the position attracted both advocates and critics in the ensuing years.[130] Prewrath advocates believe that the wrath of God is poured out sometime in the last half of Daniel's seventieth week, and that this is pictured in the bowl judgments of Revelation 16. They further argue that since God's judgment in Genesis 6 and following took place on the "day" Noah was rescued (Luke 17:26–27), so the church will be raptured on the "day" in the tribulation that the bowls of wrath are poured out. Hultberg's prewrath position does not make the "church age" a parenthesis, sees Jesus as the fulfillment of the Old Testament expectations for Israel, and does not view the tribulation as a return to the covenant with Israel, but does conclude that the 144,000 of Revelation 7 are Jews converted to Jesus.[131] While Archer's older position was close to traditional dispensationalism (with a delayed rapture till halfway through the tribulation), Hultberg's position is not.

Douglas Moo reworked his 1984 essay for the second edition of the rapture book that appeared in 2010, but the new essay is substantially similar to the earlier one. Only a brief summary of his position will be attempted here since our primary purpose lies not in fending off the various positions but in seeing how they relate to the Israel/church issue. Generally following Ladd's presentation in his *Blessed Hope* volume, Moo begins with the vocabulary of the Second Advent, *epiphaneia, apocalypsis*, and *parousia*, and shows that all three terms, every time they are used in the New Testament, refer to the posttribulational return of Christ.[132] He then examines several key texts—John 14:3;

---

[128] Gleason Archer, "Mid-Tribulationism," in Hultberg, *The Rapture* (1984), 113–46.

[129] Marvin J. Rosenthal, *The Pre-Wrath Rapture of the Church: A New Understanding of the Rapture, the Tribulation, and the Second Coming* (Nashville: Nelson, 1990).

[130] Hultberg, "A Case for the Prewrath Rapture," in Hultberg, *The Rapture* (2010), 109–54.

[131] Ibid., 110–13, 118–20, 281.

[132] Douglas Moo, "A Case for the Posttribulational Rapture," in Hultberg, *The Rapture* (2010), 194.

1 Cor 15:21, 52; and 1 Thess 4:13–18—texts that pretribulational scholars adduce to establish the two-stage coming of Christ, asking whether there are any indicators in those texts of a separation in the stages of the coming of the Lord, with a "rapture" happening before the Second Coming. He states, *"We can now conclude that no evidence for such a separation is found in any of the three principal texts on the rapture."*[133] He then surveys other relevant New Testament texts on the Second Advent, finding evidence in them that the church actually will endure the great tribulation. His conclusion on the 144,000 of Revelation is stated, "I think it very likely that the 144,000 of Rev 7:2–8 is to be identified with the church, but the identification is uncertain enough that I will not make a significant point about it here."[134] What he is clear about, though, as are Ladd, Hoekema, and others, is that there is no reason at all to conclude that the great tribulation constitutes a return to God's covenant with Israel.[135] This conclusion concurs with our hermeneutical examination earlier in this chapter. We are broadly convinced that his interpretation represents the most accurate interpretation of the language and contexts of the New Testament of any in our survey, so we would classify ourselves with the posttribulation position.

Various other events develop in the timetable of final eschatology, including the rise of Antichrist (Matt 24:15–25; 2 Thess 2:1–10; 2 John 7; Revelation 13). But, granted our discussion on the tribulation, there seems little reason to return to the Israel/church matter in regards to that. The next issue would be the actual Second Advent, but we have already shown that unless one adopts the hermeneutical position that the church age is a parenthesis (and there is no reason to do so), that becomes non-controversial as well. What remains is to offer a brief discussion of the millennial views and their implications for understanding the relationship between Israel and the church.

As in the issue of the tribulation, the interpretation of Rev 20:1–6 has brought into existence three broad schools of

---

[133] Ibid., 201.

[134] Ibid., 231.

[135] See this in Ladd: "Scripture says nothing about the end of the church age and a restoration of the Jewish age" (*Blessed Hope*, 136). Similarly, Hoekema, *Bible and the Future*, 190.

interpretation: the premillennial, the postmillennial, and the amillennial. Here we will offer a brief exegetical survey of the issue. Because our primary purpose is not to debate the millennium but only to position it over against the Israel/church debate, we will draw out the lines of disagreement, and then we will examine the theological and hermeneutical issues relative to our own thesis.

The exegetical and hermeneutical issues surrounding the interpretation of this text are enormous and beyond our scope.[136] We concur with Ladd that Revelation 4–22 ought to be taken in a roughly chronological order, but we also insist that this approach is not necessary to arrive at the conclusions we draw. If it is taken in chronological order, however, chapter 20, featuring the discussion of the thousand-year reign, follows chapter 19, which depicts the Second Advent and the defeat of the "beast." In chapter 20, verses 1–3, an angel casts Satan into the abyss and locks him there for a thousand years. This is the same creature who has been the source of temptation and woe to humanity ever since the garden, and his specter rises ever and again throughout Scripture. If there is to be any hope for peace and righteousness worldwide, he must be bound. He is sent to the abyss to keep him from "deceiving the nations any more until the thousand years were ended" (Rev 20:3 NIV). This binding is "concurrent with and inseparable from the thousand-year reign of the resurrected martyrs. For a thousand years on this earth, within history, the activity of Satan leading mankind into false worship and active rebellion against God and his people will be totally curbed under the authority of Christ in his kingdom."[137] If the reign of Christ is future, then that binding is also future, which is, again, in keeping with the chronological interpretation of Revelation.

Who are those who reign with Christ during the thousand years? Verse 4 seems to indicate that there are two groups: those who were martyred, "the souls of those who had been beheaded for their testimony" (RSV), and also "those who" (Greek *kai*

[136] Consult G. K. Beale, *The Book of Revelation*, New International Greek Testament Commentary, ed. I. Howard Marshall and Donald A. Hagner (Grand Rapids: Eerdmans, 1999), 972–1021, for a fairly complete discussion of the exegetical issues.

[137] Alan Johnson, "Revelation," *The Expositor's Bible Commentary*, vol. 12, ed. Frank E. Gaebelein (Grand Rapids: Zondervan, 1981), 582.

hotines) did not worship the beast. This raises the question as to whether those who reign with Christ in the millennium are only the saints who were persecuted by the beast in his war on the saints, and, if so, what about other believers? Are they not resurrected as well, as would seem to be the case from 1 Thess 4:13–18 and 1 Cor 15:42–44? Perhaps the best way to work out this exegetical difficulty is to see these martyrs as representing "the whole church that is faithful to Jesus whether or not they have actually been killed. They constitute a group that can be described as those who 'did not love their lives so much as to shrink from death' (12:11)," and so they are among those described as "overcomers" in Revelation chapters 2 and 3.[138]

The key to interpreting Rev 20:1–6 lies in the language of "came to life" (Gk. *ezesan*) in verses 4 and 5. These persons "came to life." This verb (from the Greek verb *zao*) is used to refer to the martyrs in verse 4 and then of the rest of the dead in verse 5, those who did not come to life until after the thousand years were completed. Two broad interpretations (with variants) have been offered. One, stemming from Augustine, sees the "came to life" in verse 4 as regeneration, while interpreting the "come to life" in verse 5 as the resurrection of the dead.[139] Generally speaking, amillennial interpreters (and often postmillennial interpreters as well) have followed this line of reasoning. Earlier church fathers, such as Justin Martyr, took the view that the first resurrection referred to the resurrection of believers at the Parousia, which was then followed by a thousand-year reign of Christ, and that the "second resurrection" of verse 5 was the resurrection of all persons after the millennium, and then anticipating the final judgment of all persons in the remaining verse of Revelation 20.[140] We are convinced that the latter interpretation is the only one that makes sense of the "came to life . . . come to life" language of verses 4 and 5. Henry Alford has famously said that if language means anything, then the usage of the same verb twice in contiguous sentences, unless some contextual marker

---

[138] Ibid., 583.

[139] Millard Erickson, *Contemporary Options in Eschatology: A Study of the Millennium* (Grand Rapids: Baker, 1977), 73–76.

[140] Brian E. Daley, *The Hope of the Early Church: A Handbook of Patristic Eschatology* (Cambridge: Cambridge University Press, 1991), 21.

specifies otherwise, ought to be construed as meaning the same thing.[141] So, the first resurrection (Gk. *anastasis*, the usual term for "resurrection" in the New Testament) is the resurrection of the saints at the time of the Second Advent, while the second resurrection is the resurrection of everyone else at the millennium's end. In this, we concur with the premillennialists. Why would there be a millennial reign after the Parousia? Why not simply go straight to the new heavens and new earth? Several plausible answers have been proposed. First, the Scriptures, and especially the Old Testament Scriptures, breathe with the expectation that there will come a time of justice and peace on earth (see, for an example, Isa 9:1–7). That is, the millennial reign will encompass, among other things, a political dimension. Second, there will come a time of harmony within the creation (Isa 11:8–9). Creation was truly harmonious before the sin of Adam, brought about and incited by the serpent tempter. Paul writes that the whole creation groans and awaits the "manifestation of the sons of God" in their glorious and resurrected adoption as signaling the end of its suffering (Rom 8:18–22). Jesus gave some hint of his power to effect such a thing in his stilling of the storm on the Sea of Galilee (Matt 8:26), but how much more will it be the case when Satan is bound and Christ rules the nations, even the cosmos? Third, the end of the millennium will make it clear that the real nature of sin and rebellion is not merely Satan but the evil in men's hearts, since, when Satan is released at the millennium's end (Rev 20:7), many of them will join him in his final rebellion.[142] Like the alliance of Orcs and Men against Aragorn and Gandalf at the battle before the black gates of Mordor in Tolkien's *The Lord of the Rings*, both are culpable, and it will be seen that it is not merely Satanic deception but human evil that is represented in Scripture. Finally, the release of Satan and his subsequent immediate demise show the invulnerability of the city of God and of Christ's kingdom, since, when the final attempted coup occurs, because of the overall plan of God, the enemy is snuffed out in an instant.[143]

[141] Henry Alford, *The Revelation* (London: Cambridge University Press, 1884), in loc.
[142] Johnson, "Revelation," in Gaebelein, *The Expositor's Bible Commentary*, 581.
[143] Ibid.

Amillennialists such as Hoekema believe that all of these things will occur, in a "historical" sense, in the new heavens and the new earth. His interpretation is probably the best amillennial interpretation of these Old Testament prophecies that we have seen, since he does not "spiritualize" lions and lambs, snakes and children, but sees a literal fulfillment in the final state.[144] But, we are convinced that these developments need to occur in *this age*. The grievances were brought in this age. Satan has worked his wiles in this age. Humans rebelled against God in this age. Some redress needs to occur in this age. But, one final Israel/church issue needs to be addressed before we conclude.

Premillennialists believe "that the millennium will occur after the second coming of Christ."[145] But, they do not all agree on just who will be the inhabitants of the millennial kingdom ruling with Christ. In classical dispensationalism (i.e., Scofield) the saints who rule with Christ in the millennium will be the nation of Israel, redeemed Jews. In that schema, the church is a heavenly people, while Israel is the earthly, Davidic kingdom. This then constitutes a separation between the kingdom of God in heaven (the church) and the kingdom of heaven (on earth).[146] This would be an eternal distinction. In revised dispensationalism (Walvoord and Ryrie), the "eternal" distinction is dropped. However, many of them still contend that the millennium is for ethnic Israel only, and that the final reconciliation of saved Israel and saved Gentiles awaits the new heavens and the new earth.[147] In such a view, the Israelite millennium would be considered the "silver age" of the earth, while the "church age" would be only the "bronze age,"[148] a position we find Christologically inconceivable. Progressive dispensationalists have largely rejected this dualism,[149] and affirm that, "the church is a vital part

---

[144] Hoekema, *Bible and the Future*, 274–87.

[145] Beale, *Revelation*, 973.

[146] Blaising and Bock, *Progressive Dispensationalism*, 30–31.

[147] Ibid., 32–33. They differed among themselves on whether the final destination was new heavens or new earth.

[148] William VanGemeren, "A Response," in Blaising and Bock, *Dispensationalism, Israel and the Church*, 346.

[149] But not all of them. Barker concurs with comments from Daniel Fuller in his work, *Gospel and Law: Contrast or Continuum?* (Grand Rapids: Eerdmans, 1971). Barker writes, "Finally, in considering Israel and the church, what becomes of Israel's land promises? Fuller rightly maintains that 'ethnic Israel will some day inhabit the land that

of *this very same plan of redemption*," that is, the plan of redemption that began in Gen 3:15.[150] For them, the church is not
an anthropological category in the same class as ideas such as
Israel, Gentiles, and so forth. Instead, "The church is precisely
redeemed humanity itself (both Jews and Gentiles) as it exists *in
this dispensation* prior to the coming of Christ."[151] The millennial kingdom of Christ will witness the church, comprised of redeemed former Jews and redeemed former Gentiles, ruling with
Christ. Though we demur from affirmation of some of the tenets
of the bulk of progressive dispensationalists (e.g., the pretribulational rapture), we certainly concur with these sentiments about
the one people of God.

Conclusion

The most famous verse in Scripture states clearly that the
God of Israel and Jesus "loved the cosmos" in such a way that
he "sent" his *monogenes* (Son) so that "whosoever believes in
him" might enter into "everlasting life." The man to whom these
words were ostensibly first spoken must have been astonished
(even incensed) by such a claim. Was not Israel alone the "beloved" of the covenant God of the Hebrew Scriptures? Was not
Israel his "first born"? How could one possibly "have eternal life"
by merely believing in *another* Son of the one and only God?
This made no sense at all to "the teacher of Israel," as Jesus had
called him earlier.

Of course, earlier in the conversation Nicodemus had been
discombobulated by the assertion that "unless one be born from
above, he cannot see the kingdom of God." The conversation became more and more obtuse to this Pharisee and rabbi steeped
in the Torah and Prophets and Writings. How could one set aside
birth from Abraham's lineage and circumcision for the sake of
something as vacuous as birth by spirit and water? No mature
human could imagine such a thing. Preposterous! Somehow

God marked out for Abraham's descendants'" (Barker, "Scope and Center," in Blaising
and Bock, *Dispensationalism, Israel and the Church*, 304). He does not offer further clarity as to how Israel and the church relate to one another in the millennium.

[150] Blaising and Bock, *Progressive Dispensationalism*, 47, emphasis original.

[151] Ibid., 49, emphasis original.

these things had never occurred to him, but Jesus clearly holds him accountable for his apparent ignorance. Wonderfully and mercifully for Nicodemus, it just so happened that this was the beginning of a journey into the marvel of the promise he later heard (perhaps as the first human ever to hear it), as he would risk first his reputation in defense of principle in the Sanhedrin and then his life in taking down the body of his interlocutor from a Roman cross. "Oh, the depth of the riches both of the wisdom and knowledge of God! How unsearchable are his judgments and unfathomable his ways!" (Rom 11:33 NASB).

This essay has sought to bring out something of the flavor of this journey into faith of a Jewish rabbi (ultimately owning allegiance to another Jewish rabbi), who found it necessary to reread his beloved scrolls in the light of Jesus, Messiah. We can forgive him for being obtuse and "slow of heart," even as we are in our day, for we need the same forgiveness despite millennia of contemplation by our churchly forebears. We in this generation, like he in his, have trouble grasping the cosmic meaning of salvation and new creation. We, too, get caught up in the minutiae of history and the mystery of things only vaguely seen through the diminished sight of sinful minds and hearts. In the end, we are all those of "the faith of Jesus Christ," cut from the same piece of wood, first out of Adam and then cut into Christ. We "see through a glass darkly" as we seek to hasten the day when all things literally will be summed up in him. For, as Paul said long ago,

> [He] is the image of the invisible God, the firstborn of all creation; for in him were all things created, in the heavens and upon the earth, things visible and things invisible, whether thrones or dominions or principalities or powers; all things have been created through him, and unto him; and he is before all things, and in him all things consist. And he is the head of the body, the church: who is the beginning, the firstborn from the dead; that in all things he might have the preeminence. (Col 1:15–18 ASV)

Even so, come!

Response by Robert L. Reymond

Brand and Pratt have coauthored a chapter, which they say takes a "middle position" (as does progressive dispensationalism, they say) between covenantal continuity of the two Testaments and traditional dispensationalism that maintains a large discontinuity between the Testaments. They propose, first, to examine the nature of righteousness to discern what it means to be in a right relationship with God; second, to examine Israel's success and failure to experience that righteousness in its worship of God; and third, to examine future eschatology to discover how Israel and the church relate to each other in the unfolding plan of God. Why do they begin with a discussion of righteousness in a volume having to do with Israel and the church in eschatological perspective? Because they contend that this whole debate is bound up in the history of salvation as that issue is revealed in the metanarrative of Scripture. While I agree with most of what they say throughout this first section, when they conclude that while traditional dispensationalism virtually requires many pathways to this salvation, traditional covenant theology "requires some form of halfway inclusion of those still unjustified in the visible people of God" and is therefore amiss and in the end unbiblical, I must respectfully demur. This assertion they make because they are Baptists standing in the Free Church tradition who reject infant baptism and the inclusion of infant children of believers in the church. But here our coauthors go astray. Because the *sacramental* continuity of the two Testaments is so strong, not to baptize infants of believers in this church age, just as God commanded Israel to circumcise its eight-day-old male children, would require an explicit word of repeal. By their conclusion here our coauthors cease to be covenantal and become themselves dispensationalists, as are all covenantal Baptists.

In their second section Brand and Pratt explain "the historical reality of ethnic Israel experiencing irreparable separation from the messianic community." They do this by mainly following James Dunn's treatment of this topic in his *The Partings of the Ways Between Christianity and Judaism and Their Significance for the Character of Christianity*. It was the temple in Jerusalem that was the early focus of conflict because

Second Temple Judaism thought that God was there, but neither Jesus nor the apostles believed so. In fact, the apostles believed that Jesus, the unique Son of God and incarnate Word and Creator, was the only proper dwelling place for the majesty of God. Stephen, is his sermon in Acts 7, declared the temple to be idolatrous—"made by hands" (v. 48), code-wording for idolatry. Our coauthors write: "This most egregious of charges against the religious establishment and its shrine would never be expunged from the relationship of ethnic Jews and messianic community until the temple was destroyed and Judaism became in a sense homeless at Jamnia." With the destruction of Jerusalem and the dispersion of the Jews, who then met in synagogues throughout the Roman Empire, Rabbinic Judaism "took up the burden of the failed political and geographical nation of Israel." Both Jews and Christians laid claim to being the authentic people of God—one now oriented toward Torah and the other toward "the faith of Jesus Christ." With nothing in this second section do I take exception. In fact, I would urge that it is a masterful summary of what took place in Second Temple Judaism before the time of Christ and in the first few centuries after Christ.

In a short section titled "The Present State of Israel," our coauthors maintain, given the facts of the second section, that it is not possible to argue that "the political entity in the Middle East of today is somehow the recipient of the promises made to Abraham." With this conclusion I am in complete accord.

In their final section titled "The Second Advent, Israel, and the Church," the coauthors turn to "an assessment of the *denouement* of history, the events related to the Second Advent of Christ." After a brief discussion of the believer's death that they maintain is part of future (I would say "personal") eschatology, they then assert that the next event on the eschatological calendar is the "great tribulation" mentioned by Jesus in Matt 24:21 that occurs just before Christ's coming. Discounting the allusions to this event in the parallel accounts of the Olivet Discourse in Mark 13 and Luke 21, Jesus uses this phrase, found only in the Matthean account of the Olivet Discourse, only this one time. Because traditional pretribulational dispensationalism sees the tribulation as a return of the covenant to Israel, it will be well worth the effort to spend a few moments discussing the Matthean form of this discourse of Jesus.

Here, Jesus intended to correct the thinking of his disciples about some aspects of his Second Advent, which will terminate this present age and usher in the age to come. As literature its genre is apocalyptic. Jesus had been teaching in the temple area and had concluded his time there by pronouncing "seven woes" against the teachers of Torah and the Pharisees because of their perfunctory religiosity, hypocrisy, and unbelief (Matt 23:13–32). In his final remarks, he declared that God's judgment against the nation's sin, which was in the process of culminating in the rejection and crucifixion of its Messiah, would be poured out on that generation of Jews (Matt 23:32, 35–36). Jesus then left the temple area, but as he was leaving, his disciples called his attention to the beauty and magnificence of the temple. Our Lord's response was terse: "Do you see all these things?" he asked. "I tell you the truth, not one stone here will be left on another; every one will be thrown down" (Matt 24:2 NIV). Here our Lord was predicting the destruction of Jerusalem and the temple that took place in AD 70.

Peter, James, John, and Andrew (Mark 13:3) came to him privately as he sat on the Mount of Olives and they asked him, "When will these things happen? And what will be the sign that they are all about to be fulfilled?" Apparently, they thought that the temple's destruction, Jesus' future coming, and the end of the age would all occur at the same time. Jesus answered their questions in the Olivet Discourse that followed in Matthew 24 and 25. But his answer was also a *corrective* to their misconception that these three events would occur simultaneously. That is to say, he distinguished temporally between the soon-to-be destruction of Jerusalem and his Second Advent and the end of the age in the distant future.

Jesus then issued a warning about false signs of Jerusalem's destruction (Matt 24:4–8) and urged them to prepare for hardship and to be faithful to the "end" (Matt 24:9–14). What end? If the "end" he intended is not the destruction of Jerusalem and the end of Israel as a nation but rather the end associated with the final *eschaton* and the end of this present age, then it must be said that, at least in its Matthean form, Jesus left unanswered the disciples' question concerning the time of the destruction of Jerusalem. And that the gospel had been preached by that time throughout the then-known world is borne out by Acts 1:5, 11; Rom 1:8; 10:17–18; and Col 1:6, 23. The disciples had asked when the destruction of the temple would occur, and in Matt 24:15–24 he told them that when they saw the "abomination that causes desolation" standing in the holy place, they could be certain that the temple's destruction would soon occur. Luke's Gospel interprets this for us, for he says: "When you see Jerusalem being surrounded by [Rome's] armies, you will know that its desolation is near" (Luke 21:20 NIV). The Judean milieu in Matthew 24 should also be noted here ("Judea," "roof of his house," "Sabbath"), for it helps to determine the "universe" within which our Lord's words should be understood. The "great distress" (Luke 21:23 NIV) has to be restricted to the Palestinian region. There is no scriptural warrant to universalize the distress to which Jesus refers and to apply it to the entire globe. Everything in the discourse to this point restricts the universe of Jesus' remarks to Judea and the destruction of Jerusalem that occurred in AD 70. Then he warned them about the appearance of false messiahs (Matt 24:23–27). In Matt 24:29–31, Jesus says that immediately after Jerusalem's destruction and as a concomitant of it, Israel as a nation would come to an end. Then all the tribes of Israel spread throughout the then-known world would mourn because of the vengeance of God upon the nation. Moreover, these tribes, Jesus said apocalyptically, would "see the Son of Man coming on the clouds of the sky with power and great glory" (NASB), not literally, but in the same sense that Jesus said that the high priest and the Sanhedrin would see the Son of Man sitting on the right hand of power and coming in the clouds of heaven (Matt 26:64)—that is, they would "experience" throughout this age his coming in wrath against Israel for its unbelief. Then Jesus said in Luke 21:31, "when you see these things happening, you know that [the coming of the kingdom of God in judgment upon Jerusalem] is near" (NIV). Then in Matt 24:34 he says: "This generation will certainly not pass away until all these things have happened"—a crucial time-text, for it places beyond reasonable doubt the propriety of the preceding interpretation of Matt 24:4–33. At Matt 24:36, Jesus' discourse takes a new direction that continues all the way to Matt 25:46. Clearly a new topic—his *Parousia*—is now before him. John A. Broadus writes, "From the point we have now reached, the destruction of Jerusalem sinks rapidly out of view . . . throughout this [new] section everything naturally suggests that final coming of Christ to judgment, which is alone brought to view in the closing paragraphs of the great discourse."[152] Jesus thereby provided the corrective to his disciples' misconception that the destruction of Jerusalem, his Second Advent, and the *eschaton* would all occur simultaneously by distinguishing between the first, which he said would occur in their lifetime, and the latter two, the time of which he said, "No one knows except the Father." So, I would contend that the "great tribulation" occurred in the distant past and is to be restricted to the Judean milieu.

I have dealt with the millennial issue in my response to Saucy. So it only remains for me to provide a short overview of my eschatology. Espousing as I do Jesus' eschatological dualism, I contend that this age will come to an end with the church's rapture at his coming (1 Thess 4:13–18) to "meet the Lord in the air" (NIV), and that this resurrected, glorified church will immediately return with Christ to this earth to judge Satan and the wicked and to usher in the eternal state known as "the new heaven and the new earth," wherein righteousness dwells. There is no pretribulation period and no intermediate age known as the literal millennium in our future.

What this has to do with Israel is exactly what it has to do with Gentiles. None will be saved apart from faith in Christ, and when the elect trust in Christ, be they Jews or Gentiles, they become Abraham's seed and heirs according to the promise (Gal 3:29), "so all Israel will be saved" (Rom 11:26 NIV) and Abraham becomes "heir of the world" (Rom 4:13 NIV).

---

[152] John A. Broadus, *Commentary on the Gospel of Matthew*, The American Commentary (Valley Forge: American Baptist Publication Society, 1886), 494.

Response by Robert L. Thomas

Thanks to the team of Brand-Pratt for their portrayal of "progressive covenantalism," terminology with which I was unfamiliar until reading their essay for this volume. It appears that "progressive covenantalism" derives partially from progressive dispensationalism and partially from traditional covenantalism. The system seems to combine the "Roman Road" approach to the gospel and the new perspective approach to the NT. I will proceed with a response to their essay, pointing out suggested needs for improvement.

An Unfortunate Understanding of Dispensationalism

Statements such as "The dispensational approach virtually requires multiple pathways to this salvation" and that the system "requires some form of halfway inclusion of those still unjustified in the visible people of God" are erroneous. The Brand-Pratt opinion derives from the fact that dispensationalists do not use the verbiage "faith in Jesus Christ" as often as they would like. Hopefully, their consideration of the dispensational perspective and response in this book will resolve that mistake.

In a similar vein, I notice in their essay a scarcity of the important term "faithfulness" in the way God keeps his OT promises, particularly those given to Abraham and his physical descendants. An emphasis on the faithfulness of God and of true believers in Christ is an important part of the dispensational perspective.

The Real Perspective on Continuity

From Genesis all the way through Revelation, dispensationalism puts great emphasis on the continuity of God's unconditional covenants with Israel. Any form of covenantalism leads to abrupt discontinuity between testaments. It has the account of his OT dealings with Israel ending abruptly with Israel's rejection of Christ at his first Advent and the day of Pentecost. In contrast, God's covenants flow smoothly throughout OT and NT.

A Neglect of Grammatical-Historical Principles of Interpretation

Brand-Pratt have little to say about hermeneutics. In fact, I was unable to find even one reference to grammatical-historical principles. They do refer to "our hermeneutical system" and "our suggested framework," but nowhere do they indicate the basis for their system, except when they refer to their personal opinions. Apparently, they eschew traditional principles of the grammatical-historical approach.

Since it is a covenantal system, one would suppose that their system has commonalities with traditional covenant theology. That similarity is evident since, like traditional covenantalism, they read the NT back into the OT. That leads them into a number of unfortunate understandings of OT passages. For example, one of the key issues of their system is that the people of God are the body of Christ, even though the body-of-Christ concept is not in the OT.

One illustration of this false assumption struck me particularly hard when they equated Paul's reference to Christ as the head of his body, the church (Eph 1:22–23; Col 1:18), with the "real" meaning of Deut 28:13. That OT verse reads, "The LORD will make you the head and not the tail, and you only will be above, and you will not be underneath, if you listen to the commandments of the LORD your God, which I charge you today, to observe them carefully" (NASB). In its OT context, that verse clearly addresses the ethnic descendants of Abraham and not Christ or the church. In Ephesians and Colossians, Paul addresses Christian churches at a much later point in history. The historical contexts of OT and NT uses of "head" must be considered in coming up with the real meaning that Moses and Paul intended in their inspired OT and NT writings. Usage of "the same kind of language" in the two places means nothing.

Spiritualizing and the Role of the Holy Spirit in Interpretation

Part of their five-part framework in showing why a dichotomy between Israel and the church is artificial and unbiblical is that "the marker of the people is the internal presence of the

Holy Spirit." They seem to ignore certain NT texts that indicate a discontinuity of the Spirit's indwelling ministry of the people of God after the day of Pentecost. In John 7:39, Jesus said, "But this He spoke of the Spirit, whom those who believed in Him were to receive; for the Spirit was not yet given, because Jesus was not yet glorified" (NASB). John later reported Jesus' words to indicate the same: "But I tell you the truth, it is to your advantage that I go away; for if I do not go away, the Helper will not come to you; but if I go, I will send Him to you" (John 16:7 NASB). As Jesus promised, his disciples were to receive the Holy Spirit in a new way on the day of Pentecost.

Under a later discussion of the "body of Christ" part of their framework, they deny a "spiritualization of the promises" as they discuss isolated texts in Revelation. Though they deny it, that is exactly what they do in viewing the text through "the lens of new creation and a new eschatological age." For example, in discussing John's two visions in Revelation 7, they equate the 144,000 in the first part of the chapter with the innumerable multitude in the last part. They thereby equate their questionable identification of 144,000 Israelites with the church composed of people from every lineage. They unquestionably handle this chapter in a nonliteral fashion. Principles of grammar and facts of history mandate that the innumerable multitude of people from a variety of ethnic backgrounds be distinct from the earlier vision in the chapter's first part. Those in the earlier vision are distinctly of Israelite lineage and differ from those in the latter vision. The Greek expression behind "after these things" in 7:9, at the beginning of the second vision, always indicates a new vision in John's Apocalypse. Exegetical issues surrounding 7:9 and the latter vision are very complex.[153] The best explanation is to see the two visions as distinct from each other and to locate the timing of the innumerable-crowd vision during the seventieth-week period of the future, not during the present "age of the Spirit" as Brand-Pratt call it.

What is also disappointing about the Brand-Pratt theory is their switch from nonliteral interpretation in some parts of

---

[153] See Robert L. Thomas, *Revelation 1–7: An Exegetical Commentary* (Chicago: Moody, 1992), 483–87.

Revelation to some principles that are quite literal when writing about the future millennium. They concur with premillennialists in interpreting parts of Revelation 20 in accord with grammatical-historical principles. They should have followed those principles in interpreting the whole book consistently; instead, they chose to follow eclectic hermeneutics, similar to G. K. Beale. That kind of hermeneutics permits them to interpret literally when it fits their system and allegorically in other places when it does not.

An authority on traditional grammatical-historical principles has written, "Calvin said that the Holy Scripture is not a tennis ball that we may bounce around at will. Rather it is the Word of God whose teachings must be learned by the most impartial and objective study of the text."[154]

The Brand-Pratt literal rendering of Revelation 20 presents their perspective with another inconsistency, their treatment of Christ's kingdom reign. At some points they see a present "heavenly kingdom" with Christ currently reigning; at others, they have him reigning in the future, during the millennium. They are not completely clear about when the present kingdom began (at the preaching of John the Baptist or at Pentecost), but they are clear that the future millennial kingdom will begin in conjunction with Christ's *Parousia* (i.e., Second Coming) at the millennium's beginning. Their explanation of how the two kingdoms differ from each other (one with Christ not personally present and the other with him personally present) is missing. The present era of Christian struggles with an adverse world system and the future era of millennial bliss must be different. Does Christ have two kinds of kingdoms?

Distortion of the Land Promises to Abraham

Brand-Pratt turn to other sources in their perspective to explain away God's promises of a particular land to Abraham. Those sources are several prominent defenders of the new perspective on Paul. For confusion over the temple and its destruction during the period of Second Temple Judaism to be offered as an

---

[154] Bernard Ramm, *Protestant Biblical Interpretation: A Textbook of Hermeneutics*, 3rd rev. ed. (Grand Rapids: Baker, 1970), 115–16.

explanation of the termination of the land promises is vastly inadequate to override the faithfulness of God in fulfilling his promises to Israel, which Scripture repeats so many times. Brand-Pratt's endorsement of a new-perspective explanation also raises questions about their dating of Synoptic Gospel origins, particularly when they place them primarily after the ministries of Paul and Peter.[155] That dating places Matthew, Mark, and Luke after their traditional dating. Early Fathers date Matthew in the AD 50s and Luke and Mark in the 60s. New-perspective authors date the three later in the first century AD and assign their authorship not to the traditional authors but to redactors who lived in significantly later periods after Matthew, Mark, and Luke had died.

In their attempt to prove that the church replaces Israel in God's program, Brand-Pratt cite Gal 6:16. A comment in my perspective essay is worth expanding in response to their identifying the church as "the Israel of God" in that verse. Those who want "the Israel of God" to refer to the church must adopt an unlikely and near-impossible meaning for the second *kai* (i.e., "even" in English) in the verse. Grammatically, the conjunction can be used ascensively to mean "even," but it can also be used explicatively to mean "even." The word order in the verse makes the explicative use a virtual impossibility.[156] Identifying the Israel of God with "those who will walk by this rule" much earlier in the Greek word order of 6:16 is the Brand-Pratt position. That requires a virtually impossible explicative use. They do not mention the ascensive possibility, which is far more probable. In other words, Paul is wishing special peace and mercy toward the ethnic Israelite believers in the Galatian church and possibly looking ahead to God's promise of their glorious future in Rom 11:26. He is not identifying the church as Israel.

Through their misuse of Gal 6:16, Brand-Pratt commit another error in citing Rom 11:26 and finding "all Israel" in the verse to refer to both Jews and Gentiles. In spite of Paul's emphasis

---

[155] For a discussion of errors, hermeneutical and others, committed by new-perspective representatives, see Robert L. Thomas, "Hermeneutics of the New Perspective on Paul," *MSJ* 16, no. 2 (Fall 2005): 293–316.

[156] For a good discussion of the meaning of *kai* in this connection, see S. Lewis Johnson Jr., "Paul and 'The Israel of God': An Exegetical and Eschatological Case-Study," in *Essays in Honor of J. Dwight Pentecost*, ed. Stanley D. Toussaint and Charles H. Dyer (Chicago: Moody, 1986), 187–88.

on ethnic Israel throughout Romans 9–11, they want to include non-Israelite Christians in what Paul teaches about the future of ethnic Israel. In the immediate context of 11:26, he notes, "From the standpoint of the gospel they are enemies for your sake, but from the standpoint of God's choice they are beloved for the sake of the fathers" (Rom 11:28 NASB). The enemies in verse 28 are the Israelites who persecuted early Christians, and the "fathers" are the patriarchs: Abraham, Isaac, and Jacob. The "all Israel" of 11:26 must be ethnic Jewish believers and must exclude Gentiles. Israelites are beloved for the sake of the patriarchs.

The NT never refers to the church as "Israel," nor does any church writing until AD 160.[157] One wonders why Brand-Pratt are so hesitant to identify the church as the new people of God. They write about a "new people" and a "new creational identity" but are hesitant to call such "the church," which Jesus planned to build after his resurrection and ascension. They struggle with terminology to portray the church's relation to Israel, suggesting and then rejecting such terms as "replacement," "transformation," "new creation," and "age of the Spirit." They seem to prefer the "new creation" terminology, but that puts them in opposition to their own "new creation" of the future. Certainly a difference exists between the new creation of Paul's day and the new creation of the future. It appears to be more accurate to call God's new program that began on the day of Pentecost "the church" rather than some form of Israel or anything else.

Contemporary Considerations

The title of this volume, *Perspectives on Israel and the Church*, appears to approve the differences between two bodies, Israel and the church. The dispensational perspective accepts the differences between the two, but, of course, it does not accept a soteriology that grants salvation to all ethnic Israelites. Today the only ones who have salvation are those who have received Christ as Savior in becoming a part of the spiritual body of Christ, the church. In such a transition, they become heirs of

---

[157] Peter Richardson, *Israel in the Apostolic Church* (Cambridge: Cambridge University Press, 1969), 74–84, 206.

Christ's promises to the church, leaving behind their heirship as descendants of Abraham.

With this in mind, the dispensational perspective marvels at how the sovereignty of God brought the state of Israel back into existence in 1948. Ethnic Israel, for the most part, is still in rebellion against God, so this could not be a fulfillment of biblical prophecy. No future fulfillment of prophecy will come until the rapture of the church and the beginning of the Day of the Lord, the latter spoken about in the OT and the NT. The present leaders of the nation Israel are probably not Christians, yet the miraculous way that God has raised up this people may be a foreshadowing of how he will raise the nation to prominence during the future seventieth week.

That week will be a time of persecution and purging for Israel and a time of suffering for the whole world as the Lord vents his wrath on a sinful creation. Dispensationalists anticipate Christ's return at any moment to meet believers in the air (1 Thess 4:13–18) because God has not destined believers in Christ to endure his future wrath (1 Thess 5:9) and has promised them deliverance from the horrors of the future seventieth week (Rev 3:10).[158] As they anticipate the Savior's return, they pray and share the good news with unbelievers, whether ethnic Israelites or those of other ethnic backgrounds.

Response by Robert L. Saucy

Brand and Pratt present an interesting and provocative perspective on the relation of Israel and the church—one with which I find many points of agreement and also deep difference.

Before responding to the five points undergirding their position, a clarifying word is needed in regard to their idea that "the entire debate over the significance of Israel and the church in eschatological perspective is bound up in the *history of salvation* as it is revealed in the metanarrative of Scripture." I am in agreement with the statement as such but not with the meaning

---

[158] Dispensationalists concur with Brand-Pratt that the seven messages of Revelation 2–3 are not localized to particular individuals or local churches but are universal to churches anywhere and at any time after Pentecost. So the promise to Philadelphian believers in the first century is still valid.

attached to it, namely that the disagreements deal with the way of salvation and thus the identity of the people of God. Specifically, the statement that dispensationalism "virtually requires multiple pathways to this salvation" is an unfortunate misunderstanding. Dispensationalists have recognized different economies through which salvation has been applied, as have nondispensationalists. But these different economies relate to the human activity in the salvation covenant, or, to phrase it differently, the administration of the covenants through which people are related to God and thus saved. For example, one expression of this faith for the Jew living under the Mosaic covenant was obedience to the laws of sacrifice whenever that was possible.[159] Believers under the new covenant do not have that particular stipulation as an expression of their faith. (The dispensational statement cited in note 12 on page 236 should be understood in this manner.) But different expressions of faith do not change the ultimate one way of salvation that dispensationalists hold with other evangelicals—salvation by grace alone through faith alone.

Thus, my understanding of the differences related to the history of salvation deal not with the way of salvation but rather with the process through which God has ordained to bring that salvation to the world. In brief, the crucial difference relates to this question: are the OT prophecies that depict God blessing the nations with salvation through the restoration and sanctification of the nation of Israel still valid and yet to be fulfilled? Or has the NT reinterpreted these prophecies as referring to Christ and the church as a new Israel?

With regard to the first point of the framework of their position, I concur that God's people are one people, that is, a people with whom God has established a saving relationship expressed in a common covenant relationship. However, as the Trinity may be described as "distinctiveness-in-unity" (n. 12), so Israel and the church are one but also distinct. If the church is understood as the final eschatological community entailing Gentiles

---

[159] Obviously it was not possible when the people of Israel were living in exile away from Jerusalem and the temple, but they clearly were saved through their faith in God and the underlying covenant of promise in Abraham. The Mosaic covenant was simply a temporary administration for the nation of Israel prior to Christ (Gal 3:16–25).

and Jews (a definition with which I have no problem, although it might not be the best definition[160]), this concept does not exclude the reality of national entities both in the present history as well as in eternity.

The concept of Israel in the Old Testament involves a people genetically related to Abraham through Jacob who formed a national entity, which also had spiritual dimension in that its existence was determined by a covenantal relationship with God. This meaning of Israel is retained throughout the OT and affirmed in the prophecies of messianic days when Egypt and Assyria would be God's people along with Israel (Isa 19:23–25; see also Zech 2:10–11). There is no evidence that the NT changed this meaning of Israel. Many nondispensationalists concur that nowhere does the NT see all the "followers" of Christ as constituting a "'new' Israel" as Brand and Pratt assert.[161]

Furthermore, if the church is the reconstituted Israel, then there would be little reason for Paul's discussion of Israel in Romans 9–11. The apostle is concerned here with the problem of the faithfulness of God in keeping his OT promises to Israel in the light of Israel's rejection of Christ and his salvation. Had the word of God failed? (Rom 9:6).

But if the NT writers taught that the church was the new or reconstituted Israel, everyone would have known that the Word of God had not failed. For the church was now the new Israel and the promises of salvation for Israel were now being fulfilled in the Israel of the church. But this is clearly not Paul's response in these chapters.

---

[160] Since "church" is never used of the saints in heaven or in eternity (Heb 12:22 probably speaks of the church enrolled in heaven but not as being in heaven), perhaps "church" is the term for God's assembly during the present history, when it is distinct from other human assemblies, and a different term is used when all people on earth are God's people in eternity.

[161] For example, Markus Barth, after noting Paul's application of salvation terminology formerly reserved for Israel to the church in Eph 1:3–10, 14, goes on to say, "But expressions such as 'new' or 'true' Israel (that seem to correspond to the 'new' covenant, the 'new' man, the 'new' Testament) are not found in this context or anywhere else in the NT" (*Ephesians 1–3*, Anchor Bible [Garden City, NY; Doubleday, 1974], 97). For more evidence, see my chapter in this book and the discussion of the meaning of Israel in the NT in my book, *The Case for Progressive Dispensationalism* (Grand Rapids: Zondervan, 1993), 194–207.

The failure to distinguish Israel and the church appears related to the fact that no reference is made in the essay to the role of Israel in salvation history. According to Brand and Pratt, Israel seems to be just the initial part of the people of God that is enlarged with the incorporation of Gentiles. But this is to overlook the role that Israel was called to play in God's plan of salvation. As explained in our chapter, God created Israel not only to be his people but to serve him as a channel of salvation for all people— to be a nation through which God revealed his glory before the nations of the world.

This explains why Jesus came originally to Israel and not to all nations. For only a converted Israel could fulfill that calling. This is also why God has uniquely preserved Israel through the centuries of exile and given numerous promises of her restoration and salvation, which, as I have shown in my chapter, are validated by the New Testament writers.

Finally, the idea that the land promise is fulfilled in the person of Christ seems to deny the physical, material nature of the human being. To be sure, all true worship is in Christ, in whom we live, and we can worship him in any place. But as bodied entities, we do worship him in a place. If, as is acknowledged in note 20, the new creation is an actual space where we worship God, then it is surely possible to see Israel restored to the land, and an actual Jerusalem with a temple where peoples come to worship, as the prophecies portray.

Regarding point 2, I concur that God's people are his by divine election and spiritual birth and that all seek the eternal city. However, I fail to see how this eternal hope negates a future earthly restoration of Jerusalem during the promised reign of the Messiah as the final age of salvation history in accord with the prophets, prior to the descent of the heavenly Jerusalem from heaven (Rev 21:10; see also 20:4). Jeremiah's prophecy of the restoration of Jerusalem is reiterated again and again. "It shall be in those days when you are multiplied and increased in the land, 'declares the Lord,' . . . At that time they will call Jerusalem 'The Throne of the LORD,' and all the nations will be gathered to it" (Jer 3:16–17 NASB; see also Isa 2:1–4 [clearly not in eternal state]; 60:14; 62:1–2; Zeph 3:14–20).

Likewise, the idea that Jesus' parable of the Tenants (Matt 21:33–34) indicates the final "death-knell of the Jewish nation with their hopes of political and religious world leadership" (p. 241, quoting A. T. Robertson) seems contrary to much biblical teaching. First, it is more likely that the tenants from whom the kingdom is taken refer to the contemporary Jewish leaders rather than the nation of Israel.[162] Second, while Jesus pronounces judgment on Jerusalem (Matt 23:37–38), he also indicates that the situation of rejection will be reversed—"You will not see Me until you say, 'Blessed is He who comes in the name of the Lord!'" (v. 39 NASB). Since Scripture indicates that *everyone* will see Jesus at his return, this statement of them calling him "blessed" seems clearly to indicate a future, repentant Israel. To assert that Israel's rejection of their Messiah signals their final rejection as a nation is also to ignore that clear teaching of prophecy that though Israel would reject their Messiah (Isaiah 53; Zech 12:10), by God's grace they would also repent and be restored (see especially all that Isaiah prophesies concerning Israel in the days of the Messiah following chap. 53).

The third point goes to the heart of the issue, namely, whether God has rejected the OT meaning of Israel as a national entity and created a new Israel in the church as its successor as the people of God. In addition to the evidence provided in my essay, I can only briefly respond to some of the specific points set forth for this understanding.[163] Concerning the olive tree in Romans 11, the root into which the Gentiles have been grafted is not identified as Israel—Israel is the natural branches. Rather, the root is Abraham and the covenant made with him and reiterated with the patriarchs, Isaac and Jacob. This covenant spoke of "the great nation" and the "families of the earth." These are nowhere in Scripture identified as the same. Moreover, Abraham is clearly identified as the father of both the Jews and Gentiles (Rom 4:10–12, 16). Therefore, Abraham's seed includes believing Gentiles without their becoming "Jewish."

---

[162] D. A. Carson, "Matthew,"in *The Expositor's Bible Commentary*, ed. Frank E. Gaebelein (Grand Rapids: Zondervan, 1984), 454; David L. Turner, *Matthew*, Baker Exegetical Commentary on the New Testament (Grand Rapids: Baker, 2008), 517–18.

[163] See also my book, *The Case for Progressive Dispensationalism*, chaps. 6–8.

THE PROGRESSIVE COVENANTAL VIEW — **297**

In addition, Ephesians 2 does not tell us that the Gentiles who were "excluded from the commonwealth of Israel" are now "included in the commonwealth of Israel." Rather both Jew (Israel) and the Gentiles are made "one new man," "one body" (2:15–16 NASB, which is never identified as Israel), and "fellow citizens with the saints" (Eph 2:19, which would include all of the saints, even those prior to Israel), that is, citizens of the kingdom of God (Phil 3:20). To understand "all Israel" as the "Israel of God" including Gentiles seems contrary to all of the other many uses of Israel in Romans 9–11, which the vast majority of contemporary commentators recognize as referring to ethnic Israel (see esp. 11:1, 7, 25). Finally, Scripture does not appear to see all outside the church as "Gentiles," therefore suggesting that the church is "Jewish" as claimed. Paul says, "Give no offense either to Jews or to Greeks or the church of God" (1 Cor 10:32 NASB; see also 9:20–21).

I agree with point 4 in that the people of God are marked by the presence of the Spirit—the promise of the new covenant—and that all are "in Christ," and that therefore only the regenerate are the people of God. But I do not see how this makes the present power of the Spirit the answer to the disciples' question concerning the restoration of the kingdom to Israel (Acts 1:6–8). Surely the present power of the Spirit does not negate the future earthly reign of Christ in power over all of the nations from Jerusalem.

The heading of point 5 is totally agreeable—"The People of God Are the Body of Christ." But a number of thoughts in this complex material seem problematic (at least to me). If I understood the essence of what is said, I take it that the authors see the church as the "reconstituted Israel," fulfilling the OT picture of the Israel the prophets were continually calling to repentance. This would seem to see the church still in "exile" and needing to repent, even as Peter told the Jews in Jerusalem, in order for Christ to return and bring "the period of restoration of all things" (Acts 3:21 NASB). At the same time, the authors see the church as the new Israel, powerfully witnessing to all nations of the coming of Jesus.

This picture of the church fulfilling the prophetic picture of Israel called to repentance prior to the kingdom has major discrepancies with the prophecies. The OT prophecies don't see a "reconstitution" or restoration of Israel as the people of God while still in exile and needing repentance. As we have just seen from Acts 3 (see also Matt 23:39), the Old Testament restoration of Israel entails the prior repentance and spiritual salvation of Israel (through the cross of Christ). Restored Israel, according to the prophecies, is no longer the object of the call to repentance. Moreover, the witness ministry of the church to the nations during this present time is not accomplishing, and will not accomplish, the salvation of the nations and their pilgrim age to Jerusalem as pictured in the prophecies (e.g., Isa 2:1–4). Thus, it is difficult to see the church as a reconstituted Israel fulfilling these prophecies.

In summary, the issues I have mentioned, along with others such as the tendency to see the prophecies concerning the nation of Israel as fulfilled in Christ and the church and thus not literally fulfilled as prophesied, all stem from a failure to recognize that the ultimate concern of the authors for one people of God through one salvation is in fact the teaching of the prophecies. The failure of Israel was prophesied, but so was the promise of its future restoration through the salvation of a new covenant. The failure, therefore, did not lead to a final rejection of the nation or a different Israel except in its new spiritual nature. The same salvation of the new covenant was to go to the nations so that all the believing peoples of all nations, along with Israel, would be related to God through the same new covenant and the same mediator of that covenant, the Messiah, Jesus Christ. This was the OT hope of the Jewish writers of the NT, and I see nothing in the their writings that denies the fulfillment of this hope.

Name Index

Abrahams, I. *172*
Adams, Michael W. *92*
Aland, Kurt *82*
Alexander, Joseph A. *178*
Alexander, Ralph H. *206*
Alford, Henry *276–77*
Archer, Gleason L. *272–73*
Arndt, W. F. *49*
Aune, David E. *118–19, 121–22, 124–26, 128–29, 131–35*

Baker, David L. *160*
Baker, J. Wayne *19*
Barcellos, Richard *92*
Barker, Kenneth L. *236, 278–79*
Barth, Markus *294*
Bauckham, Richard *257, 266*
Bauer, W. *49*
Beale, G. K. *118–23, 125, 127–29, 131–35, 247, 254–56, 262, 264, 275, 278, 289*
Beasley-Murray, G. R. *182, 199*
Beecher, W. J. *232*
Bekker, Hugo *28*
Berkouwer, G. C. *27–28*
Bigalke, Ron J. *88–89*
Blaising, Craig A. *5, 8–9, 34, 94, 136, 143, 271–72, 278–79*
Bock, Darrell L. *8–9, 34, 94, 96, 136, 143, 156, 159, 185, 271, 278–79*
Botterweck, G. Johannes *167*
Bowring, John *25*

Brand, Chad *251*
Bremer, Francis J. *251*
Bright, John *171*
Broadus, John A. *285*
Brown, Raymond E. *96*
Bruce, F. F. *183, 222*
Burton, Ernest D. *194*

Calvin, John *5, 18–20, 70, 111, 177, 207, 248, 251, 269, 289*
Carson, D. A. *47, 159, 193, 296*
Chafer, Lewis Sperry *9*
Childs, Brevard *168*
Clark, Andrew C. *184*
Clements, Ronald E. *167*
Clendenen, E. Ray *179*
Cohen, A. *172*
Cole, Graham A. *268*
Copeland, Kenneth *35*
Couch, Mal *89*
Cragoe, Thomas H. *88*
Cranfield, C. E. B. *113–15, 199*
Crouch, Matt *35*
Crouch, Paul *35*
Cullmann, Oscar *10*
Cunningham, William *19*

Daley, Brian E. *4, 276*
Danker, F. W. *49*
Davies, W. D. *107, 195, 258*
D'Elia, John A. *11*
De Witt, John Richard *153*
Diprose, Ronald E. *207*

Donaldson, James   2
Duin Julia   35
Dumbrell, William J.   79, 166, 168
Dunn, James D. G.   190, 195, 200, 207, 238, 260, 263, 265–67, 281
Durham, John I.   168
Dyson, R. W.   4

Eichrodt, Walther   179
Elliot, Mark   243–44
Ellis, E. Earle   152, 192, 204
Elwell, Walter A.   34
Erickson, Millard   276

Feinberg, John S.   231, 272
Feinberg, Paul D.   156, 161
Ferguson, Everett   3
Filson, F.   10
Foulkes, Francis   159
Franzmann, Martin H.   59
Fruchtenbaum, Arnold G.   88, 91, 271
Fuller, Daniel P.   10, 278

Garrett, James Leo, Jr.   83
Gentry, Peter J.   6–8, 10–14, 82, 84–85, 152
Gibbs, Jeffery A.   99
Gingrich, F. W.   49
Glenny, W. Edward   196
Golding, Peter   6
Goldsworthy, Graeme   239, 247–48, 253, 257
Goppelt, Leonhard   161
Grogan, Geoffrey W.   178
Grudem, Wayne   269
Gundry, Robert H.   73
Gutbrod, Walter   195

Haenchen, Ernst   187
Hamilton, James M., Jr.   260
Hankins, David E.   251
Harris, Murray   269
Harris, R. Laird   221
Hasel, Gerhard   243–44
Hayford, Jack   35

Helm, Paul   19
Hendriksen, William   50
Henry, Carl F. H.   140–41
Hinn, Benny   35
Hitchcock, Mark   75
Hoehner, Harold W.   183
Hoekema, Anthony   4, 150–51, 269, 274, 278
Holwerda, David E.   241
Horovitz, David   36
Hughes, Philip E.   269
Hultberg, Alan   270, 272–73

Jocz, Jakob   169
Johnson, Alan   275, 277
Johnson, S. Lewis   115–16, 290
Jones, David C.   28

Kaiser, Walter C., Jr.   175, 187, 200, 252
Karlberg, Mark W.   161
Keil, Carl F.   179
Kidner, Derek   177–78
Kilpatrick, Ronald   55
Kinman, Brent   58
Klassen, Bradley D.   112
Kline, Meredith G.   262
Koenig, John   199
Kraus, H.-J.   173–74
Kummel, Werner   10

Ladd, G. Eldon   10–11, 15, 30–31, 270, 273–75
Lewis, Stephen R.   88
Lincoln, Andrew T.   192
Lints, Richard   12–13, 153
Lohse, Eduard   199
Longenecker, Richard N.   151, 233, 238, 246
Lovelace, Richard F.   235
Lowery, David K.   236
Luther, Martin   5, 7, 19, 177, 267, 269

Mackintosh, H. R.   83
MacPherson, Dave   270

Macrae, Allan A. *57*
Martin-Achard, Robert *173*
Martyr, Justin *2, 4, 85, 193, 276*
McCoy, Charles S. *19*
McKnight, Scot *115*
McLain, T. Van *9*
Merrill, Eugene H. *177*
Meyer, Jason C. *11*
Mohr, J. C. B. *192*
Moo, Douglas *80, 113, 159, 273*
Morgan, Edmund S. *235, 250–52*
Motyer, J. Alec *152*
Murray, John *7, 28, 40, 114, 194,*
    200–201, 207, 247

Nägelsbach, Carl *178*
Nolland, John *96*
North, Christopher R. *172*
Noth, Martin *167–68*

Oepke, Albrecht *199, 201*
Osborne, Grant R. *118–26, 128–30,*
    132–33, 135–36
Oswalt, John N. *171–72*
Ottosson, Magnus *169*

Pao, David W. *241, 249, 253–54,*
    257–58
Parsley, Rod *35*
Pelikan, Jaroslav *207*
Peters, George N. H. *175*
Piper, John *234*
Poythress, Vern S. *90–91, 143,*
    158–59, 161, 219

Ramm, Bernard *70–71, 117, 202,*
    289
Reisinger, John G. *11, 91–92*
Reiter, Richard R. *7, 270*
Reymond, Robert L. *5–7*
Richardson, Peter *115, 120, 193,*
    195–97, 291
Ridderbos, Herman N. *115, 153*
Ringgren, Helmer *167*
Roberts, Alexander *2*
Robertson, A. T. *138, 241, 296*

Robertson, O. Palmer *13–14,*
    35–36, 41, 50, 55, 59–60, 63, 68,
    138, 200, 241, 296
Robertson, Pat *35*
Rosenthal, Marvin J. *273*
Rowley, H. H. *171*
Russell, James S. *270*
Ryrie, Charles *8–10, 271–72, 278*

Sanders, E. P. *199*
Saucy, Robert L. *34, 91, 185, 193,*
    196–97, 199, 217, 223, 271
Schaff, Philip *2*
Schleiermacher, Friedrich *83*
Schmidt, Karl L. *199*
Seccombe, David *250, 253, 257,*
    260
Seifrid, Mark A. *159*
Shedd, Russell P. *192*
Siker, Jeffrey S. *197*
Sizer, Stephen *109–11*
Skarsaune, Oskar *189*
Smith, David L. *248*
Sproul, R. C. *270*
Stewart, J. S. *83*
Stott, John *201*

Terry, Milton S. *70–71, 117*
Thomas, Robert L. *87, 120, 122–23,*
    125–26, 129–30, 132, 143, 219,
    221, 223, 288, 290
Townsend, Jeffrey L. *75*
Turner, David L. *9, 199, 272, 296*

VanGemeren, William *278*
Verhoef, Peter A. *179*
von Rad, Gerhard *159*
Vos, Geerhardus *18, 29, 48, 53,*
    211–12

Wace, Henry *2*
Wainwright, Arthur *199*
Walker, P. W. L. *60, 244*
Waltke, Bruce K. *116–18, 136, 159*
Walvoord, John *9, 75, 118, 120,*
    271–72, 278

Ware, Bruce A. *5, 9*
Watts, Rikki E. *241*
Waymeyer, Matt *114*
Weber, Timothy P. *7, 270*
Wells, Tom *11*
Wellum, Stephen J. *6–8, 10–15, 82, 84–85, 152*
Wilson, Marvin R. *197*
Wiseman, D. J. *152*
Witherington, Ben III *58, 184*

Wolff, Hans W. *206*
Wright, N. T. *233–35, 242–43, 257, 262–64*

Young, Edward J. *178*

Zaspel, Fred *11, 15*
Zimmerli, Walther *169*
Zobel, H. J. *169*

Subject Index

Abrahamic covenant   37–41, 43–44,
    48, 69–70, 78, 89–91, 95–109,
    109–16, 118–26, 165–67, 175,
    224, 237, 243, 265, 296
Armageddon   121–26
Augustine   4–5, 231, 269, 276
baptism   11, 82–84, 207–8, 231, 241,
    248–49, 251
Barnabas, Epistle of   2, 5
covenantalism (or, federalism)
    5–7, 9, 12–13, 15, 17–68, 76, 78,
    81–82, 84–85, 219, 231, 236, 240,
    281, 286
Davidic covenant   126–31, 147, 158,
    175, 186, 227, 253, 260
dispensationalism   7–10, 14, 17,
    23–25, 31–32, 34, 36–37, 57, 68,
    74, 82, 151, 155, 202–3, 206,
    208–9, 217–18, 223–24, 226, 231,
    235, 239, 271, 278–79, 282, 286,
    293
genealogical principle   6–7, 15
inaugurated eschatology   10–11,
    15, 155
Israel, future of   35, 56–58, 60, 63,
    80, 95–118, 119–31, 134–36, 138,
    143, 150, 152, 172–73, 175–76,
    193, 197–99, 201, 234, 246–47,
    253, 271, 296
Israel, modern state of   35–36, 55,
    61–63, 65–66, 74–75, 205–6,
    267–68, 292
Irenaeus   2–3

Justin Martyr   2, 84, 193, 276
kingdom of God   30–31, 80-81, 101,
    130–31, 137, 139, 144, 210, 212
land principle   8–9, 14, 37, 56–57,
    88–94, 123–25, 138, 149, 169–70,
    229
literal interpretation of Scripture
    42–44, 70, 152–53, 155, 159,
    164–65, 218–19, 223, 259, 287
millennium   9, 15, 125, 130, 133,
    136, 149, 151, 155, 204, 209,
    211–17, 258, 274–78, 285, 289
Mosaic covenant   26–27, 45, 56–57,
    167–68
Muratorian Canon   222
new covenant   27–28, 131–34,
    146–47, 175, 184
New Perspective on Paul   233–35
Origen   3
parenthesis, church as   14, 99, 139,
    151, 271
preterism   270, 285
rapture, the   14, 140, 270, 272–74
replacement theology   2–3, 14, 36,
    40, 48–49, 54, 80, 100, 151, 225,
    227–28, 257
Scofield Reference Bible   10, 24,
    29, 270
second coming of Christ   60, 141,
    174, 209, 273–75, 283–84
Shepherd of Hermas   222
Tertullian   3

tribulation, great   *9, 14–15, 269–70, 272–74, 282, 285*

typology   *42–47, 55–56, 60, 90–91, 120,138, 155–56, 159, 161–62*

Westminster Confession   *20–22, 33*

Scripture Index

Genesis

1:2 *257*
1–11 *37*
2 *42*
2:8 *42*
2:16–17 *89*
3:3 *89*
3:4–5 *89*
3:15 *17, 26, 37,
41–42, 49, 69, 77,
157–58, 165, 279*
3:17–19 *232*
3:21 *27*
4:3–5 *27*
4:4 *32*
6 *273*
6:3 *259*
9:6 *203*
12 *37, 69–71*
12:1 *10, 88*
12:1–3 *37, 42, 79, 90,
166, 218*
12:2 *88, 166, 176*
12:2–3 *79, 165*
12:3 *37, 39, 45, 56,
65, 78, 88, 139,
167, 175, 185, 196*
12:7 *42, 71, 90, 166,
169*
13:10 *42*
13:14–15 *88*
13:14–16 *37*

13:14–17 *166*
13:15 *42, 71*
13:15–16 *166*
13:16 *88*
13:17 *42, 71, 88, 259*
15:3–4 *166*
15:5 *88, 166*
15:5–6 *77*
15:6 *27*
15:12–21 *166*
15:17–21 *8, 88*
15:18 *42–43, 57, 71,
90, 166*
15:18–21 *37, 169*
17:1 *19*
17:1–2 *88*
17:1–8 *166*
17:1–16 *37*
17:2 *166*
17:5 *176*
17:5–10 *166*
17:7 *38*
17:7–8 *40*
17:8 *42, 71, 88*
17:9–14 *7*
17:16 *166*
17:19 *38*
17:19–20 *166*
18:18 *166, 176*
21:9 *51*
21:12 *166*
22:15–18 *166*
22:16–18 *37*

22:17 *88*
22:17–18 *166*
22:18 *88, 167, 175,
185*
23 *44*
25:1–2 *55*
26:3–4 *38, 166*
26:3–5 *88, 166*
26:4 *167*
26:24 *88, 166*
28:3–4 *88*
28:13–14 *166*
28:13–15 *38, 88*
28:14 *167*
30:22–24 *121*
32:12 *166*
32:28 *88, 169*
35:10 *88*
35:11–12 *166*
35:12 *38*
36:10–12 *88*
37:1–9 *121*
37:9 *120*
37:9–10 *122*
37:9–11 *121*
46:3 *166*
48:3–4 *88*
48:4 *166*
48:16 *166*
49:9 *243*
49:18 *170*
50:20 *244*

Exodus
2:24 *38*
3:1–6 *35*
3:19–20 *26*
4:5 *38*
4:22 *240*
4:22–23 *239*
6:6 *107*
6:7 *245*
12:12–13 *26*
12:17 *57*
12:21–23 *26*
12:24–27 *26*
15:1–18 *26*
19:1 *169*
19:3 *169*
19:5 *190*
19:5–6 *54*
19:6 *79, 151, 167, 176*
32:12–14 *38*
32:32 *240*
33:1 *38*
33:7–11 *244*
33:13 *167, 176*
34:29–35 *45*

Leviticus
19:9 *76*
19:19 *76*
20:26 *167*
26:12 *245*
26:40–42 *62*
26:42 *38*
28:2 *152*

Numbers
14:12 *167*
16:5 *247*
23:9 *167*

Deuteronomy
1:8 *38*
4:5–8 *168*
4:25–31 *56*
4:31 *38*

4:34 *167, 176*
6:3 *237*
7:6–8 *26*
7:7 *115*
7:8 *38, 240*
9:27 *38*
10:15 *167, 176*
10:16 *248*
26:5 *176*
26:19 *176*
28 *246*
28:12–13 *176*
28:13 *252*
28:13 *287*
28:15–68 *49, 56, 138*
29:1–30:20 *88, 91*
29:12–13 *38*
30:6 *248*
31:24–29 *49, 138*
32:1–43 *176*
32:43 *187*

Joshua
5:2–9 *246*
11:23 *259*
21:43–45 *43, 92*
21:44 *38*
23:14 *43*
24:3–4 *38*

2 Samuel
7 *128–29, 242*
7:1 *259*
7:8–16 *96*
7:12 *127*
7:12–16 *88*
7:13 *127*
7:16 *127, 181*
23:5 *88*

1 Kings
4:24 *43*
8–9 *260*
8:27 *255*
8:43 *175*
8:54–61 *259*

2 Kings
13:23 *38*

1 Chronicles
16:13–18 *92*
16:15–17 *38*

2 Chronicles
6–7 *260*
7:1–10 *239*

Ezra
7:1–10 *62*
9:9 *241*

Nehemiah
9:7–8 *38*
9:36 *240*
11:1–2 *62*

Psalms
2 *29, 33*
2:2 *130*
2:7 *240*
2:8–9 *248*
2:9 *216*
7:2 *148*
16:9–11 *27*
22:16 *27*
32:1–2 *27*
33:12 *176*
37:9–11 *92*
37:22 *92*
37:29 *92*
48:2 *240*
51:11–12 *239*
52:8 *242*
67:1–2 *172*
67:2 *175*
67:7 *172*
69:28 *240*
72:17 *175*
78:54 *35*
83:5–6 *51*
85:9 *92*
85:12 *92*
86:9 *148, 175*

87:4–6   *240*
89   *127–28*
89:3–4   *88, 96*
89:27   *127–28*
89:28   *88*
89:34   *88*
89:37   *127–28*
89:39   *88*
98:1–3   *172*
101:6   *92*
101:8   *92*
102:13   *173*
102:13–16   *172*
102:15   *148, 173, 175*
102:22   *148, 175*
104:30   *252*
105:8–10   *38*
105:8–11   *93*
105:42–43   *38*
110   *112*
110:1   *112, 144, 185,*
   238
117   *175*
117:1   *187*
118:22   *185*
127   *242*
137:22   *170*
145:7   *175*
145:11–13   *175*
147:19–20   *173*

Isaiah
2:1–4   *79, 298*
2:1–4   *295*
2:2–3   *148*
2:2–4   *81, 175*
4:3   *240*
5   *242*
5:1–7   *242*
5:7   *48, 137*
6:9–11   *256*
6:13   *242*
7:14   *27, 220*
8:3   *220*
8:14–15   *220*
9:1   *46*

9:1–7   *277*
9:6   *27*
11   *62*
11:1   *127, 129*
11:1–10   *242*
11:6–9   *46*
11:6–10   *188*
11:8–9   *277*
11:10   *148, 175, 188*
11:11   *62, 254*
11:11–16   *198*
14:1   *176, 198*
19:23–25   *294*
19:24   *176*
19:25   *175*
25:9   *170*
27:12–13   *93, 198*
32:15   *247, 254*
40:5   *181*
41:8   *170*
42:1   *240*
42:1–9   *171*
42:6   *186, 219*
42:19   *170*
43:5–6   *198*
43:7   *79, 172*
43:10   *170, 254*
43:12   *254*
44:1–2   *170*
44:3   *247*
44:8   *254*
44:23   *79*
45:4   *170*
45:18–25   *175*
48:20   *170*
49:1–7   *246*
49:1–9   *171*
49:6   *148, 186, 254*
49:8   *170*
49:8–12   *198*
50:4–11   *171*
51:1–3   *171*
51:3   *42*
52:1–2   *152*
52:10   *172*
52:11   *245*

52:13–53:12   *96, 133,*
   171, 246
52:13–53:13   *27*
53   *29, 33, 77, 96, 296*
54:1   *252*
55:3   *146*
55:4–5   *172*
55:4–7   *175*
56:7   *148, 175*
60:1–3   *172*
60:3   *186*
60:7   *79*
60:13   *79*
60:21   *79*
61   *242*
61:1–2   *162*
61:2   *162, 170*
62:6–8   *242*
63:10   *239, 247*
64:1   *248*
65:1   *177, 219*
65:3–7   *176*
65:5   *168*

Jeremiah
3:16–17   *295*
3:17   *148, 175*
4:4   *248*
5:21   *256*
11:15–16   *242*
12:14–17   *228*
16:14–15   *198*
16:15   *199*
16:19   *175*
17:23   *256*
18:7–10   *56*
23:3–8   *198*
24:4–7   *158*
24:6   *199*
29   *62*
29:10–14   *158*
29:14   *62*
30:7   *107*
30:10   *170*
31   *152*
31:5   *93*

31:7 *176*
31:8 *198*
31:12 *93*
31:31 *148, 152, 175*
31:31–33 *174*
31:31–34 *88, 132*
31:33 *133–35, 146,*
   175, 245, 248
31:34 *200*
31:36 *176*
32:38 *134*
32:39–40 *248*
34:26–27 *94*
50:19 *199*

Ezekiel
3:1–17 *243*
3:22–27 *256*
9:3 *45*
10:1–22 *45*
11:17–21 *88, 198*
11:19 *248*
11:20 *245*
12:2 *256*
13:9 *240*
16:60–63 *88*
20:33–44 *198*
20:36–37 *198*
20:41 *173*
20:42 *93*
28:13 *42*
28:25 *93, 173*
31:8 *42*
34:30 *173*
35:5 *52*
36:8–15 *158*
36:22–23 *173*
36:23 *148, 175, 197*
36:24–26 *62*
36:24–31 *206*
36:25–29 *174*
36:26–27 *248*
36:26–38 *88*
36:27 *193*
36:36 *173*
36–38 *240*

36:38 *173*
37 *228*
37:1–14 *206*
37:12–14 *174*
37:14 *173, 193*
37:20–27 *174*
37:22 *176*
37:26 *174*
37:27 *134–35*
37:28 *173*
39:13 *79*
39:21–23 *173*
39:22 *173*
39:25–29 *198*
39:27 *197*
39:27–28 *173*
39:28–29 *173*
40–48 *33*
43–44 *33*
44:9 *33*

Daniel
2 *30*
2:34 *262*
7 *192*
7:2–14 *140*
9 *75*
9:24–27 *74*
9:27 *107*
11:31 *107*
12:1 *240*
12:3 *100*
12:11 *107*

Hosea
1:6 *54*
1:9 *45*
1:9–10 *54*
1:10 *245*
3 *246*
3:5 *206*
6:7 *245*
14:6 *242*

Joel
2 *59*
2:28 *109*

2:28–30 *247*
2:28–32 *163*
3:1–21 *163*
3:17–21 *198*
3:18 *94*

Amos
5:24 *174*
9 *144, 187–88*
9:7 *206*
9:11–12 *63, 110–11,*
   186
9:11–15 *198*
9:13–15 *186*
9:14–15 *63, 94*

Micah
4 *243*
4:1–3 *175*
4:6–7 *198*
5 *243*
5:7–9 *243*
7:20 *38*

Nahum
1:7 *247*

Zephaniah
2:9 *175*
3:9 *175*
3:9–20 *243*
3:14–20 *198, 295*
3:20 *176*

Zechariah
1:16 *261*
1:17 *261*
2:4_5 *261*
2:5 *79, 172*
2:8 *36*
2:10 *175*
2:10–11 *172, 294*
2:12 *35*
4:1–10 *247*
4:6 *261*
6:12–15 *247*
8:7 *62*

9:9   *104, 175, 220*
10:6–12   *198*
12   *198*
12:10   *296*
12–14   *205*
14:9   *237*
14:9–19   *81*

Malachi
1:2   *51*
1:10   *261*
1:11   *178*
3:1   *261*
3:6   *94*
3:16–18   *244*
4:5–6   *241*
4:6   *199*

Matthew
1:1   *39*
1:16   *257*
1:23   *220*
2:15   *159*
2:16   *35*
3:2   *96, 181, 258*
3:7–10   *97, 229*
3:8   *105*
3:9   *55, 68, 241*
3:11   *162*
3:15   *241*
3:16   *247*
4:12–16   *46*
4:17   *24, 97, 181*
5–7   *97*
5:10–12   *198*
5:16   *205*
5:17–18   *85*
5:20   *97*
6:10   *97, 198, 210*
6:33   *97*
7:14   *244*
7:21–23   *210*
8:10–12   *98*
8:11   *40*
8:11–12   *183*
8:26   *277*

9:27   *44*
9:34   *100*
10:5–7   *182*
11:2   *96*
11:2–20:34   *99*
11:3   *96*
11:11–15   *85*
11:12   *209*
11:25–28   *150*
12   *99*
12:1–8   *97*
12:9–14   *97*
12:18   *181*
12:21   *181*
12:23   *98*
12:28   *99, 204, 209*
12:29   *216*
12:32   *99*
12:38–41   *242*
12:39   *73*
13   *29, 144*
13:1   *99*
13:1–3   *99*
13:3–8   *30*
13:9–17   *256*
13:11   *99*
13:11–12   *99*
13:19   *204*
13:24–30   *30*
13:31–32   *30*
13:33   *30*
13:36   *99*
13:36–43   *30*
13:43   *100*
13:44–46   *30*
13:47–50   *31*
14–28   *107*
15:24   *182*
16:13–14   *100*
16:16   *100*
16:18   *74, 100, 102, 183, 189*
16:18–19   *129*
16:19   *251*
16:21   *100*
16:21–22   *77*

16:22   *100*
16:22–23   *242*
16:24   *244*
16:27–17:3   *101*
17:5   *240*
17:11   *199*
18:20   *264*
19:16   *103*
19:23   *103*
19:25   *103*
19:28   *103, 182, 189, 199*
20:17–19   *103*
20:28   *107*
20:30–31   *44*
21   *50, 73*
21:1–11   *104*
21:5   *220*
21:9   *44, 104*
21:12–13   *105, 260*
21:18–19   *105*
21:28–22:14   *105*
21:33–34   *296*
21:33–43   *182–83*
21:33–44   *241*
21:33–45   *47, 72–73, 95, 137*
21:37   *48, 138*
21:37–38   *150*
21:43   *48, 72, 95, 105, 138, 210*
21:45   *48, 137*
22:1–14   *183*
22:41–46   *44*
23   *73*
23:1–36   *105*
23:13–32   *283*
23–24   *50*
23:29–30   *105*
23:29–39   *241*
23:31–33   *105*
23:31–36   *73*
23:32   *283*
23:34–35   *106*
23:35–36   *283*
23:36   *73–74*

23:37   *48, 137*
23:37–38   *296*
23:37–39   *182*
23:38   *49*
23:39   *74, 79, 106,*
        199, 298
24   *283–84*
24:1   *264*
24:1–3   *106*
24:1–35   *49, 138*
24:2   *183, 283*
24:3–14   *198*
24:4–8   *283*
24:4–33   *285*
24:7   *72, 95*
24:8   *75, 106*
24:9–10   *198*
24:9–14   *283*
24:14   *197*
24:15   *75, 107*
24:15–24   *284*
24:15–25   *274*
24:15–28   *49, 241*
24:21   *269, 282*
24:23–27   *284*
24–25   *74*
24:29   *163*
24:29–31   *107, 284*
24:34   *74, 106, 284*
24:36   *112, 285*
25:31   *107*
25:31–34   *210*
25:46   *285*
26:6–13   *104*
26:12   *104*
26:28   *107, 133*
26:29   *108, 210*
26:64   *284*
27:20   *50*
27:25   *50*
27:51   *264*
28:7   *47*
28:10   *47*
28:16   *47*
28:18   *248*
28:18–20   *110, 197,*

251
28:19–20   *259*

Mark
1:10   *248*
1:15   *209*
1:40–44   *149*
1:45   *149*
2:1–12   *149*
2:23–28   *97*
3:1–6   *97*
3:22   *98*
3:23–28   *149*
3:29   *99*
3:31–35   *238*
4   *144*
4:1–2   *99*
4:11   *99*
8:22–25   *150*
8:27–28   *100*
8:29   *100*
8:31   *100*
8:31–32   *77*
8:32   *100*
8:38–9:4   *101*
9:12   *199*
10:17   *103*
10:23   *103*
10:24   *103*
10:27   *103*
10:30   *244*
10:32–34   *103*
10:46–52   *150*
11:1–11   *104*
11:9–10   *104*
11:12–14   *105*
11:15–18   *105*
12:1–12   *47, 95, 105,*
        137
12:6   *48*
12:9   *49, 138*
12:28   *141*
12:29   *237*
12:38–40   *105*
13   *282*
13:1–4   *106*

13:3   *283*
13:8   *72, 75, 95, 106*
13:14   *75, 107*
13:24–25   *163*
13:24–27   *107*
13:32   *112*
14:3–9   *104*
14:24   *107, 133*
14:25   *108*
15:10   *177*

Luke
1:1–9:50   *96*
1–9:20   *96*
1:31–33   *44*
1:32–33   *96, 181*
1:35   *257*
1:46–55   *181*
1:54   *181*
1:54–55   *38*
1:68   *38*
1:68–70   *181*
1:68–77   *170*
1:69   *96, 146*
1:71–79   *181*
1:72   *146*
1:72–73   *38*
1:73   *96*
1:77   *96*
2:12   *241*
2:30   *170*
2:30–32   *181*
3:6   *181*
3:8   *105*
3:22   *247*
4:14–30   *149*
4:17–19   *162*
4:20–29   *257*
4:21   *209*
4:26–27   *77*
6:1–5   *97*
6:6–11   *97*
6:12–16   *238*
7:5   *72, 95*
8   *144*
8:4   *99*

8:10   *99*
8:26–9:31   *101*
9:18–19   *100*
9:20   *100*
9:22   *100*
9:23   *244*
9:44–45   *77*
10:8–18   *258*
10:17–20   *240*
11:13   *250*
11:14–15   *102*
11:20   *209*
13:27   *247*
13:28–29   *183*
13:31   *102*
13:34–35   *103*
14:16–24   *183*
15   *254*
16:16   *209*
17:26–27   *273*
18:15–17   *28*
18:18   *103*
18:24   *103*
18:26   *103*
18:31–33   *103*
18:31–34   *77*
19:11   *100, 145, 185, 204*
19:11–27   *145*
19:29–44   *104*
19:38   *104*
19:41   *104*
19:44   *264*
19:45–48   *105*
20:9–19   *47, 95, 105, 137*
20:16   *49, 138*
20:17–18   *220*
20:45–47   *105*
21   *282*
21:5–7   *106*
21:10   *72, 95*
21:12   *106*
21:20   *284*
21:23   *284*
21:24   *183, 199*

21:25–26   *163*
21:25–27   *107*
21:31   *185, 284*
22:18   *108*
22:20   *107, 147, 152*
22:28–29   *244*
22:29   *210*
22:30   *182, 185, 199*
22:37   *26*
23:2   *72, 95*
23:19–21   *77*
23:43   *269*
24:25   *259*
24:25–27   *26, 29*
24:27   *67*
24:44   *67*
24:45–47   *29*
24:49   *109*

John

1:1   *150*
1:11   *95*
1:13   *68*
1:18   *150*
1:29   *23, 26–27, 96*
2:14–16   *97*
2:14–22   *264*
2:18   *198*
2:18–19   *208*
3   *240*
3:1–14   *228*
3:13   *150*
3:18   *239*
4   *238*
4:22   *63, 148, 189*
5:1–18   *97*
5:9   *240*
5:17–29   *150*
5:24–25   *211, 216*
5:39   *26*
5:46   *26*
5:46–47   *67*
6:35   *150*
6:38   *150*
6:46   *150*
6:62   *150*

7:3–8   *238*
7:39   *203, 288*
8:12   *150*
8:28   *239*
8:38   *150*
8:39   *241*
8:39–44   *55*
8:39–47   *229*
8:43–44   *257*
8:56   *27, 29, 32, 39, 55*
8:58   *150*
8:59   *102*
9   *150*
9:22   *256*
9:39   *102*
9:40–41   *102*
10:1   *102*
10:1–18   *102*
10:3   *102*
10:4   *102*
10:5   *102*
10:7   *102, 150*
10:8   *102*
10:9   *102*
10:11   *102, 150*
10:12–13   *102*
10:14   *102, 247*
10:16   *102*
10:27   *247, 250*
10:30   *150*
10:30–31   *102*
11:1–44   *149*
11:25   *150*
11:45–57   *149*
11:48   *72, 95*
11:50   *72, 95*
11:51   *72, 95*
11:52   *72, 95*
12:2–8   *104*
12:12–19   *104*
12:13   *104*
12:15   *104*
12:31   *134, 216*
12:32   *239*
12:42   *256*

13:18 *26, 67*
13:33 *108*
13:35 *250*
13:36 *108*
14 *242*
14:3 *273*
14:6 *150*
14:16 *108*
14:17 *108*
14:26 *108*
15 *242*
15:1 *150*
15:13 *250*
15:20 *244*
15:26 *108*
15:26–27 *250*
16:2 *256*
16:5–7 *108*
16:7 *108, 288*
16:8–11 *250*
16:13 *108*
16:28 *150*
16:33 *244*
17:3 *237*
17:20 *108*
18:36 *55*
19:15 *242*
19:24 *26, 67*
19:28 *26, 67*
19:36–37 *26, 67*
20:9 *26, 67*
20:21 *246*
20:23 *251*
20:28 *150*

Acts
1:3 *57*
1:4 *58*
1:5 *284*
1:6 *57, 111, 150*
1:6–7 *185, 187*
1:6–8 *250, 297*
1:7 *57*
1:8 *59–60, 110, 112,*
     197, 250, 254
1:10–11 *112*

1:11 *284*
2 *112, 143, 145, 250*
2:5 *248*
2:5–13 *254*
2:16–21 *254*
2:17–18 *163*
2:17–21 *163*
2:30–31 *249*
2:30–36 *144, 182*
2:33–36 *112*
2:33–39 *185*
2:34–35 *112, 150*
2:34–36 *185*
2:36 *185*
2:39 *28*
2:44–47 *205*
2:47 *259*
3 *109, 298*
3:11–26 *183*
3:17–18 *26*
3:19–21 *109–110,*
          187, 205
3:20–21 *213*
3:21 *60, 139*
3:21 *297*
3:23 *109, 150*
3:25 *110*
3:25–26 *39, 185*
4:11 *185*
4:27 *182*
5:11 *259*
5:12 *183*
5:17 *177, 260*
5:21–26 *183*
5:42 *183*
7 *282*
7:5 *43*
7:51 *248*
7:52 *238*
8 *1*
9:16 *244*
9:31 *258*
10 *1*
10:34–35 *110, 150,*
           184, 206
10:36 *59*

10:42 *204*
10:43 *26*
11 *249*
11:17–18 *184*
13 *186*
13:1–4 *250*
13:5 *186*
13:14 *186*
13:23 *146*
13:27–30 *26*
13:32–33 *249*
13:32–35 *254*
13:34 *144*
13:45 *177*
13:46 *186*
13:47 *186, 219*
14:1 *186*
14:22 *244*
15 *143, 151, 184,*
    186–88, 249
15:5 *260*
15:8 *250*
15:9 *249*
15:13–19 *186*
15:14 *190*
15:15–17 *63*
15:15–18 *249*
15:16 *144, 187*
15:16–17 *26*
15:16–18 *110–11,*
           150
15:28 *250*
16:6–10 *250*
16:15 *28*
16:31–34 *28*
17 *95*
17:1–2 *186*
17:2–3 *26*
17:5 *177*
17:10 *186*
17:11 *37*
17:17 *186*
17:26 *72*
17:31 *204*
18:4 *186*
18:10 *190*

18:19   *186*
18:26   *186*
19:1–7   *250*
19:8   *186*
20:21   *186*
20:28   *150, 253*
20:32   *249*
24:2   *72, 95*
24:5   *260*
24:10   *72, 95*
24:15   *266*
26:22–23   *26, 192*
26:23   *186*
28:17   *186*
28:20   *266*
28:22   *260*
28:22–23   *26*

Romans

1:4   *257*
1:8   *284*
1:16   *113, 150, 186*
1:17   *232*
2:4   *214*
2:10   *113*
2:11   *206*
2:17–24   *68*
2:17–29   *65*
2:25–29   *57, 68, 84*
2:28–29   *65, 195, 237, 239*
3:1–2   *113, 150*
3:2   *173*
3:3   *113, 199*
3–8   *50*
3:9   *68*
3:21   *85*
3:21–26   *84*
3:22   *266*
3:29–30   *237*
3:31   *85*
4   *196, 238*
4:3   *77*
4:9–25   *147*
4:10–12   *296*
4:11–12   *40*

4:12   *196*
4:13   *45, 47, 56–57, 139, 228, 258, 285*
4:13–25   *229*
4:16   *196, 296*
4:18–22   *77*
5:5   *249–50*
5:12–21   *240*
5:15   *107*
5:17   *211*
5:18   *232*
5:19   *107, 232*
6   *248*
7:4   *246*
7:15   *259*
7:18–19   *259*
8:5–11   *258*
8:9   *250*
8:9–10   *193*
8:9–11   *249*
8:15–17   *249*
8:17   *244*
8:18–22   *277*
8:18–23   *259*
8:18–25   *227*
8:19–23   *43*
8:19–25   *238*
8:20   *232*
8:21   *233*
8:22–23   *60, 139*
9   *52*
9:1–5   *266*
9:3   *175*
9:3–4   *194, 199*
9:3–5   *81*
9:4   *186*
9:4–5   *66, 113, 150, 184, 187, 193*
9:5   *63*
9:6   *50, 80, 194–95, 208, 294*
9:6–8   *53, 55*
9:6–13   *37*
9:7–8   *55*
9:7–9   *51*
9–11   *79–80, 195,*

199, 235, 242, 291, 294, 297
9:11   *52*
9:11–13   *51–52*
9:13   *51*
9–16   *195*
9:24   *46*
9:25–26   *46, 190*
9:26–27   *245*
9:27   *80*
9:27–29   *50, 139*
9:30–33   *242*
9:31   *53, 80*
9:32–33   *220*
10:4   *236, 246*
10:17–18   *284*
10:19   *80*
10:19–21   *179*
10:20   *220*
10:20–21   *178*
10:21   *80*
11   *49, 54, 242, 296*
11:1–2   *114, 150, 190, 199*
11:1–5   *139*
11:2   *79–80*
11:2–5   *248*
11:5   *53–54, 183–84, 200*
11:7   *80*
11:7–10   *53, 139*
11:11   *54, 139, 177, 179, 246*
11:11–12   *80, 108*
11:11–15   *188*
11:11–36   *247*
11:12   *54, 201*
11:14   *54, 139, 177, 179*
11:15   *80*
11:16–24   *26*
11:17   *183*
11:17–18   *195*
11:17–24   *54, 227*
11:18   *190*
11:23   *242, 266*

11:23–24 *54, 139*
11:24 *184*
11:24–31 *80*
11:25 *54, 80*
11:25–31 *184*
11:25–32 *266*
11:26 *54, 75, 80, 114,*
   139, 200, 285, 290
11:28 *68, 114, 150,*
   291
11:28–29 *75, 81, 200*
11:29 *115*
11:33 *280*
12 *250*
12:1 *228*
12:2 *228*
12:6 *221*
13:7 *204*
14:17 *31, 145, 211*
15:7–12 *187*
15:8–9 *39, 187*
15:10 *187*
15:12 *127*
15:12 *188*
15:27 *190*
16:20 *157*
16:25–26 *77, 192,*
   193

1 Corinthians
1 *248*
1:16 *28*
1:18–25 *242*
2:1 *193*
2:4–5 *251*
2:7 *193*
2:10–16 *258*
4:20 *145*
5:7 *26, 57*
5:12 *204*
6:2 *142*
7:14 *28, 83*
8:3 *247*
8:4–6 *237*
9:20–21 *297*
10:1 *245*

10:1–4 *241*
10:4 *191*
10:6 *43*
10:11 *162*
10:31–32 *113, 150*
10:32 *297*
11:25 *107, 147*
11:26 *249*
12 *250*
12:2 *245*
12:12–13 *251–52*
12:13 *193*
12:28 *221*
12:31 *250*
15 *131, 258*
15:3–4 *26*
15:11 *213*
15:20–26 *211*
15:21 *274*
15:23 *142, 211*
15:24 *81, 155,*
   211–12
15:25–28 *238*
15:28 *155*
15:42–43 *142*
15:42–44 *276*
15:45 *21, 190*
15:45–49 *240*
15:47 *21*
15:52 *274*

2 Corinthians
1:20 *259*
2:14–16 *251*
3:3 *146*
3:6 *147*
3:7 *45*
3:7–16 *45, 67*
3:9 *45*
3:11 *45*
4:11–12 *253*
5:1–10 *269*
5:16 *258*
5:16–21 *229*
5:17 *252*
6:2 *170*

6:16 *148, 190*
6:16–7:1 *245*
6:16–18 *190*
11:2 *256*
11:24 *186*

Galatians
1:6–9 *266*
2:3 *57*
2:11–14 *266*
2:16 *65, 266*
2:19 *246*
3:1 *248*
3:2 *250*
3:6 *77*
3:7 *115*
3:8 *39, 45*
3:8–14 *147*
3:9 *39*
3:10 *68*
3:14 *196*
3:14 *40*
3:15–18 *238*
3:16 *39, 45*
3:16–25 *293*
3:16–29 *229*
3:17 *40*
3:20 *233, 237*
3:20 *238*
3:23–25 *77*
3:24–25 *204*
3:25–4:11 *204*
3:28 *239*
3:29 *40, 196, 233,*
   285
4:1–6 *77*
4:6 *249*
4:16 *37*
4:21–5:1 *68*
4:21–31 *51*
4:24–25 *55, 139*
4:25 *65, 241*
4:26 *44*
4:26–31 *240*
4:28 *196*
4:29 *51*

5:2–4   68
5:2–6   57
5:3–4   65
5:6   84
5:16–18   259
5:22   250
6   243
6:12–16   41
6:15   68, 115, 257
6:16   26, 41, 80,
   115–16, 120, 150,
   194, 235, 290

Ephesians
1–3   294
1:3   240, 258
1:3–10   294
1:6   240
1:13   256
1:13–14   249
1:14   294
1:15   250
1:20   258
1:22–23   248, 252,
   287
2   15, 297
2:2   134
2:4–6   216
2:6   211, 258
2:11–3:20   252
2:11–13   26, 41, 70,
   80
2:12   50, 147, 175,
   191, 245
2:14–15   153
2:15   190, 239
2:19   297
2:19–3:10   221
2:20   189
3   192, 253
3:2–12   31
3:3   221
3:3–5   222
3:3–6   247
3:3–12   29
3:4   193

3:5   221
3:6   147, 221
3:10   258
4   250
4:1–6   251
4:11   221
4:23   229
4:30   239, 249
5:18–20   250
6:19   193

Philippians
1:20   244
1:21–23   269
2:8–11   182
3:3   26, 41, 196, 237,
   246, 248
3:9   227, 238
3:18–20   240
3:20   191, 297
3:20–21   142, 211
4:3   240

Colossians
1   31
1:6   284
1:9–23   226
1:11   248
1:13   145, 211, 240
1:15–18   280
1:15–29   252
1:18   252, 287
1:23   284
1:24   253
1:25–27   31
2:2   193
2:11   246
2:11–12   57
2:15   157
2:17   43
3:1   226
3:1–4   240
3:10   229
4:3   193

1 Thessalonians
1:5   251

2:14–16   245
2:15–16   49, 63, 138
2:19   241
3:3   244
4:13–18   142, 211,
   272, 274, 276,
   285, 292
5:1–11   272
5:2   73–74
5:9   292

2 Thessalonians
1:5   244
1:5–10   142, 211
2   216
2:1–10   274
2:3–10   198

1 Timothy
2:5   238
2:6   107
3:16   193
4:1   198

2 Timothy
2:12   244
2:19   247
3:1–5   198
3:12   244
3:15   27

Titus
2:13   150, 211
2:14   190
3:3–7   229
3:6   250

Hebrews
1:2   248
1:8   150
2:5–18   240
2:14   157
2:14–15   216
4:11   91
7:11   33
7:19   203
7:27   33

8   *146–47*
8:6–7   *33*
8:7–12   *152*
8:13   *203*
9:8   *264*
9:9   *33*
9:12   *33*
9:13–14   *33*
9:22   *25*
9:25–26   *33*
9:27   *269*
9:28   *33*
10   *146–47*
10:1   *43*
10:1–2   *33*
10:10–14   *33*
10:12–14   *33*
10:19–20   *264*
11   *32*
11:1   *249–50*
11:1–40   *24*
11:8   *43*
11:8–16   *44*
11:9   *43*
11:10   *240, 242*
11:13–16   *240, 242*
11:17   *43*
11:26–27   *27*
11:39   *45*
11:39–40   *249*
11:40   *203*
12:22   *44, 65, 180, 294*
12:22–23   *191, 240*
12:22–24   *240*
12:23   *240*
13:12–13   *244*

James

1:1   *265*
1:18   *256*
2:2   *260*
4:5   *259*

1 Peter

1:1   *266*

1:10–11   *157*
1:10–12   *23*
1:13–2:12   *245*
1:20   *213*
2   *196*
2:8   *220*
2:9   *54, 80, 151, 196, 197*
2:9–10   *190*
2:10   *54*
2:12   *205*
3:20–22   *241*
3:22   *213*
5:10   *244*

2 Peter

1:1   *150*
1:11   *213–14*
1:16   *214*
1:16–19   *101*
1:17   *240*
1:21   *157*
2:7   *243*
2:9   *214*
3   *61, 214*
3:4   *214*
3:5–6   *61, 213*
3:7   *61, 213–14*
3:9   *214*
3:10   *61, 214*
3:12   *214*
3:13   *61, 213*
3:13–14   *81*
3:15   *214*
3:15–16   *214*

1 John

2:18   *198*
2:18–19   *208*
2:27   *147*
3:2–3   *142*
3:8   *157*
5:9   *240*
5:20   *150*

2 John

7   *274*

Revelation

1   *150*
1:5   *127–28, 133*
1:7   *217*
1:9   *244*
1:18   *129*
2–3   *9, 133, 292*
2:7   *42, 215*
2:9   *122, 136*
2:10   *65*
2:11   *215*
2:17   *215*
2:25–27   *215*
2:27   *216*
3:3–5   *215*
3:5   *240*
3:7   *129*
3:9   *122, 136, 257*
3:10   *73–75, 272, 292*
3:10–12   *215*
3:14   *215*
3:21   *215, 255*
4–22   *275*
5:5   *127–28*
5:5   *243*
5:6   *133*
6:10   *255*
7   *134, 136, 244, 271, 273, 288*
7:2–8   *274*
7:3   *256*
7:4   *257*
7:4–8   *120*
7:9   *133*
7:9–17   *120*
7:14   *133*
7:17   *133*
10:7   *215*
11:1–3   *122*
11:1–12   *123*
11:1–13   *122*
11:8   *240*
11:15   *128, 130–32, 204, 215*
11:18–19   *215*

12   *120–22, 134*
12:1–6   *256*
12:6   *121*
12:7–9   *157*
12:10   *130*
12:11   *132–33, 250,*
   255
12:17   *121*
13   *274*
13:8   *104, 133, 240*
13:9–10   *255*
13:14   *255*
14   *134, 136*
14:1   *133*
14:1–5   *256*
14:3   *133*
14:6   *255*
14:12–13   *255*
14:14–20   *215*
14:15   *215*
14:16   *215*
14:19   *215*
14:20   *126*
15:1   *215*

16   *273*
16:12   *125*
16:15–21   *215*
16:16   *125*
16–17   *255*
17:8   *240, 255*
19   *249*
19:6   *130*
19:7–8   *256*
19:11–20:10   *130*
19:11–21   *215*
19:16   *134*
19–20   *215*
20   *4, 116, 211–12,*
   214, 276, 289
20:1–3   *69, 133*
20:1–6   *274, 276*
20:1–10   *116, 118,*
   136
20:1–15   *216*
20:3   *133, 275*
20:4   *4, 134*
20:4–5   *201*
20:4–21:1   *81*

20:5   *4*
20:7   *277*
20:9   *125–26*
20:10   *69*
20:11–15   *217*
21:1   *216*
21:1–22:5   *9, 272*
21:1–27   *217*
21:2   *180*
21:3   *134–35, 148,*
   190
21:7   *190*
21:9–26   *44, 65*
21:10   *180, 295*
21:12   *14, 135, 153*
21:14   *135, 153*
21:27   *240*
22:4–5   *217*
22:6   *217*
22:6–21   *217*
22:9–27   *242*
22:16   *127–28*
22:17   *217*
22:20   *217*